SPENSER

AND THE NUMBERS OF TIME

SPENSER

AND THE NUMBERS
OF TIME

ALASTAIR FOWLER

NEW YORK

BARNES & NOBLE, INC.

*First published
in the United States of America
1964*

© *Alastair Fowler 1964*

Printed in Great Britain

To
JENNY

Contents

Illustrations

16. (*a*) Cybele. From Cartari's *Le imagini colla sposizione degli dei degli antichi* (Venice, 1556).

(*b*) Virgo–Astræa. From Hyginus' *Poeticon astronomicon* (Amsterdam, 1681).

Grateful acknowledgements are made to the Bodleian Library, to the Ashmolean Museum, to the Department of the History of Art in the University of Oxford, and to the Warburg Institute, for the loan of books and photographs used for reproduction. In looking for illustrative material I received much invaluable assistance from Professor Edgar Wind and Mr. J. B. Trapp, who gave liberally of their time and erudition.

Preface

THE present study has a modest aim. It is not a commentary on the *Faerie Queene*. Still less is it a general critical appraisal; even if its findings may be thought to have a bearing on interpretation of the poem's structure. It is merely an account of certain formal patterns and certain schematic arrangements of the contents that have escaped previous critical notice. The analysis of such schemes is, of course, no more than a preliminary step in reading Elizabethan poetry. A necessary preliminary only, not to be mistaken for the whole business of criticism. In the case of the *Faerie Queene*, however, the schematic element is so little understood, and a knowledge of it so indispensable to appreciation of the poet's economy of means, that a book devoted entirely to exploration of this groundwork does not seem out of place.

I should mention that in the iconographical analyses essayed in Part II the repeated use of a very few Renaissance authorities is not due only to the *lacunæ* in my reading, undeniably vast though these are; it is deliberately intended, to show the ready accessibility of the material and to obviate jig-saw construction on my own part. But the question whether Valeriano, Giraldi, and Alciati were actual sources has not much occupied my attention. It seems more useful to provide illustration than pedigree.

Part I appeared in a somewhat different form in the *Journal of the Warburg Institute*, to the editors of which I am indebted for permission to reprint the substance here. The modifications now introduced, as well as Appendix I in its entirety, are the outcome of Dr. D. P. Walker's helpful comments on the earlier version. Professor Derek J. de Solla Price and Dr. C. H. Josten assisted generously by correcting my interpretations of several astronomical and astrological passages in the poem; and Miss Frances A. Yates and Mr. J. B. Trapp, both of the Warburg Institute, offered useful suggestions at an early stage in the writing. Throughout I was saved from many imbecilities by the fruitful scepticism of the late C. S. Lewis, than whom no better teacher nor more stimulating disputant could well be imagined. I owe much also to the encouragement of the late Professor F. P. Wilson; to Professor R. B. Gottfried, Professor James Kinsley, Professor Frank Kermode, Dr. Sydney Anglo, Mr. Wallace Robson, Mr. Emrys Jones, and Mr. C. A. Robson, for their interest and their assistance; to Mr. Colin Hardie and Mr. John Burrow, for their additions to the bibliography attached to Chapter xv; and to all those undergraduates and students who have read Spenser with me. For permission to quote the passages on pp. 99 f., from Macrobius, *Commentary on the Dream of Scipio*, tr. and ed. William Harris Stahl (New York, 1952), on pp. 134 f., from Robert Ellrodt, *Neoplatonism in the Poetry of Spenser* (Geneva, 1960), and on pp. 266, 270, 281 f., from Vincent Foster Hopper, 'Spenser's "House of Temperance,"' *PMLA*, LV (1940), I am grateful to the Columbia University Press, to Librairie Droz S. A. and the author, and to the Modern Language Association of America, respectively. An especial debt should be acknowledged to my mathematical colleague Mr. John T. Lewis, who devoted much of his valuable time to calculating the probability of chance occurrence of the numerical configurations in the poem that I believe to be intentional patterns. Needless to say, he is not responsible for any misapplications I may have made of his findings. My thanks are also due to Mrs. I. Allen and Miss J. Gibbs, who typed the book in its final form.

ALASTAIR FOWLER

PART ONE
The Pythagorean Series

Creatio numerorum, rerum est creatio.

THIERRY OF CHARTRES

I

The Monad

Every student of Spenser is now indebted to Professor Kent Hieatt for his brilliant discovery of the number symbolism by which *Epithalamion* is metrically and structurally ordered.[1] He has shown us what it is almost incredible that no critic has noticed before: namely, that the twenty-four stanzas and 365 long lines of the poem represent the measure of the day in hours and of the year in days; while further line-totals imitate the apparent daily movement of the sun relative to the fixed stars. Even the proper disproportion between the hours of daylight and darkness at the summer solstice (when the action of *Epithalamion* takes place) is indicated by a change in the refrain at a numerically significant point. Nor does this numerology merely constitute an external husk, a static frame within which the real poem proceeds. As Hieatt demonstrates, the sequence of the poem's images, even the meaning of many of its lines, cannot be fully understood except in terms of the structure of number symbolism. The analogy between the repetition of the seasons and the perpetuation of life through human generation is a part of the content; so that the numerology which imitates the year's cycle makes a dynamic contribution to the unfolding of the meaning. In subtle ways (too intricate to be described briefly here) numerological form *participates* in the action of *Epithalamion*.

Besides enriching our reading of a particular poem, Hieatt has redirected our attention generally to an important element of form and meaning in Renaissance poetry. He is surely right in suspecting

[1] In *Short Time's Endless Monument: The Symbolism of the Numbers in Edmund Spenser's 'Epithalamion'* (New York, 1960).

3

that many poems of that period possess a numerical symbolism to which readers have been oblivious for many years.[1] For an outstanding example, indeed, we have to look no further than the *Faerie Queene*. Contrary to Hieatt's assumption that its numerology is limited to a planned division into twelve books dealing with twelve virtues,[2] it is in fact an astonishingly complex web of interlocking numerical patterns of many different kinds. We find numerological significance in line-, stanza-, canto-, and book-totals; in the location of these units; and even in the numbers of characters mentioned in each episode. Pythagorean number symbolism, astronomical symbolism based on orbital period figures and on Ptolemaic star catalogue totals, medieval theological number symbolism: all these strands, and more besides, are worked together into what—in this respect at least—must be one of the most intricate poetic textures ever devised. If, as seems the case, this whole numerical structure has gone almost unnoticed for many years, it is not for want of clarity on Spenser's part. Everywhere he has given indication of his purpose: not merely through oblique hints and *doubles ententes*, as in *Epithalamion*, but also through passages of explicit numerology,[3] through frequent catalogues involving arithmetical terms, even through character names (Una, Duessa) that openly announce their Pythagorean import. Only a neglect of the symbolic approach to number, and a general disregard of numerical composition as a literary mode, can have prevented several generations of readers from following up these indications. If they had done so they would have perceived a structural element that makes no small contribution to the unification of the *Faerie Queene*.

The purpose of the first part of the present work is to describe some of the simpler components in the numerological pattern. I hope to show that the themes and structural arrangements of the various books correspond, in order, to symbolic meanings traditionally attached to the several digits; and that the assignment of analogous material to similar canto positions also has a numerological basis.

[1] *Short Time's Endless Monument*, p. 77, where, however, no specific poets are mentioned. In Ch. xv below, attention is drawn to instances of numerology in Chapman, Milton, and others; see also p. 199 on Davies.

[2] Ibid., p. 76.

[3] Such as the notorious St. II. ix. 22, the only passage previously considered from this point of view.

4

According to Pythagorean doctrine, all numbers flow from the monad, the originative principle; which is accordingly good, or even above goodness. It alone existed,

> Before the Branchy head of Numbers Tree
> Sprung from the Trunk of One.[1]

Macrobius writes in this tradition when he identifies the monad with God and with *mens*:

One is called *monas*, that is Unity . . . itself not a number, but the source and origin of numbers. This monad, the beginning and ending of all things, yet itself not knowing a beginning or ending, refers to the Supreme God, and separates our understanding of him (the One, without number) from the number of things and powers following; you would not be so rash as to look for it in a sphere lower than God. It is also that Mind, sprung from the Supreme God, which, unaware of the changes of time, is always in one time, the present; and although the monad is itself not numbered, it nevertheless produces from itself, and contains within itself, innumerable patterns of created things.[2]

It is further associated with truth, the light and guiding principle both of the cosmic and the individual *mens*; and its singleness in this respect is contrasted with the multiplicity of falsehood.[3] From the monad emerges the dyad, or principle of diversity. Whereas the monad is both masculine and feminine, even and odd (added to odd it makes even; added to even, odd), the dyad, on the contrary, is only feminine. It represents 'the evil principle of the unlimited.'[4] Since it broke away from unity, the dyad was by some authors accused of rebellion;[5] sometimes it even came close to being dualistically opposed to the One. Thus, according to Porphyry, Pythagoras

[1] Abraham Cowley, *Essays, Plays, and Sundry Verses*, ed. A. R. Waller (Cambridge, 1906), p. 396.

[2] Macrobius, *In somnium Scipionis*, I. vi. 7–8; tr. and ed. William Harris Stahl (New York, 1952), pp. 100–101. See Vincent Foster Hopper, *Medieval Number Symbolism* (New York, 1938), p. 39.

[3] See, e.g., Pierio Valeriano, *Hieroglyphica, sive de sacris Ægyptiorum, aliarumque gentium literis* (Frankfort, 1613), XLIV. ii; p. 555: 'Sol unus est, eadem est veritatis hieroglyphicum, duplicia enim et multiplicia sunt veritati contraria.' Although for convenience I give references to this late edition of the *Hieroglyphica* (since it contains the valuable additional *Collectanea*), there were several earlier and accessible to Spenser, such as the 1556 and 1575 Basel editions.

[4] F. M. Cornford, 'Mysticism and Science in the Pythagorean Tradition,' *CQ*, XVII (1933), 2; see also F. E. Robbins, 'The Tradition of Greek Arithmology,' *CP*, XVI (1921), 97–123.

[5] See Cornford, p. 6.

called the better of the opposed powers monad and light and right and unvarying and firm and noble; the other, the worse power, dyad and dark and left and varying and unstable and inconstant.[1]

Through the offices of Chalcidius, Macrobius, and other digesters of antique thought, this symbolism was assimilated into medieval arithmology.[2] Pythagorean and medieval number symbolism are hardly to be distinguished, as far as the opposition of monad and dyad is concerned.

Now it is just such a near-absolute opposition that we find in the first book of the *Faerie Queene*, between Una and Duessa, the representatives of truth and falsehood, light and darkness. In fact, the name of each defines her force in the poem's number symbolism quite explicitly and directly.[3] Perhaps this is intended as an initial concession to the unprepared reader. At any rate, the numerological fitness of Holiness as a subject for the first book should have been obvious enough. Predominantly theological matter is naturally subsumed under the divinity of the monad. Moreover, holiness is the foundation of all other virtues, just as the monad is, of the numbers. And finally, holiness, as Spenser conceives it, is essentially *single-minded* virtue—the exclusive service of the truth of the one God. The particular topics of the book would have been recognized by most Elizabethan readers as equally appropriate. The unity of Truth

[1] *De vita Pythag.*, xxxviii. Cf. Plato, *De legibus*, 717A; and Plutarch, *De Iside et Osiride*, 361A, where even numbers are assigned to bad chthonic deities.

[2] For its appearance in the work of Thierry of Chartres, see N. Haring, 'The Creation and Creator of the World according to Thierry of Chartres and Clarenbaldus of Arras,' *Archives d'histoire doctrinale et littéraire du moyen âge*, XXII (1955), 195, etc., with discussion of sources; also Adolf Katzenellenbogen, *The Sculptural Programs of Chartres Cathedral* (Baltimore, 1959), pp. 19 and 111, n. 61. A typical Renaissance statement of the same ideas, using material gathered from both ancient and patristic sources (as well as from *neoterici* such as Nicholas of Cusa) will be found in Pietro Bongo, *Mysticæ numerorum significationis liber* (Bergamo, 1585): see especially Pt. I, pp. 47 ff., 'De binario.'

[3] *Una* as it stands is a Latin numeral; Duessa is recognizably connected with Italian *due* or Latin *duæ*. Hopper's 'Spenser's "House of Temperance," ' however, seems to contain the first notice of this allusion to the monadic and dyadic principles. Perhaps the allusion was once less painfully obvious than it now seems; for both Una and Duessa were common Irish names in Spenser's day. See Roland M. Smith, 'Una and Duessa,' *PMLA*, L (1935), 917–919, where *Duessa* is connected not only with the name *Dubésa*, but also, paronomastically, with *dóibhéas*, 'vice.' On *Una* as a cult name of Elizabeth's, see C. B. Millican, 'Spenser's and Drant's Poetic names for Elizabeth: Tanaquil, Gloriana and Una,' *HLQ*, II (1939), 251–263; also Roy C. Strong, 'The Popular Celebration of the Accession Day of Queen Elizabeth I,' *JWI*, XXI (1958), 86–103.

(symbolized by Una), for instance, was a commonplace both of philosophers and of popular homilists.[1] Similarly, there was numerological justification for the inclusion of ecclesiastical themes; of the various allegories of Una as the true Church; of the prominent treatment of the sacraments (I. xi); and even, perhaps, of the personifications Fidelia, Speranza, and Charissa. Simon Goulart's commentary on Du Bartas' *Sepmaines* lists all the topics just mentioned, in the course of his 'praise of the unity':

God is one, the Church is one. . . . There is . . . one Gospell, one Faith, one Baptisme, one Table of our Lord, one Hope, one Charity.[2]

If Spenser's number symbolism appeared only in the distribution of matter by books it would be of limited, though essential, interest to the critic. But the symbolism is also expressed in narrative terms, so fully that we can almost speak of the poem as having a Pythagorean form.

The opening battle against Error and her horribly prolific spawn serves as a brief emblematic statement of the subject of Book I; the contrast between Una's singleness and the profusion of evil is here a simple one. In the subtler and more detailed allegories that follow, however, the images of evil are not in themselves multiple. Instead, we find single evil characters who impersonate, and consequently *duplicate*, good characters. By simulating virtue, so that they become second members of apparent pairs, they seek to introduce the principle of duality. Thus Duessa–Fidessa, impersonating true religion, forms with Una a pair of alternatives not previously open to the Red Cross Knight. Instead of contemplating a single truth (the proper function of *mens*), he is now in doubt, like the aptly named

---

[1] Cf. p. 5, n. 3. Ficino was especially fond of this topic. Truth coming from a single divine source must itself be single: 'Unum quoque omnium esse voluit veritatem ipsius, scilicet, unius, hoc est Dei, lumen mentibus omnibus speciebusque infusum. . . . Unicam igitur veritatem, unius scilicet, Dei radium unum . . .' (Marsilio Ficino, *Opera omnia*, facsimile reprint of 1576 Basel edn., ed. Mario Sancipriano and Paul Oskar Kristeller (Turin, 1959), p. 629). The familiarity of the idea is attested by its occurrence in Francis Meres's *Palladis Tamia* (1598): 'As there is but one God: so there is but one truth' (fol. 104ʳ). In *F.Q.* itself, Arthegall tells the Giant with the Scales that 'truth is one, and right is ever one' (V. ii. 48), and in his reproof of Sir Burbon reminds him that 'Knights ought be true, and truth is one in all' (V. xi. 56).

[2] *A Learned Summary Upon the famous Poeme of William of Saluste Lord of Bartas*, tr. T. L[odge]. (London, 1621), Second Week, p. 248. Cf. the ch. 'Unus et omnis' in Van der Putte's *Pietatis thaumata* (Antwerp, 1617); also Eph. iv. 4–6.

Fradubio before him, between truth and the appearance of truth.[1] Archimago, too, is an implacable enemy of unity and individuation; he triumphs

> when his guests
> He [sees] divided into double parts.
> (I. ii. 9)

This division is achieved through the destruction of the Red Cross Knight's trust in Una by means of another simulated multiplication. Archimago raises spirits that present false appearances of her. The latter appear to the Red Cross Knight in dreams ('false shewes abuse his fantasy' (I. i. 46)); since the *phantasia* was regarded in Renaissance psychology as the immediate source of multiplicity of opinions.[2] Later, Archimago himself duplicates the Red Cross Knight to deceive Una (I. iii). Indeed, as if to emphasize the profusion of forms taken by evil, Archimago appears in Book I under many different *personæ*:

> he could take
> As many formes and shapes in seeming wise,
> As ever *Proteus* to himselfe could make.[3]

---

[1] Other aspects of the divisive principle embodied in Duessa are treated in later books. Thus the rebelliousness of the dyad (see p. 5, n. 5) is reflected in the treason Duessa is convicted of at Mercilla's Court; while her close association with Ate in the early cantos of Bk. IV is in keeping with the identification of the dyadic principle with the Empedoclean Strife—an idea Spenser may have found in Plutarch (*De Iside*, 381F). Duessa's grandmother Night has also a dyadic character, as the iconography of her 'twyfold Teme' illustrates (*F.Q.*, I. v. 28).

[2] See, e.g., Ficino, pp. 290–291, 359–360.

[3] I. ii. 10. Archimago successively disguises himself as a hermit (I. i. 35–I. ii. 9); as Redcrosse (I. ii. 10–11; I. iii. 24–39); as a pilgrim (I. vi. 34–48); and as a messenger (I. xii. 24–36).

II

The Dyad

In Book I the dyad was wholly evil, the source of corruption of simple truth and faith. From a slightly different point of view, however, the divisive principle is also the source of the material aspect of nature. Physical existence arises from the formation of pairs of elements in extreme mutual opposition. Thus the dyad comes to have a somewhat less unfavourable significance: it is

the representative of matter or existence, mother of the elements,[1] eternal but not immutable, as opposed to Essence or Idea, since everything divisible is mutable and material. It is the number of excess and defect, of manifoldness and of man, because he is both animal and reasonable.[2]

In medieval and Renaissance thought the principle of the dyad is regarded as especially manifest in human nature. For man is a creature of double natures—part spiritual, part mortally dyadic—so that the opposed principles find in him a uniquely close confrontation. The medieval tendency to schematize numerical symbolism into correspondences between numbers and particular entities leads also to an association of dyad and *corpus*, parallel to that of monad and *mens*.

When these meanings of the dyad are recalled, they are at once seen to correspond to the themes of Book II, as they do to those of no

---

[1] Cf. Martianus Capella, *De nuptiis Philologiæ et Mercurii*, ed. A. Dick (Leipzig, 1925), sect. 732, p. 368: the dyad is 'elementorum etiam mater; nam de dyade quartus elementorum numerus procreatur primaque forma paritatis est.' See also below, p. 19, n. 2.

[2] Hopper, *Medieval Number Symbolism*, p. 40 with references. Cf. Valeriano, *Hieroglyphica*, XXXVII. v; p. 456: 'dualis numerus mystico significato corpoream indicat naturam'; and Bongo, Pt. I, p. 67.

other book. The core canto of II, indeed, is the description of the Castle of Alma: an extended allegory of human nature. Moreover, an essential feature of the castle's architecture is its construction according to two different 'proportions,' symbolizing the double nature of man:

> The one imperfect, mortall, fœminine;
> Th'other immortall, perfect, masculine.
> (II. ix. 22)

Even without this piece of explicit Pythagoreanism, however, we would sense the contrast between the Castle of Alma, with its twofold interests, physical and mental, and the House of Holiness, with its solely spiritual exercises and the ascent of the mind in contemplation. Concentration on the double character of man's nature is equally evident elsewhere in Book II: most obviously perhaps is the Bower of Bliss episode, where man's animality is palpably evoked by the enchantments of a Circe-like Acrasia. The theme is already stated, however, in the opening emblem of Mordant and Amavia, that double 'image of mortalitie.'[1] Several of the intervening episodes, moreover, go to show how the extremes of temperament are rooted in elemental antinomies; this is particularly clear with the fiery Pyrochles and watery Cymochles.[2] In its details, Spenser's conception of temperance as the moderation of psychological and moral extremes is, of course, largely worked out in Aristotelian terms. But in its broad lines it is also Platonic and Pythagorean: the extremes are particular effects of the inordinate dyad.

[1] See my art. 'The Image of Mortality: *The Faerie Queene* II. i–ii,' *HLQ*, XXIV (1961), 91–110. N. S. Brooke has developed a plausible theory that the Bower episode is among other things an allegory of the corrupt human body ('C. S. Lewis and Spenser: Nature, Art, and the Bower of Bliss,' *Cambr. Journ.*, II (1949)); and Harry Berger has argued similarly with respect to the Cave of Mammon.

[2] For the theory that Pyrochles and Cymochles are dominated by particular humours, see Harry Berger, *The Allegorical Temper: Vision and Reality in Book II of Spenser's 'Faerie Queene,'* Yale Studies in English, CXXXVII (New Haven, 1957), pp. 59–61. Cymochles is clearly a contrasting type to the choleric Pyrochles; but Berger does not make the case that he is phlegmatic very convincingly. The contrast is not in fact principally between humours. It depends, rather, on a common Renaissance symbolism whereby water denotes *instability*. Cymochles should thus be compared with Chapman's 'moist man' or 'watrish thing' (from Homer's διερὸς βροτός *via* Spondanus' mistranslation *humidus homo*): a type of 'unstayed' character given over to the unstable flux of humours. See George de F. Lord, *Homeric Renaissance: The Odyssey of George Chapman* (London, 1956), pp. 93–94.

If we consider narrative structure one feature of Book II stands out with undisguised clarity. Unlike the heroes of other books, Guyon (and here Arthur as well) is confronted by pairs of enemies, whom he attempts to restrain rather than kill. In Book I the evil principle sought to undermine the unity of truth by introducing a new diversity. But in Book II the dualities of human nature are presupposed from the start. *Given* these tragic dualities (which, like Ruddymane's blemish, are ineradicable in this mortal life), Guyon has to reduce them to whatever order is possible. It is not for him to kill his enemies; to do so would be to deprive his own lower nature of the very basis of its existence. Instead, his characteristic stance is one of restraint; he seeks to impose limitation on the unlimited, order on the inordinate. Without such temperance, and without the intervention of grace, the dyadic entropy of sin would aggravate the conflicting tendencies of his elemental constitution, and produce a corrupt body of death like that represented in Maleger.[1] The fact that Guyon's double enemies are dualities resident in fallen human nature itself makes it difficult to describe them adequately as Aristotelian moral extremes. The battles with Huddibras and Sansloy, and Pyrochles and Cymochles, can no doubt be related to the *Nicomachean Ethics*; but they are also, and more obviously, an expression of the Platonic concept of a struggle between three powers of the soul. The latter concept could readily be assimilated to Pythagoreanism; as we find in Stobæus:

the soul must begin by warring against itself . . . and the one part of the soul must win victory over the others, which are more in number. It is a feud of one against two.[2]

What could be a better brief description of the narrative allegory of Book II? Conflict within man's divided nature inevitably occurs in every book of the *Faerie Queene*. But in no other book is this conflict itself the subject: nowhere else does the narrative pattern itself illustrate the dyadic principle as it appears in human nature.

So regular is the arrangement of characters in complementary pairs,

[1] On the corrupting effect of the dyadic principle, see Macrobius, ed. Stahl, p. 103 n.

[2] Stobæus, I. 41. 1a; in *Hermetica*, tr. and ed. Walter Scott, Vol. I (Oxford, 1924), 393, Excerpt II B. As Scott explains, the 'one' is mind or reason; the 'two' θυμός and ἐπιθυμία, i.e., 'repugnance' (or self-assertion against opponents) and 'desire,' the two forms of passion.

in this book, that one might almost think it a direct translation of the number symbolism into purely formal terms—a kind of Pythagorean literary ballet. Two by two the *personæ* are marshalled: Mordant and Amavia, Huddibras and Sansloy, Elissa and Perissa, Furor and Occasion, Pyrochles and Cymochles, Praysdesire and Shamefastnesse, Impatience and Impotence, Acrasia and Verdant; to list only the most prominent. Each of these pairs corresponds to some division within man's nature; or to opposed moral or temperamental extremes; or to the psychological polarities strong/weak and pleasure/pain, which are early announced as the basis of the book's classification of the passions:

> When raging passion with fierce tyrannie
> Robs reason of her due regalitie,
> And makes it servant to her basest part:
> The strong it weakens with infirmitie,
> And with bold furie armes the weakest hart;
> The strong through pleasure soonest falles,
> the weake through smart.
>
> But temperance (said he) with golden squire
> Betwixt them both can measure out a meane,
> Neither to melt in pleasures whot desire,
> Nor fry in hartlesse griefe and dolefull teene.
> Thrise happie man, who fares them both atweene.
> (II. i. 57–58)

The same is probably, thought less obviously, true of other pairs; such as the concupiscent Tantalus and the guilty Pilate in Cocytus (II. vii. 57–62), and the two naked damsels at the Bower of Bliss (one bold, the other coy: II. xii. 63–68). Moreover, just as these groupings of characters express the book's preoccupation with the dyadic character of man's nature, so also does its remarkably symmetrical episodic structure. Thus, the Alma episode, occupying two cantos (II. ix–x), is flanked by two combats of Arthur, which intervene in the adjacent cantos (II. viii and xi) as if to separate the Castle formally from the two most elaborately described places of evil, the Cave of Mammon (II. vii) and the Bower of Bliss (II. xii).[1] Between Cave and

[1] Other structural pairs in this extraordinarily symmetrical book—such as the contrasting fountains between which the action proceeds—are discussed in my 'Emblems of Temperance in *The Faerie Queene*, Book II,' *RES*, n.s. XI (1960), 143–149. The dangers encountered during the voyage to the Bower are also paired: see, e.g., II. xii. 4 and 18.

Bower, there is strong tonal contrast. The Cave offers aggressive and laborious competition, and an ordeal of physical deprivation; the Bower, voluptuous and idle ease, and an enchantment of delight. The former—'rude and strong'[1]—tempts to morally 'strong' dissatisfaction or censoriousness; the latter—'weake and thin'[2]—to weak content or sensuality. Acrasia's captives fall *below* the stature of man, to a merely sensual, animal level; whereas the error of the lovers of Philotime (False Honour) consists in their rash attempt to climb *above* their due degree in the chain of being:

> There, as in glistring glory she did sit,
> She held a great gold chaine ylincked well,
> Whose upper end to highest heaven was knit,
> And lower part did reach to lowest Hell;
> And all that preace did round about her swell,
> To catchen hold of that long chaine, thereby
> To clime aloft, and others to excell:
> That was *Ambition*, rash desire to sty [mount],
> And every lincke thereof a step of dignity.
>
> (II. vii. 46)

Even more strikingly, Sleep, which is carefully excluded from the Cave (II. vii. 25), is invariably present in the Bower, to dull and weaken the moral fibre of the unwary visitor (II. v. 30 and xii. 79). In short, the two places are as different as pain and pleasure, as hell and earthly paradise.

These and other similar dichotomies in Book II express Spenser's individual psychological and moral insights; so that we can see in them a fresh analysis of the complex interaction between superego and libido. But at the same time they should also be related to a line of thought belonging to traditional arithmology. I refer to those authors who, drawing on suggestions in Plato and Aristotle, attempted to give psychological substance to the Pythagorean doctrine of the dyad. We find a particularly complete example of such psychological description of the dyad in *The Mystical Significance of Numbers*, a compilation by the Bergamese polymath Pietro Bongo.[3] In his

---

[1] II. vii. 28. 1; cf. II. vii. 30. 2: 'coffers strong' that none could hope 'to enforce by violence.'

[2] II. xii. 43. 4; cf. II. xii. 55. 5: 'weake bowes.'

[3] A canon of Bergamo Cathedral; d. 1601. His *De mystica numerorum significatione* first appeared in 1583; my references are to the 1585 Bergamo edn., under the title *Mysticæ numerorum significationis liber.*

chapter on the dyadic principle Bongo summarizes Aristotle's account of virtue as a mean between two extremes; emphasizing, by his diagrammatic exposition, the contrast between the singleness of virtue and the doubleness of vice.[1] He goes on to essay a dichotomy of the passions, according to whether they stem from the desire for Honour, or from the attractions of the flesh. 'The passions of the soul,' he writes, 'are two-fold':

Duplices rursus animæ sunt passiones, quibus in varia hinc inde intranquilla mens divellitur, honoris scilicet, appetitio, et carnis delectatio.[2]

Pleasure lowers man; whereas 'from the desire of Honour man . . . desires to raise himself up and be superior to the mean' (*medio sui æqualitate fieri superior*). The passion of avarice, however, exerts a pull in both directions. I reproduce Bongo's diagram:

This scheme, while it is by no means identical with that of Spenser's second book, nevertheless has many points of resemblance. We have already noticed, for instance, his use of the spatial image of elevation in the Cave of Mammon. More obviously still, Philotime and Acrasia correspond respectively to Bongo's divisions *Honor* and *Illecebræ*. It could be shown that each of his honour-seeking passions finds separate representation in the Cave, each of his alluring passions in the Bower. Moreover, the same division could be demonstrated in the earlier episodes, between the passions displayed by Elissa, Huddibras, and Pyrochles, on the one hand, and by Perissa, Sansloy, and Cymochles, on the other.

In the allegory of the Castle of Alma the duality in human nature receives its most direct, yet also its most obscure, treatment. Here occurs a statement in terms of overt number symbolism: the famous architectural metaphor of II. ix. 22:

[1] 'De binario,' in *Numerorum significationis*, Pt. I, pp. 64–65.
[2] Ibid., p. 66.

The frame thereof seemd partly circulare,
And part triangulare, O worke divine;
Those two the first and last proportions are,
The one imperfect, mortall, fœminine;
Th' other immortall, perfect, masculine,
And twixt them both a quadrate was the base
Proportioned equally by seven and nine;
Nine was the circle set in heavens place,
All which compacted made a goodly diapase.

This difficult stanza calls for extended discussion in an appendix. Here we need only notice that the frame of the Castle is divided into two radically different components or 'proportions'—corresponding to man's mind, and his body or passionate part—which are described in terms clearly derived from Pythagorean and Platonic number symbolism. Vincent Foster Hopper seems quite justified in interpreting them as the monadic and dyadic principles.[1] Between these two components, in a mean position ('twixt them both'), there is the 'quadrate' or quaternion, identified in Pythagorean philosophy with the virtuous *anima*. The exertions of the latter, as it strives to reach that true proportion which constitutes the harmony of a reconstructed and integrated nature, is the subject proposed by Spenser in Book II.

Thus, the second book itself occupies a mean position, in respect of subject, among the books composing Part I. For it lies between Book I, which is primarily occupied with the *anima* in its relations with *mens*, the mind or spiritual part (the circular component of the Castle of Alma); and Book III, which is primarily occupied with the *anima* in its relations with the passionate part (the triangular component of the Castle of Alma). The two parts are harmonized, in the course of Book II, by Reason's control of the passions through the virtue of temperance—a development that makes possible Book III, with its elevation of the passionate part into a condition of ideal virtue.

This relationship between the first three books is expressed in a variety of ways. None more unambiguous, however, nor more pertinent to our present purpose, than through their numerological form. For Spenser has expressed the mean function of the second book numerically in a striking manner. He has arranged for the

[1] See his 'Spenser's "House of Temperance," ' *PMLA*, LV (1940), p. 961.

stanza-totals of certain of its cantos to be arithmetical means between totals of corresponding cantos in Books I and III.

TABLE I: STANZA-TOTALS

Book	I	II	III	IV	V	VI
Proem	4	5	5	5	11	7
Canto i	55	61	67	54	30	47
ii	45	46	52	54	54	48
iii	44	46	62	52	40	51
iv	51	46	61	48	51	40
v	53	38	55	46	57	41
vi	48	51	54	47	40	44
vii	52	66	61	47	45	50
viii	50	56	52	64	51	51
ix	54	60	53	41	50	46
x	68	77	60	58	39	44
xi	54 (1590) 55 (1596)	49	55	53	65	51
xii	42	87	47 (1590) 45 (1596)	35	43	41

As a glance at Table I will show, many of the stanza-totals in Book II are means between one or more pairs of totals in the adjoining books. But such relationships are likely to occur by chance, if not by intention. More significant are those instances where there is an *additional* numerical bond between the related cantos. Such exists in cases where they occupy similar positions within their respective books. Thus, the total for II. i (61) is the mean between those for I. i and III. i (55 and 67); while the total for II. vi (51) is the mean between those for I. vi and III. vi (48 and 54). It should be noted that, if the cantos of the poem are numbered consecutively, regardless of division into books, the ordinal numbers denoting positions of such related cantos themselves form exactly analogous relationships. For example, II. vi, placed *18th*, is in the mean position between I. vi (*6th*) and III. vi (*30th*). And the same doubly reinforced relationship links the cantos I. x, II. ix, and III. viii, even though they do not occupy similar positions within their books. If we consider totals, 60 (II. ix) is the mean between 68 (I. x) and 52 (III. viii): if we consider positions, 21 (II. ix) is the mean between 10 (I. x) and 32 (III. viii). This last triad is particularly significant in view of the subjects of the cantos concerned. The Castle of Alma could be said to maintain a mean position, not only numerologically but also substantively, between the House of Holiness and the Cave of Proteus—between, that is to say,

16

divine contemplation and the disordered flux of passion; or (to take a wider view) between heaven itself, and chaos.[1]

[1] Both passion and chaos were meanings commonly assigned to Proteus by Renaissance mythographers.

Statistically it is not significant in itself that the three sets of numbers in arithmetical progression should occur. A computer simulation which was set up at the Oxford University Computing Laboratory showed that, given the 36 actual stanza-totals of Bks. I–III, in 1001 random permutations, 16·5% of the permutations yielded 3 or more sets of numbers, one from each column of 12, in arithmetic progression of position and value. (Given 1001 random selections of numbers from a *uniform* distribution over the range 30–70, the corresponding percentage was much lower: 6·6.) As we shall see, however, several of the 36 numbers fulfil other independent conditions, so that the probability of random occurrence of the arithmetic progressions is greatly reduced. Then we have the fact that all the stanza-totals of core cantos in Bks. I–III belong to sets in arithmetic progression; with the totals of I. x and II. ix, as suits the close substantive correspondence between these cantos, belonging to one set, and that of III. vi belonging to the other. Now the probability that at least one set of 3 numbers in arithmetic progression of position and value contains the stanza-total of III. vi can be shown theoretically to be about 1 : 10. (If N sets of 3 numbers are selected from a uniform distribution over a range of M consecutive numbers, the expected number of sets in arithmetic progression is $\frac{N}{2M}$. Here N is 6, since there are 6 possible sets containing the position III. vi; and M may be taken as 30.) And the probability of the combined event—in which all the stanza-totals of core cantos are contained in sets in arithmetic progression, as described—is less than 1%. I am greatly indebted to Mr. D. C. Handscomb of the Computing Laboratory for making calculations and tests, of which the previous paragraph gives only a very summary account.

III

The Triad

With the triad, according to Pythagorean number theory, comes reversion to the limitation of oddness: unity and diversity are restored to harmony. We have seen this stage already approached in Book II. Whenever Guyon brings the principle of limitation into the dyadic field of his operations, he is seeking in effect to complete a harmonious triad. At Medina's castle, for instance, a concord is eventually reached between the three knights, that is shown to be impossible for Huddibras and Sansloy alone. Guyon provides the centre or mean term, by which these conflicting extremes are composed into an orderly triad. In other words, he strives to complete 'the Three,'

> whose inclosed Center
> Doth equally from both extreams extend.[1]

For, as Martianus Capella puts it, the triad 'centrum medietatis ad initium finemque interstitionum æqualitate componit.'[2] In numerological content, therefore, just as in narrative sequence, there is an overlap between Books II and III, similar to that between I (where the dyad already appears) and II. Such overlapping is of the essence of Spenser's structural plan: avoiding rigid schemes, he imitates the ever-changing, ever-dilating, yet fundamentally ordered growth of life itself.

Within Book III, we find the triad carrying this same force of limitation when Glauce invokes it in an attempt to control Britomart's passions by incantation:

[1] Du Bartas, *Devine Weekes and Workes*, tr. Joshua Sylvester (London, 1613), 'The Columnes,' The Second Day of the Second Week, Pt. IV, p. 361.
[2] *De nuptiis*, ed. Dick, sect. 733, pp. 368–369.

Then taking thrise three haires from off her head,
Them trebly breaded in a threefold lace,
And . . .
to the virgin said, thrise said she it;
Come daughter come, come; spit upon my face,
Spit thrise upon me, thrise upon me spit;
Th'uneven number for this businesse is most fit.

(III. ii. 50)

With characteristic humour Spenser has found a neat equivalent for a philosophical idea within the little world of his story: esoteric Pythagorean lore is here translated into homely superstition. The arithmological background of Glauce's rite is sketched for us by Goulart, who connects similar practices (in Virgil, Ovid, and Pliny) with the beliefs of 'the Pythagorists, who in their purifications and washings used the number of *three*: Numero Deus impare gaudet.'[1]

Book III is primarily devoted, however, to somewhat different metaphysical associations with the triad. An important doctrine of this number concerned its generative capacity. From the union of the opposite principles it contains—odd and even, male and female, limited and unlimited—new life is generated. Thus, early cosmogonies in the Pythagorean tradition commonly distinguished three stages of creation: (1) undifferentiated unity; (2) the separation out of two opposite powers to form the world order; and (3) the reunion of the opposites to generate life.[2] This generative union of sundered opposites in the triad was often referred to as a marriage; so that the triad was the first of the so-called marriage numbers. In the Orphic cosmogony, for example, the marriage of Heaven and Earth is mediated by a third principle, Eros.[3] It is in keeping with a recognizable metaphysical sequence, therefore, that the third book of the *Faerie Queene* should be concerned with love, and in particular with

[1] See Goulart, *A Learned Summary*, The Second Week, p. 249, quoting Virgil, *Ecl.* VIII. 75, itself a paraphrase of a Pythagorean *symbolum*.

[2] See Cornford, p. 3. Often, as in Anaximander's system, the formation of the world order was conceived as a separation out of the four elements in opposed pairs.

[3] See ibid., p. 4. Dante's use of the number three to symbolize love is noticed in Hopper, *Medieval Number Symbolism*, pp. 163, 165, 175, and 194. Evidence of Renaissance interest in early cosmogonies need hardly be given. On the artist's use of Orphic ideas, Edgar Wind's *Pagan Mysteries in the Renaissance* (London, 1958) may be consulted; and, on the influence of early philosophical systems upon Renaissance cosmology, F. R. Johnson's *Astronomical Thought in Renaissance England* (Baltimore, 1937).

the orientation of love towards generation. The medullar canto of Book III contains the myth of the Garden of Adonis: a philosophical myth of love's generation of life. Precisely what a reader would expect at this point, in fact, if he had grasped the Pythagorean laws of Spenser's poetic cosmos. The same theme unites a number of other episodes in Book III. The portion of chronicle history assigned to Merlin, for example, is cast in the form of a prophecy of the line that Arthegall and Britomart will generate. Consequently, Britomart's love has from the start a specially progenitive orientation. On the side of evil, the twins Argante and Ollyphant practise perversions in which sexuality is deflected far from its generative function. And Busyrane's love is equally thematic: he is named after the Egyptian tyrant Busiris, who cruelly sacrificed strangers to relieve the sterility afflicting his country.[1]

The prominence in the Garden of Adonis of potential forms of life —'Infinite shapes of creatures . . . And uncouth formes' (III. vi. 35) —reminds us of another closely related meaning of the triad. As the harmonious resolution of conflicting principles, it represented the perfection of ideal form. In Martianus Capella's words, the triad

mundana perfectio est; nam monadem fabricatori deo, dyadem materiæ procreanti, triadem idealibus formis consequenter aptamus.[2]

The Garden of Adonis, that sinless paradise on earth, 'so faire a place, as Nature can devize' (III. vi. 29), is certainly a vision of terrestrial perfection; while Spenser's pre-existent forms cannot be far removed from Martianus Capella's *ideales formæ*. True, the exact character of

---

[1] In 'Venus and Diana: Some Uses of Myth in *The Faerie Queene*,'*ELH*, XXVIII (1961), 101–120, Kathleen Williams connects Busyrane with the Busiris alluded to in Ovid's *Ars amatoria*, in a context of competition and hostility between the sexes. See also *Heroides*, IX. 69; Plutarch, *Life of Theseus*; Virgil, *Georgics*, III. 5; Apollodorus, II. v; Herodotus, II. lix; and Strabo, *Collectanea*, xvii. It may be suspected, however, that Spenser's main allusion is to *Metam.*, IX. 183, where Busiris is said to have 'defiled his temples with strangers' blood' (*fœdantem peregrino templa cruore . . . Busirin*)—a ready-made symbol for adultery. Hyginus (*Fabul.*, lvi) gives as a reason for Busiris' cruel sacrifices the sterility of Egypt during his reign. The kidnapping of Amoret by Busyrane (*F.Q.*, IV. i. 3) is paralleled by another action of King Busiris, related by Diodorus Siculus (IV. xxvii. 1–5): he desired to get the beautiful and chaste daughters of Atlas into his power, and had them captured by pirates; only to lose them again, when they were saved by Hercules. In this connection, we note Spenser's allusion to the Atlantides in the *chronographia* at *F.Q.*, III. i. 57 (for the identification of the Hyades with the Atlantides, see Servius on *Aen.*, I. 745).

[2] *De nuptiis*, ed. Dick, sect. 733, pp. 368–369.

the forms fathered by Adonis (III. vi. 47) and maturing in the Garden is at present under dispute. There is a choice to be made between, on the one hand, the various Platonic interpretations, that treat the forms as transcendent; and, on the other, Robert Ellrodt's (to me more convincing) theory, that they are akin to the *rationes seminales* of St. Augustine's *De Genesi*—pre-existent seeds of life, sown at an instantaneous creation.[1] But in either case, it will be agreed, the forms of Spenser's myth come within the domain of the triad, as this is defined by Martianus Capella.

If the perfection of *ideales formæ* is the undisguised subject of the Garden of Adonis episode, it is also, I believe, an underlying theme of certain of the narrative allegories, in which Florimell is a central figure. Florimell has been variously interpreted as Beauty, as Civility, and (less plausibly) as Innocence.[2] No simple abstraction, of course, can adequately define her significance. But it would seem to me at least preferable to think of her in terms of a different abstraction: Ideal Form. Since certain of her adventures have a moral import, and others are just as clearly political, some such general philosophical interpretation is surely called for. The more plausible of the particular interpretations—Beauty and Civility (or, better, Civil Order)—can

[1] Robert Ellrodt, *Neoplatonism in the Poetry of Spenser*, Travaux d'Humanisme et Renaissance, XXXV (Geneva, 1960), pp. 70–79. It may be argued that St. Augustine's *rationes* are less sharply distinct from the ideal forms of Platonism than Ellrodt maintains. Evidently Martianus Capella, at least, could conceive of forms at once *ideal* and composing a *mundane* perfection. Still, we may agree with Ellrodt that Spenser was writing a nature myth, and not a treatise on the orthodox Neoplatonic hierarchy of emanations.

[2] Beauty: C. G. Smith, 'The Ethical Allegory of the Two Florimels,' *SP*, XXXI (1934), 140–151, and Ellrodt, p. 47; Civility: Isabel E. Rathborne, 'The Political Allegory of the Florimell-Marinell Story,' *ELH*, XII (1945), 279–289, esp. 285 ff.; Innocence: Pauline Parker, *The Allegory of the 'Faerie Queene'* (Oxford, 1960), pp. 159–160. Ellrodt (pp. 47–48) rejects Smith's view that the contrast between the true and false Florimells is the Platonic opposition of ideal and phenomenal beauty; he wishes to see it instead as 'the contrast between Nature and false Art.' Certainly the magically fabricated false Florimell cannot be sensible beauty. But Ellrodt's determination to see as little Neoplatonism as he can in *F.Q.* has caused him to reject too hastily the interpretation of Florimell as ideal beauty. In Spenser, after all, truth to Nature and truth to the beauty of the Neoplatonic Venus are very closely allied. Indeed, when Ellrodt contrasts 'Nature, in all her concreteness' with the ' "ideal" model, the abstract truth of the Platonists,' he is setting in stark opposition concepts which during the Renaissance period would scarcely have been distinguished. As Ellrodt elsewhere (p. 38) has to allow, the two concepts are combined in the description of Britomart: 'That peerelesse paterne of Dame natures pride, / And heavenly image of perfection' (IV. vi. 24).

easily be accommodated as applications of the more general meaning to different spheres of experience. Beauty is the ideal form of the individual body, just as civil order is, of the body politic. As sexual desire is aroused by beauty, so is political volition, by an ideal order of society. At focal points in the allegory, such as the cestus tournament, reference to both these fields of experience is combined. The cestus itself, which Florimell borrowed from Venus (IV. v. 5), is a complex symbol for a variety of bonds of amity: it signifies political loyalty, as much as the bond of friendship or of married love. Venus, after all, was not only the goddess of beauty and desire but also of civility and of all formal order; the cestus, Spenser tells us, belonged specifically to the Acidalian Venus. Thus, the two particular interpretations of Florimell are sometimes both applicable. Neither, however, will carry us all the way. If we interpret Florimell as Beauty, for instance, we shall make very little sense of her stay at the witch's cottage.[1]

If the above view of Book III is provisionally entertained, then the possibility emerges that the themes of the first three books form philosophical triads of the order:

Divinity: Matter: Ideal Form

or, in Orphic terms,

Heaven: Earth: Eros.[2]

This opens up a very large subject, which must be left for the present, with the brief hint that there is reason to suppose that in the articulation of the books of the *Faerie Queene* such large-scale triadic arrangements play an important part. The Veritas–Virtus–Amor triad (Pls. 1a, 1b) may be mentioned as perhaps the most immediately obvious of those composing the thematic structure of Books I–III.[3]

While the themes of Book III are appropriate to the symbolism of the triad, its overall character-grouping is not. It would be quite misleading to adduce the three foresters who attack Timias, the three

[1] For the political meaning of this episode, see Rathborne, pp. 279 and 287.

[2] It is significant, in this connection, that Ellrodt (p. 102) discusses the Garden of Adonis episode against the background of Le Roy's account of generation of life—an account in which the birth of life is presented as the result of a love-relationship between Heaven (sun) and Earth.

[3] On this triad, the so-called Triad of Fidius, see P. L. Williams, 'Two Roman Reliefs in Renaissance Disguise,' *JWI*, IV (1941); also Alciati, *Emblemata* (Lyons, 1600), Embl. IX, 'Fidei symbolum,' pp. 55–57.

knights who go to the help of Florimell in Canto i, and the three who storm the Castle of Malbecco. For these patterns are unemphatic, and could easily be paralleled with examples from other books— such as the similar ambush of Timias at VI. v. 17–22. Every reader must have noticed, indeed, how frequently trios of characters occur throughout the poem. But may not we see, in this indiscriminate profusion of triple arrangements, the very reason why such grouping is without emphasis in Book III? A modification of the pattern we are tracing may have been forced upon Spenser at this point, simply because his content was everywhere so thoroughly trinitarian, his style so replete with triadic progressions circularly unfolded after the manner of Ficino.[1] To make a triadic pattern prominent in Book III, he would have had to subdue triadic formulations elsewhere. But this must remain a matter of conjecture. Fortunately, the Pythagorean series is continued in the succeeding books with a simpler and more regular consistency.

[1] Obvious instances of the formal logic of 'unfolding' are IV. ii. 41–43 and VI. v. 20; the first of which is discussed in Wind, *Pagan Mysteries*, pp. 171–172. Trios of characters occur in almost every book: e.g., in I, Sansfoy *et al.*, Fidelia *et al.*; in II, Medina *et al.*, Alma's counsellors; in III, the foresters; in IV, the Fates, Priamond *et al.*; in VI, the Graces.

IV

The Tetrad

In memory, no doubt, of the special place held by the fourth digit in Pythagorean thought, Spenser has made the fourth book of the *Faerie Queene* surpass the others in richness of number symbolism. In its core cantos—the Temple of Venus and the spousal of Thames and Medway episodes—most of the numerology is astronomical in character, and therefore beyond the scope of the present chapter. In its narrative allegories, however, the arrangement is throughout dependent upon the tetrad, conceived as a symbol of friendship and concord.

Iamblichus attributes to Pythagoras the saying φιλότης ἰσότης, ἰσότης φιλότης, 'friendship is equality, equality friendship'; which he treats as a gnomic expression of arithmological and cosmological wisdom.[1] Remote from mathematics as the cryptic phrase may now seem, it embodies an ancient conception of four as a cosmic number of concord. The *locus classicus* for this conception in later tradition is a passage in the *Timæus* (31–32) describing the creation of world-order out of the elements. Here Plato discusses the necessity for *double mean terms* between the extremes of earth and fire. As Macrobius paraphrases him, his meaning is that a union of three elements, linked by only one mean, would be relatively weak; whereas in the case of four elements, held together by two means, the bonds are stable. This is partly because

each one of the elements appears to embrace the two elements bordering on each side of it by single qualities: water binds earth to itself by coldness, and air by moisture; air is allied to water by its moisture, and to fire by warmth. . . .

[1] Iamblichus, *De vita Pythag.*, clxi; discussed in Cornford, p. 4.

24

An added mutual attraction results from the fact that the two mean terms preserve the same proportion in density with each other as with the nearest extreme; so that the densities of more distant terms are also proportional.[1] Thus, the elements are interlocked by the very qualities which make them contrary to each other. It was because four was the first number to have the requisite two means that it became a symbol of cosmic harmony and concord. 'Borrowing the means from this number,' says Macrobius, 'the Creator bound the elements together with an unbreakable chain.'

This stable concord of the tetrad, with interlocking affinities and contraries held in tension by a double mean, seems to Plato imbued with friendship:

Out of these materials, such in kind and four in number, the body of the Cosmos was harmonized by proportion and brought into existence. *These conditions secured for it Amity,* so that being united in identity with itself it became indissoluble by any agent other than Him who had bound it together.[2]

The mention of friendship brings us back to the Pythagorean *symbolum* recorded by Iamblichus. We can now see this to be a gnomic expression of the charcter of the tetrad, whose double mean terms—

[1] Macrobius, *In somn. Scip.*, I. vi. 22–33; ed. Stahl, pp. 104–106. The proportions enumerated by Macrobius may be briefly listed as follows:

water : air : : air : fire
air : water : : water : earth
earth : water : : water : air
water : air : : air : fire

and (taking more distant terms):

earth : air : : water : fire.

[2] *Timæus*, 32B–C; tr. R. G. Bury (London, 1952), p. 61 (italics mine). The tetrad is also associated with *philia* by Alexander of Aphrodisias in his comment on Aristotle, *Metaphysics*, 987ª; on which see Cornford, p. 4. It is characteristic of Aristotle himself that, in his discussion of friendship in the *Nicomachean Ethics*, even while repeatedly invoking the Pythagorean dictum φιλότης ἰσότης, he should remain silent about the number mysticism connected with it. He enlarges the meaning instead in another direction; adding the notion of reciprocity or equality in the exchange of affection (1157ᵇ). This idea, too, is worked out by Spenser in Bk. IV, both in the altruistic mutual services of Cambell and Triamond at the tournament (IV. iv) and in the business-like exchange of favours between Paridell and Blandamour (IV. i).

Ficino preceded Spenser in using the analogy between personal friendship and the concord of the four elements. In a letter to Albertus Liscus, he writes jocularly that he feels himself to be constituted the airy mean between the fire and earth of Albertus and another friend, Jacobus (probably Jacobus Linfredinus) (Ficino, *Opera omnia,* p. 844).

equal in number to the extremes—make possible an indissoluble concord. The idea is reinforced formally by the symbolic arrangement of the four words: φιλότης ἰσότης, ἰσότης φιλότης.

Some such specific conceptions as these, rather than any mere associational link, prompted Spenser's choice of fourth place for his Legend of Friendship. As the episode of the spousal of Thames and Medway shows, he thought of Friendship not only as a personal and political virtue, but also as the cosmic power of Concord:

> By her the heaven is in his course contained,
> And all the world in state unmoved stands,
> As their Almightie maker first ordained,
> And bound them with inviolable bands.
>
> (IV. x. 35)

On the side of evil, Ate's activities are also on a universal scale; she is the Empedoclean Strife:

> For all this worlds faire workmanship she tride,
> Unto his last confusion to bring.
>
> (IV. i. 30)

The selection of these subjects for the fourth book might in itself be explained as the result of association of ideas—the same association that led Palingenius to treat concord in the fourth book of his *Zodiacus vitæ*.[1] But we have to envisage a much more deliberate and organic use of Pythagorean symbolism, when we find that throughout Book IV Spenser portrays friendships as occurring, not between pairs of characters, but among groups of four. What is still more conclusive, he shows moral concord, like cosmic concord, to be dependent on the completion of tetrads with double mean terms.

The most abstract statement of the tetradic theme occurs in the Temple of Venus episode, in an emblematic description of Dame Concord herself. Concord presents four aspects. Two are the extremes of Love and Hate, who appear as half-brothers 'of contrarie natures' standing on either side of her, whom she, from a mean position in the centre,

> tempred both,
> That she them forced hand to joyne in hand.
>
> (IV. x. 33)

[1] *The Zodiake of Life*, tr. Barnabe Googe, ed. Rosemond Tuve (New York, 1947), Bk. IV, 'Cancer,' pp. 51–61, where the peace, friendship, and concord of the elements are taken up in turn.

Dame Concord also, however, gives issue to 'blessed *Peace*, and *Friendship* trew,' her twins.[1] These are not only the result of mediation, but also aspects of the act itself. It is *by means of* reconciliation (Peace) and of personal friendship, that Scudamour is to negotiate, in his approach to Amoret, the conflicting extremes of sexual passion and sexual hostility. The disposition of the four emotional elements, two of contrary nature and two of similar, recalls the conditions of stable concord defined by Plato. Peace and Friendship are double mean terms in a system holding affinity and repulsion in tension:

FIRE	warm	dry	LOVE	affinity	extreme
AIR	warm	moist	FRIENDSHIP	affinity	mean
WATER	cold	moist	PEACE	no affinity	mean
EARTH	cold	dry	HATE	no affinity	extreme

If we added the concept of Love as 'the enimy of peace' from III. vi. 14, we would even have proportional relationships between alternate terms; but the cosmic analogy is perhaps not intended to be so detailed at this point.

The quartet to which the titular heroes belong displays the ideal operation of the tetrad in a more personal fashion. Between Cambell and Triamond themselves there is initially a mortal opposition of contraries. Both feel an affinity for Canacee; but Cambell's is 'the deare affection unto kindred sweet' and Triamond's the 'raging fire of love to woman kind.'[2] Inadequately resolved by Canacee, these competitive affinities can lead only to conflict *à outrance*. The intervention of Cambina as a second mean, however, leads to immediate reconciliation, and to a system of interlocking relationships linking all four characters permanently together. Cambell marries Cambina, and Triamond marries Canacee; while between each pair of the same sex 'true friendship and affection sweet' develops (IV. iii. 50–51). The double match is not arranged just to secure a happy ending; nor in

[1] IV. x. 32–34; notice the use of the scheme *chiasmus*, the same scheme as in the Pythagorean *symbolum* quoted above, whose ABBA arrangement echoes the structure of the tetrad. Spenser uses *chiasmus* also at IV. iii. 50. 9, IV. iv. 1, and IV. x. 32. 6–7: on each occasion while describing a tetrad. Wind (*Pagan Mysteries*, p. 172) regards Spenser's allegory of Concord, Love, and Hate as an instance of ' "infolding" of opposites into one'; the one, however, is itself *unfolded* into two—Peace and Friendship.

[2] Quotations from IV. ix. 1: an important stanza, from the schematic point of view, listing as it does the three kinds of competing affinities.

27

the interests of mere symmetry; nor to recommend the aristocratic custom of close intermarriage. Morally, it symbolizes the satisfactory resolution of the claims of family loyalty and of love: a resolution that Canacee herself found impossible. But there are obvious philosophical overtones. Although we are dealing here with individualized characters and not with abstract principles, the correspondence with the tetrad at the Temple of Venus is evidently close. Triamond and Cambell ('Whylome . . . foes the fellonest on ground' (IV. ii. 32)) are like the antipathetic extreme terms Love and Hate. Appropriate to these rôles are the magical aids they receive from their families. Thus, the ring of chastity given to Cambell to render him immune from (emotional) hurt indicates his rejection of love; while the souls incorporated in Triamond's are souls given in love.[1] Canacee, who at first feels affection (IV. iii. 35. 5) but not love (IV. ii. 37), takes the rôle of Friendship. Even more clearly, Cambina corresponds to Dame Concord's other daughter; for in her right hand she bears a caduceus particularly described as 'a rod of peace,' in her left the nepenthe of forgiveness that establishes 'sweet peace.'[2] United in 'bands of mutuall couplement,' the four friends at length enjoy the same concord that binds the macrocosm together. Indeed, their interlocking relationships exactly match those of the elements as formulated by Macrobius in the passage quoted above. We may demonstrate this by attempting a parody of Macrobius; casting Triamond as fire, Canacee as air, Cambina as water, and Cambell as earth:

> Cambina binds Cambell to herself by sexual love, and Canacee by friendship; Canacee is allied to Cambina by friendship and to Triamond by sexual love; Triamond mingles with Cambina because of sexual love, and with Cambell because of friendship.

Moreover, since the relationship of Triamond to Cambina is the same as that of Cambell to Canacee (that is, brother to sister), we

[1] A full discussion of Triamond's threefold life will be found in Seabury M. Blair, 'The Succession of Lives in Spenser's Three Sons of Agape,' *MLQ*, II (1941), 109–114. Tracing the idea that friendship doubles one's life-span to passages in Cicero and Ficino, Blair rejects 'the Feronia–Erulus analogy in the *Aeneid* noted by Upton' (112). The Virgilian passage, however, is no mere narrative analogue: what Upton did not note was that since Servius the threefold lives of Erulus had been interpreted as a symbol of man's multiplicity of souls.

[2] IV. iii. 42–43. I mention only similarities to the appropriate term of the archetypal tetrad; not the additional individual features that define Cambina's rôle more particularly.

even have an equivalent for the proportionality of alternate terms:

'As earth is to air, so water is to fire'[1]
As Cambell is to Canacee, so Cambina is to Triamond.

The story of the faithful friends Amyas and Placidas presents another variation of the tetradic pattern. Here the rival affinities, discussed abstractly in the three moralizing stanzas IV. ix. 1–3, are differently disposed. Æmylia, whose love has quenched her affection for kindred (IV. vii. 16), represents one extreme; while Pœana, whose love turns to grief and bitterness when she loses Amyas (IV. ix. 7–9, 13–14), is the other. Amyas, whose friendship for Placidas surpasses his love for Æmylia (IV. viii. 57), corresponds to the mean of Friendship; Placidas, as his name indicates, ought to act as the other mean, Peace. The two squires, though not twins by birth like Dame Concord's daughters, are nevertheless physically identical (IV. viii. 55 and ix. 10). It is this likeness, indeed, that makes possible the stratagem which leads to Amyas' release. And the function of the second mean is again emphasized; for the actions of Placidas are decisive in precipitating the solution of the plot.

The interlocking affinities and repulsions of the tetrad here find equivalents in the conflicting loyalties of an intricate emotional situation. Placidas, for instance, finds Pœana attractive,

Yet did this trustie Squire with proud disdaine
For his friends sake her offred favours scorne.
(IV. ix. 3)

Similarly, it is in the interests of Amyas' love that he should be impersonated by Placidas; but friendship towards the latter makes him oppose the plan (IV. viii. 58). Each of the four, we notice, has a tendency to overvalue one loyalty at the expense of another. Thus Æmylia sins against love of kindred; and Placidas, by being immoderately loyal to his friend, lacks the forgiveness required by his role as peacemaker (IV. ix. 15). Expressing the relationships schematically, one might say that the tetrad is defective because Friendship and Peace have changed places; so that Friendship and Love now compete, instead of being linked adjacent terms.

Arthur's additional mediation is needed to restore the tangled situation to 'peace and setled rest' (IV. ix. 17). When he has at last 'shut up all in frendly love,' another double match is arranged; and,

---

[1] Macrobius, *In somn. Scip.*, I. vi. 33; ed. Stahl, p. 106.

as before, this is permanently conclusive—'so stinted all their strife' (IV. ix. 15). Nowhere else in the book do we see more clearly the implication of Spenser's emphasis on the need for a second mean. Friendship by itself is not enough: only with reconciliation, forgiveness, and mutual adaptation, can there be any stable and peaceful relationship.

Where the friendships of Book IV involve evil characters, we find only gross travesties of the tetrad. So it is with the first group of friends, Paridell, Blandamour, Ate, and Duessa. Here, the friendship of Paridell and Blandamour is unstable because of the falsity of the system's mean terms. Instead of a peaceful mean to restrain aggression, there is Ate, 'mother of debate,' who finds

> fit opportunity
> To stirre up strife, twixt love and spight and ire
> (IV. ii. 11)

—strife, that is to say, between affinity and repulsion. For a mean on the side of attachment, there is only Duessa; so that the friendship is false and lacking in unity. Significantly, when Duessa mediates between Blandamour and Scudamour in a further variation of the tetrad, she proposes as ground for agreement the false principle that 'love is free, and led with selfe delight' (IV. i. 46). Nor has she the chastity and moderation requisite in the mean of Friendship. Consequently, since it is not 'combynd with vertues meet' (IV. ix. 1), the relationship between Blandamour and Paridell lacks any real basis, and must be unstable. It cannot survive the difference of interest that comes with the false Florimell. Conflict results between what are now directly opposed terms: a conflict that would be irreconcilable (as Spenser remarks at IV. ii. 20), if the Squire of Dames did not intervene as a new mean term, bringing a new common interest, the tournament.

Passing over the convergence of the various quartets of friends on the cestus tournament (where 'the knights in couples marcht, with ladies linckt attone' (IV. iv. 14)), and the succeeding realignments, we come to the reconciliation between Britomart and Arthegall in Canto vi. In this variation of the tetrad, the conflicting terms are for the first time of different sex. Scudamour, the patron of love, and the virtuous Arthegall, who has previously despised women (IV. vi. 28) and been 'rebellious unto love' (IV. vi. 31), are both at first opposed to Britomart. The conflict arises out of a series of errors about her

30

identity (that is, about the nature of love itself). In particular, a failure to recognize her femininity has led to rivalries and aggressions inappropriate between the sexes. Moreover, Scudamour's confusion between friendship and erotic passion has allowed Ate to instil into him a jealousy that makes his love immoderate. Britomart is here cast in the rôle of a mean term of the tetrad (the mean of Peace, as a later chapter will show); but it is only with the assistance of a second mean, Glauce, that all is 'upknit' (IV. vi. 30) in concord. This reconciliation has a structural function; for it initiates the treatment of concord between the sexes in the second half of the book.

Immediately before Scudamour's tale of the Temple of Venus there comes a final variation of the tetrad. In this, as in the last variation, the problem is not to harmonize different kinds of affinity, but different attitudes to the one affinity, sexual love. Britomart and Scudamour come upon four knights fighting among themselves:

> sterne *Druon,* and lewd *Claribell,*
> Love-lavish *Blandamour,* and lustfull *Paridell.*
> (IV. ix. 20)

The attitudes that the knights represent are defined with reference to two distinct polarities. These are the polarity Love/Rejection of love, and the polarity Constancy/Inconstancy:

> *Druons* delight was all in single life,
> And unto Ladies love would lend no leasure:
> The more was *Claribell* enraged rife
> With fervent flames, and loved out of measure:
> So eke lov'd *Blandamour,* but yet at pleasure
> Would change his liking, and new Lemans prove:
> But *Paridell* of love did make no threasure,
> But lusted after all, that him did move.
> So diversly these foure disposed were to love.
> (IV. ix. 21)

The knights' alignments repeatedly shift, in a confused manner, from the one axis to the other. Sometimes those who love—Blandamour and Claribell—join against those who do not (IV. ix. 26); sometimes the fickle and promiscuous—Blandamour and Paridell—join against those who, in whichever way, are more deeply committed to one course (IV. ix. 25). If this social system is considered as a form of the tetrad its most outstanding feature is the absence of mean terms. More than one pair of knights may be regarded as outer extremes; so that there can be nothing corresponding to the fixed sequence of the elements. Between the two possible schematizations, there is nothing to choose:

CLARIBELL	love	constancy	CLARIBELL	love	constancy
BLANDAMOUR	love	inconstancy	DRUON	disdain	constancy
PARIDELL	disdain	inconstancy	PARIDELL	disdain	inconstancy
DRUON	disdain	constancy	BLANDAMOUR	love	inconstancy

In fact, the complete disorder of such unmoderated, unharmonized inclinations, continually in conflict, continually in a state of flux, is an exact moral equivalent of chaos among the elements. And this is just the point Spenser himself makes; for he likens the battle to the 'rude unruliment' of winds that 'from all foure parts of heaven' confound the world 'as if in stead thereof they *Chaos* would restore' (IV. ix. 23).

Britomart and Scudamour attempt to mediate, but are outnumbered. Emphasis is laid, we note, on the proportion in which the extremes exceed the means: 'Foure charged two, and two surcharged one.'[1] The mean terms thus being unequal to the extreme terms, conflict must continue, until the arrival of Arthur and Amoret restores equality. The result is a harmonious double tetrad. In accordance with the specifically sexual focus (appropriate as we near the Temple), the mean position on the side of affinity is taken by Scudamour, the true lover, who bears as arms 'the God of love, with wings displayed wide' (IV. i. 39), and who was opposed in the preceding *mêlée* by Druon and Paridell, the two without love (IV. ix. 30). Similarly, the mean position on the side of restraint is occupied by Britomart, the exemplar of chastity, who was opposed by Claribell and Blandamour, the two immoderate lovers. The fact that both mediators require Arthur's help symbolizes the need for a twofold grace in the attainment of sexual harmony: an idea that is further developed in his subsequent reproof of the immoderate knights. This speech, which is couched in the language of the tournament allegory, reconciles the values of freedom and restraint; affirming the inviolability of the marital relationship ('Ye seemen much to blame,/To rip up wrong, that battell once hath tried'), but also its dependence on the lady's free choice ('the world this franchise ever yeelded' (IV. ix. 37)).

[1] On the word-play in this passage, see Linwood E. Orange, 'Spenser's *The Faerie Queene*, Book Four, IX. xxx. 5–9,' *Explicator*, XVII (1958), Comment 22.

While the above account of Book IV has been mostly confined to the narrative cantos, it is actually in the descriptive cantos that the most complex and accomplished number symbolism is to be found. The whole book, in fact, is saturated with numerology, as if Spenser had been possessed with a vision of number as the chain of concord binding the world's workmanship together. In the core cantos, however, although Pythagorean numbers abound, the main schemes are astronomical and must await analysis in a later chapter. For the present, we may consider it established that the matter of Book IV is selected in accordance with the Pythagorean symbolism of the fourth digit, and shaped to an appropriate arithmological pattern. Throughout the intricate dance, in which its formations of friends, relatives, and lovers group and regroup, the basic figure, as we have seen, is always a *pas de quatre*. Each episode has its four principals, linked by interlocking emotional bonds, in imitation of the cosmic tetrad.

V

The Pentad

i

I F the tetrad is the combination that unlocks the allegory of Book IV, the pentad is almost equally helpful in approaching Book V. The fifth digit had a varied range of meanings, as everyone knows who has visited Sir Thomas Browne's *Garden of Cyrus*. Its principal Pythagorean epithet, however, was Justice:

To enlarge this contemplation unto all the mysteries and secrets, accommodable unto this number, were inexcusable Pythagorisme, yet cannot omit the ancient conceit of five surnamed the number of justice; as justly dividing between the digits,[1] and hanging in the centre of Nine, described by square numeration, which angularly divided will make the decussated number. . . . And might be the originall of that common game among us, wherein the fifth place is Soveraigne, and carrieth the chief intention. The Ancients wisely instructing youth, even in their recreations unto virtue, that is, early to drive at the middle point and Central Seat of justice. . . . The Ancients have named it the Divisive Number, justly dividing the Entities of the world.[2]

[1] Cf. Iamblichus, *Theologoumena arithmeticæ*, ed. V. de Falco (Leipzig, 1922), pp. 39 f. Ficino, following Plato, finds a different, more metaphysical significance in the division of the numbers of the decad by five: see his *Commentary on the Timæus*, Ch. xxviii; *Opera omnia*, p. 1451.

[2] *The Garden of Cyrus*, Ch. v; ed. J. Carter (Cambridge, 1958), p. 108. Not only does five occupy a central position among the nine digits; but when nine points are described in three parallel rows of three ('square numeration') the diagonal rows consist of five points, arranged in the quincunxial ('decussated') shape that is Browne's subject. (Note that *The Garden of Cyrus* has, inevitably, just five chapters.) The ancient identification of five as Justice (see, e.g., Iamblichus, *Theolog. arith.*, ed. de Falco, p. 41) was reinforced in the Middle Ages by the association of the Law with the Pentateuch. Dante was familiar with the symbolism, for in the *Paradiso*, in the Heaven of Jupiter, the holy lights forming the

34

With what ease must Browne have been able to grasp the numerical plan of the *Faerie Queene*! The cluster of associations with the pentad that he lists here correspond exactly to the principal subjects of Spenser's fifth book. The Pythagorean conception of five as divisive justice, for instance, is reflected in the poem's vision of a former age when 'Justice . . . did divide her dred beheasts' (Proem, 9); in the encounter with the Giant with the scales (V. ii. 29–54); and in the arbitration between the sons of Milesio (V. iv. 4–20), where we see Arthegall 'justly dividing the Entities of the world' in the shape of territorial and marine wealth. As for the meaning sovereignty, this is a theme not only of the trial of Duessa but also of the Radigund episode, and of the liberation of Belge and Irena from foreign tyrants. Even the 'Central Seat of justice' figures in the book. Isis and Mercilla both occupy such a throne. Isis', as we shall see, is numerologically central; while the sovereign position of Mercilla's, between Arthur and Arthegall, is mentioned explicitly (V. ix. 37).

Another epithet of the pentad is Marriage. Plutarch explains that five is named Marriage because it is generated by a combination of two and three: the first of the even (feminine) and the first of the odd (masculine) numbers.[1] As Browne puts it, five is

the Conjugall Number, which ancient Numerists made out by two and three, the first parity and imparity, the active and passive digits, the materiall and formall principles in generative Societies.

In this connection it is perhaps significant that the public spousal of Marinell and Florimell is held back until Book V. Books III–V, through which the stories of Florimell and Britomart are continued, share the subject of love; but each of the three concentrates on a single aspect of it. While III is concerned with chastity, and the orientation of desire towards generation, IV is concerned with love as a personal friendship. By the same token, in so far as V deals with love, it is concerned with its expression in marriage *considered as an institution*.[2] It is when love is so considered that those problems of

[1] The monad not being counted a number. See *De E apud Delphos*, 388A, and cf. Cornford, p. 2.

[2] According to Ficino (loc. cit., p. 34, n. 1 above), five symbolizes the embodiment of virtue in action.

Eagle's eyebrow-arch number five; cf. Hopper, *Medieval Number Symbolism*, pp. 86. 115, and 180. For the less common attachment of the epithet Justice to the tetrad and octad, based on a different application of the idea of equal division, see Macrobius, *In somn. Scip.*, I. v. 17; ed. Stahl, p. 98 and n.

male sovereignty arise, which are touched on in the Radigund episode. Similarly, all we are told about the relationships between Amidas and Bracidas and their wives has to do with dowry disputes, and thus with the legal, institutional aspect of marriage.

ii

Can it be coincidence that the numbers of these books, 3, 4, and 5, denote the Pythagorean zoogonic triangle, which provides the basis for the Nuptial Number or Number of the State in Plato's *Republic*?[1] If we say that it is coincidental, then we must be prepared to explain away further 'coincidences.' For Book V contains many other allusions to the Platonic Number. Most obvious is the representation of the Pythagorean triangle in the stanza-totals of certain significantly placed cantos. Few cantos of the *Faerie Queene* have round-number stanza-totals; and of these nearly half occur in this book, where Cantos i, iii, vi, and ix have the totals 30, 40, 40, and 50 respectively.[2] (Multiplication of the sides of the 3, 4, 5 triangle by 10—an operation not affecting their ratio—is forced on Spenser by the need to maintain a reasonable canto-length; but it also enables him to give to the core canto, V. ix, containing the episode of Mercilla's Court, the total 50: itself in Philo's view the Platonic Number.[3]) The repetition

[1] *Republic*, 546. This passage received as much attention as any other, in the Renaissance; see, e.g., Ficino's long *Expositio circa numerum nuptialem* (*Opera omnia*, pp. 1414–25), and Barozzi's *Commentarium in locum Platonicum obscurissimum* (Bologna, 1566). Outstanding among more recent commentaries is James Adam, *The Republic of Plato*, Vol. II (Cambridge, 1929), 201–209 and 264–312, which presents a solution of the Number accepted by Marc Denkinger in his fuller analysis of the mathematical aspects, 'L'Enigme du nombre de Platon et la loi des dispositifs de M. Diès,' *Revue des Études Grecques*, LXVIII (1955), 38–76. Consult also Robert S. Brumbaugh, *Plato's Mathematical Imagination* (Bloomington, Ind., 1954). For convenience, I append Adam's translation of the passage: 'The number of a human creature is the first number in which root and square increases, having received three distances and four limits, of elements that make both like and unlike and wax and wane, render all things conversable and rational with one another. Of which the numbers 4, 3, married with 5, furnish two harmonies when thrice increased, the one equal an equal number of times, so many times 100, the other of equal length one way, but oblong—on the one side of 100 squares rising from rational diameters of five diminished by one each, or if from irrational diameters, by two; on the other, of 100 cubes of 3.'

[2] It may be significant that the numerical *positions* of three of the cantos, with stanza-totals 30, 40, and 50, form the series 1, 3, 9. This is one of the so-called *lambda* series of the *Timæus*, and has sometimes been thought to underly the Nuptial Number: see B. Jowett, *The Republic of Plato* (Oxford, 1881), p. cxv.

[3] See ibid. $50 = 3^2 + 4^2 + 5^2$, the squares of the three sides of the Pythagorean triangle.

of the 40 total seems to be intended to produce a sequence of four terms, that will recall Plato's statement that in the first part of his Number the 'increases' receive 'three distances and four limits';[1] as well as to allude to the tetrad of concord (with its twin means), on whose prior establishment the justice of Book V is based.

Ancient and Renaissance commentators agreed that Plato made use of the Pythagorean triangle in constructing his Number;[2] though there were many theories as to how exactly he did so. James Adam[3] has shown that Aristotle (*Pol.* E 12. 1316ª) and several other early authorities gave the first part of the Number the arithmetical solution $3^3 + 4^3 + 5^3 = 6^3 = 216$. Plato's phrase 'the number of a human creature,' he convincingly argues, must mean the period of human gestation.[4] 216 is such a number,

known to the Pythagoreans as the ψυχογονικὸς κύβος . . . because it expresses the period of the seven months' child, counted in days. It is also the cube of the number 6, which the Pythagoreans called the marriage number, owing, as we are told, to the fact that 6 represents the union of the first male number 3 and the first female number 2 ($3 \times 2 = 6$). In other respects also the number 216 maintains its character as a matrimonial and generative force: for it is the cube of the area of the zoogonic triangle and the product of the cubes of the first male and female numbers ($2^3 \times 3^3 = 216$). 216 . . . was suited to express the meaning which is here attached to it, that is to say the number of the seven months' child. I will only add, in conclusion, that the number of the ἐννεάμηνον γεννητόν [nine months' child] was itself also connected with the smaller number by adding thereto the product of the sides of the triangle . . . $3 \times 4 \times 5 + 216 = 276$.

The second part of the Number, with its two 'harmonies,' Adam interprets as $(3 \times 4 \times 5)^4 = 3600^2 = 4800 \times 2700$. Again with the support of Aristotle, he connects these two 'harmonies' of the *Republic* with the two cycles of the *Politicus*. He identifies the second

---

[1] *Rep.*, 546B: τρεῖς ἀποστάσεις, τέτταρας δὲ ὅρους λαβοῦσαι. As Adam shows (pp. 270–272), the ἀποστάσεις are the three dimensions, and the ὅροι the attendant limits, of a solid figure; properly understood, the phrase as a whole refers to the operation of cubing. It has, however, been given other interpretations. Ficino (pp. 1414–15) translates 'tres distantias atque quatuor terminos'; taking the phrase to mean a series of four *numbers* (namely the first two cubic primes with their mean proportionals).

[2] See Adam, pp. 266–267, citing Aristotle, *Pol.*, E 12.1316ª; Plutarch, *De Iside*, 373F; Proclus; and Aristides Quintilianus.

[3] Pp. 267–275 and 291–295.

[4] Pp. 268 and 293, from where the following quotation (stripped of its documentation) is also taken.

part of the Number, moreover, with the Platonic Great Year: the cycle in which the heavenly bodies go through all their possible courses and return to their original position relative to each other.[1] Thus 3600^2, or $360^2 \times 100$, expresses in days the duration of a Great Year in the life of the universe; expressed in years, the figure is 36,000, since Plato customarily used an ideal division of 360 days to the year. Plato also counted the ideal duration of human life as 100 years, or 36,000 days; so that a day in the life of man, it follows, will correspond to a year in the aeon of the macrocosm.[2] Further, the Great Year may be denoted by

a rectangle whose sides are respectively the longer period and the sum of the longer and shorter periods of gestation in the race of man, after it has been multiplied by the square of the Pythagorean perfect number 10. As the Universe is a 'magnus homo,' and man a 'brevis mundus,' these and similar analogies may well have seemed significant to the Pythagoreans.[3]

Ficino's solution of the Number should also be mentioned. He too uses the Pythagorean triangle; but he apparently takes Aristotle's phrase 'when the number of this diagram is made solid' to refer to the cubing of the sum of the sides of the triangle, rather than of its area. Accordingly, he arrives at the number $(3 + 4 + 5)^3 = 12^3 = 1728$. For this solution he finds support in Plato's frequent veneration of the duodecad, not to speak of its association with the zodiacal signs and with the orbital periods of certain planets governing the conditions of birth.[4] He argues, moreover, that 1728 is *dignus* because it yields the numbers 1000, 728, 700, and 28, to each of which he assigns Pythagorean meanings more or less relevant to the Platonic passage.[5]

[1] See Adam, pp. 295–302.

[2] See ibid., pp. 202, 301.

[3] I.e., $360^2 \times 10^2 = 270 \times (270 + 210) \times 10^2$.

[4] Such as Sol (12-month orbit) and Jupiter (12 years): see Ficino, *Opera omnia*, pp. 1415–16.

[5] Thus, 1000 is the cube of 10, and itself a cosmic number relating to the firmament of fixed stars; 700 'is appropriate to the 7 planets following the firmament'; and 28, besides having an association with the lunar cycle, is a perfect number (ibid., pp. 1422 f.). The use of the number 700 at this point is of interest in view of its appearance as the most inclusive stanza-total of Bk. II of *F.Q.* Throughout, Ficino's exposition is based upon an astrological interpretation of the title of the Platonic Number, 'lord of better and of worse births'—see especially pp. 1414–15, and Ch. xvii: 'De numero perfecto, et generatione divina, et observatione cœlestium,' pp. 1424–25.

These interpretations of the Platonic Number have been summarized at some length, because they seem to me to throw an unexpected light on the numerology not only of Book V, but of the poem as a whole. Let us consider, firstly, the stanza-total[1] of Book V, the number 576. We notice that it is a square number ($576 = 24^2$). This is appropriate to the book's subject, for all square numbers carried the meaning Justice.[2] But what is more remarkable, 576 is exactly one-third of Ficino's value for the Platonic Number. The Number itself, 1728, is the total of distinct rhymes in Book V. Another property of the stanza-total, which may well, however, be accidental (and to which, in consequence, I do not attach such importance), is that $576 = 216 + 360$. That is to say, it represents an addition of the two parts of the Nuptial Number, according to Aristotle's solution—Plato's 'number of a human creature' and the root of his 'number of the macrocosm.'[3]

These numerological features encourage us to enquire whether the whole structure of the *Faerie Queene* may not be built upon mathematical analogies between the periodical cycles of the universe and of the life of man; just as Hieatt has shown to be the case in *Epithalamion*. An astronomical structure is indeed revealed by this line of investigation, and will be dealt with in its proper place. One aspect of the structure may be mentioned here, however, since it concerns the Platonic Number. It is natural to suppose that, if the *Faerie Queene* has a numerical and astronomical pattern comparable with that of *Epithalamion*, its overall line-count will be similarly significant. In the latter poem, we recall, the total of long lines is 365, the number of days in the solar year. Now, there is only one periodical cycle with a phase of such magnitude as to correspond to the line-total of the whole *Faerie Queene*, a number which runs into many thousands.

[1] Counting proem stanzas, but not argument stanzas.
[2] For the evidence that square numbers symbolized Justice, see Hopper, 'Spenser's "House of Temperance." '
[3] Omitting the factor 100, which is introduced towards the end of Plato's account of the Number. For the addition of the two parts of the Number, I know of no direct precedent; though there is something not unlike it in Aristides Quintilianus' addition $216 + 3 \times 4 \times 5 = 276$, to form the period of a 9-month birth: see Adam, p. 293. The ancient significance of the number 216 was also known to the Renaissance through Vitruvius' observation (*De architectura*, V, Preface, 3–4) that the Pythagoreans 'wrote their rules cube fashion' and fixed upon the modulus of 216 lines—i.e., 6^3—to represent the cube. On this point, see Ch. xv below.

That is the Platonic Great Year. The identification of this cycle as a 36,000-year period was well known in the Renaissance from such text-books as Barozzi's *Cosmographia* and Sacrobosco's *De sphæra*.[1] It was therefore possible for Spenser to have used it as an easily recognizable figure for his line-total. Moreover, if our interpretation of the numerology of Book V is correct, it was logical that he should use such a figure; the allusions to the Number of the State strongly encourage the reader to expect the macrocosmic number in the over-all line-count.

We find that Spenser did in fact so use the number of the Great Year cycle. As a simple calculation shows, the line-total of Part I of *The Faerie Queene*, in the 1590 edition,[2] is exactly 18,000.

Why Spenser should have abandoned this modulus in Part II (where the line-total is only 15,741), I am unable to say.[3] We may reasonably suppose, nevertheless, that the line-total of 18,000 for Part I implies a grand line-total for the completed *Faerie Queene* in twelve books, of 36,000 × 2. Thus the numerological movement of

---

[1] See Adam, pp. 302–305, where it is pointed out that the fact that the Great Year was called the *annus platonicus* indicates a Ptolemaic tradition of correct interpretation of Plato's Number. Various other figures for the Great Year were, of course, proposed; among the most prominent of those not listed in Adam are the 15,000 years of Macrobius, *In somn. Scip.* II. xi. 5–11 (ed. Stahl, pp. 220–221 and n.), and the 12,954 years of Servius, on *Aen.* III. 284. For the continuation of the idea of a Great Year through the Middle Ages, see Lynn Thorndike, *A History of Magic and Experimental Science*, 6 vols. (New York, 1923–41), index, s.v. '*annus magnus*,' and George Sarton, *Introduction to the History of Science*, Carnegie Inst. of Washington Pubs., CCCLXXVI, 2 vols. (Baltimore, 1927–31), index, s.v. 'world year.'

[2] See Table II. With regard to this total, four points should be observed: (1) The stanza I. xi. 3, which first appeared in 1596, is not included. (2) In the 1596 edn. the altered conclusion of Bk. III is two stanzas shorter than in the 1590 edn.—a change only partly compensated for by the addition of I. xi. 3. The count applies, therefore, only to the first, 1590 edn. (3) Both proem and argument stanzas are included in the count. The latter have been treated throughout as couplets in fourteeners; a form often printed as four lines at the printer's convenience. Commonly in *F.Q.* the second halves of the fourteener lines are not begun with a capital letter. (4) It is assumed that the text stanzas are uniform in length. The significance of the defective stanza in Bk. I is discussed below, p. 144, n. 1; where also the probability of chance occurrence of the 18,000 total is estimated.

[3] The obvious explanation—that the 1596 edn. was put through the press too hastily for its numerology to be fully worked out—seems to me improbable, in view of the many complex symmetries actually present in Pt. II. In any case, I am unwilling to engage in speculation about stages of composition; we must deal with the poem we have, and not another.

the whole poem would have corresponded to *two* Great Years, and embraced Plato's two cycles—each of them a Great Year in duration —the peaceful progressive cycle of Uniformity, and the discordant retrogressive cycle of Dissimilarity.[1] This result affords an experimental verification of the main drift, at least, of my interpretation of Book V.

We have now to consider the more immediate structural implications of Spenser's allusions to the Nuptial Number. These allusions may be thought to support our original hypothesis, that, in distribut-

TABLE II: LINE TOTALS

	Cantos only		Cantos and proem		Cantos, proem, and arguments	
	Stanza total	Line total	Stanza total	Line total	Stanza total	Line total
Book I (1590)	616	5544	620	5580	632	5604
(1596)	617	5553	621	5589	633	5613
II	683	6147	688	6192	700	6216
III (1590)	679	6111	684	6156	696	6180
(1596)	677	6093	682	6138	694	6162
IV	599	5391	604	5436	616	5460
V	565	5085	576	5184	588	5208
VI	554	4986	561	5049	573	5073
Part I (1590)	1978	17,802	1992	17,928	2028	18,000
(1596)	1977	17,793	1991	17,919	2027	17,991
II	1718	15,462	1741	15,669	1777	15,741

ing his treatment of sexual love between books bearing the numbers 3, 4, and 5, he had in mind the Pythagorean zoogonic triangle which governs the increase of life.[2] But a further possibility now occurs: namely that he may be proposing an imaginative solution of the Platonic Number. Does he mean to imply that a right proportion

[1] On the connection of the two cycles of the *Politicus* with the Number of the *Republic*, see Adam, pp. 297–302. Note that 18,000 is itself Heraclitus' value for the Great Year, according to Stobæus (see Adam, p. 303 and n.).

[2] On the significance of the zoogonic triangle, see Adam, pp. 291, 293, and 299–300.

between the different elements of marriage (sexual relation, personal relation, social institution) is the key to those 'laws of prosperous birth or infertility,' inaccessible to reasoning alone (*Republic*, 546 A–B), but enshrined by Plato in his mysterious Number?[1]

We are on surer ground when we turn to the implications for Book V itself. Relating the book to the Platonic Number clearly puts us in a better position to understand the unity underlying its combination of marital and political topics. The Number describes the cycles of growth and of dissolution to which all created life (even that of ideal cities) is subject; and Spenser's use of it here is yet another expression of a theme ubiquitous in his work—the purpose of sexual generation in renewing the life of the state and of the universe. More particularly, the book's number symbolism helps us to see the full relevance of the proem. Its complaint about the decay of the macrocosm, and its circumstantial account of the changing relative positions of the heavenly bodies since 'they first tooke/Their setting forth' now stand out as an astronomical description of Plato's second cycle of discord and strife, the movement of ἀνομοιότης that constitutes the present age. The displacement of the zodiacal constellations, described in Proem, 5–6, is a phenomenon produced by the cyclic precession of the equinoxes. Since Hipparchus, the period of this cycle had been estimated at 36,000 years—the same as the *annus platonicus*, with which it was commonly identified, or perhaps confused.[2] Spenser draws attention to the period of cosmic deterioration by his references to specific intervals of time: 'these few thousand yeares'; 'since the terme of fourteene hundred yeres' (Proem, 5, 7). Moreover, his mention of solar ἀνακύκλησις in Proem 8 recalls the allusion to the same phenomenon in the introduction to the myth of the two cycles in the *Politicus*; such legends handed down from 'Ægyptian Wisards old' were often regarded as mythical expressions of the transition from one cyclical movement to another.[3] It need hardly be said that Spenser, as a Christian of his time, cannot have accepted Plato's conception of repeated cycles in its entirety. To

---

[1] This view would seem to gain support from the first episode in Bk. V, where Arthegall's adjudication between Sir Sanglier and the squire is essentially an affirmation that legal right in marriage depends upon a relationship of love.

[2] On the question whether the agreement between the precessional period and the Great Year can have been a coincidence, see Macrobius, *In somn. Scip.*, ed. Stahl, p. 221 n. and Adam, pp. 304–305.

[3] *Politicus*, 268E; see Adam, p. 298.

Spenser, the movement of the heavens towards 'their last ruinous decay' (Proem 6) must have seemed historically final: a movement to be succeeded, not by the natural renovation of a new cycle, but by a 'time when no more *Change* shall be' (VII. viii. 2). Strictly speaking, therefore, the *annus platonicus* should have been analogous to the *total* term of the life of the universe. Nevertheless, the idea of transition between cycles could be assimilated, so long as it applied to the remote past. In the *Politicus* myth, our own era with its discordant movement is said to have been preceded by a golden age of concord and harmony; and at the beginning of Book V Spenser adumbrates just such an age, by his allusions to the myths of Astræa and the *saturnia regna*.[1] It should be noticed, too, that Book V comes immediately after the three harmonious cantos which conclude Book IV. This sequence is underlined numerologically; for the immediately preceding canto, IV. xii (where Marinell and Florimell are reconciled), has a stanza-total of 35: a number which the Pythagoreans thought of as a 'harmony,' and which, for this reason, contributed in various ways to both parts of the Platonic Number.[2]

[1] Plato's myth of the retrogressive movement of the cosmos should be seen against the background of an early cosmogonic tradition which imagined a whole succession of ages, each of them characterized by a symbolic metal. In particular, he drew on a passage in Hesiod concerning the end of the *fifth* era, our own age of iron (see Adam, pp. 296–297). Spenser seems to have been influenced by the same passage, for he makes extensive use of this imagery in his fifth book. Not only is Talus an 'yron man' bearing an iron flail, but the description of Grantorto at V. xii. 14 ('a cote of yron plate,' 'a steele cap . . . Of colour rustie browne,' 'an huge Polaxe . . . Whose steale was yron studded') and of the Soldan's chariot at V. viii. 41–42 repeatedly refer to the same metal. By contrast, Astræa gives Arthegall a sword Chrysaor 'garnisht all with gold,' and Mercilla appears in a blaze of gold (V. ix. 27–28). On the topical application of Earth's metallic ages in chiliastic and apocalyptic literature, see Ernest Lee Tuveson, *Millennium and Utopia* (Berkeley and Los Angeles, 1949), p. 40, etc.; and Frances A. Yates, 'Queen Elizabeth as Astræa,' *JWI*, X (1947), 27–28 and 82.

[2] See Adam, pp. 294, 301–302. On 35 as a harmony, see Plutarch, *De animæ procreatione*, 1017F. Aspects of the harmonious 35 which are particularly relevant to its use at this point in Bk. IV are its union of the male and female cubes 27 and 8 (see Macrobius, *In somn. Scip.*, I. vi. 14–16; ed. Stahl, p. 102), and its significance as the ideal age for marriage (see Ficino, *Opera omnia*, p. 1424). It is interesting to note that A. C. Hamilton has arrived, by quite a different route, at the view that Bk. V represents an apocalyptic stage of history, after the cosmic harmony of Bk. IV: see his *The Structure of Allegory in 'The Faerie Queene'* (Oxford, 1961), Ch. v, *passim*, and p. 221: 'At the end of Book IV when the marriage of the Medway and the Thames heralds the bursting of the waters which precedes the rebirth of England, and the return of Spring in the person of Florimell completes the natural cycle, Plato's Great Year stands

Some may object that Spenser is not likely to have used the Platonic Number so extensively without making some verbal allusion to its mathematical form. As it happens, however, he does make just such an allusion. It will be remembered that all interpreters agreed in regarding the Number as essentially a cubic construction. Now, when Astræa left Earth, she furnished Arthegall with an iron man, Talus. As is well known, Spenser found the material for this allegory in the legend of a brazen law-giver recounted by Plato, Apollonius Rhodius, and Apollodorus. Plato's guardian of Crete, however, was not called *Talus*, but *Talo*.[1] This is surely no casual alteration; for *talus* is a Latin word meaning 'cube.' Being the most stable of all solid shapes, the cube was an emblem of virtue:[2] a symbolism referred to in the description of Talus as 'immoveable' (V. i. 12). But it seems plausible also to find in his name a covert allusion to the construction of the Platonic Number.

iii

In the episodic struction of Book V, numerical arrangement is again highly significant. The somewhat intricate design may be clarified by the table on page 45.

We notice that the action of the book is divided into two equal parts by Arthegall's captivity among the Amazons, during which Britomart assumes the patronage of justice, in the two central cantos, V. vi and vii. Thus, sovereign power has in a double sense fallen into female hands. Before the central section, there are *five* cantos in which Arthegall represents sovereign Justice *simpliciter*. After his reinstatement, however, he owes his authority to Britomart, and later to the commission granted by Mercilla; so that it is a new Arthegall, exercising Justice tempered with Equity, who in the remaining *five* cantos

[1] Nom. Τάλως. See Spenser, *Works*, ed. H. J. Todd, Vol. II (London, 1805), pp. xlviii–1 n.

[2] On this meaning of the cube, see Guy de Tervarent, *Attributs et Symboles dans l'art profane 1450–1600*, Travaux D'Humanisme et Renaissance, XXIX (Geneva, 1958), cols. 136–137. Vitruvius (see p. 39, n. 3 above) had specified the number 216 as the immovable cube *par excellence*.

poised to turn down into another cycle.' The numerological pattern which I have been describing (and on which I had stumbled before reading Hamilton's book) corroborates his daring interpretation in a most striking manner; it is not often in literary criticism that such an objective, almost mathematical, verification is possible.

(V. viii–xii) co-operates with Arthur. This change is symbolized by Britomart's dream at Isis Church, in which the sovereign power of Arthegall–Osiris is subdued to the grace and equity of Britomart–Isis. The exact bisection of the book is emphasized by the positioning of the Isis Church canto, V. vii. Introducing the second half, its first three stanzas announce a new theme, Equity—'that part of Justice' with which Spenser is now to deal.[1] At this point, moreover, there falls the arithmetical centre of the book: V. vii. 4, a stanza concerning the 'like race in equall justice' of sun and moon which, as we shall see, occupies a key position in the astronomical structure of the poem. All this is in accordance with the meaning of the goddess Isis herself. For we are told that she represents Equity; and we know that her name was sometimes connected with the Greek ἴσος, 'equal.' Appropriately, Spenser so places her temple that it exemplifies equal division in a formal manner.

Canto number	Episode	Episode number
i	Sanglier	1
ii	Pollente and Munera	2
ii	The Giant with the scales	3
iii	The spousal of Marinell and Florimell	4
iv	The sons of Milesio	5
iv–v	Arthegall among the Amazons	6
vi	Britomart and Dolon	7
vii	ISIS CHURCH	1
vii	Britomart among the Amazons	2
viii	Samient and the Soldan	3
ix	Guyle	4
ix	MERCILLA'S COURT	5
x	Gerioneo's Seneschal	6
xi	Gerioneo	7
xi	Burbon	8
xii	Grantorto	9

So much is obvious; even if it has not in fact previously been demonstrated. The numerical disposition of episodes, however, is less obvious. As the table will show, the first of the two equal divisions of the book contains 7 episodes, the second 9. (Of the 9 episodes in the second half, Mercilla's Court takes fifth place; so that she occupies a

[1] See esp. V. vii. 3; and cf. V. x. 1–3, a justification of the treatment of Mercy as a part of Justice. Hamilton (p. 189) comes to a similar conclusion regarding the division of Bk. V between Justice and Mercy.

'Central Seat of justice' in the sovereign position.[1]) Moreover, the two medullar cantos, containing the Isis Church and Mercilla's Court episodes, are again numbered vii and ix. Why this emphasis on the numbers 7 and 9? I would suggest that we are meant to recall, here, the numerical description of the Castle of Alma:

> a quadrate was the base
> Proportioned equally by seven and nine;
> Nine was the circle set in heavens place,
> All which compacted made a goodly diapase.
>
> (II. ix. 22)

Book V, it seems, is also 'proportioned equally by seven and nine.' The same parallel explains why the episodes of Book V are proportioned 7 : 9, and not 9 : 7. As Sir Kenelm Digby observes in connection with the Castle of Alma,[2] 7 signifies the mortal, mutable part of man, 9 the immortal, heavenly part. How suitable, then, that it should be the second half of Book V that contains 9 episodes: the half concerned with the perfected virtue of gracious Justice, Justice mingled with a Mercy 'borne of heavenly race' (V. x. 1).

Spenser's desire to proportion Book V by 7 and 9 may have been an additional reason for the repetition of the number 40 in the series of round-number stanza-totals. As we saw, this series runs 30, 40, 40, 50. We now notice that $30 + 40 = 7 \times 10$, $40 + 50 = 9 \times 10$, and $30 + 40 + 40 + 50 = 16 \times 10$. Thus the series makes yet another allusion to the quadrate (signifying Justice[3]) proportioned equally by 7 and 9. Finally, it should be remembered that the numbers 7 and 9, being the measure in months of the shorter and longer periods of human gestation respectively, contributed to the Platonic Number. Indeed, Aristides Quintilianus' discussion of the Pythagorean triangle contains an arithmetical operation very similar to Spenser's. He notices that the sides 3 and 4 add to 7, the period of the ἑπτάμηνος, and the sides 4 and 5 to 9, that of the ἐννεάμηνος.[4]

---

[1] The stanza V. x. 1, which concerns Mercy's origin in the 'Almighties everlasting seat' is actually the centre *stanza* in the second half of the book, being 145 stanzas from the end, and 145 stanzas from the centre of the whole book at V. vii. 4.

[2] *Observations;* in *Variorum Spenser* [*Var. Sp.*], II, 475–477.

[3] See above, p. 39, n. 2.

[4] See Adam, p. 294 n. Spenser's multiplication of these numbers by ten can also be paralleled: Macrobius (*In somn. Scip.*, I. vi. 17; ed. Stahl, p. 103) notes that 'the embryo moves either on the seventieth or the ninetieth day after conception. Multiply these numbers by three and you get in the one case a term of

By contrast with these complexities, the book's schemes of characters present a welcome simplicity. Arrangement by fives is only less regular here than tetradic arrangement in Book IV. The episodes of Sir Sanglier; of Pollente; of the sons of Milesio; of Dolon; and of Grantorto: all have five characters.[1] Throughout the Court of Mercilla, too, five is the modulus. Thus, the attendants upon Mercilla's throne number five, even though Spenser has to make up this total by adding to the traditional three *Litæ* (Dice, Eunomie, Eirene) the two virtues Temperance and Reverence. The personified values who give evidence for and against Duessa are also marshalled in groups of five;[2] and after Ate turns Queen's evidence there is a further group of five prosecution witnesses (V. ix. 47–48).

[1] Arthegall, Talus, Sanglier, squire, and lady; Arthegall, Talus, Dony, Pollente, and Munera; Arthegall, Amidas, Bracidas, Lucy, and Philtra (Talus not participating); Britomart, Talus, Dolon, and Dolon's two sons; Arthegall, Talus, Sergis, Irena, and Grantorto.

[2] V. ix. 43–45. In the case for the prosecution there are actually more than five items, but only five individual named plaintiffs—an instance of Spenser having his numerological cake and eating it.

---

seven months [measured in days], and in the other a term of nine.' In the action of *F.Q.*, the seven-month period is twice used prominently. The confinement of Florimell is of this duration (IV. xi. 4); and so is that of Amoret (IV. i. 4). In this connection it is interesting that Hamilton interprets the tearing and loss of Florimell's girdle as the loss of her maidenhead (p. 150); and relates the spousal of Thames and Medway to the 'bursting of the waters which precedes the rebirth of England' (p. 221).

VI

The Hexad

T HE matter of Book VI appears to be less closely related than that of any preceding book to the Pythagorean theory of number. Perhaps the virtue of Courtesy resisted arithmological treatment; or perhaps Spenser felt the need of a change of mode at this stage in the poem. At any rate, there is no symbolic conception of the hexad known to me that can constitute a centre for all the themes of the sixth book. Only partial connections with the symbolic number series suggest themselves.

Six was, as we have seen, a Pythagorean marriage number, being the product of the first feminine and first masculine numbers. It was given the epithet ζωογονητική, 'procreative.'[1] Spenser possibly means us to recognize the selection of a corresponding sphere of life for Book VI, in its concern with children, the *product* of marital union. This concern is shown not only in the stories directly involving children and their parents (Priscilla and her father; Aladine and his father Aldus; Matilda and the foundling; Pastorella and Meliboe; Pastorella, Bellamour, and Claribell), which are far more numerous here than in any other book; but also in the various treatments of problems of nurture, and of the effects upon character of noble or base birth. So far as I can tell, this numerological decorum is not reinforced by any formal pattern of characters or episodes. Nevertheless, it is not difficult to grasp the sequence of thought that leads

[1] Robbins (p. 105) discusses Philo's statement that six is γεννητικώτατος. Pythagorean embryological theory provided various reasons for the epithet ζωογονητική; these were easily accessible in Macrobius, who discusses at some length the presence of six as a factor in the period of gestation (*In. somn. Scip.*, I. vi. 14–17).

on from the books of the zoogonic triangle to Book VI. Where these three preceding books were concerned with sexual love and with the increase of life, Book VI moves on to the result of this: the child. In particular, where the numerology of Book V expressed the laws of change which govern 'better and worse births,' Book VI examines the effects of heredity and environment in greater detail.

The medullar canto, with its vision of the Graces, expresses a different symbolism of the hexad. As portrayed by Spenser, the Graces have several functions which account for their inclusion in the Legend of Courtesy. They bestow all those personal adornments which are the complements of courtesy (VI. x. 23); they teach the social graces of civility; and by their iconographical posture they symbolize liberality.[1] The Graces had also, however, a simpler and more obvious meaning, which was so much taken for granted as to need no explicit statement. Whatever particular triads of qualities Renaissance philosophers interpreted the Graces as unfolding, the root assumption was that their dance symbolized the *harmony* of these qualities.[2] Sometimes, indeed, the Graces served as an image of musical harmony itself; as when Gafurio, in the frontispiece to his *Practica musice*, gives them a prominent place, as an archetype of the harmony of the cosmos.[3] It is on this philosophical tradition that Spenser draws, when he emphasizes the musical character of the Graces by having them dance to the pipe of Colin. Not only do we have here almost the sole occasion in the poem when a named character plays a musical instrument; but also one in which the music has a specially symbolic value, owing to Colin's unique rôle as the poet's own persona.[4] The vision he describes is nothing less than a vision of the ideal harmony into which Spenser sought to bring all the elements of his poetic world. Now, harmony was one of the chief associations of the hexad: an association based partly on the fact that there are six tones in the octave.[5] Most of the section Martianus Capella devotes to the number is occupied with this topic; and,

---

[1] VI. x. 24; see Wind, *Pagan Mysteries*, p. 33 and Ch. ii *passim*.

[2] For a survey of Renaissance interpretations of the Graces, with this under-lying idea of harmony, see ibid., Ch. iii.

[3] Reproduced ibid., p. 47, and discussed p. 46 n.

[4] Note also the musical imagery, uncommon in Spenser, at VI. x. 27–28. The music of Arion in IV. xi has also, as we shall see, a philosophical significance.

[5] See Martianus Capella, *De nuptiis*, ed. Dick, sect. 737, p. 372: 'totius harmoniæ toni sunt sex . . . unde Venus Harmoniæ mater perhibetur.'

among Renaissance authorities, Giorgio's *De harmonia mundi totius* elaborates it at very considerable length. Martianus Capella even refers to Venus, to whom the hexad, in its zoogenetic capacity, was ascribed, as 'the Mother of harmony.' And Spenser seems to have had these same association of the hexad in mind, when he placed the dance of the 'handmaides of *Venus*' (VI. x. 15) at the culminating point of his sixth book.

VII

Canto Placement

i

LACKING the second half of the *Faerie Queene*, we have no means of knowing whether the series of symbolic numbers was to have been continued. We may suppose, however, that Spenser meant to proceed through the decad, until the creative generation of number, symbolizing at once the creation of the universe and the fashioning of a gentleman, was brought to completion. We have only two pieces of firm evidence about the complete scheme of books projected by Spenser. One is his statement in the Letter to Raleigh, that in the first instance twelve books were planned; the other is the programme of publication which he actually followed, whereby the poem came out in 'parts' consisting of three books each. From the statement in the Letter, which I see no reason to question, it is to be inferred that the Pythagorean series did not provide the sole basis of the complete numerological scheme; for the duodecad had comparatively little significance in the Pythagorean system. Nevertheless, the choice of a twelve-book scheme was not guided merely by the literary precedent established by Virgil and Statius. It was essentially a numerological choice, for a poet with Spenser's interests. Such a scheme implied the notion, essentially astronomical in origin, that the duodecad represents a completed cycle.[1] Epics were in twelve books because they imitated the entire zodiac of life—a symbolism also exhibited, in a more obvious way, by Spenser's *Shepheardes Calender*. As the pervasive astronomical symbolism of the *Faerie Queene* testifies, its duodecad was intended to be similarly expressive. It would be a mistake to

[1] On the duodecad as completion, see Hopper, *Medieval Number Symbolism*, p. 19.

think of a numerological poet such as Spenser as passively adhering to a Virgilian convention of structure, or blindly following a tradition which happened to number the virtues in Aristotle's *Ethics* twelve.[1]

As for the parts defined by the procedure of publication, these seem to be the outcome of a deliberate division of the poem's structure, rather than of the accidental exigencies of Spenser's career. For the division of twelve books into four groups of three, there was again a famous precedent. St. Augustine included such an arrangement of books in his *Civitas Dei*, to symbolize the apostolate by which the Gospel of the Trinity is carried into the four corners of the world; and subsequently the pattern became quite commonplace.[2] It seems quite likely that this numerological tradition influenced Spenser's publication programme. We can be certain, however, that the division represents more than mere obedience to a tradition. It is also an organic division, corresponding to the triadic articulation of books mentioned above. In applying such a scheme to a poetical work, Spenser ran the risk that his epic would fall apart into separate three-book poems. But he has avoided this danger by making an unusually close narrative suture in the case of Books III and IV; as well as by articulating the themes of Books III–V into a triad cutting across the main division. These measures have, indeed, been so successful that the principal triads have been lost from sight.

ii

The discovery that there is a numerological arrangement of books, episodes, and characters[3] leads on to a further enquiry. May not the

---

[1] On this tradition, see V. B. Hulbert (*Var. Sp.*, I, 353–356), who traces it to the time of Aquinas. For Equicola's adherence to this tradition, and possible influence on Spenser, see Ellrodt, p. 110; Jusserand, however, and Josephine W. Bennett (*The Evolution of 'The Faerie Queene'* (Chicago, 1942), pp. 229–230) believe that the tradition reached Spenser *via* Piccolomini and Bryskett.

[2] See Hopper, *Medieval Number Symbolism*, pp. 86, 87, 99, 102; among others, St. Thomas Aquinas is cited.

[3] Besides the Pythagorean schemes of characters already considered, and the astronomical schemes I consider below, there are also a great many incidental schemes of the kind classified by Curtius under the heading 'numerical apophthegms' (Ernst Robert Curtius, *European Literature and the Latin Middle Ages*, tr. Williard R. Trask (London, 1953), Excursus xvi, pp. 510–514). Random specimens of this group—which have been given no apparent numerological application by Spenser—are: the five mermaids at II. xii. 30 (the five senses), Malecasta's six knights (a variation on the Ladder of Lechery motif), and the twelve troops of Maleger (seven deadly sins, plus temptations of the five senses).

distribution of matter between cantos similarly obey a logic of number?

We do not find any continuous numerological scheme governing canto placement; narrative requirements, after all, must sometimes have decided the sequence. But a significant proportion of episodes prove to be symbolically placed. At least twice, moreover, the correlation between subject and canto number occurs in five of the six books at the same point, and thus contributes to what W. J. B. Owen has called the element of repetitive structure in the poem.[1]

Several critics have noticed, without explaining, the regularity of Arthur's interventions, which occur in the eighth canto of almost every book. This is not always an equivalent point in the narrative development: sometimes Arthur delivers the titular hero of the book, sometimes only a minor character. Why, then, always at this numerical place? Clearly it is no coincidence that in medieval arithmology eight was the number of regeneration. This association derived from another. Eight first signified eternity, succeeding the mutability of seven, the number of the present universe; then, since regeneration was the putting on of eternal life, this meaning, too, accrued to eight.[2] There were confirmatory associations with the resurrection (on the eighth day after the beginning of Holy Week); with circumcision (on the eighth day after birth); even—among the more speculative arithmologists—with the number of souls in the Ark. In accordance with this symbolism, baptismal fonts were often octagonal in form, as were the shafts of cathedral pillars.[3] Given these familiar associations, an early reader of the *Faerie Queene* must have felt a sense of the reliability both of God's providence and Spenser's design, when he found deliverance repeatedly brought by the Prince of Grace in an eighth canto.[4] Placidas in IV, Samient in V, Mirabella in VI: all are

[1] W. J. B. Owen, ' "In These XII Books Severally Handled and Discoursed," ' *ELH*, XIX (1952).

[2] See Hopper, *Medieval Number Symbolism*, pp. 77, 85, 90, and 101.

[3] See ibid., p. 114, and, for Dante's application of the symbolism, p. 178. On the use of the octagon in the design of Chartres Cathedral, see Otto von Simson, *The Gothic Cathedral*, Bollingen Series, XLVIII (New York, 1956), pp. 21, 40, 48, and 144; also Ernst Levy's mathematical appendix to the same volume, pp. 240–250, 257, and 258–259. Von Simson (p. 40) relates the symbolism to St. Augustine's analogy between the consonance of the octave, and Christ's work of reconciliation, considered as a restoration of harmony.

[4] Except in Bk. III, where Arthur rescues no one (Britomart having assumed the redemptive rôle); the *theme* of divine grace is introduced at the usual point, but not in the form of narrative (III. viii. 27–29; cf. II. viii. 1–2). In Bks. II, IV, V,

E   53

rescued by Arthur at this same numerical juncture; while in I and II, which are more centrally concerned with regeneration, his deliverances of the Red Cross Knight and of Guyon from spiritual death make the eighth cantos turning-points of the whole action.

Just as noticeably, in every book except IV an elaborately described image of evil is assigned to the eleventh canto. Sometimes, the representative of evil is encountered by the knight patron of the contrasting virtue (as with the dragon in I, Busyrane in III, and the brigands in VI); sometimes, instead, the champion of virtue is Arthur himself (as with Maleger in II and Geryoneo in V). In Books II, V, and VI victory over this evil is gained immediately; in I and III it is deferred until the final canto. But these variations do not obscure the common feature; a principal image of evil, elaborately treated, occurring in each eleventh canto. This is another clear instance of numerological decorum. St. Augustine's authority had early established eleven as the number of sin. Did it not go beyond—'trangress'—the ten of the decalogue?[1] Later, Dante followed the same symbol-

---

[1] 'Numerus undenarius, quoniam transgreditur denarium, transgressionem legis ac per hoc peccatum significat' (*Civitas Dei*, XV. xx); see Hopper, *Medieval Number Symbolism*, pp. 87, 101, and (on Dante's use of the number) 152.

---

and VI Arthur also achieves one or more additional rescue; only in I, where the scheme has to be unambiguously inaugurated, does his *sole* intervention fall in Canto viii. In the case of Bk. I numerological decorum extends also to the stanza-total of the redemptive canto. For the stanza-total of I. viii is 50, a number that was associated with the advent of the Holy Spirit (on the fiftieth day after the Resurrection), and with the Hebrew Jubilee (fiftieth) Year, the year of remission when slaves were liberated, exiles recalled, and debtors forgiven. See Valeriano, *Hieroglyphica*, XXXVII. xliv and xlvi; pp. 465 f.: 'Erat autem hic numerus remissioni et indulgentiæ consecratus. . . . Utcunque autem quinquagenarius numerus describatur, spiritalis vitæ hieroglyphicum est. . . .' The stanza-totals of several other cantos display a similar decorum. E.g., II. xi, containing Arthur's battle with Maleger, has a stanza-total of 49, a number denoting the first or bodily climacteric, believed to be a critical age for man's physical constitution, when the forces of mortality were particularly strong (see Ficino, p. 528, and Sir Thomas Browne, cit. *Var. Sp.*, II, 484); V. iii, containing the spousals of Marinell and Florimell, has a total of 30, the only large number denoting marriage (a symbolism based on the digital gesture for 30: see Valeriano, *Hieroglyphica*, XXXVII. xxxvi, p. 463); and no fewer than three cantos in the second book—II. ii, iii, and iv—have the appropriate total of 46, a number that denoted 'edification' or the building of the regenerate body (see Bongo, Pt. II, p. 104: 'Numerus 46 significat ædificationem templi corporei, quod sibi Christus ædificavit ex carne Adae, cuius nomen tam apud Hebræos, quam Græcos ex litteris numerum 46 comprehendentibus conflatur, quot diebus Salvatoris Christi Corpus in utero Mariæ virginis fuit absolutam, quo ad augmentum, non tamen quo adformationem, quæ instanti facta fuit. . . .').

ism when he mapped out the dimensions of the *bolge* in his *Inferno*.

By contrast, third place is favourable: *numero Deus impare gaudet*. Accordingly, in this position we find an image of virtue, or at least a fortunate turn in the action. In I we have the reforms executed by Una and her lion; in II Belphœbe's defence of true honour; in III the prophecy of Britomart's line; in IV the ideal friendship of Cambell and Triamond; in V the spousals of Florimell and Marinell; and in VI Calidore's safe return of Priscilla and (less conclusive) his rescue of Serena from the Blatant Beast.

It is easy, of course, to exaggerate the regularity of the canto scheme. We are dealing, not with a rigidly repetitive mechanism, but with an organism whose cycles of metabolism and of growth obey certain numerical laws of nature. Spenser, delighting in his poem's proliferating variety, meant the thread of number symbolism to be more of a clue than a ligature. Flexibility of placement was made possible, happily, by the considerable (though not unlimited) range of associations that most numbers were endowed with. An example of this is seen in the case of the medullary episodes, which we might expect to be placed with especial deliberation. Since they present complete and perfect images of the virtues, these episodes would seem best suited to the tenth position. In Pythagorean thought the decad was a symbol of perfection; being mystically identified with the monad, and revered as the number in which the multiplicity of the digits returned to divine unity. According to Porphyry's characteristic eulogy, ten is

a perfect number—rather, the most perfect of all numbers; comprehending in itself, as it does, every numerical difference and proportion.[1]

Three medullary episodes in fact occur in tenth place: the House of Holiness, the Temple of Venus, and Mount Acidale. The ninth place, however, also has a claim to the principal image of a virtue. Nine, the perfect form of the perfect three, was the number of the heavens and of the angelic hierarchy, which the virtuous human mind resembled. Spenser himself follows this line of thought when he makes nine the rational proportion of the Castle of Alma: 'Nine was the circle set in

---

[1] Porphyry, *De vita Pythag.*, lii; cf. Hopper, *Medieval Number Symbolism*, pp. 34, 44, 46, 117, etc. Hopper traces the idea from Pythagorean to scholastic authors (p. 102) and to Dante (pp. 144, 149). Roger Bacon writes: 'every whole and perfect thing is ten.'

heavens place.' Moreover, nine aptly symbolizes the goal or end of moral effort, since it is the last of the digits—*quod primi versus finem tenet*.[1] In ninth place, accordingly, we find the Castle of Alma and the Court of Mercilla, principal images of the cardinal virtues Temperance and Justice; and also (if we accord it similar status) the House of Meliboe.

There remain three differently placed episodes, which must clearly be regarded nevertheless as medullar: the Garden of Adonis at III. vi, the spousal of Thames and Medway at IV. xi, and Isis Church at V. vii. Of these, the placing of one, Isis Church, has already been discussed in connection with the episodic structure of Book V. The spousal of Thames and Medway is a more prominent exception; since it not only falls outside both the normal positions for a medullar episode (only one of which, the tenth, is pre-empted by the Temple of Venus), but occupies the eleventh place, elsewhere reserved for a principal image of evil. The consequent absence of an image of evil, where we have been conditioned to expect one, is so emphatic that precisely in this must lie the effect Spenser desired to achieve. In a book which is concerned with Concord, and which, for reasons given above, had to leave an altogether harmonious impression upon the reader, there was literally no place among the concluding cantos for an image of evil with the conflict it would have given rise to.

The placing of the Garden of Adonis episode is to some extent immediately intelligible. As a methological treatment of generation, it would naturally be connected with one of the Pythagorean marriage numbers, and placed, accordingly, third, fifth, or sixth. The choice between these possibilities, however, is determined by a less obvious and much more precise allusion. One of the main features of the Garden is Genius' clothing of 'naked babes' with 'fleshly weeds.' This has been interpreted as a mythological expression of the infusion into the human embryo either of the soul or, as Ellrodt has it, the pre-existent vegetable soul.[2] Now, the infusion of the soul is an office specifically of the hexad. Nicomachus tells us that the Pythagoreans revered [the hexad] with distinguished praises, saying that the world is endowed with a soul in accordance with it . . . and that animals and

[1] Martianus Capella, *De nuptiis*, ed. Dick, sect. 741, p. 375; in the same passage the perfection of the ennead is discussed.

[2] See Ellrodt, pp. 70–90, for an intelligent critique of previous interpretations of the Garden, and a new theory based on more accurate information about Spenser's sources.

plants get completeness and persistence and careful health by its joining them, and its share in their birth;

while his editor has remarked that

no number is more able to fit the soul than the hexad; no other would be called so much an articulation of the universe set up as a maker of soul.[1]

iii

An unintended convenience of Spenser's numerology is that it throws new light on the vexed question of the rubrics attached to the posthumously published *Cantos of mutabilitie*. What position did Spenser intend those cantos to occupy in the completed *Faerie Queene*? Their title in the 1609 Folio runs:

Two Cantos of mutabilitie: Which, both for Forme and Matter, appeare to be parcell of some following Booke of the Faerie Queene, under the legend of Constancie.

It is not known from external evidence whether the running title 'VII. Booke,' and the canto numbers vi, vii, and viii, derive from Spenser's manuscript. These rubrics have consequently come under scrutiny, and their internal probability has more than once been questioned by the more speculative Spenserian critics. Most recently, Miss Pauline Parker has remarked:

as I am not the first to perceive, the more one tries to enter into Spenser's mind and follow his construction of the poem, the less likely it appears that this [the *Mutabilitie* fragment] could have been part of a seventh book. . . . its obvious position would be in Book Eleven.[2]

The basis of her conviction is that she finds the theme of the *Mutabilitie Cantos* too large for any middle book; while the twelfth book of her *Faerie Queene* is already devoted to a Legend of Magnificence. On numerological grounds, however, we have the very strongest reasons for dismissing all such speculations, and for upholding the authority of the running title and canto rubrics.[3]

[1] Nicomachus, *Introduction to Arithmetic*, tr. M. L. D'Ooge (New York, 1926), p. 97.

[2] *The Allegory of the 'Faerie Queene,'* p. 260. Throughout her discussion of the position of the *Mutabilitie Cantos* (pp. 260–265), Miss Parker is influenced by the similar speculations of Janet Spens in *Spenser's Faerie Queene: An Interpretation* (London, 1934). The rubrics are also queried by Church: see *Var. Sp.*, VI, Critical Notes on the Text.

[3] Strictly speaking, the numerological evidence can support only the suitability, not the authority, of the rubrics. It is just possible that someone other than Spenser arrived at them by numerological inference.

Seven was in medieval tradition the number of the mutable world; being contrasted, as we have seen, with the eight of resurrection, eternity, and final glory.[1] It was also 'the Number of th' unfixed Fires of Heav'n';[2] of universality; of the established order of the cosmos; and of the age of the world.[3] Macrobius bases a whole chapter on Cicero's remark that seven is 'the key to the universe.'[4] What more appropriate place than seventh, then, for a book concerned with the extent of mutability in the natural order? Such is the strange logic of number that the seventh place is equally appropriate, moreover, for Mutability's anti-type, Constancy. Because it was the only 'unbegotten' (prime) number that does not 'beget' (that is, yield as a factor any number less than ten), seven had a reputation for *immunity from change*. Valeriano likens it in this respect to the impassible and unalterable aspect of God.[5] The symbolic associations of seven thus embrace not only the subject of the *Mutabilitie Cantos*, but also the presumptive subject of Book VII as a whole. The associations of no other number will do this.

The canto rubrics are just as appropriate. Placed seventh is the assembly of the orders of creation as witnesses to Mutability, but also, in a deeper sense, to the order underlying a historical creation. The imperfect Canto viii, on the other hand, looks forward to the last things. It opens with a prayer of aspiration towards the great Sabbath when 'all shall rest eternally': that eighth day when the seven-fold cosmos will be made new and eternal. Spenser here echoes the hope of St. Augustine, who tells us, in a fine passage of number symbolism in the *Epistles*, that there was no evening of the seventh day of creation because

the first life was not eternal; but the final rest is eternal, and for this reason too the eighth day will hold eternal blessedness: because that rest, which is eternal, is received from the eighth day, not ended by it (or else it would

---

[1] E.g., Hugo of St. Victor, *Exegetica*, xv (Migne, *Patrolog. lat.*, CLXXV, 22–23), cit. Hopper, *Medieval Number Symbolism*, p. 101.

[2] Du Bartas, The Second Day of the Second Week, Pt. IV, 'The Columnes'; p. 361.

[3] See Hopper, *Medieval Number Symbolism*, pp. 31, 44, 46, 53, 84–85, and 112.

[4] *In somn. Scip.* I. vi. 34; ed. Stahl, p. 106.

[5] *Hieroglyphica*, XXXVII. xxi; p. 459: 'septenarius sine motu est, neque quicquam patitur. Nam alii numeri partim generant non geniti: partim generantur, cum minime generent: alii utrunque obeunt munus: solus vero septenarius utriusque conditionis immunis.' Seven is like God, 'singularis et immobilis.' See also Macrobius, *In somn. Scip.*, ed. Stahl, p. 102 n.

not be eternal). So, then, what was the first day will be the eighth; so that the first life will be restored—but eternized.[1]

This is not the place for a general evaluation of the numerology of the *Faerie Queene*. It is right, however, to reflect at this stage on the relative preponderance of Pythagorean ideas in those parts of the numerical structure that we have been able to explore. The results of our enquiries are novel; but they should not be altogether surprising. From its earliest period, Neoplatonism had drawn on Pythagorean doctrines of number; the triad itself, indeed, was an arithmological concept.[2] Besides, Pythagorean number theory was a fashionable—and, from a scientific point of view, significant—strain in Renaissance thought.[3] At the same time, I do not wish to give the impression that Spenser was in any systematic way an orthodox Pythagorean. More than once, we have seen his Pythagorean symbolism bear traces of its medieval transmission. Spenser used any ideas that could contribute to his vision of divine order, whether they were Pythagorean, Platonic, or Patristic, ancient, medieval, or contemporary.

It is difficult for us, perhaps, to take Spenser's Neopythagorean interests as seriously as we can his other Orphic enthusiasms. But we can at least agree that he found in this strange mode of thought a valid system of poetic belief. It proved an abundant source of structural ideas, enabling him to organize content and form according to a single plan. Number does not, of course, provide the only structural framework used in the poem. Nevertheless, it may be doubted whether access to the inward unity of *The Faerie Queene* can be achieved without the key of numerology. Curtius' comment on Dante's compositional scheme applies with even greater force to Spenser's: 'Here number is no longer an outer framework, but a symbol of the cosmic *ordo*.'[4]

[1] *Epist*. LV. ix. 17.
[2] See Proclus, *Elements of Theology*, ed. E. R. Dodds (Oxford, 1933), p. 208 and index, s.v. 'Pythagoreanism.'
[3] For the influence of Neopythagoreanism upon Renaissance cosmology, see Johnson, *Astronomical Thought in Renaissance England*, pp. 28 ff.
[4] *European Literature and the Latin Middle Ages*, p. 509.

PART TWO
The Planetary Week

But now my teme begins to faint and fayle,
All woxen weary of their journall toyle:
Therefore I will their sweatie yokes assoyle
At this same furrowes end, till a new day. . . .
The Faerie Queene, III. xii. 47 (1590)

Time's purpled maskers, then do them advance,
As by sweet music in a measur'd dance. . . .

He only who you made, decipher can
Your notes; heaven's eyes, ye blind the eyes of man.
WILLIAM DRUMMOND, 'An Hymn of the Fairest Fair'

Weisst wie viele Sterne stehen
In dem blauen Himmelszelt? . . .

Gott der Herr hat sie gezählet
Dass ihm auch nicht eines fehlet
Von der ganzen grossen Zahl.
JOHANN W. HEY

VIII

The Book of the Sun

The hypothesis has often been advanced that the *Faerie Queene* may contain an underlying structure of astronomical or astrological symbolism; but no very definite suggestions have been made as to what form this symbolism takes.[1] It is my present purpose to explore the astronomical symbolism sustaining the poem. As I hope will become clear, its symbolic structure is not merely an external scheme determining distribution of topics, but an organic morphosis, expressing Spenser's vision of cosmic order and of the generation of the microcosmic soul. It is a dynamic or temporal structure: a cycle manifested in the action itself, and contributing to the identities of the principal characters, each of whom is assigned a planetary rôle. Moreover, the astronomical symbolism is matched by an elaborate formal accompaniment in the poem's numerology; particularly in the number-patterns of characters in descriptive cantos. It will thus be possible to complete the numerological description begun in the previous chapters.

There I argued that, while the poem's numerical organization is almost unimaginably intricate, nevertheless its main lines can be

[1] Except by J. H. Walter (' "The Faerie Queene": Alterations and Structure,' *MLR*, XXXVI (1941), 37–58, especially pp. 53 ff.), who proposes a schematic distribution of themes in accordance with the same calendrical arrangement as in Palingenius' *Zodiacus vitæ*. But little firm evidence is offered in support of this view, which seems to me untenable. In particular, Walter fails to realize that the distribution of subjects in Palingenius is as much according to the associations of the Pythagorean symbolic numbers and of the fixed houses of the horoscope as according to the associations of the zodiacal signs. This is not to say that Spenser does not occasionally share with Palingenius certain particular associations. Indeed, his use of Palingenius has been established by Rosemond Tuve in 'Spenser and the "Zodiake of Life," ' *JEGP*, XXXIV (1935), 1–19.

easily grasped, once you see that Spenser is using the Pythagorean series of symbolic numbers. In his astronomical symbolism, similarly, the poet uses a series well known to his readers; so that all can appreciate at least some of the cosmic rhythms he adumbrates. In fact, the series he has chosen is one of such domestic familiarity that there is something grotesque about uncovering it with all the ceremonies of scholarship. It is simply the planetary week: the series of deities whose guardianship is acknowledged in the names we still apply to our seven days. True, Spenser's use of the astrological week is subtle and implicit. But he could easily afford to be indirect, since the notion of the week as a structural frame was quite a usual one. Such a frame was not only inevitable in hexaemeral literature itself but was also common in the divine poetry that developed out of the hexaemeral tradition. It was used in Tasso's *Le sette giornate* (1592), and it was used in Du Bartas' *Sepmaines*, the most widely read vernacular long poem of Spenser's time. In the latter poem each major division corresponds either to a day in the week of creation, or to a day in a great week of human history.

The astrological week of antiquity[1] is as follows:

I	Dies Solis
II	Dies Lunæ
III	Dies Martis
IV	Dies Mercurii
V	Dies Iovis
VI	Dies Veneris
VII	Dies Saturni

It is in this same sequence that the planetary gods make their veiled appearances in the successive books of the *Faerie Queene*. Moreover, where signs of the zodiac are introduced this is not done in simple calendar order (Aries, Taurus, Gemini, etc.), but in an order mainly determined by their associations with one or another of the planetary deities, as these follow in diurnal sequence.

[1] Originally, the sequence in which the planetary deities followed each other through the week had in itself no immediate significance. It was determined, though only indirectly, by the order of remoteness of the planets from Earth in the Babylonian system. According to that order, each of the twenty-four hours of the day was consecrated in turn to one of the deities; and the deity who happened to preside over the first hour of a day was regarded as presiding over the whole of that day. See J. L. E. Dreyer, *A History of Astronomy from Thales to Kepler* (London, 1953), p. 169.

The allotment of signs to planets is usually in accordance with the normal astrological system—the system set out, for example, in Ptolemy's *Tetrabiblos*:

TABLE III: HOUSES, EXALTATIONS, AND DEPRESSIONS

Planet	Solar house	Lunar house	Exaltation	Depression
Sol	Leo	——	Aries	Libra
Luna	——	Cancer	Taurus	Scorpio
Mars	Scorpio	Aries	Capricornus	Cancer
Mercurius	Virgo	Gemini	Virgo	Pisces
Iuppiter	Sagittarius	Pisces	Cancer	Capricornus
Venus	Libra	Taurus	Pisces	Virgo
Saturnus	Capricornus	Aquarius	Libra	Aries

There was also, however, another system, the Manilian,[1] in which each of the signs was allotted to one of the twelve Olympian guardians (only six of whom were planetary deities). This system was not a purely astrological one, and it differed radically from the Ptolemaic, as a glance at Table IV will show:

TABLE IV: THE MANILIAN AND PTOLEMAIC SYSTEMS

Sign	Guardian deity	
	Manilian system	Ptolemaic system
1. Aries	Pallas	Mars
2. Taurus	Venus	Venus
3. Gemini	Apollo	Mercurius
4. Cancer	Mercurius	Luna
5. Leo	Iuppiter and Iuno	Sol
6. Virgo	Ceres	Mercurius
7. Libra	Vulcan	Venus
8. Scorpio	Mars	Mars
9. Sagittarius	Diana	Iuppiter
10. Capricornus	Vesta	Saturnus
11. Aquarius	Iuno and Iuppiter	Saturnus
12. Pisces	Neptunus	Iuppiter

[1] Manilius, *Astronomicon*, II. 433–452; and see A. E. Housman's analysis of the system in his edition of Manilius (Vol. II (Cambridge, 1937), Introd., p. xvi). The standard Renaissance edition of Manilius was Joseph Scaliger's *Astronomicωn libri quinque* (Paris, 1579), the astrological commentary in which is superior to Housman's. Accounts of the twelve Olympian guardians were, of course, available in many other authors: as, e.g., in L. G. Giraldi's *De diis gentium* (Basel, 1548), *syntagma* I, p. 24 (with references to ancient authorities, such as Seneca's *Nat. Quaest.*, II). Note that according to Ficino (*Theolog. Platon.*, IV. i; p. 126) the system was Pythagorean in origin: see Giovanni–Battista Riccioli, *Almagestum novum* (Bologna, 1651), I, 398.

The system of Manilius is used by Spenser, but in a subsidiary way, to facilitate the orderly introduction of non-planetary deities.

It has long been recognized that the allegory of the *Faerie Queene*, Book I, is conceived in terms of the imagery of the Revelation of St. John. Sometimes Spenser handled the Biblical material as Bunyan was later to do: combining a large number of short texts, directly applied to contemporary life, into a single but multi-partite allegorical fable. At his best, however, he worked in a different manner. He would develop a few of the Biblical images in a more extended symbolism, and make these the dominating poetic features of the book. Thus, the character of Una, and the outline of her story, are based on the passage in the twelfth chapter of Revelation about 'a woman clothed with the sun' who fled into the wilderness to escape a persecuting dragon—a passage interpreted by Reformation exegetes as a prophecy of the sufferings of the true Church.[1] It is in accordance with this symbolism that Una is repeatedly described as bright,[2] or even associated directly with the sun. Her brightness is transcendent, a 'celestiall sight':

> The blazing brightnesse of her beauties beame,
> And glorious light of her sunshyny face
> To tell, were as to strive against the streame.
> (I. xii. 23)

Evidently this illumination is related to Una's philosophical significance as Truth, and to her special endowment with grace. We are told that

> Her angels face
> As the great eye of heaven shyned bright,
> And made a sunshine in the shadie place;
> Did never mortall eye behold such heavenly grace.
> (I. iii. 4)

Now, underlying this solar imagery is an exegetical tradition in which the sun of the Revelation passage is interpreted as an image of Christ; 'clothed with the sun' being taken to refer to the incorporation of the Church in the body of Christ. The sun, in fact, is specifically the *Sol iustitiæ*. Thus, Van der Noodt's *Theatre* (a book which Spenser helped

---

[1] See J. E. Hankins, 'Spenser and the Revelation of St. John,' *PMLA*, LX (1945), 364–381. Hankins (pp. 370–371) shows that Spenser has conflated this Biblical passage with another, traditionally associated with it: the account of the Bride's search for her lover (allegorically, Christ) in Song of Songs.

[2] Cf. ibid., 371.

to translate) explains that in 'I saw an angel standing in the sun' (Rev. xix. 17) the sun intended is 'the bright and cleare sunne of righteousnesse, which is Christ Jesu, that amiable and shining morning starre.'[1]

The apocalyptic concept of the *Sol iustitiæ* had had a powerful appeal during the preceding century. It derived its Biblical authority from a prophecy by Malachi, which is cited by Van der Noodt:

For, behold, the day cometh, that shall burn as an oven; and all the proud, yea, and all that do wickedly, shall be stubble: and the day that cometh shall burn them up, saith the Lord of hosts, that it shall leave them neither root nor branch. But unto you that fear my name shall the Sun of righteousness arise with healing in his wings.

(Mal. iv. 1–2)

The most famous representation of this motif in graphic art is undoubtedly the engraving by Dürer (Pl. 2a), which portrays Christ as a stern judge, with sword in right hand and scales in left. Flames issue from his eyes as he sits upon a grim lion. In his analysis of this engraving Professor Panofsky shows that it draws its iconography from an allegorization of Malachi by the medieval commentator and encyclopædist Pierre Bersuire. Bersuire's influential exegesis, which applies the prophecy to Christ's coming in judgement, develops its first verse in an astronomical sense:

as the sun, when in the centre of his orbit, that is to say, at the midday point, is hottest, so shall Christ be when He shall appear in the centre of heaven and earth, that is to say, in Judgment. . . . In summer, when he is in the Lion, the sun withers the herbs, which have blossomed in the spring, by his heat. So shall Christ, in that heat of the Judgment, appear as a man fierce and leonine; He shall wither the sinners and shall destroy the prosperity of men which they had enjoyed in the world.[2]

In view of this background special significance attaches to the fact that Una, Spenser's 'woman clothed with the sun,' is attended by leonine companions.

The most obvious of these companions is the lion of Canto iii, who pities Una's wronged innocence and goes with her to the house of

---

[1] John Van der Noodt, *A Theatre for voluptuous worldlings* (London, 1569), fol. 67^v; confirmatory texts cited are Mal. iv, Rev. xx, and Heb. x.

[2] Pierre Bersuire, *Dictionarium seu repertorium morale* (Nuremberg, 1489), s.v. 'Sol' (Vol. III, fol. cxciv^r), cit. Erwin Panofsky, *Meaning in the Visual Arts* (New York, 1955), p. 262. Panofsky's whole discussion of the type (pp. 257–265) is relevant here; as is his further treatment of it in *Albrecht Dürer* (Princeton, 1948), I, 78–79.

Corceca, where it not only terrifies the female occupants but also tears Abessa's lover Kirkrapine to pieces. The first part of this episode utilizes an antique emblem of *iustitia*, in which a lion's domestication at the hand of a woman represents the power of justice over ferocious passions.[1] Before its 'proud submission' to Una's humble weakness, the lion was savagely wrathful and revengeful: as the poet exclaims, 'O how can beautie maister the most strong,/And simple truth subdue avenging wrong?' (I. iii. 6) Afterwards, it is diligent in its devotion to Truth, 'with humble service to her will prepar'd' (I. iii. 9). Now that the lion acts as an instrument of divine retribution, however, the connection with the *Sol iustitiæ* motif is drawn closer. Prophetic applications of Revelation to contemporary situations have always included denunciation of ecclesiastical abuses. Thus, the dreadful irruption of Una's lion upon Corceca's superstitious piety, and upon Kirkrapine's appropriation of Church property and removal of ornaments and vestments, comes as an apocalyptic judgement. To borrow the imagery of another emblem,[2] it seems as if God has assumed his lion mask and pronounced wrathful judgement. But the Spenser who wrote *The Shepheardes Calender* was well aware that the correction of abuses by force, though it may be just, is spiritually dangerous; so that Ruskin was probably not far wrong in believing that the episode shows 'how Truth, separated from Godliness, does indeed put an end to the abuses of Superstition, but does so violently and desperately.'[3] This point is underlined by the eventual fate of the lion; its

[1] Valeriano (*Hieroglyphica*, I. xxx; pp. 15–16) describes the emblem of a woman seated upon a lion, with the inscription 'IUSTITIA,' as it occurred on an ancient coin (our Pl. 2b). His interpretation of the emblem is that followed above.

[2] Hermann Hugo, *Pia desideria* (Antwerp, 1624), Embl. II. xix, on the text Ps. cxix. 120: 'Confige timore tuo carnes meas, a iudiciis enim tuis timui.' The engraving shows the divine Eros wearing a lion-mask and wielding a thunderbolt (our Pl. 3a, from the 1628 Antwerp edn.); while the epigram contains a prayer for a true fear of God—as distinct from the false fears of the guilty, who 'dread a *Lion*, when a *Mouse* they hear,' and who, when there is thunder and lightning 'ruin from each accident presage' (tr. E. Arwaker (London, 1686), p. 107). The same emblem may serve to illustrate a passage in the *Cantos of Mutabilitie*, where we are told that some explain the concealment of Natura's features as a device to disguise the terror beneath: 'For that her face did like a Lion shew, / That eye of wight could not indure to view' (VII. vii. 6).

[3] *The Stones of Venice*, III, App. ii, 'Theology of Spenser'; though in view of Paul E. McLane, *Spenser's 'Shepheardes Calender'* (Notre Dame, 1961), pp. 97–98 and 100–101, it may be concluded that Spenser refers to contemporary, and not pre-Reformation, spoliation of the Church.

defeat by Sansloy ('Without Law') implies that forcible reformation can easily succumb to a tendency to lawlessness.

The lion of the third canto thus falls short of complete embodiment of the power of the Sun of righteousness. Una is associated with another lion, however, who proves in the end more virtuous—the Red Cross Knight. Red Cross, whom she calls 'my Lyon, and my noble Lord' (I. iii. 7) is her proper companion. Only because he has abandoned his faith in her, does she need the support of the other, revengeful, lion. Later, the Red Cross Knight re-enters the service of Una; though not before he has undergone an amendment, penance, remorse, and repentance so painful 'that like a Lyon he would cry and rore.'[1] At the House of Holiness the *miles christianus* puts on the armour of Christ more decisively than before. His three-day battle with the dragon, and the subsequent release of Una's parents, re-enact Christ's victory over sin and death and his harrowing of hell; while his betrothal to Una in the last canto alludes anagogically to the marriage of the Church with the Heavenly Bridegroom.[2] In these final cantos the Red Cross Knight's rôle seems often to be specifically that of *Sol iustitiæ*. Thus, emphasis is laid on the simultaneity of his resting with the sun's setting, and of his rising with the sun's.[3] Even the wings of Malachi's rising sun are echoed in the 'newly budded pineons' of the eagle upstarting 'fresh out of the Ocean wave' (I. xi. 34), to which the Red Cross Knight is compared, and which in turn parallels the rise 'out of the sea' of *Titan's* 'deawy face' in the previous stanza. At first it seems contradictory that the rôle of *Sol iustitiæ* should be taken sometimes by Una and sometimes by the Red Cross Knight. So long as we do not press for a single mechanically consistent allegory, however, there need be no difficulty. As a symbol of Divine Truth, Una is closely identified with Christ, whom she—as the Church—must in any case represent upon earth during his absence. It is when parted from the Red Cross Knight that Una

---

[1] I. x. 28. Here the symbolism is further complicated by the introduction of another emblematic lion, the lion of human sin subdued by Christ: on which see Ruskin, *The Bible of Amiens*, Ch. iv, sect. 34.

[2] Hankins (art. cit., pp. 371–372, 374) lists many details in the later cantos which point to Redcrosse's assumption of this theological rôle.

[3] See *F.Q.*, I. xi. 31, 33–34, and 49–52. We may note in passing that the Well of Life in which Redcrosse bathes is likened to 'th'English *Bath*' (I. xi. 30. 7), whose Latin name was *Aquæ Solis* (Camden, *Britannia*, 'Somersetshire' (London, 1600), p. 200). If this is not coincidence, it is a characteristic piece of amplificatory texturing.

most explicitly assumes a solar rôle; reunited with him, she is imaged as the morning star preceding the sun and prophesying 'that dawning day is drawing neare,/And to the world does bring long wished light.'[1] What is important for our present purpose, however, is simply to establish that both Una and the Red Cross Knight are conceived in terms of the *Sol iustitiæ* concept.

Panofsky has shown Dürer's *Sol iustitiæ* engraving to be related to a very common type of representation of the planet Sol, in which a lion is introduced, not because of any connection with Justice, but merely as the appropriate zodiacal house.[2] Dürer's use of this purely astrological motif, as we have seen, has its literary authority in Bersuire. It expresses the idea that Sol is at his most powerful in his own sign Leo, at the height of summer; or, more abstractly, it implies an 'equation of the astrological notion, *medium cæli*, with the theological notion, *medium cæli et terræ*, presumed to be the seat of the Judge.'[3] Now the related symbolism in the first book of the *Faerie Queene* similarly has its astrological aspect. True, this springs naturally from the apocalyptic images on which it is based; there is no question of an independent allegory. Nevertheless, Spenser must have known that the simple astrological implication of his sun and lion imagery would be at least as familiar as its theological content. Moreover, he would also count on the image of a woman with a lion having direct mythological associations with the sun, for those of his readers who knew Valeriano's account of Adad and Adargatis, or had studied the iconographical engraving of the Assyrian Apollo in Cartari's *Imagini degli dei*.[4] A possible inference is that Spenser in-

---

[1] I. xii. 21; cf. xi. 33, where Una rises a little before Redcrosse.

[2] *Meaning in the Visual Arts*, p. 264, n. 87. Panofsky describes the motif of Sol *seated* on his lion—as in the capitals on the Palace of the Doges in Venice—as of rare occurrence in Dürer's time. That particular attitude, however, is not in question here; and the wider class of representations, of Sol *with* his zodiacal sign, was of course ubiquitous.

[3] Ibid., p. 262.

[4] See Jean Seznec, *The Survival of the Pagan Gods* (New York, 1953), p. 238; and our Pl. 3b, which reproduces the engraving. Cartari portrays Apollo with Adad and Adargatis; the last seated upon a lion. While Adad (or Hadad) was a sun god, Adargatis (Atargatis) was properly an earth goddess—though Valeriano (*Hieroglyphica*, I. xxvii, pp. 14–15) connects her, via *Ceres legifera*, with Justice and hence with the emblem described above. (The lion he interprets as symbolizing in its fore parts the power of the sun, in its hind parts the earth.) It is perhaps worth noting that from the 1575 Basel edition onwards, Valeriano's woodcuts confuse Adad and Adargatis; so that the male deity is labelled 'Terra,' and the

tended the symbolism of the first book to have a definite astrological value. Book I is governed by Sol in a way that—as we shall see—no later book is; so that we are encouraged to think of it as in some sense his special province.

As soon as this possibility is entertained, a new appropriateness is seen in much of the material of the book. I do not mean, merely, that there are many verbal allusions to the sun; though this is certainly the case—even the Muse being referred to, in this book, as 'faire ympe of *Phoebus*, and his aged bride.'[1] Nor am I mainly concerned with explicit astronomical indications, such as the *chronographia* at I. ii. 1, which places the sun in a summer sign, if not in Leo itself.[2] What is more important is that the solar metaphor deeply influences the portrayal of the principal characters, and the conduct of the action.

Consider the turning-point of the action in the seventh canto: Redcrosse's defeat by Orgoglio. The occasion of the knight's fall is his slothful dalliance with Fidessa, beside a fountain in a woodland

[1] I. xi. 5. In addition to solar images already mentioned, we may note I. v. 20, I. v. 43–44, I. vi. 6 and 35, and I. ix. 18. A rough tally of verbal mentions of the sun (based on the frequency of such words as *sun* (together with compounds such as *sun-bright*), Apollo, Titan, *Phœbus*, etc.) shows that these predominate in Bk. I. The count is: Bk. I: 40; Bk. II: 23; Bk. III: 32; Bk. IV: 11; Bk. V: 17; and Bk. VI: 10.

[2] See F. R. Johnson, *Astronomical Thought in Renaissance England* (Baltimore, 1937), p. 194 and n. 80. On the basis of an erroneous supposition that the whole action of *F.Q.* takes place in summer, Johnson believed that I. iii. 16 demonstrates Spenser's ignorance of astronomy. In fact, much of the action takes place at other seasons of the year, particularly in spring (e.g., III. x. 44: 'their May-lady they had newly made'; VI. vii. 32: '*Cupid* kept his court, / As he is wont at each Saint Valentide'); and in any case Spenser's astronomy is schematic and allusive, not naturalistic. It is possible, e.g., that the two *chronographiæ* at I. ii. 1 and I. iii. 16 describe the state of the heavens at the solstices, when Sol is in Cancer and Capricorn respectively. Known as the 'portals of the sun,' these tropical signs, which limit the sun's path, were regarded symbolically as forming gates through which the soul enters and leaves the body (see Macrobius, *In somn. Scip.*, I. xii. 1–5, ed. Stahl, pp. 133–134, where the soul's descent is followed out in detail, and described as a change from monad to dyad; also Ficino, *Opera omnia*, p. 917). The appropriateness of this allusion—if it is intentional—near the opening of the poem needs no explanation.

female deity 'Sol' (see Pls. 4a and 4b). Spenser may possibly have been influenced by this error in his conception of Una; though it is much more likely that he chose elements from both deities—the name and solar character from one, the female sex from the other—with deliberate eclecticism. More distant folklore analogues for the woman with a lion protector, as well as romance precedents (such as the *Alphabet of Tales*) are listed by Irving Ribner in 'Una's Lion: a Folklore Analogue,' *N & Q*, CXCVI (1951), 114–115.

glade, where he has sought relief from the 'boyling heat' of the sun.
We are told that the fountain was once a nymph of Phœbe's band,
who

> quite tyr'd with heat of scorching ayre
> Sat downe to rest in middest of the race

and who was metamorphosed by the wrathful goddess into a
magically enervating fountain. Dreadful judgement similarly descends
upon Redcrosse, when he sits down to rest and drinks of the fountain.
What we should notice here is the timing. Judgement comes when the
knight turns aside from the heat of the summer sun in its power—
from the righteousness and truth, that is, of the *Sol iustitiæ*. Moreover,
the judgement is in accordance with Bersuire's astronomical development of Malachi.[1] For it occurs 'in the centre of the sun's orbit, that
is to say, at the midday point (*in medio orbis, sc. in puncto meridiei*)
. . . In summer'—not only in narrative terms, but also formally, in
that it is placed just half-way through Book I. This is underlined for
us numerologically, since the exact mid-point in the stanza-count of
the book comes at I. vii. 5, where the nymph, Redcrosse's mythological counterpart, also fails 'in middest of the race.'[2]

Professor C. S. Lewis has well remarked that the large-scale
imagery of the first book is predominantly of light and darkness.[3]
Altering the emphasis slightly, one may also speak of a conflict
between *sunlight* and darkness. Indeed, the most explicit statement of
the antinomy, which comes in a later book from the lips of Arthur
(III. iv. 55–60), ends in a prayer to the sun. The opposition is not
only expressed in the places already mentioned, but in descriptive
passages throughout Book I. Evil creatures such as Error and Despaire inhabit places of sunless gloom; while a whole canto is devoted
to a splendid evocation of Night and her dynasty. In the latter episode
the incident of Sansjoy's medical treatment illustrates the leitmotif
with particular clarity. The surgeon Æsculapius is only competent to
take the case because he is the 'farre renowmed sonne/Of great
Apollo' (I. v. 43). This infernal therapy is obviously intended as an

[1] See p. 67, n. 2. Many texts authorizing a similar symbolic interpretation of
the meridian are gathered in the *Collectanea* added to Valeriano's *Hieroglyphica*
(see the Ch. 'Sol Iustitiæ,' pp. 204D–207D, especially p. 205D). With Redcrosse's
scorching by the sun in fulfilment of Malachi's prophecy, cf. Fradubio's similar
fate (I. ii. 33).

[2] Spenser's frequent use of *race* in an astronomical sense (= orbit) is discussed
below.

[3] *The Allegory of Love* (Oxford, 1938), pp. 313–315.

antonym (suitably modulated into a pagan mythological mode) to the healing of Redcrosse at the House of Holiness and at the Well of Life—where the restorative power of the *Sol iustitiæ*—the 'healing in his wings'—is displayed more directly.[1]

Evil may also, however, consist in a false appearance of light. Thus, Duessa, when in her Fidessa disguise she counterfeits Truth, is like Truth called 'sunny bright' (I. v. 21). She outshines Fraelissa, who is compared, like Una her counterpart, to the morning star (I. ii. 36). Lucifera's brilliance is even more striking. Her name probably alludes to the morning star, Lucifer; though it was also an epithet of Day itself.[2] She goes to her coach

> As faire *Aurora* in her purple pall,
> Out of the East the dawning day doth call:
> So forth she comes: her brightnesse brode doth blaze . . .
>
> Her glorious glitterand light doth all mens eyes amaze.
>
> (I. iv. 16)

But we miss the full degree of Lucifera's pride unless we also notice the pretence to a rôle of solar supremacy that is implied in the protocol of her court. It will be remembered that she is accompanied by six attendants, her counsellors, who ride the beasts that pull her coach (I. iv. 17–36). From a moral point of view, of course, these six counsellors, together with Lucifera herself, represent the Seven Deadly Sins. But the description of six mounted attendants and a brilliant coach, moving as if 'through heavens bras-paved way,' is also a deliberate travesty of the conventional representation of Sol with his retinue of lesser planets. The best-known poetic rendering of this motif occurs in Du Bartas' *Sepmaines*, in a passage which Spenser is known to have had by heart:

[1] A prominent aspect of the symbol, based again on Malachi's prophecy. See the *Collectanea*, added to Valeriano, p. 207A, where the comparison between *Sol iustitiæ* and Apollo the healer is developed at some length. Upton (*Var. Sp.*, I, 285) connects the serpent in Fidelia's cup with Æsculapius' serpent of renewal.

[2] See Kitchin's discussion of the name, in his note to *F.Q.*, I. iv. 12. Throughout Bk. I, Spenser plays upon the ambiguous associations of the morning star, which might shine either with pride (like Lucifer) or as a harbinger of the sun (like Una at I. xii. 21, and Fraelissa at I. ii. 36). Dr. Sydney Anglo draws my attention to a use of this same ambiguity (which stems originally from patristic allegorical exegesis) in the 1501 pageants for Katharine of Aragon. See his 'The London Pageants for the Reception of Katharine of Aragon: November 1501,' forthcoming in *JWI*.

Daies glorious Eye![1] even as a mighty King,
About his Countrie stately Progressing,
Is compast round with *Dukes, Earls, Lords,* and *Knights,*
(Orderly marshall'd in their noble Rites)
Esquires and *Gentlemen,* in courtly kinde
And then his *Guard* before him and behinde;
And there is nought in all his Royal Muster,
But to his greatness addeth grace and lustre:
So, while about the World thou ridest ay,
Which only lives by vertue of thy Ray,
Six Heav'nly Princes, mounted evermore,
Wayt on thy Coach, three behinde, three before,
Besides the Hoasts of th'upper Twinklers bright,
To whom, for pay thou givest onely Light.[2]

Lucifera's aspiration to a solar dignity is also indicated by the extended comparison with Phæton—she 'exceeding shone, like *Phœbus* fairest childe,/That did presume his fathers firie wayne'—as well as by the description of the Queen's throne ('as bright as sunny day') and of her own person 'that shone as *Titans* ray.'[3]

---

[1] Cf. *F.Q.*, I. iii. 4, where Una's face 'as the great eye of heaven shyned bright, / And made a sunshine in the shadie place; / Did never mortall eye behold such heavenly grace.' Adam's note to *Republic* 508B. 9 traces a wide distribution of this solar epithet in ancient authors. In the Renaissance, however, it seems to have been regarded as distinctively Orphic: see, e.g., Ficino, *De Sole,* Ch. vi, 'Antiquorum laudes in Solem, et quomodo cœlestium vires in Sole, et a Sole sunt omnes': 'Orpheus called Apollo the life-giving eye of heaven' (*Opera omnia,* p. 968).

[2] The Fourth Day of the First Week, 11. 551–564; p. 106. A similar symbolism may underlie a later episode in *F.Q.* (III. i), where Redcrosse encounters the six knights of Malecasta. Contrary to expectation, the number of these knights is not to be accounted for in terms of numerical apophthegm; for the *points d'amour* (which they represent in the moral allegory) numbered five, not six. See my 'Six Knights at Castle Joyous,' *SP,* LVI (1959), 583–599, where references to earlier material will be found.

[3] Another detail in the description of Lucifera's palace may also be related to the themes under discussion. Many have been puzzled by the line 'And on the top a Diall told the timely howres' (I. iv. 4), which A. C. Hamilton explains simply as meaning that Lucifera's pride is pride in *temporal* things (*The Structure of Allegory,* p. 67: 'the dial shows that [the palace] belongs to the fallen world of time'). If, however, we ask why a *dial* should be specified, we are led back to solar imagery, and in particular to the 'Dial of Ahaz' motif. This image was a very familiar one, from its inclusion in Holbein's *Icones Historiarum Veteris Testamenti* (Fig. 1), as well as in the Bibles of de Lyra and Paul of Burgos (on which see James Strachan, *Early Bible Illustrations* (Cambridge, 1957), notes to his Figs. 23–25). The return of the shadow on the dial of Ahaz (Isaiah, xxxviii. 8) was a sign to Hezekiah that the city would be delivered out of that proud tyrant's hands. Since this story was not infrequently given a topical prophetic

The solar imagery we have been examining had its source in primitive religion; its focus in the Biblical myths that provided Spenser with his matter; and its diffraction in medieval exegetical tradition.[1] It also underwent, however, a further phase of modification; and we do not grasp its full value in the first book of the *Faerie Queene*, unless we keep in mind the special significance of the sun in Renaissance Neoplatonism. Ficino, continuing a philosophical tradition

FIG. 1

which goes back through Proclus and Pseudo-Dionysius to Plato himself, devoted a whole treatise, the *De Sole*, to the theology of the sun. Countless passages throughout his works, moreover, develop the Platonic doctrine that light, the purest quality apprehended by the

[1] See H. Flanders Dunbar, *Symbolism in Medieval Thought and its Consummation in the Divine Comedy* (New Haven, 1929); and Panofsky, *Meaning in the Visual Arts*, pp. 259 ff.

application in Reformation polemic, we ought, perhaps, to treat the dial of Lucifera not only as an amplification of her pride but also as yet another small indication that, in its political orientation, Book I is conceived as 'realized apocalypse.' Note that the incident of the dial of Ahaz is referred to more directly at I. x. 20: Fidelia's words have such power that 'when she list poure out her larger spright, / She would commaund the hastie sunne to . . . backward turne his course from heavens hight.'

75

senses, is the most complete manifestation of the nature of good.[1] Bringing with it nourishing warmth, light generates, fosters, and moves all things, imitating the divine emanations by which the universe consists. The chief light, the sun, is consequently regarded in Orphic and Platonic theology as the most adequate image of God.[2] More particularly, the concept of the sun as a symbol of divine truth (and so, also, of faith) occurs very frequently in Ficino, and is widely current among Renaissance iconographers: 'just as the light of the sun is to the eye of the body, so is the light of truth to the eye of the soul.'[3] Thus, the dominant solar imagery in the first book of the *Faerie Queene* is adjusted in the most organic way to its philosophical themes. Truth, as conceived by Spenser, is indeed the first-born of 'Dayes dearest children.'[4]

The astrological character of Book I is also related to its numerical symbolism. For, in almost all schemes in which symbolic numbers were conferred upon the planets, the monad was allotted to Sol.[5] The sun was not placed first in order of proximity to the centre of the system either by Plato, or by Ptolemy, or by the Pythagoreans; nevertheless, it had an obvious priority of importance. Moreover, it

---

[1] Cf., e.g., *Epist.*, lib. VI, 'Orphica comparatio Solis ad Deum' (*Opera omnia*, p. 825); and the 'Commentary on Dionysius' *De divin. nom.*, chapters entitled 'Lumen est imago boni. Sol est cœlestium dominus et imago Dei,' 'Similitudo luminis atque Solis ad Deum' (pp. 1056–57), and 'Comparatio Solis ad Deum' (p. 1097). Outstanding is the exalted passage in *De immortalitate animorum*, iii, where he speaks of the light of the sun as God in the body of the universe (p. 205): 'Adore the light of the sun beyond all other things—or rather, love it alone! Love God alone, love light alone O soul!'

[2] As Ficino puts it, 'Sol vero maxime Deum ipsum tibi significare potest.' See his *De Sole*, ii, 'Quomodo Solis lumen sit ipsi bono scilicet Deo, simile' (p. 966). Valeriano reviews the ancient and early Christian authorities for the solar analogy, in his chapter 'Deus Optimus Maximus' (*Hieroglyphica*, XLIV. ii; p. 555).

[3] See Ficino, *De immort. anim.*, I. vi (*Opera omnia*, p. 90) for a typical development of this Platonic metaphor, which goes back to *Republic* 508B–D. Note that Ficino identifies the eye of the soul (*animæ oculum*) as the *mens*: a point that will have some bearing when we come to estimate the symbolic relationship of Spenser's first two books.

[4] *F.Q.*, III. iv. 59. On the allegorical ancestry of Truth, see Rudolf Wittkower, 'Chance, Time and Virtue,' *JWI*, I (1937), 313–321; and Donald Gordon, ' "Veritas Filia Temporis": Hadrianus Junius and Geoffrey Whitney,' *JWI*, III (1940), 228–240.

[5] Typical, except for their detailed elaboration, are the schemes or *scalæ* in H. C. Agrippa's *De occulta philosophia* (Antwerp and Paris, 1531), II. iv ('Scala unitatis,' 'Scala binarii,' etc.).

initiated the sequence of the astrological week: an influential consideration for Spenser.

In Pythagorean and Orphic thought Sol was associated with the monad because both were key images of deity. This conception of the sun dominated all others. Thus, Ficino, fond as he may be of demonstrating Proclus' cyclic triad of causes in the creative action of the sun,[1] never fails to stress even more vigorously its unity. In the commentary on the *De divinis nominibus*, for instance, his paraphrase of Dionysius' *Comparatio solis ad deum* constantly returns to this theme:

A single sun with a single light generates, nourishes, vivifies, moves, distinguishes, and unites, the natures of all sensible things . . . the single nature of the sun . . . various effects under one sun . . . a variety of virtues proceeding by light and a single motion . . . God creates the most diverse things through a single nature.[2]

Valeriano, who has a chapter on the unity of the sun, finds authority for the idea not only in Orpheus and Plato but also in the evidence of etymology. The name *Sol*, he assures us, is *a solitudine deductum, sive potius a Sole ipso fiat solitudo*.[3] It is the singleness of the sun that makes it a symbol of truth:

for the same reason as the sun is unity, it is also a symbol of truth; since those things which are duplicitous and labyrinthine or changeable (*multiplicia*) are contrary to the truth. Therefore it is necessary for a thing to be simple, if it is to be considered true.[4]

Thus, a new significance attaches to Spenser's choice of the name Una for his 'woman clothed with the sun,' who is also a personification of Truth. The choice was certainly made in awareness of the symbological background outlined above. It may even be possible to fix on a particular source. For Macrobius, in his discussion of Adad and Adargatis—the solar and earth deities whose iconography we have already connected with the portrayal of Una in Canto iii— explains *Adad* as meaning *unus unus*.[5] It is useful to recognize that each book of the *Faerie Queene* develops a different cult image of

---

[1] See Wind, *Pagan Mysteries*, p. 40, nn. 4 and 5.

[2] Ficino, *Opera omnia*, pp. 1097–98; cf. p. 538.

[3] *Hieroglyphica*, XLIV. iii, 'Unitas,' p. 555; cf. Goulart, *Learned Summary*, p. 182. This derivation goes back to Cicero, *De nat. deorum*, II. xxvii.

[4] Ibid., XLIV. iv, 'Veritas' (p. 555).

[5] *Saturnalia*, I. xxiii. 17–18 (ed. Eyssenhardt (Leipzig, 1893), p. 127). This work, which was a main source both for Valeriano and for Cartari, was also extensively quarried by Spenser: its syncretism seems to have had a strong attraction for him.

Elizabeth; and that in this first book, in the person of Una, we are meeting Elizabeth as the sun.[1] A fresh meaning has thus been given to a name already endowed with cultic associations. The name *Una* asserted the Queen's imperial dignity: her office as a Godly Prince, Christ's representative, the administrative head—in the words of the Supremacy Act, 'the only supreme governor'—of the True Church persecuted in vain by the dragon of the Romish Antichrist.[2] To this complex of ideas Spenser adds an association with the unique sun's imperial sway over the lesser planets.

We have seen that the image of the sun, which is also the Christ in his unity, holds together, by its symbolic implications, the themes of Book I. Themes of faith, of apocalyptic judgement, of sovereignty, of truth's singleness against error's multiplicity, of the sole authority of Elizabeth: all find their embodiment in this solar image, to which so much Platonic speculation and Biblical allegorizing had been devoted. It is doubtful whether the relevance of the book's parts can be properly understood, without allowance being made for this schematic element —without regarding it, that is to say, as in some sense the Book of Sol. Certainly we would fail to appreciate the cosmic movement that is initiated here and that continues, as we shall see, through the cycle of the poem's week. In that movement, the sphere of the sun has a primacy of function. Just as Holiness underlies and empowers all the other virtues, so in the macrocosm it is the sun which strengthens and regulates and informs with particular virtues all the other planets: they will be powerful *quando in unitate Solis extiterunt*.[3] A. C. Hamil-

---

[1] For this suggestion, as for several other points made in this chapter, I am indebted to Miss Frances A. Yates. With Spenser's unfolding of the successive spheres of the Queen's glory may be compared the well-known illustration to John Case's *Sphæra civitatis* (London, 1588), which shows a moralized planetary system held in the arms of Elizabeth the One Monarch (Pl. 5). See Frances Yates, 'Queen Elizabeth as Astræa,' p. 61.

[2] On *Una* as a cult name for Elizabeth, see C. B. Millican, 'Spenser's and Drant's Poetic Names for Elizabeth: Tanaquil, Gloriana and Una,' *HLQ*, II (1939); E. C. Wilson, *England's Eliza* (Cambridge, Mass., 1939), p. 78 etc.; Roy C. Strong, 'The popular celebration of the accession day of Queen Elizabeth I,' *JWI*, XXI (1958), 86–103; and Frances Yates, 'Queen Elizabeth as Astræa,' p. 68, where Una's imperial claim is discussed.

[3] Ficino, *Opera omnia*, p. 538; cf. p. 968, on the fundamental importance of the sun's motion: 'Astronomi per motum Solis iam compertum Planetarum motus inveniunt, atque metiuntur. . . .' In Ficino's account of the planets' rôles in creation, as we shall see, each is conceived as a special mode of operation of the sun.

ton's theory that the pattern of Book I may be said to 'contain the action of the whole poem'[1] perhaps requires a fuller substantiation than it has been given in *The Structure of Allegory*; but at least it encounters no obstacle in the allocation of this book to Sol and to the all-inclusive monad.

[1] *The Structure of Allegory*, p. 128. This theory is developed at some length throughout his fourth chapter; cf. also pp. 89–90: 'Book I is central and unifying within the poem's structure.'

IX

The Book of the Moon

i

IF any planetary deity presides over the second book of the *Faerie Queene* it must be one whose relationship with Sol is especially close. Its symbolic province would have to be complementary to his. For the formal relationship between their respective books would be of this nature: structurally, the second book is a modified reflection of the first, matching it far more intimately than any other. Both in narrative order and in allegorical development, the adventure of Guyon keeps pace with that of Redcrosse, in such a way that it covers exactly complementary ground.

The full extent of this thematic and formal relationship was first indicated a few years ago in a brilliant essay by A. C. Hamilton.[1] Hamilton called his paper '"Like Race to Runne,"' in allusion to a speech of the Palmer's addressed to the Red Cross Knight:

> enrolled is your glorious name
> In heavenly Registers above the Sunne,
> Where you a Saint with Saints your seat have wonne:
> But wretched we, where ye have left your marke,
> Must now anew begin, like race to runne.
>
> (II. i. 32)

[1] ' "Like Race to Runne": The Parallel Structure of *The Faerie Queene*, Books I and II,' *PMLA*, LXXIII (1958); included as Ch. iii in *The Structure of Allegory in 'The Faerie Queene.*' A. S. P. Woodhouse ('Nature and Grace in *The Faerie Queene*,' *ELH*, XVI (1949), 204–208) made an earlier attempt to explain the same formal antithesis; but his theory, which exaggerates the contrast between Books I and II, and denies to the second any considerable theological content, has not met with general acceptance. To the bibliography given in Hamilton, *Structure of*

This resonant phrase, which primarily alludes to the Biblical metaphor of the race of life,[1] can at the same time be taken as an artistic statement: a notice of the similarity between the courses followed by the first two books. It is important to realize, however, that the words also have yet another sense. The image of running a race or a 'course' was almost habitually used by Spenser to describe the fulfilment of an astronomical periodic cycle.[2] Moreover, the metaphor is used in an explicitly astronomical sense in a passage which may well be thought to have some connection with II. i. 32. I refer to the description of the priests in the temple of Isis:

> They wore rich Mitres shaped like the Moone,
> To shew that *Isis* doth the Moone portend;
> Like as *Osyris* signifies the Sunne.
> For that they both like race in equall justice runne.
>
> (V. vii. 4)

The 'races' of the sun and moon are alike in equal justice for at least two reasons: because each runs a daily course across the sky from East to West; and because, one being the chief diurnal luminary and the other the chief nocturnal luminary, their annual course eventually accomplishes an *equal sharing* of the total hours of day and night.[3]

[1] I Cor. ix. 24; Heb. xii. I.

[2] Cf., e.g., *F.Q.*, I. v. 44 ('The mother of dread darknesse . . . tooke her wonted way, / To runne her timely race') and I. xi. 3 ('*Titan* rose to runne his daily race'); *Amor.*, lxii ('The weary yeare his race now having run'); and *Epith.*, ll. 149–150 ('Lyke Phœbe from her chamber of the East, / Arysing forth to run her mighty race'). The same metaphor was common with Du Bartas (e.g., The Fourth Day of the First Week, ll. 391–392 (p. 101), apostrophizing Sol: 'Thou, in three hundred threescore dayes and five, / Doost to the period of thy Race arrive'), who develops it into an elaborate *allegoria* in his famous analogy between Sol's course and the course run by the Queen's Champion, Sir Henry Lee: 'Thou glorious Champion, in thy Heav'nly Race . . .' (ibid., ll. 597–608; p. 107). From the last passage we may perhaps conclude that the metaphor was not uncommon in the symbolism of politico-cosmic pageantry.

[3] Hieatt has attempted to show that the equalization of day and night finds formal expression in the structural pattern of *Epithalamion* (see *Short Time's Endless Monument*, Ch. ii). My hypothesis of a comparable symbolism in *F.Q.* ought to make his case more plausible; and vice versa.

Allegory, p. 91, add T. M. Gang, 'Nature and Grace in *The Faerie Queene*, the problem reviewed,' *ELH*, XXVI (1959); Woodhouse, 'Nature and Grace: Mr. Gang's mode of argument reviewed,' *ELH*, XXVII (1960); and my own 'The Image of Mortality.' Hamilton (p. 91) ostensibly accepts Woodhouse's dichotomy; but then in effect subverts it by giving a theological interpretation of Bk. II.

Comparison of the two passages prompts the suggestion that Book II, which has 'like race to runne' with the Book of Sol, may belong to Luna. Now Luna admirably fulfils our requirement of a unique relationship with Sol. The two were naturally associated as the chief luminaries; so that in every astrological scheme acknowledging pairs of planets they had their place together.[1] Even in Manilius' list of Olympian guardians, Apollo and Diana are linked. For the list is so arranged that, when its summer and winter halves are placed in opposition, each pair of months is presided over by a pair of male and female deities:

Minerva (Aries)	Vulcanus (Libra)
Venus (Taurus)	Mars (Scorpio)
APOLLO (Gemini)	DIANA (Sagittarius)
Mercurius (Cancer)	Vesta (Capricornus)
Iuppiter (Leo)	Iuno (Aquarius)
Ceres (Virgo)	Neptunus (Pisces)[2]

The connection between the first two guardians of the planetary week was further reinforced by a mythological relationship; since Apollo and Diana were brother and sister. They were the 'faire twins' of Latona 'which . . . did rule the night and day' (II. xii. 13).

The moon's guardianship over Book II is exerted in a variety of ways. Operating mythologically, for example, it occasions in several episodes the appearance of representatives of the lunar deity. Thus, Guyon, after descending through the Cave of Mammon (where the light is like that of 'the Moone cloathed with clowdy night'), comes to the Garden of Proserpina: a goddess often regarded as one of the three aspects of Luna.[3] And indeed Guyon himself re-enacts the myth of Proserpina. Like her, he is enticed beneath the earth—not by Pluto himself, it is true, but by a god

[1] E.g. the scheme in Ficino's letter entitled 'Saepe in cœlestibus gemini sunt. . . . Marsilius Ficinus Martino Uranio Germano, amico unico,' to which my attention was directed by Mr. J. B. Trapp. 'Non solum in firmamento gemini sunt illi Dioscuri, sed inter planetas sunt quoque Germani,' writes Ficino, punning on his friend's name. The pairs he gives are Mercurius/Saturnus (on the ground that 'ingeniis utrique præsunt'); Iuppiter/Venus; and Phœbus/Phœbe. Mars is left out, as being 'superbior' (*Epistolæ*, lib. XII; p. 949). Cf. Agrippa's 'Scala binarii,' which also links Sol and Luna.

[2] For a discussion of these Manilian pairs, see Housman's Introd., Vol. II, p. xvii.

[3] See, e.g., Valeriano, *Hieroglyphica*, XLIV. xvii (p. 559), and Conti, *Mythologiæ*, III. xvi, *ad fin.*

often confused with Pluto[1]—and his freedom to return to the upper world, like hers, depends on whether he takes a symbolic fruit. Only, being a more virtuous Proserpina, Guyon refuses the 'goodly golden fruit'; so that he escapes with a shorter term in the Underworld.

In the third canto, a point at which, in the first book, there came an image directly based on solar iconography (Una and the lion), the second book has an image just as clearly lunar. This is the embodiment of true Honour and Temperance in the person of Belphœbe. From a mythological point of view, Belphœbe is predominantly conceived as a surrogate of the moon-goddess, Phœbe. Indeed, as we are told at III. vi. 28, she began life as Diana's foster-child; just as her twin sister Amoret was the foster-child of Venus. In that later book Belphœbe proves to have an admixture of other planetary influences; in particular, she is sometimes to be thought of as a Venus–Diana figure.[2] Her first splendid description in II. iii, however, presents simply the mythological ideal of Diana. As Belphœbe appears to Trompart, she is a 'queen and huntress, chaste and fair,'

> Such as *Diana* by the sandie shore
> Of swift *Eurotas*, or on *Cynthus* greene,
> Where all the Nymphes have her unwares forlore,
> Wandreth alone with bow and arrowes keene,
> To seeke her game.
>
> (II. iii. 31)

---

[1] Ploutos, the god of wealth, was often confused with Pluto (i.e., Plouton), the ravisher of Proserpina. We may note in passing that Pluto's presence in Bk. II is numerologically appropriate, since the unfortunate dyad was often ascribed to him.

[2] Her geniture combines Jupiter, Venus, and Sol in favourable aspect—'In th' *Horoscope* of her nativitee, / . . . *Jove* laught on *Venus* from his soveraigne see, / And *Phoebus* with faire beames did her adorne' (III. vi. 2). The significance of this geniture is that in Neoplatonic mythology Jupiter Venus and Sol were regarded as corresponding to the three Graces (see Ficino, *De vita*, III. v; pp. 536 ff.). Spenser means that Belphœbe is endowed by nature with those qualities which are in the gift of the Graces: nobility, personal grace, beauty, liberality, etc. Merritt Hughes finds hints of the Venus component in Belphœbe's character as early as II. iii: see his 'Virgilian Allegory and *The Faerie Queene*,' *PMLA*, XLIV (1929), 696–705. On Venus–Diana as a composite deity in the Renaissance, consult Wind, *Pagan Mysteries*, especially pp. 73 ff., 85, 88, 164, 166, and 168. That the sophisticated notion of an ideal mixture of Venus and Diana was within the mental reach of a literate Elizabethan is shown by its casual introduction in *Astrophel and Stella*, LXXII.

As Jonson's poem reminds us, Elizabeth was widely celebrated as Diana or Luna—a persona which she projected more successfully, perhaps, than any other.[1] We have it on Spenser's own authority that Belphœbe was intended as a contribution to this cult:

For considering she [Elizabeth] beareth two persons, the one of a most royall Queene or Empresse, the other of a most vertuous and beautifull Lady, this latter part in some places I doe expresse in Belphœbe, fashioning her name according to your owne [i.e., Raleigh's] excellent conceipt of Cynthia, (Phœbe and Cynthia being both names of Diana.)[2]

Belphœbe, like Una, is meant to shadow forth the person of the queen. But she constitutes a different sphere of the cosmic Elizabeth: Elizabeth as Luna.

Among incidental allusions to the moon in Book II,[3] one occurring in the same third canto is especially significant. Braggadocchio boasts that he has always pursued honour, "endevouring [his] dreadded name to raise / Above the Moone' (II. iii. 38). This boast contrasts with the Palmer's earlier praise of Redcrosse's achievements, for which his 'glorious name' is enrolled 'in heavenly Registers above the Sunne' (II. i. 32). The contrast reflects the different values prevailing in the first two books. Not only Braggadocchio, but Guyon, Belphœbe, and Pyrochles too, are devoted to the pursuit of honour; achievement, as they understand it, brings *honourable* fame. Redcrosse, on the other hand, is concerned with the achievement of glory, in a more exclusively religious sense. This antithesis, which extends throughout the two books, at times seems almost to amount to a dichotomy of interest between the sacred and the secular, the heavenly and the earthly. Such a dichotomy could be expressed very appropriately in terms of a contrast of solar and lunar realms. As a 'little earth',[4] the moon might symbolize what was earthly, in opposition to the divinity of the sun. Moreover, since the first men after the Flood were reported to have believed themselves descended from the moon, the latter came to be associated with the secular values of nobility and honour.[5] At the same

[1] On the prevalence of Elizabeth's Diana cult, see Wilson, *England's Eliza*, Ch. v.

[2] Letter to Raleigh.

[3] These are more numerous than in Bk. I, but not significantly so.

[4] In the Renaissance the view that the moon is a 'celestial Earth' was regarded as Pythagorean: see, e.g., Valeriano, *Hieroglyphica*, XLIV. xv; p. 558.

[5] See ibid., XLIV. xxiii, 'Nobilitas' (pp. 560–561).

time, any theory which describes the relationship of Book II to Book I in terms of a theological dichotomy (such as that between Nature and Grace) is in my view bound to prove inadequate. Guyon experiences spiritual crisis, exhaustion, and regeneration, as well as the Red Cross Knight. Besides, the structure of the *Faerie Queene* is not static and compartmented, but constantly dilating and evolving. Each book after the first is built upon the preceding book, and takes for granted the spiritual territory already conquered. Thus, Guyon and the Palmer must begin their race *where Redcrosse left off*: 'wretched we, where ye have left your marke,/ Must now anew begin' (II. i. 32). Book II is much occupied with honour; but its values are far from being limited to those of the secular world. Confronted with Mammon's offer of Philotime, Guyon refuses such honour as the world can give.

In a different symbolic application the moon was thought of as celestial: set over against earth, and reflecting upon it the light of the sun. Regarded in this way, the moon could represent the secondary source of illumination, doctrine. The emblem of the fountain of Diana in II. i-ii, which brings home to Mordant his mortal guilt, develops this aspect of lunar symbolism. Elsewhere[1] I have shown that this magical fountain *formed* by Diana is derived from Solinus' account of a mythical river with similar properties *named* the Diana. The antique myth has in the interval been allegorized by Bersuire, who interprets *Diana* as meaning 'manifest' (*clara*), and the water as signifying doctrine. Spenser's use of this fountain symbolism does not end with the death of Mordant (allegorically, the Old Adam) and the baptism of Ruddymane (the New Man). The waters of revealed doctrine have further to be transmitted to the natural order by Guyon (himself named after Gæon, one of the four rivers of paradise):[2] a process which is not completed until he has run his full course from the Nymph's well to the fountain of Acrasia. Thus, it would appear that, just as Bersuire's *Sol iustitiæ* furnished a key image for the first book of the *Faerie Queene*, so his river Diana provides the symbolic framework for the second.

Its theme of mediation of doctrine to the natural order differentiates

---

[1] 'The Image of Mortality,' p. 95, and 'Emblems of Temperance,' pp. 148–149.

[2] See my note, 'The River Guyon,' *MLN*, LXXV (1960), 289–292, which shows that from the time of Philo the four rivers named in Gen. ii. 10–14 were allegorized as the four cardinal virtues; Gæon being usually allotted to Temperance.

the province of Book II from that of its predecessor more subtly than in Professor Woodhouse's partition. The first book dealt with faith in revealed truth; and with conflict against error, pride, despair, and other enemies of truth at a spiritual and intellectual level. Book II, however, deals with applications of the same truth to the psychological and moral sphere; and hence with conflict against the passions. Now, practical application of truth is an office of the reason (*ratio: anima*); while belief in truth is an office rather of the intellect (*mens*). I would suggest, therefore, that the division of labour between Books I and II is best thought of, not as a division between Orders of Grace and Nature, but as a division between the tasks appropriate to *mens* and *ratio* together, on the one hand, and those appropriate to *ratio* in its dealings with the lower parts of the mind, on the other. This schematic relationship is seen most clearly, perhaps, in the two medullar cantos. In the Castle of Alma is portrayed *anima*—indeed, *alma* is Italian for *anima*—ordering the body in accordance with counsel; whereas in the House of Holiness is portrayed *mens*, the spiritual faculty of mind, believing and contemplating.

It so happens that precisely the same relationship between *mens* and *ratio* was not infrequently explained by Renaissance Neoplatonists in terms of an analogy with the relationship between sun and moon. The analogy had its source in the Orphic and Platonic theology of the sun. Writers in this tradition customarily compared *mens* with the sun;[1] and the natural concomitant, comparison of *anima* with the moon, was only less common.[2] It was left to Leone Ebreo, however, to develop the full metaphysical possibilities of the double analogy. A large part of his *Dialoghi d'Amore* is taken up with a speculative *schema* in which the sun and moon are found to correspond analogically to complementary faculties of the mind, as well as to different stages of cosmic emanation. The sun is for Ebreo an 'image of divine Intellect, on which every intellect depends; and the moon is an image of the Anima Mundi, from which every *anima* proceeds.'[3] In view of the symbolic mean position that Spen-

[1] E.g. Ficino, *Opera omnia*, p. 90. The comparison is probably based upon the same passage in Plato (*Rep.*, 508B–D) already mentioned in a similar connection; though Valeriano (*Hieroglyphica*, XXXIII. ii, p. 392) finds further sources for it in Cicero and Plutarch.

[2] See, e.g., Fortunio Liceti, *Hieroglyphica* (Padua, 1653), p. 438D.

[3] Leone Ebreo (i.e., Giuda Abarbanel), *Dialoghi d'Amore*, ed. S. Caramella (Bari, 1929), p. 179.

ser's second book occupies between the first and the third, special interest attaches to Ebreo's account of the intermediate place of moon and *anima*:

Just as *anima* comes between intellect and body, and is formed compositely, out of intellectual stability and unity on the one hand, and corporeal diversity and changeableness on the other; so the moon comes between the sun—an image of intellect—and the corporeal earth, and is formed compositely, out of unified stable solar light, and diversified mutable terrestrial shade.[1]

Underlying all such speculative analogies is the notion that the relationship of *ratio* or *anima* (reason) to *mens* (intellect) is a *reflective* one, and therefore appropriately likened to the moon's reflection of the sun. The 'like race' of the first two books of the *Faerie Queene* is thus a faithful enactment of Ebreo's analogy. Their formal correlation renders, on the moral plane, the interplay of mental faculties; on the plane of astronomical symbolism, the interdependence of solar and lunar movements.

In a closely related but more specific sense, the moon was sometimes a symbol of *anima* in its form-bestowing capacity: the builder, that is to say, of the human body.[2] Thus, in Chapman's 'Hymnus in Cynthiam' it is Cynthia herself who commissions Form to raise her bodily temple according to a geometrical plan: a plan that is fulfilled 'by bewtious Forme, as her great mistresse wild.' This aspect of the symbolic Luna is given ample attention by Spenser in his allegory of the Castle of Alma—a canto which Chapman's poem resembles in many ways.

From the mythographic encyclopædists a clear impression can be formed of the range of ideas that fell within the lunar province. And we find that the symbolic meanings of the moon coincide to a significant extent with the subjects of Spenser's second book. Theologically considered, that book deals with Original Sin or concupiscence; with Regeneration and Edification (the building of the 'goodly frame of Temperance'); with the mortification of fleshly human nature and its passions; and with the putting on of the temperate nature of the New Man—in short, with the Christian

---

[1] Leone Ebreo, p. 187; cf. Ficino, *Opera omnia*, p. 1468.
[2] An idea which goes back to Macrobius, *In somn. Scip.*, I. xi. 7.

doctrine of man, or of human nature.[1] Closely similar meanings were attributed to the moon. Thus, Valeriano gathers authorities for the view that 'by the symbol of Luna is expressed human nature.'[2] In explanation, he refers to the Pythagorean conception of the moon as a celestial Earth; notices that the moon has a 'shadow side'; and recalls the analogy between the rapidly changing face of the moon, and the variable passions of man. (This last symbolism was so familiar that Trissino could give his lunar goddess Selene the succinct title 'Lady of humours.'[3]) The hieroglyphist Liceti, drawing on similar material, adds that Luna may be interpreted as 'human nature translated to the heavens on account of worthy deeds previously performed in life.'[4] His elaboration of this idea is particularly relevant:

Just as the woman in Holy Scripture clothed with the sun, having the moon under her feet . . . is everywhere and with justice applied to the great Virgin Mother, wholly pervaded by the divine Sun, who has always trodden underfoot the earthly passions of human nature; so also it can fitly be interpreted with reference simply to human nature, sanctified in heaven—where it wholly and fully enjoys the divine Sun, and is illuminated by his light, as the physical moon is bathed in the light of the physical sun. . . . The moon can also signify the soul.

Did Spenser have some such symbolism as this in mind when he turned from the 'woman clothed with the sun' in his first book to an analysis of human passions in his second? At least we can be sure that the episode of the Castle of Alma presents his vision of sanctified human nature.

A more elusive question is that of the emotional tone of Book II. This, though not lacking in affirmativeness, is distinguished by a virginal coolness, if we compare it with the tone of, say, Book III. At a time when the planetary deities had definite emotional auras,

[1] For discussions of the theological content of Bk. II, see Hamilton's *The Structure of Allegory*, Ch. ii, and my 'The Image of Mortality.'
[2] *Hieroglyphica*, XLIV. xv, 'Natura Humana' (p. 558): 'Sole pro sublimioris naturæ imagine constituto, fuere qui per Lunæ hieroglyphicum naturam humanam exprimi differerent.'
[3] *La Italia liberata* (Rome, 1547), fol. 108ʳ; cf. Du Bartas, The Fourth Day of the First Week, l. 412 (p. 102) where Luna is 'regent of humours.' These titles depend on the notion that, in the generation of life, Luna is responsible for the provision of *humor*, or moisture.
[4] Liceti, *Hieroglyphica*, p. 438C–D. The tradition in which Liceti here writes can be traced to Bersuire, *Dictionarium*, s.v. 'Luna' (Vol. II, fol. cclviiiᵛ–cclixʳ).

such tonal gradation between parts of a mythological work were probably keenly appreciated. In particular, the connection of temperance with chaste Diana and with Luna was a traditional one.[1] It was not for nothing that Spenser based the early episode of the Nymph's well on Bersuire's allegorization of the river Diana: the 'home key' of Book II is at the outset established as lunar, and would thereafter be felt as such by a trained reader.

Finally, a minor aspect of Book II, that is stressed—perhaps over-stressed—by Berger,[2] is its treatment of man's subjection to *Tyche*, chance or fortune. It is doubtful, however, whether this theme is at all independent from that of the mortality of dyadic human nature. Significantly, when Valeriano assigns to Luna the meaning *Tyche*, he explains: 'Luna is *Tyche* because she is guardian of bodies, which are swayed by alterations of fortune.'[3] If the changeableness of the moon and her earthly constitution were emphasized to the exclusion of her borrowed light, she might even represent body itself.

It will be recalled that some of the themes of Book II, that have here been related to Luna, were in an earlier chapter related also (though for somewhat different reasons) to the dyad. Are we to draw the depressing conclusion that in this field anything can be related to anything else? By no means. Our procedure is justified, for the reason that the series of Pythagorean symbolic numbers and the series of planetary guardians *are not fully independent systems*. From a very early date, symbolic numbers were linked with Olympian deities, mainly in accordance with the sequence of the astrological week. The ascription of the dyad to Luna for example, goes back at least as far as Iamblichus.[4] Later, numerical and planetary symbolisms developed in the most intimate association with one another. Indeed, without such interdependence, structural decorum of the kind Spenser aimed at would have been impossible.

[1] Bersuire, fol. cclix[r]: 'Luna temperat ardorem.' We note that the specific quality of shamefastness or *pudicitia*, which Guyon discovers at II. ix. 43 to be the well-head of his moral life, is referred by Valeriano to Luna (*Hieroglyphica*, p. 559).

[2] In *The Allegorical Temper*; see my review of Berger, in *EC*, X (1960), 334–341.

[3] *Hieroglyphica*, p. 187.

[4] *Theologoumena arithmeticæ*, ed. de Falco, p. 14, l. 9; cf. Goulart, *A Learned Summary*, Second Week, p. 249.

ii

There is also a connection of quite a different sort between the numerical and the astronomical elements of the *Faerie Queene*. For Spenser has chosen to give the astronomical symbolism formal expression in numerological terms. In a most remarkable manner, he has allowed astronomical constants, such as orbital period figures, to determine the placing of significant passages; so that the numerical movement of the poem mimes the courses of planets figuring symbolically in its action. The formal proportions of the *Faerie Queene* are the proportions of the cosmos itself.

As we now know, a similar numerical symbolism underlies another poem by Spenser, *Epithalamion*.[1] Understandably, the formal patterns of the *Faerie Queene* have been more resistant to analysis. Not only is the numerology of a longer poem more extended and more complicated, but in this case there are two additional factors that combine to cause difficulty. First, what is measured is for the most part the internal division of the action itself, rather than the external division of the poem into book and canto. This makes for a more organic and expressive formal decorum; but it has the incidental result that the most obvious points of entry for numerological analysis—stanza-totals of whole books or cantos—lead to no immediate result.[2] We are prepared for this feature, however, by the overlapping of each patron knight's adventure beyond the boundaries of his own book (Redcrosse does not leave the action until II. i, Guyon until III. i, and so on); as well as by the *entrelacement* that characterizes the narrative structure generally. The other factor that renders the numerology less obvious is that in reckoning orbital cycles Spenser usually counts the days and nights in the period separately.[3] Thus, a solar year is represented by the figure

---

[1] See the ref. to Hieatt, above p. 3, n. 1; also the discussion in my concluding chapter of other poems whose numerology is based on astronomical numbers.

[2] None, that is, in the pattern of astronomical number symbolism. As we have seen, the stanza-totals sometimes have Pythagorean or theological significance.

[3] Such reckoning was not without precedent. Plato's number expressing the relation between King and Tyrant with respect to justice and injustice (*Rep.*, IX, 587–588) is 729: a number that Adam (n. to *Rep.*, 558A) explains as $2 \times 364\frac{1}{2}$, that is, twice the number of days (or nights) in the year of Philolaus. As Adam notices, 729 is also the number of months in the Great Year of Philolaus; a point we should bear in mind, in view of the frequent appearances of Great Year figures in the numerology of *F.Q.*

730 (not 365); a synodic lunar year by 708 (not 354); and a sidereal lunar year by 656 (not 328). The reason for this may simply be that the smaller numbers would have given too narrow a scheme. More probably, however, it is because the alternation of day and night has a particular importance in Spenser's cosmic symbolism. As Kent Hieatt has shown, the whole structure of *Epithalamion* is an imitation of the seasonal changes in the relation between day and night: a relation which is developed poetically in the direction of nature myth and sexual symbolism. And we have every reason to believe that a similar symbolism underlines much of the *Faerie Queene* as well. The pageant of time in the *Mutabilitie Cantos* suggests a further consideration. There we find, closely juxtaposed, not only '*Day*, and *Night*, /Riding together both with equall pase,' and the daughter Hours who measure their interaction; but also Life and Death. Perhaps it is because, in Spenser's vision, darkness, death, and night are woven into the very texture of existence that he measures their duration so carefully together with the warp of light, life, and day.

The most obvious use of orbital period numbers is in the positioning of the various stanzas which recount how certain of the patron knights departed on their missions. Thus, Guyon relates his departure from Gloriana's court at II. ii. 44, itself a chronographical stanza:

> Now hath faire Phœbe with her silver face
> Thrise seene the shadowes of the neather world,
> Sith last I left that honorable place.

Reckoning from the very beginning of the poem, these words come after just 730 stanzas.[1] That is to say, the beginning of Guyon's adventure occurs when the solar year of Redcrosse's adventure has run its numerological course. Further, if we count forwards from II. ii. 44 we arrive, after exactly a *lunar* year of 708 stanzas, at Britomart's account of *her* departure from home (III. iii. 7). This is not the only way in which Guyon's adventure is connected numerologically with the period of the moon's course. The most inclusive stanza-total of Book II, 700,[2] is close to, though curiously short of, the number of the synodic lunar year. But observe! Guyon's mission is not quite complete at the end of Book II. Not until

[1] In the 1596 edn.; 729 stanzas in the 1590 edn. Unless otherwise stated, proem stanzas, but not argument stanzas, are included in the count.

[2] That is, counting proem and argument stanzas. 700 is itself a symbolic round number appropriate to the content of Bk. II; since it denotes the seven planets

III. i. 2 has he sent the captive Acrasia to Gloriana's court and gone on himself with Arthur in search of new adventures. Reckoning to the end of this stanza, we find that the total now comes to exactly 708, the number denoting the lunar year of Guyon's adventure.[1]

Perhaps the most remarkable of this class of patterns concerns the meeting between Guyon and Redcrosse. Several moments in this episode, significant from the present point of view, should be distinguished. First, the moment when the two knights, having begun to fight—'He gan rencounter him in equall race./They bene ymet'—discover their mutual error (II. i. 27–28); second, their reconciliation (II. i. 29); third, the transition from Redcrosse's to Guyon's pageant, explicitly noticed by the Palmer—'wretched we . . . Must now anew begin, like race to runne' (II. i. 32). Redcrosse also remarks in II. i. 33 that Guyon's 'pageant next ensewes,' and in the following stanza Guyon goes off with the Palmer guiding 'his race with reason'; so that the transition from pageant to pageant must be considered as falling between II. i. 33 and 34. The whole passage is rich in numerological harmonies. For example, the transition between pageants comes 650 stanzas after the opening of Book I, and 650 stanzas before the end of Book II (counting canto stanzas only). Thus, the stanzas of the first two books are divided in 'equall justice' between the race of the sun and the race of the moon. Moreover, halfway through the first 650 stanzas is the entry of Arthur 'like glauncing light of *Phœbus* brightest ray' (I. vii. 29); halfway through the second 650 stanzas, the appearance of the guardian angel 'like *Phœbus* face adorned with sunny rayes' (II. viii. 5)—both crucial interventions of divine grace. Next, if we include proem stanzas in the count we find that the mid-point of Books I and II together falls at II. i. 29, the stanza describing the reconciliation of Redcrosse and Guyon: 'So bene they both attone.' The equity of their relationship is expressed numerically; reckoned from this point, too, their courses have the same temporal measure.[2]

[1] We should note that 708 is also the number of hours in a 29½-day lunar month.

[2] Guyon, like Redcrosse, is spiritually at his lowest ebb at the mid-point of the book. The end of II. vii falls at the 354th stanza—exactly halfway through the days and nights of the lunar year, or the hours of the lunar month.

governing the body (see p. 38, n. 5, above). Bongo tells us that 700 also signifies the reign of a just king: a symbolism utilized by Spenser in the 'seven hundred Princes' of his Elfin chronicle (II. x. 74).

But the numerology of the episode goes beyond mere symmetry. Consider the position of the knights' discovery of their mutual error. Not counting proem or arguments, it comes 27 stanzas from the beginning of Book II, and 656 stanzas—the number of a sidereal lunar year—from its end. Why such redoubled allusion to the sidereal lunar period? We may best approach this problem by paying close attention to the text at the exact point where the sidereal lunar period (27 days 8 hours) is symbolically completed, after 27 stanzas and a fraction:

> But when he heard him speake, streight way he knew
> His error, and himselfe inclyning sayd;
> Ah deare Sir *Guyon*, well becommeth you,
> But me behoveth rather to upbrayd,
> Whose hastie hand so farre from reason strayd.

The error, whose occurrence somehow accompanies completion of the moon's sidereal period, is attributed to Redcrosse's *haste*—the haste, that is to say, of Sol's representative. Stated in these terms, the astronomical sense of the passage is immediately apparent. The sidereal lunar period is the time taken by the moon to return to the same point relative to the zodiac. This is not, however, the same time as it takes the moon to return to the same position (say, conjunction) relative to the sun; since the sun has meanwhile passed on in its own zodiacal course.[1] Thus, the sidereal lunar period is insufficient to re-establish the original conjunction; and it may be said to bring a discrepancy or *error* in the spatial relation of sun to moon. This error, which is due to the sun's 'haste,' is not adjusted until the *synodic* lunar period ($29\frac{1}{2}$ days) is completed. It is from the 29th stanza, therefore, that we find Redcrosse and Guyon 'both attone.'

But if the discrepancy after the sidereal lunar period can be attributed to the sun's haste, could it not equally well be attributed to the moon's tardiness? Certainly; and we find that Spenser has allowed for this possibility in a later episode. As Guyon approached

[1] A simple account of the elements of the moon's motion, from the present point of view, was available to Spenser in Macrobius, *In somn. Scip.*, I. vi. 49–53 (ed. Stahl, pp. 109–110). An allegorical application of the various phases of the moon, including conjunction with the sun, was also accessible in Bersuire's *Dictionarium* (s.v. 'Luna,' Vol. II, fols. cclviii[v] and cclix[v]). For Bersuire, too, conjunction carries a favourable meaning: namely that man 'is united with God the *Sol iustitiæ* through grace and charity.'

the end of his mission, he was guilty of a temporary moral lapse: he was attracted by the sight of two bathing nymphs, who caused him 'to slacke his pace,' until the Palmer corrected his race with reason and 'him forward thence did draw' (II. xii. 68–69). This error of Guyon's comes 27 stanzas and a fraction—the number denoting a lunar sidereal period—from the end of his adventure at III. i. 2.[1] Similarly, counting from the beginning of the same twelfth canto, Guyon erred in being attracted by the doleful maid after 27 stanzas and a fraction; but submitted to the Palmer and 'held on his course' in the 29th stanza.

iii

The zodiacal sign which is featured most prominently in the imagery of Book II is Aquarius. Much of the book's theological allegory is focused upon two emblematic fountains, the Nymph's and Acrasia's, which confront each other from its opposite ends. The first fountain is a Fountain of Wisdom, the second a Fountain of Concupiscence; and Guyon's mission is to go from one to the other—to form, as it were, a human conduit. It is by his moral course that the waters of doctrine and grace are communicated to corrupt nature; just as, in Trissino's *La Italia*, Spenser's model, 'water of salvation' is carried in a bottle from the fountain of Sinesia (Conscience) to the fountain of Acratia (Concupiscence).[2] This motif of the bringing together of two fluids, one life-giving and the other death-dealing, is closely related to a very familiar emblem of Temperance: the mingling of wine and water.[3] Moreover, as we have seen, Spenser's river of doctrine is connected with Diana, the planetary deity presiding over Book II. But, in a more obvious way, the fountain imagery also alludes to Aquarius, the Water-Pourer. Often this sign was represented as a river-god, from whose tilted urn a stream takes origin. Alternatively, it might be represented as a young man serving drink:

---

[1] Counting proem and argument stanzas.

[2] For a fuller discussion of this fountain symbolism, which is too intricate to be summarized adequately here, see my three articles, cit. above, p. 85, nn. 1, 2.

[3] One of the commonest types of representation of the virtue consists of a human figure pouring water from one receptacle into another that contains wine (Pl. 7b). See Tervarent, s.v. 'Aiguière,' i, and 'Vase,' vi, cols. 8–9 and 394; also my 'Emblems of Temperance,' pp. 147–149.

the *Skinker* [i.e., tapster] from his starry spout,
After the *Goat*, a silver stream pours-out;
Distilling still out of his radiant Fire
Rivers of Water.[1]

There was thus an iconographical similarity between representations of Aquarius and of the virtue Temperance, whose commonest emblem was also a figure pouring water from an ewer. Even the second receptacle, usual in the emblem of Temperance, is occasionally to be found in representations of Aquarius.[2] This formal connection was confirmed by others. Aquarius being a winter sign, for example, its water was cool, allied to the *aqua refrigerativa* of piety and virtue, rather than to the warm Egyptian fountain of worldly pleasure.[3] To these associations of Aquarius with Temperance in general may be added another with Spenser's particular theological treatment of the virtue. Temperance in Book II is conceived as a mortification of the Old Man and an edification of the New: in short, as baptism implemented. It may be, therefore, that when we interpret Guyon's washing of Ruddymane in the Nymph's fountain we are meant to recall the application of Aquarius as a symbol of baptismal regeneration. In Du Bartas' *Devine Weekes*, for example, Aquarius is:

the deer Son of dumb *Zacharias*,
Gods Harbinger, fore-runner of *Messias*:
Who in clear *Jordan* washeth clean the sin
Of all that rightly do repent with-in.[4]

The symbolic appropriateness of Aquarius to the themes of Book II is readily appreciated. From an astrological point of view, however, it is at first more difficult to see what the sign Aquarius has to do with the book's planetary guardian. Aquarius is neither the House, nor the Exaltation, nor the Depression of Luna. Why, then, should it be linked so closely with this planet, not only in the same book, but even in the single image of the Nymph's fountain? In Book I a simple connection between planet and domiciliary sign led directly

[1] Du Bartas, The Fourth Day of the First Week, ll. 267–270 (p. 98).
[2] E.g., in Falconetto's sequence of the months in the Salone dello Zodiaco at the Palazzo di Bagno at Mantua, where Aquarius appears as a celestial youth pouring water from a ewer into a large laver (Pls. 6, 7a). Aquarius could thus be represented iconographically in all three ways in which the water of the Nymph's well is symbolically considered by Spenser: (*a*) as a river; (*b*) as drinking water (*F.Q.*, II. i. 55); and (*c*) as water for washing (*F.Q.*, II. ii. 3–10).
[3] For this traditional opposition, see my 'Emblems of Temperance,' p. 146.
[4] Du Bartas, 'The Columnes,' p. 372.

to symbolic developments. But it now appears either that Spenser does not use astronomical images with any systematic consistency or else that his astrological scheme is a complex one.

A partial explanation of the connection of Luna with Aquarius is to be found in the astrology of character-formation. In his account of how to combine and 'temper' the three graces bestowed by Jupiter, Sol, and Venus—significantly, the same planets which figure in Belphœbe's geniture—Ficino stresses the importance of Luna's assistance. The much-desired gifts of the three fortunate planets are transmitted through Mercury and Luna, he tells us, but most readily through the latter. To be able to carry out this transmissive function, however, as well as to strengthen Iuppiter as a temperate mean between Sol and Venus, Luna must fulfil certain conditions. In particular,

it should be borne in mind that, when integrating those tendencies which nourish and strengthen the heart and mind, Luna will have her most powerful unifying effect if, besides these other favourable aspects, she has this one also, that she moves within an airy sign, especially within Aquarius, which is considered to be the airiest.[1]

While this passage certainly throws light on the psychological content of Book II (helping us to see how it, too, is concerned with the integration, rather than with the mere avoidance, of extremes), it still does not resolve our difficulty. For, if the first two books are in reflective and complementary apposition we must expect this to be true also of the zodiacal signs most dominant in them. The logic of the pattern so far established demands that Leo and Aquarius should bear some symbolic relation to one another, corresponding to that between Books I and II, or between Sol and Luna.

As it turns out, there are at least three such connections. The first follows directly from the notion that Books I and II imitate the 'like race' of sun and moon. As we saw, the hours were divided in

---

[1] *De vita cœlitus comparanda*, III. v: 'Quod tres Gratiæ sint Iupiter et Sol et Venus, et quod Iupiter sit Gratia geminarum media, et maxime nobis accommodata' (*Opera omnia*, pp. 536–537). Another passage in the same chapter is interesting in connection with Spenser's combination of the influences of Luna and Venus in Bk. III: 'Abhis quidem tribus cœli Gratiis, et a stellis eiusdem generis Astrologi gratias et sperant, et deligenter exquirunt, easque per Mercurium atque Lunam, quasi nuncios transmitti putant atque curant, facile vero communiterque per Lunam, Lunam quidem cum Iove coniunctam, aut Venere feliciorem esse putant, quam si per sextilem aspexerit, aut trinum.'

'equall justice' between day and night; the diurnal hours being allotted to the sun, the nocturnal to the moon. By a more arbitrary system, however, the zodiacal signs were also shared between the two chief luminaries. This division of signs into solar and lunar could be carried out on various plans;[1] the commonest of these, the one followed in Ptolemy's *Tetrabiblos*, is shown in Fig. 2:

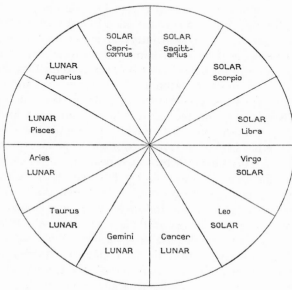

FIG. 2

Ptolemy explains that

since of the twelve signs the most northern, which are closer than the others to our zenith and therefore most productive of heat and of warmth are Cancer and Leo, they assigned these to the greatest and most powerful heavenly bodies, that is, to the luminaries, as houses, Leo, which is masculine, to the sun and Cancer, feminine, to the moon. In keeping with this they assumed the semicircle from Leo to Capricorn to be solar and that from Aquarius to Cancer to be lunar, so that in each of the semi-circles one sign might be assigned to each of the five planets as its own, one bearing aspect to the sun and the other to the moon.[2]

[1] For an account of various divisions of the signs into diurnal and nocturnal, see Housman's Introd., in Manilius, *Astronomicon*, Vol. II, pp. vii–viii.
[2] *Tetrabiblos*, I. xvii (ed. Robbins, pp. 79–81).

It will be noticed that the sign of Spenser's first book, Leo, is not only the House of Sol but also the first of the solar or diurnal signs; while the sign of his second book, Aquarius, is the last of the lunar or nocturnal signs. From this point of view, therefore, the two signs are at opposite ends of the zodiacal gamut.

The second relationship between the two signs has an astronomical content. Since Aquarius occupies a segment of the zodiacal circle diametrically opposite to the segment of Leo, the sun will complete its apparent journey from one to the other in just six months. By the end of that period the gradual interchange between the night sky and the day sky will have accomplished an exact reversal of the original position of the firmament with respect to the sun. When the sun is in Leo (in northern latitudes) that sign is near the zenith at noon; while Aquarius, invisible by day, is near the zenith at midnight. It is summer, and the sidereal hours above the horizon by day far exceed those above it by night. Six months later, however, when the sun has arrived in Aquarius, *Aquarius* is near the zenith at noon; and Leo, invisible now by day, is near the zenith at midnight. Moreover, the sidereal hours visible by night now exceed those visible by day in the same proportion by which they were before exceeded.[1] Thus, the sequence followed by Spenser in moving from Leo (Book I) to Aquarius (Book II) is a natural one, responsive to the complementary or reflective relationship of the two books. It gives further substance, also, to the theme of 'equall justice,' or adjustment, between the seasonal races of day and night. For this purpose, any other pair of diametrically opposed signs (such as Sagittarius and Gemini) would, of course, have served; but no other pair would have served equally well. Leo and Aquarius alone reinforced the symbolism doubly, by evoking in addition Ptolemy's equal sharing of the signs into diurnal and nocturnal, solar and lunar.

The third symbolic connection between Aquarius and Leo is of a different order, though ultimately it, too, depends upon the spatial

---

[1] Cf. Hieatt's account (pp. 35–38) of the similar symbolism of paired dia-metrically-opposed sidereal hours used by Spenser in *Epithalamion*, the stanzas of which have a function analogous to the books of *F.Q.* This part of Hieatt's interpretation has been adversely criticized (see, e.g., Joan Grundy's notice in *MLR*, LVII (1962), 143–144), but in my opinion can withstand scrutiny. See further my review, *RES*, n.s., XII (1961), 418–419, and Hieatt's resumption of his argument in 'The Daughters of Horus.'

opposition of the signs. It belongs to the Neopolatonic doctrine of the soul's descent into bodily incorporation. As Macrobius informs us,[1] this descent was conceived as a journey through the spheres, during which the soul collected the various attributes that it would later exercise. The journey began at the two tropical signs, Capricorn and Cancer, which were named 'the portals of the sun,' since

the solstices lie athwart the sun's path on either side, checking farther progress and causing it to retrace its course across the belt beyond whose limits it never trespasses. Souls are believed to pass through these portals when going from the sky to the earth and returning from the earth to the sky. For this reason one is called the portal of men and the other the portal of gods: Cancer, the portal of men, because through it descent is made to the infernal regions.[2]

It is the next phase of the descent which is critical from the present standpoint:

So long as the souls heading downwards still remain in Cancer they are considered in the company of the gods, since in that position they have not yet left the Milky Way. But when in their descent they have reached Leo, they enter upon the first stages of their future condition. Since the first steps of birth and certain primary traces of human nature are found in Leo, and moreover, since Aquarius is in opposition to Leo, setting just as it is rising, the festival in honor of the dead is celebrated when the sun is in Aquarius, that is, in a sign contrary and hostile to human life.[3]

Macrobius' continuation is so generally relevant to the philosophical allegory of the *Faerie Queene* that a further quotation may be forgiven:

The soul, descending from the place where the zodiac and the Milky Way intersect, is protracted in its downward course from a sphere, which is the only divine form, into a cone, just as a line is sprung from a point and passes from this indivisible state into length; from its point, which is a monad, it here comes into a dyad, which is its first protraction. . . . When the soul is being drawn towards a body in this first protraction of itself it begins to experience a tumultuous influx of matter rushing upon it. This is what Plato alludes to when he speaks in the *Phaedo* of a soul suddenly staggering as if drunk as it is being drawn into the body; he wishes to imply the recent draught of onrushing matter by which the soul, defiled and weighted down, is pressed earthwards. Another clue to this secret is the location of the constellation of the Bowl of Bacchus in the region between

---

[1] *In somn. Scip.*, I. xii (ed. Stahl, pp. 133–137).
[2] Ibid. I. xii. 1–2 (pp. 133–134).
[3] Ibid., 4 (p. 134).

Cancer and Leo, indicating that there for the first time intoxication over-takes descending souls with the influx of matter; whence the companion of intoxication, forgetfulness, also begins to steal quietly upon souls at that point. Now if souls were to bring with them to their bodies a memory of the divine order of which they were conscious in the sky, there would be no disagreement among men in regard to divinity; but, indeed, all of them in their descent drink of forgetfulness, some more, some less. Consequently, although the truth is not evident to all on earth, all nevertheless have an opinion, since opinion is born of failure of the memory.

Sir Kenelm Digby refers to this Neoplatonic theory in his explana-tion of the number symbolism of the Castle of Alma.[1] Even without the benefit of this hint, however, every careful reader of Spenser's second book must have remarked its allusions to the doctrine of the soul's descent. One of the book's most prominent images, for ex-ample, is the Bacchic bowl dispensed by Acrasia.[2] In those who drink from it, like Mordant, its material draught produces forget-fulness of divinity. (Mordant's counterpart in Book I, Fradubio, exemplifies the other evil consequence of the soul's descent—the doubt (*dubio*) that follows 'protraction' into the dyad (Duessa).) By contrast with the intoxicated oblivion of Mordant, Cymochles, and Verdant, the regenerate human nature of Alma's temperate frame has a formidable memory, in the person of Eumnestes. Within Eumnestes' only partly ruined chamber, Arthur and Guyon are able to linger for more than a canto, studying the records that remain there 'incorrupted.'

In view of Macrobius' observation about the 'festival in honour of the dead' (the Parentalia) being 'celebrated when the sun is in Aquarius,' it is significant that in his second book Spenser should make such a point of the honourable burial of Ruddymane's parents (II. i. 58–61), and should devote a whole canto (II. viii) to the dispute over the disposal of Guyon's supposed body. Moreover, in a sense Book II is concerned throughout with tendencies 'hostile to human life'; since it treats the forces disturbing temperance—forces that have their extreme realization in the deathly Maleger—as causes of human mortality. It is the book which deals with the condition of Amavia who 'loves to live' and of Mordant, 'him that death does give.'

[1] *Var. Sp.* II, 476–477.
[2] On the Bacchic imagery in Bk. II, see my 'Emblems of Temperance,' p. 146.

iv

Aquarius was regarded as 'contrary to human life' not only because it was in opposition to Leo but also because its lord was Saturn, the most malevolent of the planets.[1] The dominance of Aquarius in Book II thus warns us to look for Saturn's dire influence. Even so, we are hardly prepared to find it exerted in the Castle of Alma itself. Yet Phantastes, one of Alma's counsellors, is undoubtedly a child of Saturn:

> Of swarth complexion, and of crabbed hew,
> That him full of melancholy did shew;
> Bent hollow beetle browes, sharpe staring eyes,
> That mad or foolish seemd: one by his vew
> Mote deeme him borne with ill disposed skyes,
> When oblique *Saturne* sate in the house of agonyes.
>
> (II. ix. 52)

Although the astrological particulars of this stanza may be obscure,[2] its general drift is clear. The physiognomic information shows, and indeed Spenser explicitly states, that Phantastes is 'full of melancholy.' 'Black colour,' according to Gratanarolus, 'argues natural melancholy; so doth leanness, hirsuteness, broad veins, much hair on the brows [Spenser's 'beetle browes'].'[3] A bodily conformation like this might be attributed to various astrological causes, of which the most familiar was the influence of Saturn in the geniture. Ptolemy's *Tetrabiblos*—the ultimate source of most Renaissance astrologies—tells us that Saturn's power in a nativity,

if he is in the orient, makes his subjects in appearance dark-skinned [compare Spenser's 'swarth complexion'], robust, black-haired, curly-haired, hairy-chested, with eyes of moderate size, of middling stature, and in temperament having an excess of the moist and cold. If Saturn is setting, in appearance he makes them dark, slender, small, straight-haired, with little hair on the body, rather graceful, and black-eyed; in temperament, sharing most in the cold and dry [that is, melancholy].[4]

[1] As Stahl (p. 134) notes. Ficino, we may observe, attributes the unfortunate character of Saturn to the fact that, of his houses Aquarius and Capricorn, one stands opposite to the house of Sol (Leo), the other to that of Luna (Cancer) (*De Sole*, viii (*Opera omnia*, p. 970)).
[2] Some comments on it will be found in Appendix ii.
[3] Cit. Burton, *Anatomy*, Pt. I, Sec. ii, Mem. 1, Subs. 4.
[4] *Tetrabiblos*, III. xi; ed. Robbins, p. 309.

It is also clear that the melancholy with which Phantastes is filled is not of a wholly desirable variety: he has the appearance of one 'borne with ill disposed skyes.' This is a surprising feature of the Castle, and one that commands our closest attention.

Spenser probably had several reasons for including such an extreme saturnine trait within Alma's turret, the mental part of the temperate human edifice. The brain was not assigned to Saturn in the most usual planetary melothesia (in which he figures as 'lord of the right ear, the spleen, the bladder, the phlegm, and the bones');[1] nevertheless, as Ficino reminds us, 'the ancient theologians attributed mind itself to Saturn.'[2] It cannot, however, be only in his functional capacity, as the father of contemplation and of speculative thought, that Saturn operates in Alma's turret. For Spenser's portrayal of the melancholic Phantastes emphasizes the ambivalence of Saturn's influence in a most striking way. While Phantastes 'had a sharpe foresight, and working wit,/That never idle was, ne once could rest a whit,' as well as a 'quicke prejudize'; yet, on the other hand, his eyes seemed 'mad or foolish.' This last observation does not express any general distrust of the imagination; it relates to Phantastes' specifically melancholic disposition. The passage should be referred, I believe, to the context of Renaissance discussions about the psychological strain of prolonged intellectual application. To this ancient problem, which can be regarded as the type of all those problems raised by the strains of civilized life, Renaissance thinkers sometimes responded with analyses of an astrological order. One might say, although this is to oversimplify, that dissatisfactions and neuroses which Freud describes psychologically in *Civilization and its Discontents* were considered then as effects of Saturn. The roots of this conception of Saturn can be traced as far as Ptolemy's *Tetrabiblos*. Describing Saturn's effect as ruler of the soul, dominating the moon, he finds that at best Saturn will make his subjects

strong-minded, deep thinkers, austere, of a single purpose, laborious, dictatorial, ready to punish, lovers of property, avaricious, violent, amassing treasure, and jealous;

[1] Cf., e.g., *Tetrabiblos*, III. xii (p. 319); and see Franz J. Boll and Karl W. O. Gundel, *Sternglaube u. Sterndeutung* (Leipzig, 1926).

[2] *Opera omnia*, p. 1618.

whereas, if his position is without dignity, he makes them 'sordid, petty, mean-spirited . . . fond of toil, unfeeling, devisers of plots against their friends, gloomy, taking no care of the body.'[1]

In the Renaissance no one was more aware of the ambivalence of Saturn than Marsilio Ficino. As Professor Seznec has noticed,[2] Ficino's letters often betray a deep fear of Saturn's influence, a fear that all Cavalcanti's sceptical reassurances could not remove. At other times Ficino tried to make the best of his melancholic temperament—remembering that he was free to select and to foster the desirable element in Saturn's influence, his gift of speculative intellect. Then he would himself attack deterministic astrology with the most rigorous scepticism; exposing its contradictions and absurdities, or demonstrating with ingenious sophistry why, according to its own tenets, Saturn must be the most beneficent of planets.[3] Or else, still speaking in astrological terms, but really dealing with psychological concepts, he would attempt a serious reinstatement of the saturnian condition as the necessary way of intellectual life: the way by which man is withdrawn from the animal life of the senses to a higher life within. 'It is Mercury,' he writes, 'who attracts us to inquire after learning, and Saturn who causes us to persevere in acquiring it, and to preserve our discoveries.'[4] Saturn's effects were essential to thought; even the coldness and dryness and conglutination, which were sterifying and contrary to life, contributed the centripetal concentration on which thought depended.[5]

[1] *Tetrabiblos*, III. xiii; p. 341.

[2] *The Survival of the Pagan Gods*, p. 61 and n. 93, where Ficino's account of his own horoscope is noticed: 'This melancholy temperament seems to have been imposed on me from the beginning by Saturn, set almost in the centre of my ascendant sign, Aquarius, and being met by Mars in the same sign, and by the Moon in Capricorn—while looking toward the Sun and Mercury in the Scorpion, occupying the ninth zone of Heaven.'

[3] Ficino, *In librum Enneadis sec. comment.*, III. v ('Errata Astrologorum de Saturno, et Marte, et Luna') and III. vi ('Quod in cœlo sit tantum lumen, et calor, et humor . . .'); pp. 1616 (wrongly paginated as 1619) and 1618.

[4] *De vita*, I. iv, 'Quot sint causæ, quibus literati melancholici sint, vel fiant' (*Opera omnia*, p. 496).

[5] See ibid.: 'The natural cause [why intellectuals are melancholy] seems to be that, especially in the pursuit of difficult branches of learning, the mind has to be withdrawn from external to internal things, as if from its circumference to its centre; and while it speculates it has to remain with the greatest stability at man's very centre. But to be gathered together from the circumference to the centre, and

Ficino was fond of describing the process of thought as the mind's withdrawal from peripheral involvements to its stable centre, where it could focus with maximum concentration. And always it was Saturn who produced concentration in the material of life, both before and after birth, 'by his marvellous power of collecting, gathering, and containing . . . a power of leading back from the circumference to the centre . . . contracting like a hand into a fist.'[1] Saturn gave, as it were, the continence and density of libido, that made possible directed thought.

Beneath these special pleadings, beneath the brave determination to see favourable possibilities in a melancholy temperament, there no doubt lay the ancient fear of the malevolence of *impius Saturnus*, the planetary deity who happened to be lord of Ficino's own nativity. At the same time he seems also to have had an objective recognition that man's intellectual efforts and the whole cultural advance 'to the summits of comprehension' tend to be accompanied by the compulsive, life-negating malaise, melancholy.[2] And from his tone we can infer that he expected many of his readers to share this insight.[3]

This point has been developed at length, to show that when Spenser portrays Alma's counsellor as melancholic he has in mind an infirmity common in those devoted to intellectual pursuits: perhaps, even, one to which the virtuous, temperate man (who denies himself many sensual gratifications) is particularly prone. A melancholic is located in Alma's turret, the intellectual part of her castle, because this condition is specifically associated with man's Saturn-influenced aspiration above the merely sensual to the rational and contemplative.

[1] *In librum Enneadis sec. comment.*, III. vi; p. 1618. In this piece of special pleading Ficino denies the coldness and dryness of Saturn: this cannot be the nature of his power, for, if it were, *exordium vitæ peteretur a contrario vitæ.*

[2] *De vita*, I. iv (p. 496). Paradoxically, as Ficino explains, contemplation not only draws the thinker down to his centre but also, since Saturn is the highest of the planets, draws him up to the heights as well.

[3] For further material on sixteenth-century views about the connection between learning and melancholy, see E. Panofsky and F. Saxl, *Dürers Melencolia I* (Leipzig, 1923); also L. Babb, *The Elizabethan Malady* (East Lansing, 1951).

---

to be fixed at the centre, is very much the property of earth, to which black bile is most similar. Melancholy, therefore, stimulates the mind, so that it concentrates itself into a unified state and contemplates assiduously.

In Phantastes the maleficence of Saturn is only potentially fatal. It has caused a disposition to melancholy; but this, like all other tendencies dangerous to life, is in the Castle of Alma 'kept in sober government.' Certain characters outside the Castle, however, display more extreme saturnine traits. Most malignant of all is Maleger's evil disease of unnatural melancholy, which Berger has contrasted with the natural melancholy of Phantastes.[1] From our present point of view, we can see that Maleger manifests, in his pale, wan, ashen complexion and his 'cold and dreary' withered body, the worst effects of 'pale Saturnus the colde,'[2] Saturn as death-bringer (*mortifer*). Huddibras, a character composed in a more narrowly psychological mode, is also saturnine. He is 'like a Malecontent'; 'Sterne melancholy [does] his courage pas'; and with Elissa he despises the pleasures of the feast, preferring the inward torment of censorious virtue.[3] The word used for Huddibras' and Elissa's perverseness—'froward' (II. ii. 38) —is in itself an indication; for Gavin Douglas applies this term to Saturn ('frawart *Saturne* from his mortall spere [i.e., sphere]'), and so does Du Bartas' translator ('His froward beams disast'rous frouns').[4] Finally, Mammon, though like Maleger he is too complex a figure to be thought of merely as a temperamental extreme, nevertheless has many of the qualities of the saturnine soul. His miserly amassing of treasure, for instance, is so common a perversion of Saturn's 'marvellous power of collecting, gathering' that it finds a place in Ptolemy's list of the god's effects. Physically, Mammon's staring eyes, dark skin, and neglected body—his beard 'ill bedight,' his 'nayles like clawes'—all betray the influence of his baleful patron.[5] The whole life of his Cave, indeed, is an exaggerated social projection of the saturnine temperament at its darkest. In this gloomy place, where labour is so incessant that

---

[1] *The Allegorical Temper*, pp. 84–85; though of course I would not agree with Berger's view that Phantastes is melancholy because he is 'dominated by man's earthly part and corporeal powers.'

[2] Chaucer, *Knight's Tale*, I (A) 2443.

[3] *F.Q.*, II. ii, especially Sts. 17, 37, and 38.

[4] 'The prologue of the XII Booke of *Eneados*,' l. 7; The Fourth Day of the First Week, l. 376 (p. 101). At II. ii. 34, however, Spenser uses the word more loosely, to apply to both Medina's sisters. Elissa's frowns (II. ii. 35) are also a familiar characteristic of Saturn: cf. Henry Constable, *The Poems*, ed. Joan Grundy (Liverpool, 1960), p. 205: 'thy frownes hold *Saturne*.'

[5] *F.Q.*, II. vii. 3–6; cf. Ptolemy, *Tetrabiblos*, III. xiii (ed. Robbins, p. 341)— 'taking no care of the body.'

sleep is banished, sensual gratification must for ever be impossible. Inhabited by Despight, Disloyall Treason, Gealosie, Payne, and Strife—all personifications of qualities attributed to Saturn by astrologers[1]—the Cave is indeed a 'house of agonyes.'

If Saturn's influence is so widely felt in Book II, what becomes of our theory that the guardian deity is Luna? Are we to look for some significant relationship between the operations of Saturn and Luna? The key to this problem seems again to lie in the astrology of character formation.[2] Before we can hope to find it, therefore, still more planetary influences will have to be noticed, and the question of the book's guardianship temporarily obscured yet further.

The moral topic proposed in Book II is 'The arrest of concupiscence.' In astrological terms, this topic might be restated as 'The cultivation of a planetary influence that will offset the harmful influence of Venus.' Whatever else Acrasia's island may signify, it is clearly intended to portray the venerean disposition at its most ungoverned. Animals there are enraged by 'Venus sting'; bathing damsels are like the new-born '*Cyprian* goddesse'; and even the porter is an evil counterpart of Agdistes, the true porter of the garden of Venus.[3] Acrasia herself, who is eventually trapped in a magically subtle net (though of the Palmer's, not Vulcan's, framing), is a descendent of the disreputable *Venus naturalis* of medieval art. Since Venus is a temperate planet, the island is disturbed neither by 'scorching heat, nor cold intemperate'; instead, 'the milde aire with season moderate/Gently attempered.' But this 'temperance' is deceptive. The exclusion of all obvious danger and unpleasantness from the Bower, and the hidden poison with which Acrasia, like some sinister Circe,[4] unmans her victims, allude to familiar characteristics of the bad Venus' harmful influence. The same character-

---

[1] See ibid. With the incessant labour of the Cave (*F.Q.*, II. vii. 8 and 35 ff.), cf. Ptolemy's epithets ἐπιμόχθος (laborious) and φιλομόχθος (fond of toil).

[2] There was also an astronomical relation between Luna and Saturn, in that one had the nearest and fastest, the other the farthest and slowest, of the planetary orbits—a contrast underlined by the numerical coincidence that the synodic orbital period of the moon in days was the same as the orbital period of Saturn in years. This relationship was occasionally given a symbolic development by other authors (e.g., Ficino, *Opera omnia*, p. 1468); but there is no sign that Spenser thought of the two influences as constituting opposite extremes.

[3] See II. xii. 39, 65, and 47–48.

[4] On Spenser's use of the Circe myth in this episode, see M. Y. Hughes, 'Spenser's Acrasia and the Circe of the Renaissance,' *JHI*, IV (1943).

istics are described in not dissimilar imagery by Ficino. 'Deceitful Venus prepares wonderful allurements,' he warns; 'and captured by these you lose your lives secretly, like wretches, every day.' Why blame Mars and Saturn? Their maleficence is at least open:

only Venus comes to you apparently as a friend, covertly as an enemy. You should rather blame her, if it is right to blame any god. . . . Stop your ears against her enticing promises, as you would against the fatal songs of the Sirens. Accept, therefore, the fruits of my foresight, by which you may avoid the potions of this Circe.[1]

I shall return presently to the advice that Ficino gives—the same advice, it seems, that Spenser means to give in Book II. First, however, we must look at a different solution to the problem of enslavement by Venus, which was not fully accepted by Spenser, but which has its place in the book, and occasions the introduction of yet another planetary deity.

The latter solution, perhaps the most widely approved in Spenser's time, consisted in mobilizing the irascible faculty in support of the rational faculty, against the concupiscible. This moral strategy had been advocated by Plato, and could be illustrated from many medieval and Renaissance moral philosophies. What is more immediately relevant, it forms the basis of the action of one of Spenser's models, the *Gerusalemme Liberata*. Tasso's hero Rinaldo, who is captivated by Armida much as Spenser's Verdant is captivated by Acrasia, regains his freedom by responding to a virile call to arms from Ubaldo. Roused from his post-coital lethargy by a reminder of his true rôle as *fatal guerriero*, Rinaldo is soon possessed by a new passion:

> Ma, poi che diè vergogna a sdegno loco,
> sdegno guerrier de la ragion feroce,
> e ch'al rossor del vólto un novo foco
> successe, che più avampa e che più coce,
> squarciossi i vani fregi, e quelle indegne
> pompe, di servitù misere insegne.
>
> (XVI. 34)

For Tasso, escape from concupiscence depended upon stimulation of an irascible disdain that fought on reason's behalf against the baser passions. Virtue, in short, consisted in opposing Mars to Venus. Tasso was deeply committed to this view of morality;

---

[1] *De vita*, II. xv (*Opera omnia*, p. 522).

though, as the Gernando episode shows, he was aware that the irascible faculty was not always a reliable servant of reason. He notices this difficulty in his 'Allegory of the Poem,' which I quote in Fairfax's translation:

Godfrey, which holdeth the principal place in this story, is no other in the allegory but the Understanding. . . . Rinaldo, which in Action is in the second degree of honour, ought also to be placed in the Allegory in the answerable degree. But what this power of the mind, holding the second degree of dignity, is, shall be now manifested. The Ireful Virtue is that, which amongst all the powers of the mind, is less estranged from the nobility of the soul, insomuch that Plato, doubting, seeketh whether it differeth from reason or no. And such is it in the mind, as the chieftain is an assembly of soldiers: for as of these the office is to obey their princes, which do give directions and commandments to fight against their enemies: so is it the duty of the ireful, warlike, and sovereign part of the mind, to be armed with reason against concupiscence. . . . But when it doth not obey reason, but suffers itself to be carried of her own violence, it falleth out, that it fighteth not against concupiscence but by concupiscence. . . . This violent, fierce, and unbridled fury, as it cannot be fully noted by one man of war, is nevertheless principally signified by Rinaldo. . . . Wherein, whilst fighting against Gernando, he did pass the bounds of civil revenge . . . his return and reconciliation to Godfrey noteth obedience, causing the ireful power to yield to the reasonable. . . . As the reasonable part ought not,—for herein the Stoics were very much deceived,—to exclude the ireful from actions, nor usurp the offices thereof, for this usurpation should be against nature and justice, but it ought to make her her companion and handmaid, so ought not Godfrey to attempt the adventure of the wood himself, thereby arrogating to himself the other offices belonging to Rinaldo.[1]

Now Spenser's portrayal of virtue has a strikingly different emphasis. After his visit to Alma, at least, Guyon shows little sign of any emotion that could be called irascible or '*sdegno*.'[2] He resists concupiscence not by the substitution of any opposite passion, but by his integration: by the spiritual 'edification' of his nature, and by the rational understanding of it which he has arrived at through the

---

[1] *Jerusalem Delivered*, tr. Edward Fairfax, ed. H. Morley (London, 1890), pp. 441–442.

[2] Except at *F.Q.*, II. xii. 83, where Guyon shows 'rigour pittilesse' in turning the pleasantness of the Bower to 'balefulnesse.' But this action is designed to put an end to the deceitfulness of the place, and (in the theological allegory) to destroy the 'body of sin'; it could hardly be interpreted as a use of Mars' severity to modify and temper the excessive pleasantness of Venus. Certainly the *dénouement* is in no way made to depend on the inculcation of irascibility.

instruction of Alma and the Palmer. As for Verdant, he is roused by no Martian call to arms, but 'formally' netted—subjected to rational analysis—then freed 'and counsell sage in steed thereof to him applyde.'[1] It is true that Spenser has another episode that resembles Tasso's much more closely. In the fifth canto Atin exhorts Cymochles in the Bower of Bliss, just as Ubaldo exhorts Rinaldo; until 'inflam'd with fell despight' he arms himself, and goes to fight at the side of his brother Pyrochles—a character whose fiery shield, red steed, and contentious nature proclaims him to be a child of Mars.[2] But this is a scene played out entirely by evil characters: the martian transformation of Cymochles can hardly be regarded as Spenser's recommended correction for an excessively venerean disposition.

In general, Spenser accepted the Orphic theory that each of the gods is potentially both an inciting and a moderating influence.[3] Thus, we often find him presenting first an excessive, then an ideal version of the same mythological deity: the 'good' Venus of the Garden of Adonis, for instance, after the 'bad' Venus of the Bower of Bliss. Nevertheless, he seems to have been chary of the use of Mars as a corrective to Venus. In his view, appeal to the irascible passions against the concupiscible was calculated to produce a wavering 'watrish' character such as Cymochles, swayed in a dangerous tide between the weak pleasures of Acrasia's bower and the strong martian fury of Pyrochles' quarrels. We may suppose that he disliked enlisting the irascible passions because of the danger of aggressiveness (as Cymochles, after his 'reform' by Atin, is aggressive towards Guyon); and because any equilibrium between diametrically opposed extremes such as Mars and Venus was apt to be

[1] Cf., however, the magic book that guides Ubaldo through Armida's labyrinthine palace: this may symbolize a similar rational understanding of the passionate heart.

[2] For descriptions of Pyrochles and his accoutrements, see, e.g., *F.Q.*, II. iv. 38 and II. v. 2–3. The characterization of Pyrochles (πῦρ κλέος, fire and glory) shows Spenser's keen appreciation of the dangers of an unreflecting aspiration to nobility. For a useful survey of the connections between aspiration and courage and irascibility in ancient moral philosophy, see Paul Tillich, *The Courage to Be* (London, 1952), especially Ch. i.

[3] On this conception of the gods, see Wind, *Pagan Mysteries*, pp. 81 ff., where the theory of correction of one influence by another is also discussed—especially Venus' moderation of the rigour and strife of Mars. On Ficino's connection of Mars with 'strong' passions, see also E. H. Gombrich, 'Botticelli's Mythologies: A Study in the Neoplatonic Symbolism of his Circle,' *JWI*, VIII (1945), 13.

strained and unstable. The difference between Tasso's view and Spenser's, however, had also its social correlative. Tasso's ideal of virtue as a lofty *disdegno* was too close a reflection of the proud aspirations of the d'Estes and their like to have any but a dyslogistic equivalent in the *Faerie Queene*. It becomes the 'despight' of Atin's dart (II. iv.38), or the 'Disdayne' of the Cave of Mammon (II. vii. 41).

As for the contrary transformation, of rough Mars' rigour by the softness of Venus, Spenser does not doubt its efficacy in producing a sort of moderation; but in this book at least he seems distrustful none the less of its prudence. It is the careless Phædria, after all, who assuages the rancour of Guyon and Cymochles with the appeal:

> *Mars* is *Cupidoes* frend,
> And is for *Venus* loves renowmed more,
> Then all his wars and spoiles, the which he did of yore.
> (II. vi. 35)

Just as the influence of Mars might be opposed to that of Venus, so might the influence of Saturn. If Mars exchanges the pleasures of the Bower for the rigours of the camp, Saturn promises an equally extreme denial of sensual gratification, through contemplation, or through laborious effort. Thus, the saturnian characters in Book II, no less than the martian, are antonyms of Acrasia. However, while Spenser recognizes the saturnian mode as a diametrically opposed alternative to the venerean, he shows no sign of preferring it. He seems as wary about cultivating Saturn at the expense of Venus as he is about cultivating Mars.

At this point we are ready to hear Ficino's advice on escape from captivity to Venus: advice that provides an illuminating analogue to Spenser's mythological argument. For he, too, considers pitting Saturn against Venus, and he, too, sees in this a danger.

As one might expect with a Neoplatonist, Ficino begins by counselling preference for the pleasures of the less material senses: better still, for those of the imagination and the reason. But then, less predictably, he continues with a warning against the hazards of Saturn:

Just as I advised you, though, to beware of deceitful Venus in the pleasures of touching and tasting, so in this more removed and too assiduous pleasure of the contemplative mind, beware of Saturn; for often he devours his own children.[1]

[1] *De vita*, II. xv; p. 522.

110

Carrying away his devotees with ever more sublime contemplations, Saturn will 'steal earthly life from those who are not careful.' Accordingly, we should remember the doctrine *æquus Iuppiter* taught to Pythagoras and Plato: that 'a certain equable proportion' should be preserved in human life between soul and body. In his next chapter Ficino enlarges on the reasons why·saturnian traits should not be cultivated as an antidote to Venus. When astrologers call Venus and Saturn mutually hostile, he tells us, this is to be interpreted as meaning 'diverse in their effects.' Saturn posits pleasure, our spiritual food, at our centre; but Venus, at our periphery:

Thus Venus and Saturn await the movement of our spirit on opposite sides. She through her pleasure attracts towards external things, while he through his recalls to the world within. And so they pull the spirit asunder and dissipate it. . . . Nothing can be more destructive to the contemplative man or the careful enquirer, than the venereal act; nothing, on the contrary, more foreign to the libertine than care and contemplation.[1]

So far, the saturnian extreme Ficino has in mind seems to be that embodied in Phantastes, rather than in Huddibras or Mammon. But now he extends the saturnian category: 'in the same class with the contemplative person we may number anyone who is very thoughtful about his work, and liable to heavy cares.' Because of the extreme difference between the two influences, if we wanted to relieve someone weighed down by saturnian care it would be useless to do it through venery, games, and hilarity 'as if essaying as remedies things far removed.' By the same token,

if we wanted to moderate someone lost in venery, or extravagantly given to play and hilarity, we would not easily manage to reform him through the severity of Saturn. *The best discipline is rather to recall him to the mean* through certain applications of Phœbus and of Jove (who are means between Saturn and Venus).[2]

And, as Ficino has already explained, these moderating influences of Sol and Jupiter are mediated by Luna.[3]

No doubt Ficino's and Spenser's concepts of Saturn and Venus differed in many particulars. But the same general conception that underlies the *De vita producenda* seems also to inform Spenser's

---

[1] *De vita*, xvi; p. 523.
[2] Ibid. (my itals.).
[3] E.g., ibid., xv; p. 522: 'Quos enim vos in rebus sapores percipitis, mediocri quadam temperie gratos, hos Diana, hæc Apollinis Iovisque munere tradidit.'

astrological structure. It is now clear how the lunar and other planetary influences in Book II are related. Luna stands as a mean between Mars and Saturn, on the one hand, and Venus, on the other.
She mediates the right influences to moderate Venus, whereas the
others are too violently opposed to do so. Accordingly the book's
martian and saturnian characters, though often placed in opposition
to venerean characters, are presented as no less aberrant. At the
Castle of Medina, for instance, Sansloy, who courts Perissa (excess
of sensual pleasure), errs in the direction of Venus. The behaviour
of this 'forward paire'—their hilarity, their enjoyment of the grosser
pleasures of touching and tasting, their wanton looseness—all
betrays the effect of this planetary influence. Huddibras, on the
contrary, and his ideal, Elissa (deficiency of sensual pleasure), are
saturnian and martian. Their 'frowardness' is perhaps specifically
saturnian; but the influences of the two maleficent planets are here
not separately distinguished. Elissa's contempt for the baseness of
Medina's fare might spring either from rejection of material pleasures, or from aristocratic *disdegno*; while Huddibras' rashness was
a quality produced by the combined influence of Saturn and Mars.[1]
What seems to me significant is that both sisters quarrel with Medina,
and both knights with Guyon, so that the whole episode has a symmetrical character. Spenser more than once draws attention to this
by the form of his rhetoric. It is true that Huddibras is critical of
Sansloy's immorality (II. ii. 37); but there is no suggestion that the
froward pair is less culpable, or that they should be made allies
against the children of Venus. Huddibras cast in the rôle of *guerrier de
la ragion feroce* would hardly be Spenser's conception of temperance.

The pattern set in this initial episode is continued—though on a
much larger scale, and complicated by additional structural relationships—through the remainder of the book. Thus, the Cave of
Mammon and the Bower of Acrasia can be regarded as saturnian-
martian and venerean extremes respectively, set over against the
lunar mean of the Castle of Alma. Even within the Castle the same
pattern obtains; for the chamber of the saturnian Phantastes and
the honourable and martial muniments of Eumnestes, both in the
Turret, are answered by a Parlour below, where 'little *Cupid* playd/
His wanton sports' (II. ix. 34).

[1] *F.Q.*, II. ii. 17. On the influence of Saturn allied with Mars, see Ptolemy,
Tetrabiblos, III. xiii (ed. Robbins, p. 343).

Guyon's task is to communicate the mediating influence of Luna. But this is not to say that he succeeds in doing so with ideal consistency. For he has a temperamental inclination towards the rigour of Mars and the self-denial of Saturn. If these characteristics make him in a sense a natural champion against Acrasia the virtue they lead to is yet far short of temperance. It is not until he has cultivated the lunar element in his personality, under Alma's instruction, that he is ready to complete his mission.

No sooner has the book begun than we find Archimago tempting Guyon in a Martian direction:

> Faire sonne of *Mars*, that seeke with warlike spoile,
> And great atchiev'ments great your selfe to make.
>
> (II. i. 8)

The effects of Martian influence are to be seen not only in the attack on Redcrosse but also in Guyon's inability, by himself, to pacify Huddibras and Sansloy. Later, an erroneous correction of Venus can also be diagnosed in Guyon's treatment of Phædria, an embodiment of venerean *hilaritas*. To her, he seemed

> Still solemne sad, or still disdainfull coy,
> Delighting all in armes and cruell warre,
> That her sweet peace and pleasure did annoy,
> Troubled with terrour and unquiet jarre.
>
> (II. vi. 37)

However successful Guyon's resistance to her charms may be, we feel uneasy with the savageness of his solitary and self-feeding virtue. It is but a short step to pouring 'bitter scorne' (II. vii. 18) upon Mammon, who has to 'beare the rigour of his bold mesprise' (II. vii. 39) through many accusing lectures and haughty reminders of his station. Indeed, Guyon's attitude has in it so much aristocratic *disdegno*, that in the same episode he is easily reconciled with the stern giant Disdayne (II. vii. 41–43). As for the saturnian element in the Cave's temptation, it is by no means confined to the obvious allurement to avarice. As Berger has argued, Guyon's prolonged researches under the world's surface have a marked quality of curiosity; and curious learning was the especial domain of Saturn. Appropriately, Guyon's contemplative journey takes a centripetal course towards the earth's centre. Moreover, in his too assiduous pursuit of truth he neglects his body to the point where he almost loses his earthly life. Again, his censoriousness towards the suffering Tantalus comes perilously near to that 'readiness to punish' which Ptolemy noted as a characteristic of the saturnian soul.[1]

After he has been redeemed by Arthur, and has learned from Alma the shame-inspired nature of his own virtue, Guyon is able to achieve a true temperance. In her castle he is shown how the 'quick prejudize' of Phantastes and the passions of the parlour of Cupid can together be obedient to the mean, in an ideal proportion of mind and body. Informed by the doctrine of Luna, and of that other mediating and integrating planet, Mercury (whose harmonizing power is symbolized by the Palmer's caduceus), Guyon can at last proceed to his calm liberation of Verdant. He is not now too rigorous to feel the attractions of bathing damsels; yet he is capable of rigour, when the Bower has to be destroyed. Mars and Venus are equally within his power.

v

In the above account of Book II I have stressed its mythological and astrological elements disproportionately. Some such approach is necessary, however, if we are to grasp the principle of decorum that governs its formal organization. For the astrological symbolism we have been tracing has its counterpart in an important area of the book's numerology, not yet considered: the character-grouping in the main episodes.

The character-totals in Spenser's descriptive cantos are astronomical numbers; more precisely, numbers from the Star Catalogue in Ptolemy's *Almagest*. If the use of so technical a source seems inherently unlikely it should be recalled that Ptolemy's Catalogue differed in several ways from such modern counterparts as the Shapley-Ames or New General Catalogues. First, it indicated position in terms of membership of one or other of the constellations, which had each their definite complement of stars. Secondly, the authority of the *Almagest* was such that, in spite of advances both in astronomical theory and in observational technique, after fifteen centuries it still continued in use; by which time Latin translations and popular vernacular versions had given its less difficult contents a wide currency among laymen. In particular, its settings of the

---

[1] *Tetrabiblos*, III. xiii; p. 341; cf. the influence of Saturn allied with Mars (ibid. p. 343): 'without pity . . . unmoved by pleading.'

different constellations were well known, even though there were rival sets of figures, both ancient and modern.[1] It can be shown that Ptolemy's totals for the constellations were not only used by poets but also by the designers of pageants meant to be understood by general audiences.[2] Spenser seems to have been alone, however, in conceiving the idea that the Ptolemaic numbers might be used for more than an occasional allusion: that they might provide the basis of a continuous structural pattern.

A rule observed by Spenser in his use of the Ptolemaic numbers is that only characters *individually enumerated and actually present* contribute to the principal count. Thus, mentions of characters off-scene are ignored, as are all numerically vague references to crowds of extras, even if they participate in the action. Inevitably there are doubtful cases; but these can ingeniously be turned to account, by making them provide a second indication of the Catalogue number in question. For, as the accompanying table will show, most of the

TABLE V: PTOLEMY'S CONSTELLATION TOTALS

Constellation	Principal total of stars	Inclusive total, counting *stellæ informatæ*
Aries	13	18
Taurus	33	43
Gemini	18	25
Cancer	9	13
Leo	27	35
Virgo	26	32
Libra	8	17
Scorpio	21	24
Sagittarius	31	—
Capricornus	28	—
Aquarius	42	45
Pisces	34	38

[1] E.g., the figures given by Hyginus, who was also a well-known authority, mostly differ from Ptolemy's. Drayton can allude to Hyginus' total for even an extra-zodiacal constellation quite casually: 'And thou brave Perseus in the northern ayre, / . . . / In seaventeene glorious lights are stellified' (*Endimion and Phœbe*, ll. 365–368; cf. l. 946, alluding to the total for Lyra). The special prestige of Ptolemy's figures may be judged from the fact that they are adopted by Goulart in his commentary on Du Bartas (The Fourth Day of the First Week), though he knows and cites not only Hyginus, Firmicus, and Manilius, but even the *neotericus* Piccolomini.

[2] This was the case as late as 1633, when Drummond of Hawthornden's *Entertainment* for King Charles included a representation of Virgo 'beautified with six-and-twenty stars.' See below, pp. 199–200.

constellations are assigned two totals in the *Almagest* Catalogue.[1] Normally, Spenser uses only the smaller and more familiar figure, which totals the stars in the constellation proper. Sometimes, however, where two character-totals could be arrived at, he employs also the larger figure, which includes peripheral stars or *informatæ*, as an additional check.

So it is in the principal episodes of Book II. If the character-total of the Bower of Bliss episode alludes to any zodiacal constellation, on the basis of our earlier analysis we should expect it to allude to Libra. Not only is this the House of Venus;[2] but it was also known as *Bacchum ministrans Libra*, because of its association with the wine-harvest.[3] It therefore fitly presides over the Bacchic draught administered in Acrasia's venerean bower. Now Libra's total in the *Almagest* Catalogue is eight; and eight characters take part in the action inside the Bower of Bliss: Guyon, the Palmer, Genius, Excesse, two damsels, Acrasia, and Verdant. At this point it may be objected that such a correspondence could have occurred by chance. After all, if the probable range of character-totals is no more than from eight to forty-eight (no narrower range can be set, since several episodes have eight characters or less, and several have more than fifty), the Ptolemaic number of one of the four signs connected with Venus will occur in nearly 10% of a sufficiently large sample of character-totals. Such odds are not long. But the probability of chance correspondence is greatly reduced by the occurrence of a second Libra total in the same canto. A larger character-total for the episode can be arrived at by including the characters met during

[1] Claudius Ptolemæus, Μαθηματική σύνταξις: *Composition Mathématique*, tr. and ed. M. Halma (Paris, 1816), VII. v. Note that Halma gives an erroneous total, 32, for Taurus. Latin translations of the *Almagest* Catalogue appeared frequently in the sixteenth century, not only together with the rest of the *Syntaxis* (as in *Claudii Ptolemæi omnia quæ extant opera, præter Geographiam* (Basel, 1566)), but also separately (as in *Phaenomena, stellarum MXXII. fixarum ad hanc ætatem reducta*, tr. G. Trapezuntius (Cologne, 1537)).

[2] See Table III, above, p. 65. Constellations and signs are really, of course, quite different entities. Due to the precession of the equinoxes, deplored in the Proem to Bk. V of *F.Q.*, the constellation Libra is no longer in that sector of the heavens which is still called the *sign* Libra. Spenser, however, has to ignore this distinction. We may either think of him as treating the Ptolemaic totals as conventional labels not only for the constellations whose stars they number but also for the signs bearing the same names; or we may think of him as setting his poem in an antique world in which each constellation is still in its appropriate sign.

[3] Manilius, *Astronomicon*, II. 658–659.

116

the voyage to Acrasia's island, as well as Grill, who is also outside the Bower. This larger total introduces no ambiguity: it is seventeen, Ptolemy's inclusive total for Libra with its *stellæ informatæ*.[1]

The probability of double correspondences of this kind occurring by chance can be calculated in the following manner. Let the episodes be labelled with pairs of numbers (n_1, n_2), where n_1 is the number of characters in the whole episode and n_2 is the number of characters within the house or other enclosure portrayed in the episode (here the Bower), so that $n_1 \geqslant n_2$. The number of characters n_1 may range from N to n; N being the largest number of characters likely to occur in an episode of the poem, and n the smallest number likely to occur. Then the total number of distinct labels is arrived at by considering the array

$$(N,N), (N,N-1) \quad . \quad . \quad . \quad . \quad (N, n)$$
$$(N-1, N-1). \quad . \quad . \quad (N-1, n)$$
$$. \quad . \quad . \quad . \quad .$$
$$(n+1, n+1), (n+1, n)$$
$$(n, n)$$

There are $(N - n + 1)$ labels in the first row, $(N - n)$ in the second row . . . and 1 in the $(N - n + 1)$ th row. Thus the total number of labels is

$$(N - n + 1) + (N - n) . . . + 1 = \frac{N - n + 1}{2} (N - n + 2)$$

If we assume that each label is equally probable, then the probability of any particular label occurring by chance is

$$\frac{2}{(N - n + 1)(N - n + 2)}.$$

And if S labels are regarded as being significant the probability of an episode having a significant label is $\dfrac{2S}{(N - n + 1)(N - n + 2)}$.

Now, we may safely take N as, say, 47, and n as 8; while S must be 4 since 4 labels—that is, pairs of Ptolemaic numbers—could conceivably be appropriate to a single planetary deity. Hence the probability of an episode having a significant pair of character-totals, where only one planetary deity is involved, is approximately

---

[1] I.e., the boatman, Phædria, the 'dolefull Mayd' of II. xii. 28, five mermaids, and Grill—in all, nine characters—together with the eight inside the enclosure, already counted; 9 + 8 = 17.

$$\frac{2 \times 4}{(47 - 8 + 1) \ (47 - 8 + 2)} = \frac{1}{205}.$$ The joint incidence of many

such improbable correspondences, in different episodes of the poem, virtually excludes any possibility of chance occurrence.

In the Cave of Mammon there are twenty-one characters certainly present: the *Almagest* Catalogue total for Scorpio.[1] Three additional characters are mentioned, however, whose presence during the action is doubtful. These are Force, Fraud, and Sleep (II. vii. 25); Care, we are told, ceaselessly prevents their approach. Unless we are prepared to take a high Neocritical line here, how can we tell whether characters thus introduced by exclusion should be listed in the count? Fortunately a decision is unnecessary. For, if we do include them, the character-total will come to twenty-four, Ptolemy's inclusive figure for the same constellation, Scorpio. The choice of Scorpio for the Cave has the air of inevitability. Not only is this sign the solar house of Mars, just as Libra is the solar House of Venus; but it is also the sign in diametric opposition to Libra in the zodiacal circle. Moreover, Scorpio is the Depression of Luna:[2] a particularly unfortunate house, therefore, for Guyon—as, indeed, the action shows Mammon's house to be. Incidentally, Scorpio's own nature is conformable to the moral character of the Cave. The sign was always thought of as *acer Scorpius*:[3]

> The spitefull *Scorpion*, next the *Skale* addrest,
> With two bright Lamps covers his loathsom brest;
> And fain, from both ends, with his double sting,
> Would spet his venom over every thing.[4]

---

[1] The characters are: Guyon, Mammon, Payne, Strife, Revenge, Despight, Treason, Hate, Gealosie, Feare, Sorrow, Shame, Horrour, Celeno, Care, the 'feend' of II. vii. 26, the 'Spright' of II. vii. 32, Disdayne, Philotime, Tantalus, and Pilate.

[2] It is probably for this reason that a meeting of Saturn and Luna in Scorpio was supposed to produce a particularly bad melancholy: see Burton, *Anatomy*, Pt. I, Sec. ii, Mem. 1, Subs. 4. It may be noted that the symmetry of Bks. I and II is in this respect complete; for the Despaire episode at I. ix, which occupies a similar structural position to that of Mammon at II. vii (i.e., both are episodes leading to the hero's downfall, just before the core canto of the book), employs a total of eight characters: the number denoting Libra, the Depression of Sol. (The characters present in I. ix are: Arthur, Una, Despaire, Redcrosse, Terwin, Trevisan, and—by inference—Arthur's squire and Una's dwarf.)

[3] Manilius, *Astronomicon*, II. 513.

[4] Du Bartas, The Fourth Day of the First Week, ll. 255–258; p. 98. The association of Scorpio with poison may throw some light on the arbour of poisonous

It was regarded as a symbol of earth.[1] And, according to a well-established medieval tradition, it was connected with the art of dialectic.[2] This last association is particularly interesting in view of the fact that the Mammon episode contains the only prolonged debate in the whole poem.

The more sophisticated numerology of the Castle of Alma calls for fuller analysis. Fortunately, Spenser has assisted us by signalizing the various divisions of the Castle. Transitions are indicated by Alma redirecting the attention of her guests. She never allows them to occupy themselves disproportionately with any one part of the human frame: 'First she them led up to the Castle wall': 'Thence she them brought into a stately Hall'; 'Thence backe againe faire *Alma* led them right'. Even their studies in the chamber of Eumnestes are interrupted in the interests of health:

> gentle *Alma* seeing it so late,
> Perforce their studies broke, and them besought
> To thinke, how supper did them long awaite.
> (II. x. 77)

Since the episode takes the form of a conducted tour, the number of characters present during the action in each part of the Castle exceeds the number permanently resident in that part. The totals of characters *present* in the various parts correspond to *Almagest* constellation totals. And, as the accompanying table shows, the astrological pattern symbolized is again a pattern of saturnian and venerean influence balanced by Luna.

Starting with the Castle's 'other frame,' the Turret, we find nine characters present—four residents, that is, together with the touring party of five (Alma, Guyon and palmer, Arthur and squire). By a fortunate coincidence, this nine happens to denote the 'circle set in heavens place'; but its primary allusion is to the Ptolemaic figure for Cancer, Luna's house. Appropriately, the governing part of the Castle is dominated by the influence of the mediating planet. Next below the Turret comes the Parlour, belonging to the first frame,

---

[1] See Valeriano, *Hieroglyphica*, XVI. xviii; p. 195.
[2] See Émile Mâle, *The Gothic Image* (London, 1961), pp. 80, 84.

plants at *F.Q.*, II. vii. 52. Similarly, the imagery of claws or hands recurrent throughout the episode (e.g., II. vii. 3. 9 ('nayles like clawes'); 27. 2; 34. 6; 58. 4; 61. 4–9; and 62. 8) contains an incidental allusion to the 'ugly craples' of the 'monstrous Scorpion' (V. viii. 40).

119

THE CASTLE OF ALMA

Locality	Division of castle		Permanent inhabitants	Number of characters present
II. ix. 21–32	First frame	Between the two gates	Porter 2 × 16 warders Diet Appetite Concoction Digestion	42
II. ix. 33–44		Parlour	Cupid Prays-desire Shamefastnesse	8
II. ix. 45–60	'Other wondrous frame'	Turret	Phantastes Second counsellor Eumnestes Anamnestes	9

but set off from the other parts by the action that takes place in it. There are eight characters in the Parlour: the figure for Libra, the House of Venus also symbolized by the character-totals of the Bower of Bliss. Thus, Venus' influence in the Castle finds numerological expression in the population of the room where 'little *Cupid* playd.' The remaining parts of the Castle can be considered as a single unit, since they all lie between the oral gate (II. ix. 23) and the Esquiline gate (II. ix. 32). Spenser is here playing a joke on us—if a somewhat obscure one—by presenting the body of man as a Water-Pourer. For the number of characters certainly present between the two gates is forty-two, the Ptolemaic figure for Aquarius.[1] In short, the human proportions of the House of Alma express the temperature of the planetary influences we have traced elsewhere in the book. The saturnian extreme (represented by Aquarius) and the

[1] Cf. Balthazar's disillusioned view of man, in Lawrence Durrell's *Justine*: 'after all the work of the philosophers on his soul and the doctors on his body, what can we say we really know about man? That he is, when all is said and done, just a passage for liquids and solids, a pipe of flesh.' The total of 42 is made up of 37 characters resident in the parts visited, together with the 5 of the touring party. It might be argued, however, that the watchman of II. ix. 11, as well as Alma's two damsels (II. ix. 19) have a claim to be included in this section. If they are, the larger total of 45 is reached; but without ambiguity, since 45 is the larger Ptolemaic figure for Aquarius.

venerean (represented by Libra) are moderated by the lunar mean of Alma's equable government (represented by Cancer).[1]

[1] The pattern is made more emphatic by the fact that each of the parts occupies an almost equal number of stanzas—though the venerean portion is slightly deficient, and the saturnian portion slightly excessive. Thus, exactly 12 stanzas are devoted to the three counsellors in the Tower (ix. 49–60); somewhat less than 12 to the Parlour (ix. 33. 5–44. 7); and somewhat more than 12 to the remainder of the first frame (ix. 21. 1–33. 4). There may well be other instances of number symbolism in the canto; but the risk of obscuring the main lines of the numerology, as well as the dictates of reason and common sense, deter me from pursuing the investigation further. A typical problem is presented by the 'ten steps of Alablaster wrought' by which Alma leads her guests to the Turret. Are these the ten steps to knowledge, mentioned in cabalistic lore (see, e.g., Johann Reuchlin, *De arte cabalistica*, cit. Thorndike, VI, 444)? Or are they—as William Austin thought—the ten vertebræ of the neck?

X

The Book of Minerva and Venus

i

As we move into the third book of the *Faerie Queene*, the mythological pattern becomes still more complex. Evidently the poem is not to develop consecutively, by seriatim concentration on one planetary sphere after another. Instead, it ramifies and burgeons in everchanging efflorescence, each new mythological influence joining those already present, transmuting and revealing new possibilities in them. As the greater number includes the less, so each book of the poem contains the themes of all earlier books: the structural diagram would resemble a tree's growth rings, not a row of separate globes. The prodigality with which always more themes are taken up than laid aside nowhere manifests itself more strikingly than in the portrayal of Britomart. We may conveniently begin, therefore, by tracing some of the diverse mythological components of her character.

The logic of the structural pattern we have been tracing so far leads us to expect Mars as the third guardian; since the third day of the planetary week is assigned to that deity. This expectation is confirmed to some slight extent by the unusually high frequency of verbal allusions to Mars in Book III.[1] At the same time it is obvious that the pattern must have been modified at this point, for there is no character capable of carrying the martian rôle, as Redcrosse did the solar, and Guyon the lunar. This modification may partly have been

---

[1] See Osgood's *Concordance*, s.v. 'Mars,' 'Mart,' 'Martiall,' 'Martian,' and 'the God of warre.' The statistics are: Bk. I: 8 mentions; Bk. II: 7; Bk. III: 11; Bk. IV: 2; Bk. V: 2; and Bk. VI: 0. A few narrative motifs point in the same direction. For example, the boldness repeatedly called for at the House of Busyrane was a pre-eminently Martian quality (see, e.g., Macrobius, *In Somn. Scip.*, I. xii. 14).

occasioned, as we shall see, by the exigencies of an additional structural pattern, in which Books I–III form an interrelated triad; and partly by Spenser's unwillingness to entrust a book to the unqualified guardianship of a maleficent deity. But the principal reason may well have been that he wished another divine persona of the Queen to follow those already developed, Elizabeth as the 'woman clothed with the sun,' and Elizabeth as Diana.

Simply by choosing a female knight patron, Spenser effects a modulation out of the martian mode. True, Britomart is more than once compared with Bellona, the ancient goddess of war and the sister (or wife) of Mars himself.[1] Also, Britomart's warlike qualities give the poet several opportunities to compliment Elizabeth upon her recently demonstrated prowess as a war-leader, and to place her in a tradition of valiant female warriors that extends from 'bold *Penthesilee*' and 'stout *Debora*' (the rarity of whose kind is lamented at the beginning of the fourth canto) to 'bold *Bunduca*,' 'renowmed *Martia*,' and the other notable examples invoked by Glauce— especially Angela, who 'hath the leading of a Martiall/ And mighty people,' the English. We may even say that when Britomart assumes the Saxon queen's arms and becomes a *British* 'mayd Martiall' (III. iii. 53–61) Spenser is inventing a new cult image for the queen, and celebrating her as a British Mars.[2] Nevertheless, even if Britomart's rôle is to some degree that of a female Mars, the mere fact of her sex must modify this ideal. Britomart may be a Mars 'trained up in warlike stowre' from her earliest years, and may despise feminine pursuits (III. ii. 6); but she is also a Mars softened by tenderness and love—though not to the point where courage is subverted. She represents, as it were, a better resolution of Mars and Venus than was accomplished between Cymochles and Acrasia or Cymochles and Phædria. One element in Britomart's mythological character, in fact, is that paradoxical Renaissance composite deity, the bellicose Venus

---

[1] III. ix. 22 (1590 version only) and IV. i. 14.

[2] It was J. W. Draper ('Classical Coinage in the *Faerie Queene*,' *PMLA*, XLVII (1932), 100) who first suggested that *Britomart* = *Brito[n]* + *Mart* (a common Spenserian variant of *Mars*). I am aware that Spenser had other reasons (some of which are discussed below) for choosing the name Britomart. Nevertheless, Draper's theory gains support from the many reminders in the poem that Britomart is British, as distinct from Saxon or Elfish: e.g., III. ii. 4: 'Briton Mayd.' On Bellona as a cult name of Queen Elizabeth after her appearance at Tilbury, see Wilson, *England's Eliza*, p. 88.

or *Venus armata*.[1] As Professor Wind has justly remarked, often 'the
martial Venus may stand for the strength that comes from love';
alternatively, she may signify a pure love guarded and braced by
virtue.[2] Both these conceptions are relevant to Britomart, who is
first inspired to enter on her perilous enterprise by a vision of
Arthegall granted to her as she views herself—Venus' classic stance—
in a looking-glass.[3] Whatever Britomart may signify in the moral
allegory, it is certainly some form of love.

The armour of a martial Venus, however, was as often borrowed
from Minerva as from Mars. And so it proves to be with Britomart.
Indeed, the closer we look, the more evident it becomes that her
principal mythological rôle is that of a Minerva. The goddesses
Minerva, Bellona, and Pallas were usually regarded as one and the
same—a view which the 1596 revision of the simile describing Britomart at III. ix. 22 perhaps shows Spenser himself to have taken.[4] But,
as Church has remarked, the name Bellona was used when the goddess was thought of as presiding only in war; while Minerva had a
much wider connotation. Unless we recognize this more varied complex of associations, then the co-ordinating principle of much of the
material in Book III must elude us.

From an iconographical point of view, many features in the
portrayal of Britomart point to distinctive attributes of Minerva.
From the first, attention is directed towards her accoutrements,
which are clearly endowed with a symbolic value. She overthrows
Guyon with an 'enchaunted speare' against which the Palmer warns
him not to fight:

[1] On this Venus, see Wind, *Pagan Mysteries*, pp. 74, 85 f., and 164; also the
same author's *Bellini's Feast of the Gods* (Cambridge, Mass., 1948), pp. 49 ff.

[2] *Pagan Mysteries*, p. 86. For this second notion, see Valeriano's explanation
why the Lacedæmonian Venus was armed: *Hieroglyphica*, XLII. ii: 'Muliebris
Virtus' (p. 524).

[3] For the 'looking glasse' (*F.Q.*, III. ii. 18) or 'glassie globe' (III. ii. 21) as an
attribute of Venus, see Tervarent, s.v. 'Miroir,' v, and 'Boule,' iii, cols. 274 and
52. It seems probable, however, in view of Spenser's reference to the mirror of the
faithless Phao (III. ii. 20), that Britomart's glass also embodies a more specific
symbolism: namely, 'perfect but fragile marital union.' On this significance of
the glass globe in Renaissance iconography, see Panofsky, *Studies in Iconology*
(New York and Evanston, 1962), p. 162; also Tervarent, s.v. 'Sphère trans-
parente,' ii, col. 363.

[4] 1590: 'Like as Bellona'; 1596: 'Like as Minerva.' The evil genealogy given to
Bellona at VII. vi. 3 and 33, however, may mean that the change was made
because Spenser had decided to introduce a distinction between the good Minerva
and the evil (or at least ambivalent) Bellona.

For by his mightie Science he had seene
The secret vertue of that weapon keene.
(III. i. 10)

To such an extent is it her distinguishing feature, that at the tournament of the cestus it is she 'whom all men term'd Knight of the
Hebene speare.'[1] Now, the sharp spear was a conventional attribute
of Minerva, tracing its lineage back to the 'strong lance with steel
made keen,/ Great, massy, active' of Homer's Pallas.[2] It was interpreted, usually, as the power of wisdom: a symbolism still enshrined
in the metaphorical epithets we ourselves apply to intellect ('keen,'
'piercing,' 'penetrating').[3] That Spenser intended Britomart's spear
to carry a similar meaning can be deduced from what he says of its
origin. It is the same 'which *Bladud* made by Magick art of yore'
(III. iii. 60)—Bladud, the king commemorated in Eumnestes'
chronicle for his Grecian arts and 'sweet science' (II. x. 25).

Britomart's helmet is even more prominently treated. Its voluntary
or involuntary opening or removal is invariably the occasion for an
elaborate simile evoking her divine appearance to the awed on-
lookers.[4] This is not surprising; for the helmet was a familiar attribute of Minerva—whose Ciceronian epithet, indeed, was *galeata*.[5]
The distinguishing mark of Minerva's helmet, at least from the time
of Martianus Capella's *De nuptiis*, was a high crest or plume.[6] And

[1] *F.Q.*, IV. v. 8; cf. IV. vi. 6.

[2] *Odyssey*, I. 123–126 (Chapman's tr., I. 165–166). For the spear as an attribute
of Minerva, see Tervarent, s.v. 'Lance,' i, col. 230.

[3] See, e.g., Conti, *Mythologiæ*, IV. v; p. 306: 'Cuspis vero tribuitur propter
necessarium acumen ingenii: nam qui crasso ingenio est ab ipsa natura præditus,
neque munus Dei clarissimum acceperit iudicium, hunc vel decem Minervæ
expolire nunquam poterunt.' Cf. Alciati, *Emblemata* (Lyons, 1600), Embl. xxii,
'Custodiendas virgines,' under the heading 'Cur armata Pallas' (p. 105): she
carries a long lance 'because she makes an impression from a distance, by
eloquence.' Also Valeriano, *Hieroglyphica*, XLII. xix ('De Hasta: Sapientiæ Vis'),
where the lance of Pallas is said to manifest 'the power and quickness of intelligence' (*ingenii vim atque promptitudinem*); one thinks of Britomart's penchant for
striking the first blow. Valeriano cites Martianus Capella's explanation: 'Hasta
etiam vibrans penetrabile monstrat acumen.'

[4] III. i. 42–43; III. ix. 20–22; IV. i. 13–14; and IV. vi. 19–21.

[5] *De natura deorum*, I. xxxvi. See Tervarent, s.v. 'Casque,' i, col. 62; and cf. our
Pls. 13b and 14a.

[6] See Tervarent, ibid. Alciati (p. 105) remarks that Pallas 'has a crested helmet
on her head, which should be referred to Judgement and Constancy, by which the
wise man's *cerebrum*—the citadel and fortress of his soul—can best be strengthened'; while Conti (p. 306) tells us that 'a crest and a helmet are attributed to
[Minerva] because it is proper to use not strength alone, but also courtesy.' But

Britomart's, we find, is constructed to the same specification: when she falls in love with Arthegall's image, 'thenceforth the feather in her loftie crest,/ Ruffed of love, gan lowly to availe.'[1] Again, Britomart's great reluctance to disarm is explained at the narrative level by her wish to preserve her disguise. But it acquires added point, particularly as regards the Malecasta episode, when we reflect that the armour of Minerva is an armour of virtue: a protection against passion offered by prudence and wisdom.[2] All these iconographical details would speak for themselves to many Elizabethan readers. For the benefit of others, Spenser notices the opinion of certain observers that Britomart wore 'shield and armour fit' for Bellona or Minerva.[3]

The early seventeenth-century Cambridge Marginalian detected an allusion to yet another attribute of Minerva in the name of Britomart's nurse; for his gloss on *Glauce* is 'Γλαυξ noctua.'[4] The owl

---

[1] III. ii. 27; and again at the House of Malbecco, 'vailed was her loftie crest' (III. ix. 20).

[2] We find a very practical application of the idea in Liceti (*Hieroglyphica*, p. 155B–C): 'Minerva is portrayed armed with helmet, shield, and javelin, and fully clothed, so as to show the virgin goddess opposed to the lust of wanton Vulcan, and contending with it; and because virgins, where they have no other resource, should defend their modesty, from the violence offered by impure men, by covering themselves with their clothing. In particular, Minerva is represented armed with helmet, shield, and spear, because a virgin ought to guard her own integrity with prudence, constancy, and strength, against every wanton aggressor.' See also Alciati, p. 105: 'the armed girl signifies a wise man arming himself against all perturbations of mind, and resisting vices with a strong hand.'

[3] IV. i. 14.

[4] See Anon., 'MS Notes to Spenser's *Faerie Queene*,' *N & Q*, CCII (1957), 510, where the note is wrongly taken to mean that 'Glauce . . . is associated somewhat unkindly with . . . the screech owl.' In fact, she is being associated with the clear-sighted owl: as Giraldi reminds us, Pallas was by some believed to be called *Glaucopis* 'because she had the eyes τῆς γλαύκης, that is, of an owl—the bird which was ascribed to her' (*De diis gentium*, pp. 472 f.). Thus the Cambridge Marginalian's explanation is undoubtedly correct. At the same time we should note an additional possibility. There was also a Glauce whom Cicero mentions as the mother of Diana (*De natura deorum*, III. xxiii); and, as we shall see, the Diana element in Britomart's character is an important one. This mythological ambiguity is an excellent example of the richness of texture which is so common in *F.Q. Glauce* may fitly denote the attendant either of Britomart *qua* Diana or of Britomart *qua* Minerva. The former association accounts for Glauce's motherly character; the latter for her prudence (on the owl as a symbol of prudence, see Alciati, Embl. XIX, 'Prudens magis quam loquens'; p. 97).

---

beside these should be set other more arbitrary interpretations, such as that implied in a poem in the *Arundel Harington MS* (ed. Ruth Hughey (Columbus, Ohio, 1960), No. 247): 'A prudent head Dame Pallas perfect crest.'

was consecrated to Minerva, according to Conti, 'because wisdom, wherever it is placed, can see; also because it can discern things that are obscure to others.'[1] Glauce, it is true, gives little sign of profound sapience. But she certainly shows common sense and the wisdom of the heart, both in understanding Britomart's disturbed emotions after the vision of Arthegall and in pacifying combatants—'Glauce thus gan wisely all upknit' (IV. vi. 30). Moreover, it is through her that Britomart comes to be protected by her symbolic armour.

The influence of Minerva, however, goes far beyond this matter of symbolic attributes. Indeed, the real significance of the iconographical indications is that they embolden us to correlate all the narrative motifs in the book that have as their archetypes myths of Minerva. Thus, the most explicit statement of Britomart's mythological rôle—

> Like as *Minerva*, being late returnd
> From slaughter of the Giaunts conquered;
> Where proud *Encelade*, whose wide nosethrils burnd
> With breathed flames, like to a furnace red,
> Transfixed with the speare, downe tombled ded
> From top of *Hemus*, by him heaped hye;
> Hath loosd her helmet from her lofty hed,
> And her *Gorgonian* shield gins to untye
> From her left arme, to rest in glorious victorye.
>
> (III. ix. 22)

—is far more than a simile illustrating her appearance to Malbecco's other guests. Its main function is as mythographical comment: retrospectively, upon the battle with the Giantess Argante (that 'daughter of the *Titans* which did make/ Warre against heaven'), two cantos earlier;[2] prospectively, upon the pursuit of the Giant Ollyphant, Argante's brother, in Canto xi. Minerva's battle with the Giants warring against Jupiter was one of her most famous exploits, and the immediate occasion for her warlike attributes and bellicose reputation. Sometimes the myth was interpreted as signifying a conflict between divinely inspired wisdom and human rebelliousness:

[1] *Mythologiæ*, IV. v; p. 306.
[2] In III. vii it is not Britomart, but Palladine, who pursues Argante. Josephine Bennett (*The Evolution of 'The Faerie Queene*,' pp. 20, 146 n., and 169) plausibly argues that Palladine is a relic from an older version of the poem, in which Britomart bore this name. Whether this is so or not, our knowledge of Spenser's practice in name-formation certainly permits us to connect *Palladine* with *Pallas*. If the name *Palladine* is left over from an earlier version, then the scheme we are tracing would appear to have obtained in it too.

Conti's 'boldness and vain arrogance.'[1] Spenser, however, gives it a sexual application. Argante's and Ollyphant's wilfulness rebels specifically against the natural law of normal sexuality; while Palladine and Britomart, who curtail their activities, exemplify that particular wisdom which consists in an understanding and a chaste direction of libidinal urges.

In Renaissance art generally, indeed, we find that Minerva most often embodies an ideal of wise virtue or chastity, opposed either to the bestiality of vice or to the passion of Venus and Cupid. One thinks of Mantegna's *Wisdom Overcoming the Vices* (Pl. 8), in which Minerva, assisted by Diana and Chastity, puts Venus and a swarm of attendant vices to rout; or Perugino's *Combat of Love and Chastity* (Pl. 9), where Pallas and Diana again unite, this time against Venus and Amor. [2] It is to such a context that Britomart's main adventure in Book III, her defeat of Busyrane, ought to be referred. Busyrane's masque is a Triumph of Cupid,[3] in which the conjured cruel-seeming image of the god is accompanied by 'maladies' comparable with the vices attendant on Mantegna's Venus. All these appearances are dispelled at once by the bold irruption of Britomart; whose adventure thus corresponds to Minerva's expulsion of false Cupid (though Britomart, far from being *semper virgo*, herself loves passionately). At the beginning of the same episode Britomart's encounter with 'cruell *Mulciber*'—the flames at the porch—is similarly a re-enactment of the archetypal myth; for the lustful Vulcan (alias Mulciber) was Minerva's traditional opponent.[4]

And the catalogue of minervan features could be extended. For instance, much of the action in which Britomart participates turns on

---

[1] *Mythologiæ*, IV. v; pp. 298 f. and 305 f.

[2] See Seznec, *The Survival of the Pagan Gods*, pp. 5, 109, and 111; also Wind, *Bellini's Feast of the Gods*, p. 19. For Minerva as a patroness of chastity in Botticelli's painting, see E. H. Gombrich, 'Botticelli's mythologies,' pp. 21, 23. Cf. Alciati's Embl. XXII, 'Custodiendas virgines,' where Minerva appears as *virginum custodia* (Pl. 13b).

[3] Cupid's triumph is solemnized not only in the masque of III. xii but also in the tapestry of III. xi. It may be noted that it is in accordance with numerological decorum to place a triumph at the culmination of Bk. III and a celebration of alliance (the spousal of Thames and Medway) at the corresponding point in Bk. IV. Thenaud of Mellynays described the triangle as the shape for triumph, the quadrilateral as the shape for alliance (Thorndike, VI, 454).

[4] Britomart's passage through the flames is related at III. xi. 21–26. For the opposition of Minerva and Vulcan, see, e.g., Liceti, loc. cit. p. 126, n. 2; and for their pairing in the Manilian scheme, see p. 82.

128

mistakes about her identity, like that made by Malecasta.[1] Misapprehensions of this kind do not occur with any of the other good characters; but they are appropriate with Britomart, because Minerva was a goddess of many disguises, not least masculine ones.[2] Again, Minerva's patronage of the arts, particularly of tapestry, is amply reflected in Book III. The only two tapestries that are elaborately described anywhere in the poem are Malecasta's and Busyrane's: both in the book under the guardianship of Minerva. It is hard to resist the conclusion that the tapestries are evil not because they are artificial (as Lewis supposes); but because they issue, like Arachne's in competition with Minerva, from presumptuous wilfulness, and because they celebrate a love contrary to the virtue of the chaste goddess.[3]

The reader may be left the pleasure, which I have too long usurped, of noticing other minervan features in the book. One further aspect may be noticed here, however, since it is important for the overall allegory of the poem. I refer to Minerva's significance as a goddess not only of war but also of peace; and therefore of an armed or wise peace. Unless we grasp Britomart's embodiment of this ideal, then the political import of her love and search for Arthegall will be lost to us, and we shall have to fall back on a recent critic's ineffabilities about Chastity seeking Justice. If, however, we keep Minerva's dual character in mind we shall recognize that the theme of Britomart's promised union with Arthegall is related to a traditional festival motif, the Reconciliation of Peace and Righteousness.[4] This motif

[1] III. i. 47. Comparable errors are made by Amoret and Scudamour in IV. i and vi.

[2] On Chapman's interpretation of Minerva's disguises, see Lord, *Homeric Renaissance*, p. 83.

[3] The principal authority for the connection of Minerva with tapestry-making was Ovid, *Metam.*, VI. Later, however, the connection became conventional. Thus, tapestries appear under the Triumph of Minerva in the Schifanoia frescoes, a calendrical series based on the Manilian astrology (Pls. 10, 11). Manilius himself had connected Minerva with weaving, and alluded to Ovid's story of Arachne and Minerva, in treating of her sign, the fleecy Ram, under which the wool industry was pursued (*Astronomicon*, IV. 130–136).

[4] For this motif, which was based on a literalistic translation into visual terms of Ps. lxxxv. 10 ('Mercy and truth are met together; righteousness and peace have kissed each other'), see Tervarent, s.v. 'Corne d'Abondance,' iv, col. 118. A notable English example, contemporary with Spenser's writing of *F.Q.*, is the frontispiece to Saxton's *Atlas* of 1579 (our Pls. 12, 13a), where, in an oval above Queen Elizabeth's head, there occurs a representation of Peace and Justice embracing. (On this engraving, see further McLane, *Spenser's 'Shepheardes*

did not spring from a pacifist belief that Peace was the necessary concomitant of Righteousness. Indeed, their joint occurrence, though desirable, was rare enough to be worth celebrating; to have about it, even, a millennial quality. Until the time came when Peace and Righteousness were united, justice was likely to be achieved only by conflict. So it is that Britomart must engage in many battles before being reconciled with Arthegall, and, even after that, must twice suffer a separation when he departs to fight on behalf of Belge and Irena. Peace, as far as is compatible with Righteousness: it is a political ideal very like the one officially pursued by Elizabeth's own government. The kind of armed peace such a policy could produce— a peace maintained by maritime power[1] and interrupted by expeditions in the interests of righteousness—is imaged in Merlin's prophecy for Britomart:

> Thenceforth eternall union shall be made
> Betweene the nations different afore,
> And sacred Peace shall lovingly perswade
> The warlike minds, to learne her goodly lore,
> And civile armes to exercise no more:
> Then shall a royall virgin raine, which shall
> Stretch her white rod over the Belgicke shore,
> And the great Castle smite so sore with all,
> That it shall make him shake, and shortly learne to fall.
>
> (III. iii. 49)

—where the emphasis, as befits Spenser's patriotic Protestantism, is on the belligerence of Minerva. One sees that the political convenience of so flexible an ideal as armed peacefulness must have done much to encourage Elizabeth's Minerva cult.[2]

Clearly we must accept the dominance of Minerva's influence in Book III. Yet this view entails difficulties of a schematic order. To substitute Minerva for the planetary deity Mars is to take, it seems, a considerable liberty. Since Minerva was a goddess much richer in

---

[1] Critics agree that maritime power—another object, incidentally, of Minerva's patronage—is a sub-theme of Bks. III–IV: see Isabel Rathborne, 'The Political Allegory of the Florimell–Marinell Story,' 279–289.

[2] On this cult, see Wilson, *England's Eliza*. Another important factor was, of course, the appropriateness to Elizabeth of the minervan epithet *semper virgo*.

Calender,' n. to Pl. I.) There were almost always *Astræa redux* or millennarian implications in the motif; as witness *F.Q.*, V. Proem 9, and the whole tenor of the fifth book.

meaning than the merely warlike Bellona, it is not enough simply to describe the change as a feminine modulation of the martian mode.

As it happens, however, the substitution was not without precedent in traditional astrological schemes. Spenser could appeal to the authority of calendrical art based upon the Manilian system of twelve Olympian guardians. For in this system Minerva is the *third* guardian, presiding over the month of March, which is assigned in the Ptolemaic system to Mars.[1]

There are, besides, numerological reasons why Minerva should come third. In ancient and Renaissance symbology she is persistently associated with the number three, or with the three-sided figure, the triangle.[2] This association is based on the goddess's surname, Tritonia or Tritogenia. Thus, Conti, who gathers a variety of explanations of these names, notes that some find in them an allusion to the three parts of the head (the member from which Minerva sprang); others, an allusion to the three faculties of the soul.[3] Several of the theories that he outlines point to a connection between Minerva and Luna, in tracing which he displays a Plutarchan syncretizing tendency common among Renaissance mythographers. For example, he tells us that Callisthenes believed Minerva to be called Tritonia

because she had been born on the third day of the moon; and on this basis constructed his explanation why that day was consecrated to Pallas by the Athenians. . . . Others believed that the moon was called this, because she was accustomed to appear on the third day from conjunction.

As Valeriano had pointed out, these were not really rival theories, since 'most interpret Pallas and Luna as one and the same.'[4] This

---

[1] See p. 65, Table IV; and cf. Tervarent, s.v. 'Minerve,' i.

[2] As Valeriano explains, 'the Pythagoreans consecrated not only numbers, but also geometrical figures, to the names of the gods; seeing that they called the equilateral triangle Minerva, Verticigena, and Tritogenia' (*Hieroglyphica*, XXXIX. xlii; p. 495). The point of this attribution was that an equilateral triangle 'is bisected by the three perpendicular lines drawn from its three angles,' and hence symbolizes the virtuous mean; also that the triad was already attributed to Minerva. The latter association gives added force to Glauce's ritual invocation of the power of three at *F.Q.*, III. ii. 50: 'thrise upon me spit; / Th'uneven number for this businesse is most fit.'

[3] *Mythologiæ*, IV. v (p. 305); cf. Valeriano, *Hieroglyphica*, XXXIX. xliii, 'Minerva' (p. 495). Among other theories proposed, one traces the association to the three seasons of the Egyptian year; another, to the fact that air, the element usually attributed to Minerva, comes third—always assuming that one counts from earth upwards.

[4] Valeriano, ibid., following Plutarch (e.g., *De facie*, 938B: 'The Moon which is Athena in name and fact').

identification of Minerva and Luna should not be thought of as the abstruse lucubration of a comparative mythographer. For it was a natural and general consequence of the moralizing of mythology that the chaste virgin goddesses should be closely associated; as they are in the Mantegna and Perugino paintings mentioned above.

We are not surprised, therefore, to find subordinate traits of Luna or Diana in the portrayal of Britomart, who is in any case too complex a character to be rendered in terms of a single mythological deity. Britomart's lunar rôle is not fully developed until the Isis Church episode in the fifth book, where her dream mysteriously assigns her the part of Isis, who 'doth the Moone portend' (V. vii. 4 and 22). This identification is prepared for, however, by similes in which Britomart is compared to Cynthia (notably that describing the opening of her umbrere: 'as when faire *Cynthia*, in darkesome night'[1]); as well as by the allusion contained in her name. For, whatever else it may imply, *Britomart* is clearly derived from *Britomartis*, a surname of Diana. [2] The longer form, indeed, is used by Spenser as a fairly common variant—for example, at III. i. 67 and III. iv. 29.

All this is not to say that lunar elements dominate the mythological portrayal of Britomart. She has Diana's chastity, yet she is chaste in quite a different manner from Guyon. Above all, she is a woman in love, whose passion is not to be ordered by self-denial, but by chaste fulfilment in her promised marriage with Arthegall.[3]

ii

The various mythological traits condensed or infolded in Britomart herself are given a separate treatment in the parts of Book III where she does not appear. To some extent, the rest of the book completes

[1] III. i. 43. Contrast, however, the simile at III. ix. 20, in which Britomart's hair is compared with the beams of the sun.

[2] See J. E. Hankins, 'The Sources of Spenser's Britomartis,' *MLN*, LVIII (1943). The idea of Britomartis as British may have been suggested to Spenser by the tradition, mentioned by various Elizabethan antiquarians, that Diana was anciently worshipped in Britain under that name.

[3] It has always been recognized that Britomart represents chaste love, rather than chastity in any sense that is opposed to love; and her embodiment of specific characteristics of Venus is noticed by Hamilton (*The Structure of Allegory*, pp. 142 f.). But by far the best study of the mythological opposites reconciled in Britomart is Kathleen Williams' 'Venus and Diana: some uses of myth in *The Faerie Queene*.' Quite independently of the present enquiry, and by a different route, this article arrives at a similar conclusion, that in Britomart 'Venus and Diana, Venus and Mars, are in true and unsurreptitious relation' (p. 115).

patterns already distinguished. Thus, the debate between Diana and Venus in III. vi complements, though at a more abstract and explicit level, the conflict between Minerva and Cupid in the concluding episode. It will be remembered that the same two pairs of adversaries are matched in Perugino's *Combat*;[1] though the theme of that painting (as the detailed instructions issued by Isabella d'Este confirm[2]) is the eternally equal conflict of Diana and Venus, whereas Spenser is more interested in a concordat, in a mode of sentiment uniting virtue and pleasure.[3] At the same time, however, there are other mythological elements which, because of their profuse variety, present more difficulty from a structural point of view. It seems at first that the many mythological narratives of Book II must elude any formal net of analysis.

Fortunately, this problem has been simplified through the insight of Mr. A. C. Hamilton, who has shown that several of the narratives have as their underlying pattern either the myth of Venus and Adonis or the myth of Cupid and Psyche. It is true that, for the purposes of any complete reading of the poem, differences between episodes are as important as similarities. Also, that referring a mythological narrative to its archetype does not determine its precise moral or psychological import in the development of this particular book. For the limited purposes of our present enquiry, however, we may willingly accept Hamilton's findings about the extent to which the activities of Venus and Cupid between them pervade the action. We may accept, as a useful rationalization of the structure of Book III, his view that the Venus and Adonis myth, which is directly presented in the description of Malecasta's tapestry and in the Garden of Adonis episode, provides in addition the symbolic basis for the stories of Marinell and of Timias; further, that the Cupid and Psyche myth (again directly treated in the core canto) reappears in the stories of Amoret

---

[1] Similarly, it is in the Malecasta episode, where she is matched against an evil Venus, that Britomart's Diana rôle is most marked (see, e.g., III. i. 43). The point about Britomart containing within herself the mythological traits developed at large throughout the book has been made, from a somewhat different point of view, by Hamilton (*The Structure of Allegory*, p. 144).

[2] See Braghirolli, *Giornale d. Erudiz. Artist.*, II (1873), 163–166; also Wind, *Bellini's Feast of the Gods*, p. 19 and n. 41.

[3] Hence the reconciliation at III. vi. 25; where it is Venus, we should not fail to note, who gives way—or has grace to relent. The connection between Minerva's and Diana's opposition to love is briefly glanced at in Venus' contemptuous reference to 'loftie creasts' at III. vi. 22.

and of Florimell. (The two myths are complementary, in the sense that the sex of the sufferer differs; so that it is possible for both to be combined in the story of Marinell and Florimell.) As Hamilton explains, the Psyche myth was sometimes given a cosmic as well as a moral interpretation by Renaissance mythographers; and Spenser follows this tradition, treating Psyche as a Proserpina figure, whose sufferings and imprisonment image the state of winter, as her release does the coming of spring or (with wider reference) the return of the golden age.[1] Hence the imagery of winter in the portrayal of Proteus (III. viii. 34–35), and the imagery of spring accompanying Florimell's reunion with Marinell (IV. xii. 34). It should be said, however, that the pattern of Florimell's story is more complex than Hamilton gives us any reason to believe. For example, her flight from the witch's monster, her smearing with fish-scales (which is not simply erotic allegory), her descent under the sea, and her acceptance into the company of sea gods, all glance at the myth of Venus' flight from Typhon and metamorphosis into the fish that later became the constellation Pisces.[2] Thus, Florimell—as, indeed, one might expect from her possession of the cestus—is a Venus to Marinell's Adonis, as well as a Psyche to his Cupid.

To this it may be added that the Venus and Adonis myth, which Hamilton rightly traces through the various instances of wounding in Book III, was also given a seasonal interpretation in the Renaissance. Since Upton, this cosmological interpretation of the myth has been applied to Spenser's Garden of Adonis; most effectively by Professor Ellrodt, whose often laudable purpose it has been to redirect attention away from theories of an orthodox Neoplatonic content, to the less debatable element of nature myth. Elldrodt reminds us that

Natalis Comes offered two cosmological interpretations [of the myth of Venus and Adonis]. One saw in the dying and reviving hero an image of the fate of corn, which stays six months underground with Proserpina and enjoys Venus, that is the mildness of the air, for the remaining months. The myth could be extended to the general cycle of vegetation. But far more space was devoted to another interpretation. Adonis was identified with the Sun, 'father of germination,' and the boar with Winter. Comes traced this symbolism to the Orphic Hymns. A more elaborate exposition

[1] *The Structure of Allegory*, pp. 140, 143–152.
[2] Alternatively, the Giant Typhœus might be the pursuer; as in Ovid, *Metam.*, V. 325–331.

could be found in the *Saturnalia* of Macrobius. It had been reproduced in the *De Genealogia Deorum* of Boccaccio and commended for its ingenuity. This consensus of opinion among his favourite authorities could not but impress Spenser. Though his own adaptation of the Adonis myth could be referred to the cycle of vegetation in general outline, some statements imply that a sun myth was intended. The Sun, indeed, 'may not / For ever dye, and ever buried bee / In balefull night' (st. 47. 2–3), but is 'by succession made perpetuall,' for 'needs mote he live, that living gives to all' (47. 6, 9). The boar is the emblem of Winter for, in the words of Macrobius, 'Winter is as a wound to the Sun, whose light and heat it lessens, which happens through death in all living beings.' That the boar should now be imprisoned in a rocky Cave hewn underneath the Mount (st. 48. 5–9) agrees with the earlier description of the Garden, since 'There is continuall spring, and harvest there / Continuall, both meeting at one time' (st. 42. 1–2). This would be a simple explanation of the *stable* immortality there enjoyed by Adonis: the Sun always shines over Eden and all Earthly Paradises. Adonis would be set in the 'thickest cover' (44. 1) of a 'gloomy grove' (41. 3) because such Paradises are 'hid from the world' (46. 6) of our experience, because Adonis must be shown to be alive even when out of our sight and because privacy is required for the love sports in which 'fayre Venus' and 'the wanton boy' indulge 'in secret,' 'Lapped in flowres and pretious spycery.'[1]

The voluptuousness of the descriptive passage indicates, in Ellrodt's view, a sexual, even an anatomical, application of the myth. (It compensates, as it were, for the conspicuous absence of the organs of generation from the body allegorized in the Castle of Alma.) As authority for such an application, Ellrodt cites a passage in Equicola, where an interpretation of the myth in terms of sexual symbolism, and a seasonal interpretation, are juxtaposed:

Plutarch scrive che in Siria Venere da gli habitanti è chiamata Giunone, laquale dà principio a tutte le cose che nascono. I poeti dissero essere stata innamorata di Adone, il quale significa il Sole secondo la religione de gli Assiri, osservata da Fenici. . . . La terra è divisa in due hemisperii. Questo superiore, c'habitiamo noi, si dice di Venere: nell' inferiore de gli Antipodi, secondo li antichi habita Proserpina. Sei mesi piange Venere, cioè quel tempo che'l Sole è nel altro hemisperio. Il porco ciguale, il quale ammazzo Adone, intendono la vernata.

Altri dicono, che Adon nacque di Mirrha cosa grata a Venere, appropriata al coito, e come Petronio dice incitamento di Venere. E ammazzato Adone; cioè la libidine, laquale cessa con l'età e non risorge. Leggiamo in Platone, e in Plinio, che Adone da' suoi horti significa suavità.

[1] R. Ellrodt, *Neoplatonism in the Poetry of Spenser*, pp. 87 f.

135

Professor C. S. Lewis, however, though he accepts the sexual interpretation, challenges the validity of Ellrodt's cosmological approach.[1] For example, he rejects the solar theory on the grounds that while it is conceptually congruous, it is imaginatively unacceptable. Adonis feels 'obstinately un-solar'; inhabiting, as he does, 'a "gloomy grove," a thicket of "shady boughes" (43) where "Phoebus beams"—his own beams, if he were the sun!—can never reach him (44),' in a garden of 'eternal moisture' upon earth.

Perhaps the difficulty here arises from this: that Spenser himself has declined to follow any particular application of the myth consecutively throughout the canto. Instead, he elects to modulate, smoothly but rapidly, from one application to another—sometimes within a single stanza or even a line. Now he explores the myth as a symbol of the generation of physical nature; now as the cyclical pattern of generation in nature's seasonal death and rebirth; now as the little death of the sexual act; and now as all of these together. Spenser may have adopted this particular mode of symbolism for either of two reasons. It may have been that he was interested primarily in the Adonis myth itself, in the multifarious pattern of natural generation, rather than in any individual enactment of it. His aims may have been akin to those of Marino in *L'Adone*, which is, after all, the Renaissance poem closest to his own in subject and in range of narrative motifs. Or else, and this seems to me more likely, Spenser may have intermingled different forms of creativity so as to evoke the symbolic relationships that set human generation (a main concern of Book III) within a philosophical and cosmological design. In other words, his purpose is to show how human love, when it is orientated to generation, enters into the divinely ordained creative pattern of nature herself.[2]

That the Garden canto contains an allegory of human generation

[1] See his rev. of *Neoplatonism in the poetry of Spenser*, in *Études Anglaises*, XIV (1961), 107–116, especially 112. Among other criticisms made by Lewis that have a bearing on this canto is his refutation of Ellrodt's theory that the 'naked babes' are either 'seeds of bodies' or the vegetable souls of men. Lewis is undoubtedly right in arguing that the babes are instead human souls. This is clearly how the passage was read by Sir Kenelm Digby, to judge by his use of it in his discussion of the incarnation of the soul (*Observations*; *Var. Sp.*, II, 476 f.)—a discussion which strangely has never been brought into the controversy about the Garden of Adonis. On the other hand, Digby's consideration of the possibility that souls 'have been created ever since the beginning of the world, and reserv'd in some fit place till due time' greatly strengthens Ellrodt's contention that Spenser's myth has its background in the Augustinian theory of an instantaneous total creation.

[2] Cf. here Ellrodt, p. 85.

is beyond question; when Spenser says 'well I wote by tryall, that this same / All other pleasant places doth excell' (III. vi. 29), he means that he has made love, and enjoyed it. Even Ellrodt's identification of the Mount with the *mons veneris* (a hypothesis rightly accepted by Lewis) need not have been so tentative, nor so dependent on Equicola's authority. Sexual interpretations of the Adonis myth were quite common in the Renaissance, and can be illustrated from so familiar an author as Alciati.[1] More particularly, when we read of the 'gloomy grove of mirtle trees . . . / Whose shadie boughes sharpe steele did never lop' (III. vi. 43)—words that Ellrodt contents himself with italicizing—we recall Valeriano's remark: 'it should not be disguised that the myrtle signifies the female pudendum.'[2] Building on the anatomical interpretation of the myth, and on the fact of Adonis' passivity, Lewis constructs the interesting theory that Spenser has reversed the sexual rôles; so that Venus is here the form-giver, while Adonis, ' "eterne in mutabilitie" and "transformed oft," ' corresponds to matter. If, however, we follow the sexual symbolism through closely, noticing how Spenser has related it to seasonal symbolism, it is possible to escape the many difficulties this theory gives rise to. Adonis has a passive rôle not because he symbolizes matter, but because *his life is poured out as seed*. And when Venus descends to the life of the womb (in her own, not Adonis', Garden), it is of the seed's 'sweetnesse' that she 'takes her fill' (46. 9). Only thus can we fully understand the statement that Adonis is 'by succession made perpetuall' (47. 6)—by the line of succession of the seed, that is to say, from generation to generation. But, equally, he is perpetual from season to season; for the Adonis of vegetation myth was also associated with seed.[3] Transitions from the one meaning of seed to the other are accomplished through such metaphors as

[1] Embl. LXXVII; pp. 287 f.

[2] *Hieroglyphica*, L. xxv (p. 639), carried over into Liceti, p. 377D. But most of the mythographers mention more abstract or psychological meanings also: e.g., that the myrtle signifies pleasure, or fantasies, or the wounds of love. The feature of the Garden that seems to Lewis to count most against the solar interpretation of Adonis—namely, that the myrtle grove is 'gloomy,' giving such thick shade 'that nether *Phœbus* beams could through them throng'—belongs to the anatomical allegory. Cf. Chapman, *Hymnus in Cynthiam*, ll. 185–187, where Cynthia conjures Form to make 'that blissful court of hers,' the human body, 'to shine / With all accomplishment of Architect, / That not the eye of Phebus could detect.'

[3] See, e.g., Conti, *Mythologiæ*, V. xvi (p. 525), rendering Theocritus: 'Adonis frumentum est satum, quod sex menses degit sub terra: sex menses illum habet Venus. . . .'

'reape sweet pleasure' (46. 3). Indeed, we may say that generation through seeds of various kinds is the theme of the whole canto. Even its philosophical content, as Ellrodt has shown, is a version of Augustine's theory of *rationes seminales*. Now, whether seed is 'transformed oft' in the darkness of the womb or in that of the earth, is not its share in the generative process always a passive one?

The seasonal element in the myth could be traced through such details as the flowers on the Mount (all wounded and metamorphosed lovers who were associated with fertility myths),[1] or the imprisonment of the boar of winter.[2] But the episode is so patently concerned with the life-cycle as a repetitive phenomenon that this seems an unnecessary labour. One point, however, ought to be noticed: the part played in the vegetation myth by the equinoxes. We recall that in the Garden

> There is continuall spring, and harvest there
> Continuall, both meeting at one time.

This coincidence of the beginning and the end of the growing season implies that in the Garden it is never winter: that in the ideal perfection of generative love creativity is continuous and uninterrupted. Now, almost all the mythographers who interpreted the Adonis myth agreed in referring it to the contrast between the six months of autumn and winter and the six months of spring and summer. We have met this idea in Equicola and in Macrobius; and other instances could easily be multiplied.[3] In this connection Ellrodt cites a passage from the *Saturnalia;* but his quotation does not give an adequate impression of the emphasis placed upon the exact duration of the contrasted seasons. For Macrobius allots considerable space to explaining the dichotomy between the six superior (northern) signs of the zodiac and the six inferior signs; and to describing the Assyrian

---

[1] See T. P. Harrison, 'Divinity in Spenser's Garden of Adonis,' *Univ. of Texas Studies in Eng.*, XIX (Austin, 1939), 51.

[2] Though the boar also has a meaning at the individual moral level, where it is the counterpart of Grill outside the Bower of Bliss at II. xii. 86. True Pleasure can be an inhabitant of the Garden of Adonis, because the boar of lust has been confined. See Valeriano, *Hieroglyphica*, IX. xx–xxiii ('Æstas et Hyems,' 'Venus,' 'Adonis,' and 'Chaos': pp. 106 f.), where the three traditional interpretations of the boar, as winter, as impurity, and as Chaos, are very closely related. Thus, the darkness of the wintry boar is a moral darkness, etc.

[3] See, e.g., Valeriano, ibid., xx; and Conti, *Mythologiæ*, V. xvi (pp. 525 f.).

belief that when the sun (Adonis) is in the latter Venus mourns his loss:

And they will have it that Adonis returns once more to Venus, when the sun, having struggled free from the six signs of the lower world, begins to illuminate our hemisphere with the increase of light and of days. . . . When the sun emerges from the lower parts of the earth, and as the day lengthens crosses the line of the vernal equinox, then is Venus joyful, and the fields flourish a beautiful green with corn, the meadows with grass, the trees with leaves. For this reason our elders named April the month of Venus.[1]

As we shall see, this connection between the season of growth and the sun's position with respect to the equinoctial line is of some structural importance in the *Faerie Queene*. For instance, the two books (III and IV) which deal with love and the increase of life turn out to be situated between symbolic presentations of the equinoctial points. At the moment, however, I wish only to notice that Macrobius' emphasis on the return of Adonis *in the seventh month after his loss* lends support to Hamilton's extension of the pattern of seasonal myth to the stories of Amoret and Florimell. Each of these was imprisoned— Florimell by the wintry Proteus, Amoret by the sterile Busyrane— for a period of seven months.[2]

The Venus of the Garden of Adonis episode clearly embodies an aspect of divine creativity. Her descent to earth (III. vi. 12, 29, 46), and her manifestation in human sexuality and in the vegetative cycle, serve to show that these activities have a larger setting: that they share in a cosmic movement of creative generation. In the myth of Chrysogone, however, that immediately precedes the Garden myth, we find two other deities associated with human generation:

> . . . the fruitfull seades
> Of all things living, through impression
> Of the sunbeames in moyst complexion,
> Doe life conceive and quickned are by kynd:
> So after *Nilus* inundation,
> Infinite shapes of creatures men do fynd,
> Informed in the mud, on which the Sunne hath shynd.

---

[1] *Saturnalia*, I. xxi.
[2] See III. xi. 10 and IV. xi. 4. I should add that I believe the primary meaning of Amoret's story to be moral and psychological, and the primary meaning of Florimell's to be political and philosophical; but it is not to my present purpose to give a detailed exposition of either.

> Great father he of generation
> Is rightly cald, th'author of life and light;
> And his faire sister for creation
> Ministreth matter fit, which tempred right
> With heate and humour, breedes the living wight.
> So sprong these twinnes in wombe of *Chrysogone*.
>
> (III. vi. 8–9)

Ellrodt, indeed, finds *three* powers referred to in the passage: sun, moon, and earth. His comment is that

The sun and moon preside at the birth of man. The sun because he is the life-giver. The moon, because bodies are in her charge. That is why she 'ministreth matter fit for creation' (III. vi. 9. 4), a puzzling phrase which led some to identify the sun's fair sister with the earth.[1]

One may agree with all of this, except the last sentence. It is hard to see how the matter of living bodies can have two quite separate sources. True, Spenser describes the sun as activating mud, that is, matter received from earth; while Chrysogone, the sun's 'faire sister,' who 'ministreth matter'—surely, *provides* matter—is just as certainly the moon. But may it not be assumed that the traditional identification applies here, between the material of earth and of the moon (on the basis of which the moon was called a 'little earth')? There was also a mythological connection between earth and moon. Indeed, throughout the *Faerie Queene*, earth goddesses such as Isis are allotted a lunar rôle, after the manner of late antique syncretism.[2] In any case, even if we distinguish (with Ellrodt) between the provision and the ministering of matter, there are only two *deities* in question; since earth is not personified in the Chrysogone passage.

Still, taking the canto as a whole, we are left with three deities associated with the generation of life: Titan (the sun); 'his faire sister' (the moon); and Venus. It is in determining the interactions of these three deities that the real difficulty lies.

In his perceptive account of the canto, Ellrodt (pp. 102–103) speaks of Spenser's imagination playing upon different 'mythological and cosmological couples . . . sun–earth, form–matter, Adonis–Venus.' Couples occurring at different points in the canto, he stresses, are not to be identified with one another. Thus, the Adonis–Venus polarity

---

[1] *Neoplatonism in the Poetry of Spenser*, p. 103, n. 46.
[2] At V. vii. 4 the identification of Isis with the moon becomes explicit, being stated in so many words: '*Isis* doth the Moone portend.'

must not be confused with the form–matter polarity: such 'allegorical reiteration of a plain statement would be pointless' (p. 87). In this insight, as well as in his subsequent suggestion that both Venus and Adonis are in some way parents of forms, Ellrodt does much to clarify Spenser's meaning. The relation of the Adonis myth with the earlier myth of Titan and Chrysogone, however, remains obscure. Granted that Venus is a form-giver—as Spenser himself seems to infer at III. vi. 12—how are the operations of sun, moon, and Venus related in the generation of life?

It may help to observe that the different 'mythological and cosmological couples upon which [Spenser's] imagination plays' do not succeed one another at random; but that they are arranged in a logical order. This order, in its broad lines at least, follows the stages of a definite Platonic cosmogony. For a prose statement of the latter, we may turn to Ficino, who, in his commentary on the *Timæus*, explains the position of the sun's sphere between the spheres of Luna and Venus in terms of the relative functions of the three planets in the generation of life. As the 'mother of generation,' the moon has the lowest position. Being nearest to the material elements, and having a proportion with them that the sun does not have, she is interposed as a temperate mediator. Ficino continues:

Rightly is the sun, the father of generation, placed next to the mother of generation: the first heat to the first moisture [*humor*], the illuminator to the illuminated. . . . The sun through lunar moisture lays the foundations of generations; through the moisture of Venus, he brings to completion or sets free the forms of the creatures generated [*Sol per lunarem humorem generationes inchoat, per Venereum generabilium formas absolvit*].[1]

We find a similar sequence of the same two aspects of generation in Spenser's myths of Chrysogone and of Adonis. In the first myth there is quickening of the seeds of living things by the interaction of the sun and his fair sister the moon 'through impression / Of the sun-beames in moyst complexion.' At this stage the matter of the seeds is 'tempred right / With heate and humour': Ficino's 'first heat' and 'first *humor*.' (Notice that in this myth there is no mention at all of the *forms* of life.) Then, secondly, considering a different aspect of generation, we have the completion of the forms of life in the Garden of Adonis, through the interaction of Venus the form-giver and 'the Father of all formes' (III. vi. 47), the sun. Here again there is

[1] *In Timæum*, Ch. xx, 'Planetarum dispositio, annus magnus'; p. 1468.

moisture; but this time it is supplied by Venus, not the moon. Gum flows from the myrtles of the Mount, and all the things of the Garden 'in themselves eternall moisture . . . imply' (III. vi. 34).

We are therefore inclined to envisage not only mythological and cosmological *couples* but also a generative *triad*: sun, moon, and Venus. This notion gains support from Ellrodt's demonstration (p. 102) that Spenser derived many suggestions for the core canto of Book III from the *Sympose* of Le Roy, a work that describes 'the birth of living beings as the result of a love-relationship between heaven (meaning the sun) and earth.' For, behind Le Roy's philosophy there lies the fundamental Orphic triad, Heaven, Earth, and Love. We recall that Spenser's Garden, as well as being the seminary where forms are completed and generated, is also a garden of love. It is the place where Amoret, Venus' foster-child, is nurtured, and where Cupid himself lives and generates pleasure. At the same time, though we may speak of a triad, this does not mean that the three powers concerned have equal prominence. Venus clearly predominates (even, as Lewis notices, in her relation with Adonis); while the power of the sun, and the tempering ministration of the moon, are represented in a summary or subordinate manner.

The structural inferences to be drawn from the above seem to me of the greatest interest. First, consider Ficino's statement that through the moisture of Venus the sun *generabilium formas absolvit*; remembering that *absolvit* implies a loosening as well as a perfecting action. May not this phrase be regarded as the explicit expression of an idea rendered implicitly and formally in the structural peculiarities of Book III? I do not mean merely that the episodic structure of this book is *looser* than that of any other, except Book VI—though many readers have remarked the abrupt change to a more fluid and Ariostan narrative method at this point. What is even more striking is the multitude of respects in which Book III constitutes a break in otherwise uniform schemes and structural regularities running throughout the poem. As we have seen, Book III is exceptional in the early placing of its core canto; in its departure from the scheme whereby in other books the character-totals of narrative cantos follow the Pythagorean series; and in the omission of a deliverance by Arthur in its eighth canto. It also differs from the other books in that its official champion, Scudamour, fails to carry out his mission, and is replaced by Britomart. In the scheme of planetary guardians, moreover, Book

III finds the proper guardian of the third day, Mars, replaced by Minerva, Venus, and other subsidiary mythological powers. The joint occurrence of these and other departures from formal regularity, all in the same book, is surely intentional. May it be that we are to see the departures, not as exceptions at all, but as instances of a subtle decorum? Are they the formal correlatives of Venus' power to set free and loosen the forms of life? Since the creative action that generates these forms is in touch with chaos both at the Cave of Proteus and at the Garden of Adonis, may we not recognize in its structure, too, something of the quality of the chaos from which new life emerges? If so, then Book IV—which, as we shall see, is Mercury's book—certainly fulfils the office assigned to that deity: namely, giving to the liberated forms a fixed order and proportion. Itself a highly symmetrical and closely proportioned structure, Book IV draws together the loose threads of the preceding book, concluding or bringing to harmony its unfinished narratives.

Secondly, the mythological triad which we distinguished in the core canto of Book III—Sol, Luna, Venus—also carries far-reaching structural implications. Sol and Luna were the guardians of Books I and II; so that the subsidiary solar and lunar influences in Book III are carried on from preceding books. The participation of Sol and Luna in a triad with Venus, a principal deity of Book III, therefore, suggests that, in their whole substance, the first three books may similarly bear triadic relationships with each other. This way of looking at the first part of the *Faerie Queene*, which we have had independent reasons to consider in a previous chapter, is so fruitful that it calls for separate treatment. Here we can only mention that, in addition to implicit moral schemes connecting the three books, such as the triad of Fidius (Veritas–Virtus–Amor[1]), there are also more overt indications of a triadic structure. Consider, for example, the scheme embodied in Aveugle's three sons, Sansfoy, Sansloy, and Sansjoy. All three appear in the first book, but only one of them— appropriately, Sansfoy—is decisively conquered there. The encounter of Redcrosse with Sansfoy is nevertheless the most perfunctorily described. Why? Because its purpose is only to summarize a conflict that receives expanded treatment, in other modes of symbolism, throughout Book I. The second son, Sansloy, who is subdued at the Castle of Medina in Book II, is a brief representation,

[1] See above, p. 22.

143

similarly, of the intemperance against which Guyon's mission is directed. It is true that the third son, Sansjoy, makes no appearance by name in Book III. But he is none the less implicitly vanquished there. For sexual joy and the obstacles to sexual joy are preoccupations of this book. The joy of lovers is its recurrent theme; whether it be the false joy of Malecasta's Castle Joyous or the true joy of the Garden where 'wont faire *Venus* often to enjoy / Her deare *Adonis* joyous company' (III. vi. 46). Against the joy of the *Venus læta* of spring, neither the suffering of wounded lovers, nor the cruelty of Busyrane's mastery, nor Malbecco's attempt to keep Hellenore 'depriv'd of kindly joy' (III. ix. 5), can for long prevail. In short, we may say that the family relationship of Aveugle's sons is a symbolic statement of a triadic scheme implemented on a large scale throughout Books I–III.

If the first three books have a triadic structure this argues a certain completeness in them. With the conclusion of the third book there should be a relative finality. More particularly, Venus' power as form-giver—the power by which forms are *perfected*—carries a similar implication. Moreover, if Hamilton's cosmological interpretation is correct, then the release of Amoret from the House of Busyrane in III. xii, while it is far from being the end of her story in the 1596 version of the poem, at least represents the completion of a seasonal cycle. One of the reasons for Minerva's place among the guardians, we recall, was that this number represented the three seasons of the complete Egyptian year. Considerations such as these may lie behind the numerological division by which Spenser has set the first three books apart as constituting a complete unit. I refer not only to the division of the poem into parts but also to the remarkable 'harmony' whereby the lines of Part I add to 18,000. For this is the number of the Platonic generative cycle or *annus magnus*. The physical duration of Part I thus mimes the cycle whose completion sees the unfolding of the generative triad, Sol–Luna–Venus. For, as Ficino describes it, that triad belongs to the divine activity of the Great Year, the period in which each of the planets completely fulfils its creative function.[1]

---

[1] See his ch. 'Planetarum dispositio, annus magnus' (p. 1468). The 18,000 line-total for Pt. I of *F.Q.* is discussed above, p. 40. It is based on the presupposition, surely one that Spenser would expect most of his readers to share, that the

iii

If the astrological pattern of Book III is examined in the light of the foregoing discussion some theories previously advanced find additional support. Most obvious, perhaps, is the *chronographia* at III. i. 57 describing the state of the heavens at the moment when the company at the House of Malecasta retire for the night:

> By this th'eternall lampes, wherewith high *Jove*
> Doth light the lower world, were halfe yspent,
> And the moist daughters of huge *Atlas* strove
> Into the *Ocean* deepe to drive their weary drove.

The information conveyed in these lines enables us to fix the date of the event as the vernal equinox. For we are told that it is midnight (Jove's lamps are 'halfe yspent'), and that the Hyades ('moist daughters of huge *Atlas*') are on the point of setting. Now it can easily be determined from tables—and any Elizabethan interested in astronomy would have known—that the Hyades set at midnight on

---

stanzas of the poem are all of equal length. For readers with a more microscopic eye, however, the poet had a further marvel in store. For, in all the earliest editions one line is lacking from the stanza describing Fidelia's miraculous powers. We are told that she could stop the sun or change his direction; and, immediately after, the poem itself stops, for the interval of a silent line (I. x. 20. [5]). This irregularity throws out the 18,000 count, but introduces instead a new harmony. Those who noticed it would surely also notice that it brings the least inclusive line-total for Bk. I to 5552—Aretes' value for the Great Year. This use of the missing line is particularly striking in view of the fact that change of direction of the sun (*anakuklesis*) was a sign of transition from one Platonic cycle to another.

The probability that Great Year figures should twice appear among the line-totals of books and parts of *F.Q.* is less than 1 : 2500. The calculation assumes, for the sake of rigour, that the possible line-totals for a single book range only from 4986 (the least inclusive total for the shortest actual book, Bk. VI) to 6216 (the most inclusive total for the longest actual book, Bk. II). If, however, the permissible range of possible line-totals were wider—as it must properly be considered—the probability of chance occurrence of any particular total would, of course, be much less. Allowance has been made for the variation of line-totals between the 1590 and 1596 editions, which increases the probability of chance occurrence; and for the existence of several Great Year figures and half-Year figures within the specified range (half Herodotus' 10,800, half Dion's 10,884, Aretes' 5552, and half Orpheus' 12,000, within the range for a single book; Macrobius' 15,000 and half Plato's 36,000, within the range for a part), which also increases the probability. The calculation cannot, however, take any account of the striking congruence between the symbolic values of the formal numbers and the content of the poem.

or about the vernal equinox, in the latitudes of Northern Europe around the date 1590.[1] We may therefore assume, in the absence of any more specific information, that the vernal equinox itself is referred to. It follows that the zodiacal houses indicated are Pisces and Aries, between which the vernal equinoctial point falls.[2] The second of these houses, Aries, is the house of Mars; while the first, Pisces, is the Exaltation of Venus, and was often associated with that planet, rather than with its proper guardian Jupiter.[3] The images from which the *chronographia* is composed—'moist daughters' and '*Ocean* deepe' —point to Pisces, which was a particularly moist sign. As Ptolemy informs us,

> Venus . . . as she is moist by nature and increases her own proper power all the more in Pisces, where the beginning of the moist spring is indicated, has her exaltation in Pisces and her depression in Virgo.[4]

In this connection between Pisces and Venus (whose weeping for Adonis was regarded by Macrobius and others as a symbol of the rainy season) lies the aptness of the astronomical image at III. i. 57. The moist sign Pisces and the rain-bearing constellation Hyades[5]— situated at the head of the Bull—fitly usher in a book which deals with the generative power of Venus. As we have seen, this power was believed to operate during a fruitful season initiated when the sun, leaving Pisces at the vernal equinoctial point, passed from the signs of darkness into the signs of light, and when the seed was exposed to the moist air of Venus. The *chronographia* may once have had the effect of alerting the instructed reader to the element of astrological symbolism running through much of the succeeding action. Not only are images of the ocean 'fertile . . . in generation' (IV. xii. 1) far more

[1] At this point I am indebted to Professor D. J. de Solla Price for his generous assistance.

[2] Due to the precession of the equinoxes, in Spenser's time the vernal equinoctial point no longer fell, of course, between the *constellations* Pisces and Aries, but instead about 5° from the beginning of the constellation Pisces. My astrological argument remains unaffected, however, since it refers to the fixed houses of the firmament, not to the constellations.

[3] See Hieatt, *Short Time's Endless Monument*, pp. 23–25, where examples in Dante, Chaucer, and a possible example in Spenser, *Epithalamion*, St. xvi, are discussed.

[4] *Tetrabiblos*, I. xix; ed. Robbins, p. 91.

[5] It is not impossible, however, that the Hyades were also chosen because they formed (and were said to be named after) the Greek letter Υ, which signified the choice between pleasure and virtue. See Hyginus, *Fab.*, cxcii.

prominent in this and the following book than in any other of the poem—one thinks of the 'surges hore' at the Rich Strond, and of the sea on which Florimell in her flight embarks and beneath which she is imprisoned[1]—but there is also an allusion to the sign Pisces in the fish-scales with which Florimell is smeared in the fisherman's boat.[2] Finally, we may notice the rain storm in the Malbecco episode (III. ix. 11).

Another stanza with a specifically astrological implication is that describing the descent of Venus in search of Cupid:

> Him for to seeke, she left her heavenly hous,
> The house of goodly formes and faire aspects,
> Whence all the world derives the glorious
> Features of beautie, and all shapes select,
> With which high God his workmanship hath deckt;
> And searched every way, through which his wings
> Had borne him. . . .
>
> (III. vi. 12)

Ellrodt (p. 90) contents himself with rejecting the Neoplatonic interpretation of these lines, and with a general reference to the influence of the planet Venus. But perhaps it is not too fanciful to see, in the story of Venus' descent and temporary sojourn upon earth, a more detailed astrological allegory, tracing her course through the signs of the fruitful season. When Venus meets Diana, she (1) has 'lately left' Cupid 'in *Mars* his bed' (III. vi. 24), and (2) has also left her own 'heavenly hous' (III. vi. 13); next, Venus and Diana together search and (3) find the twins Amoret and Belphœbe. Do these stages of the myth correspond to the first three zodiacal signs of the fruitful season? These signs are (1) Aries, the House of Mars, (2) Taurus, the House of Venus, and (3) Gemini, the Twins. (The signs adjacent to the Twins are a House of Venus, Taurus, and the House of Luna or Diana, Cancer.)

The numerology of the descriptive cantos offers further points of agreement. In each case the character-total indicates a sign associated with Venus. Thus, in the Garden of Adonis there are eight characters

[1] III. iv and vii. Due to the overlapping effect mentioned above, the influence of Venus is already felt in II. xii. The oceanic images of the first part of that canto indicate that the transition from Aquarius to Pisces is beginning; nor should we miss the allusion to Venus 'newly borne / Of th'Oceans fruitfull froth' at II. xii. 65.

[2] Naturally this allusion does not exhaust the meaning of the incident. For a sexual interpretation, see Hamilton, *The Structure of Allegory*, p. 151.

present: Venus, Adonis, Genius, Time, Cupid, Psyche, Pleasure, and Amoret. This is the Ptolemaic total for Libra, the solar House of Venus. Its association with the harvest and with the completion of the season's growth make Libra particularly appropriate for the canto portraying the perfection of generative love. As we have seen, the total for Libra also occurs in that false simulacrum of the Garden of Venus, the Bower of Bliss. Thus, the similarities between the true and the false version of the Garden extend to numerical and astrological properties.

At the house of Busyrane Ptolemaic numbers are used in a particularly emphatic manner, both in the tapestries of Cupid's wars and in the masque of Cupid. But, as Spenser himself warns us (while at the same time encouraging us with a direct allusion to the cataloguing of stars and therefore to the Ptolemaic totals), the numerology of the tapestries will not be easy to disentangle:

> But to declare the mournfull Tragedyes,
> And spoiles, wherewith he all the ground did strow,
> More eath to number, with how many eyes
> High heaven beholds sad lovers nightly theeveryes.[1]

It seems prudent, therefore, to defer consideration of the tapestries until the simpler masque of Cupid in the following canto has been examined.

It will be remembered that the masquers parade round an outer room where Britomart keeps vigil, then retire to an inner room, leaving her excluded. Hence Britomart, whose rôle is purely that of a spectator, falls into a different category from that of the masquers themselves. We may therefore expect that their numerical arrangement will be to some extent self-contained. Moreover, Spenser's hint that Busyrane's company march 'in manner of a maske, enranged orderly' (III. xii. 5) implies that their internal grouping is significant. Accordingly, the order of the masque is analysed in the table on p. 149.

The different sections of the procession are clearly distinguished by rubrical lines, in a style that has seemed flat to readers uninterested in numerology: 'Thus marched these six couples forth in faire degree./ After all these there marcht a most faire Dame'; 'Next after her the winged God himselfe'; 'Behinde him was *Reproch, Repentance,*

---

[1] III. xi. 45; cf. IV. xii. 1. This comparison was not original with Spenser: as editors have noted, there are close parallels in Ariosto (*Orl. Fur.*, XIV. 99) and Tasso (*Gerus. Lib.*, xii. 22).

1(a). *Fidei symbolum*

1(b). *Fidii simulacrum*

23(a) Dürer, St. John

23(b) Dürer, St. John

3(b). Apollo with Adad and Adargatis

3(a). The Mask of Judgement

4(b). 'Terra'

4(a). 'Sol'

SPHÆRA CIVITATIS

QVAM benè CœLESTI CIVILIS machina formæ
Congruat, & quàm sit panibus distincta figuris,
Viuca pro multis Reipublicæ nostra loquetur.
Aspicis alterno circumgyrantia cursu
Sidera, & æquali causas quæ pondere librat
IVSTITIAS, nostri centrum inuariabile mundi?
Aspicis emensos SEPTEM spatia ampla PLANETAS,
Quorum quisque suo studiosè præsidet orbi?
VBERTAS RERVM, Luna:& FACVNDIA, Regni
Mercurius: Venus esse potest CLEMENTIA Regis.
Par soli PIETAS medijs diffunditur Astris.
VIS ANIMI iustis Mauortem spirat in armis.
Nata Iouem simulat PRVDENTIA prouida patrem
Saturnumq; graui MAIESTAS plena timore.
Hæ sunt quæ nostras collustrant Lampades oras
Præcipuæ: verùm his Octauam apponere Sphæram
Luminibus fixis, clarisq; varijsq; micantem
Iam libet, yrcq; olim STELLATVM dicere CœLVM.
Cœlum Stellatum CAMERA est STELLATA Britannis,
Consilijs munita pijs, Procerumq; frequenti
Nobilium stipata manu, qui munia Regni
Ardua procurant, & magna negotia versant.
Omnibus impēdet globus is, cui MOBILE PRIMVM
Nomen, & amplex nexus qui continet omnes,
Tu VIRGO, REGINA Potens, tu MOBILE PRIMVM
ELISABETHA, rapis tecum molimina Gentis.
Inde reluctantes animos, mentesq; rebelles
Debilitas, MOTVq; trahis Suprema DIVRNO.
Hic ordo sic conspirat status ORBIS, & VRBIS:
Hæc tamen hoc tanctum discrimine distat ab ILLO,
Quòd non perpetuò firmari possit viv ILLE.
Ergò diu SPHÆRÆ SVMMA MOTRICE ferantur,
Ergò diu SPHÆRAS & MOTRIX SVMMA gubernet.

RICHARDVS LATE—WAR, Collegij
D.Iohannis Præcursoris Socius.

§2.

5. Queen Elizabeth as *primum mobile*

6. Falconetto, Aquarius Presiding over the Month of January

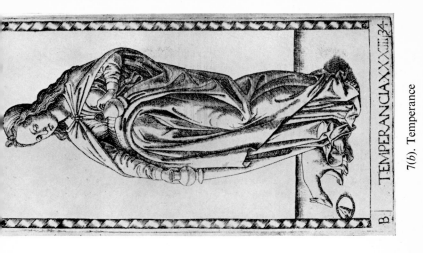

7(b). Temperance

7(a). Falconetto, Aquarius Pouring into a Laver (detail)

8. Mantegna, Wisdom Overcoming the Vices

9. Perugino, Combat of Love and Chastity

10. Cossa, Triumph of Minerva

11. Cossa, Tapestry Weavers (detail)

12. Queen Elizabeth Enthroned

13(a). Righteousness and Peace (detail)

13(b). Minerva

14(a) Goltzius, Minerva and Mercury

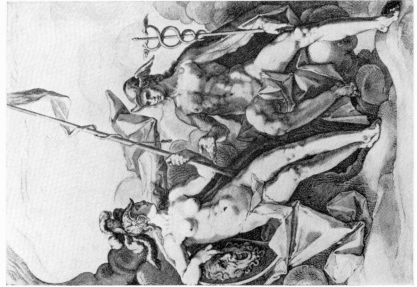

14(b) Mercury and Peace

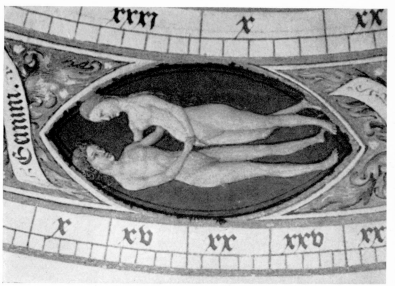

15(b). Gemini as Androgyne

15(a). Falconetto, Gemini as Male Twins (detail)

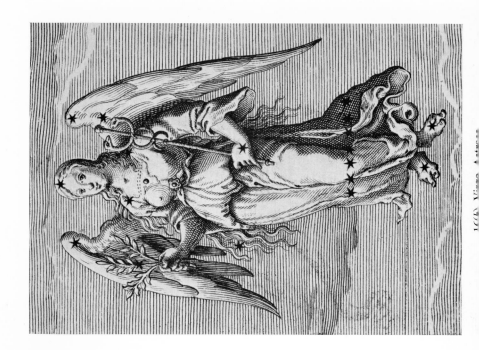

16(b) Virgo Aquena

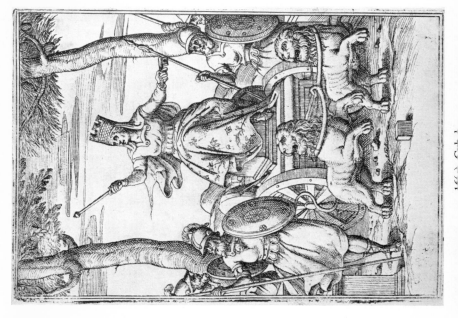

16(a) Cybele

THE MASQUE OF CUPID

Locality	Characters		Numbers of characters
III. xii. 3–18		Ease	1 ⎫
	'sixe couples'	Fancy Desyre Doubt Daunger Feare Hope Dissemblance Suspect Griefe Fury Displeasure Pleasance	12 ⎪
III. xii. 19–24	Cupid's party	Despight Dame Cruelty CUPID Reproch Shame Repentance	1 + 6 ⎬33
III. xii. 25	'rude confused rout'	Strife Anger Care Unthriftihead Losse of Time Sorrow Chaunge Disloyaltie Riotise Dread Infirmitie Povertie Death	13 ⎭

Shame'; 'And after them a rude confused rout / Of persons flockt, whose names is hard to read.' The most outstanding feature in the arrangement is, of course, the contrast between the orderly grouping of the characters (phases of emotional experience) that precede the triumphant god and the hurried confusion of the rout that follows. This is clearly meant to convey the difference between earlier and later stages of a sexual relationship; the later stages showing the cruel and chaotic effects of Cupid at his most despotic. Less obvious is the significance of the exactly central position of the god, who comes seventeenth in the procession of thirty-three *personæ*. In a general way this arrangement is appropriate for a triumph, since the central position was considered sovereign. More particularly, however, Cupid also comes at the centre of a sub-group of seven; reminding us of similar placings of Lucifera and Malecasta. These, we saw, implied usurpation of cosmic sovereignty. Finally, it may be noted that the total number of masquers, thirty-three, is the Ptolemaic number of Taurus. This sign was the house of Venus, and in consequence was directly associated with love.[1]

A puzzling feature of the masque's numerology is the effect of Britomart's presence as a witness. If she were included in the count the character-total would be brought to thirty-four, the Ptolemaic number of Pisces. True, Pisces is the Exaltation of Venus; but it is hard to see why Britomart should effect such a shift from the House to the Exaltation of Venus.[2] This problem is seen to be a real one, as soon as we turn to the tapestries of Cupid's wars. For we find that *the numerological pattern of the tapestries is closely similar to that of the masque.*

THE TAPESTRIES OF CUPID'S WARS

God	Metamorphosis	Lover	Metamorphosis	Locality
	Ram	HELLE	—	Stanza 30
	Bull	EUROPA	—	Stanza 30
	Golden shower	DANAE	—	Stanza 31
	Swan	LEDA	—	Stanza 32
	Sovereign majesty	SEMELE	—	Stanza 33
JUPITER	Amphitryon	ALCMENA	—	Stanza 33
	Eagle	ASTERIA	[Quail]	Stanza 34
	Eagle	[GANYMEDE]	—	Stanza 34
	Satyr	ANTIOPE	—	Stanza 35
	Fire	ÆGINA	—	Stanza 35
	Shepherd	MNEMOSYNE	—	Stanza 35
	Serpent	[DEOIS]	—	Stanza 35

[1] As, indeed, was the animal itself: see Valeriano, *Hieroglyphica*, p. 750. It is worth noting that Valeriano (p. 41) derives the name *Busiris* (from which Spenser's *Busyrane* is formed) from *bos* (βοῦς), synonymous with *taurus*. Miss Williams ('Venus and Diana,' p. 114) rightly connects Busyrane with the cruel Busiris of Ovid's *Ars amatoria*. But there are also other reasons for the use of the name. E.g., in view of the fact that Busyrane kidnaps Amoret, it is significant that Diodorus Siculus (IV. xxvii. 1–5) relates that Busiris so desired the Atlantides, daughters of Atlas, that he had them carried off by pirates. (The Atlantides—i.e., Hyades—are alluded to by Spenser at III. i. 57.) Another Ovidian passage, *Metam.*, IX. 183, seems to me almost equally relevant. There King Busiris is said to have defiled his temples with strangers' blood: a ready-made symbol, it may have seemed to Spenser, for adultery.

[2] The arrangement by which Ease remains outside the masque proper, on the other hand, is easily understood. Its purpose is to make the masque itself consist of Cupid together with thirty-one other actors; for thirty-one is the Ptolemaic total of Draco, and the Cupid of the Tapestry is portrayed surmounting a dragon: 'A wounded Dragon under him did ly, / Whose hideous tayle his left foot did enfold, / And with a shaft was shot through either eye, / That no man forth might draw, ne no man remedye' (III. xi. 48).

THE TAPESTRIES OF CUPID'S WARS (*contd.*)

God	Metamorphosis	Lover	Metamorphosis	Locality
CUPID	—	—	—	Stanza 35
	—	DAPHNE	'gyrlond ever greene'	Stanza 36
	—	HYACINTHUS	'Paunce'	Stanza 37
PHŒBUS	—	CORONIS	'breare'	Stanza 37
	—	[PHÆTON]	—	Stanza 38
	Cowherd	ISSE	—	Stanza 39
	Lion	—	—	Stanza 39
	Stag	—	—	Stanza 39
	Falcon	—	—	Stanza 39
	[Ram]	BISALTIS	[Sheep]	Stanza 41
	[Enipeus]	IPHIMEDIA	—	Stanza 42
NEPTUNE	Steer	ARNE	[Jackdaw]	Stanza 42
	Dolphin	[MELANTHO]	—	Stanza 42
	Winged horse	MEDUSA	[Snaky hair]	Stanza 42
SATURN	Centaur	ERIGONE	[Constellation Virgo]	Stanza 43
BACCHUS	Vine	PHILYRA	[Linden tree]	Stanza 43
MARS	—	Venus	[Alectryon into a cock]	Stanza 44
VENUS	—	—	—	Stanza 45
Cupid	—	[PSYCHE]	—	Stanza 45

Square brackets indicate that the name of a lover, or the form taken in a metamorphosis, is not directly stated by Spenser.

From the table it will be seen that the total of gods and lovers appearing in the tapestries is again thirty-three, the Ptolemaic number of Taurus. Moreover, the various sections of the tapestries catalogue correspond exactly with the sections of the masque; as will be obvious if the two schemes are summarized:

Tapestries	Number of *personœ*	Masque
Jupiter and his twelve loves	1 + 12	Ease and 'six couples'
CUPID, with Phœbus and his loves	1 + 6	CUPID, with Amoret and others
Various gods and their loves	13	'confused rout'

As if the construction of these correspondences did not offer enough of a formal challenge, Spenser goes on to reproduce the same pattern yet again in the metamorphoses occasioned by the gods' amours. If the series of transformations induced by love is carefully followed it is found to arrive, by a most ingenious route, at an independent summation of thirty-three. Thus, in addition to the twelve metamorphoses of Jupiter one of his mortal loves, Asteria, also suffered a change of form;[1] so that the total for this section is by a neat compensation brought to thirteen. In the second section, only four changes of Phœbus are catalogued;[2] but there are three metamorphoses of his lovers—Daphne's, Hyacinthus', and Coronis'. Similarly, though the amours of the other gods lead to only five explicitly specified metamorphoses, the myths alluded to involve an additional seven, all of them familiar ones to readers of Ovid or Hyginus. For the love of Neptune and Bisaltis led to his metamorphosis into a ram, hers into a sheep;[3] Arne was changed by Neptune into a girl, after being born a foal as a result of Æolus' amour with her mother;[4] Neptune took the form of Enipeus to win Iphimedeia;[5] Medusa's beautiful hair (which had attracted Neptune and occasioned his pollution of Minerva's temple) was turned into writhing serpents by the angry goddess; Erigone became the constellation Virgo[6] and Philyra a linden tree;[7] and the love of Mars and Venus occasioned the transformation of Alectryon, their sleepy sentry, into a cock.[8] Thus, although the series of metamorphoses is quite distinct from that of the *personae*, it too consists of thirty-three terms.

It is remarkable enough that in the same episode we should meet three independent occurrences of the total 33, a number that is itself appropriate to the content.[9] Added to this, however, is the triple agreement in the manner of partition of 33. The masquers, the gods and lovers in the tapestries, and the metamorphoses in the tapestries: all three sets are arranged in such a way that 33 is divided into the portions 1, 12, 1, 6, and 13. Even if my count of the metamorphoses

[1] Asteria was changed into a quail when she lost Jupiter's favour (Hyginus, *Fab.*, liii).

[2] The mortals who occasioned Phœbus' assumption of the forms of lion, stag, and falcon remain unspecified in Spenser's source (Ovid, *Metam.*, VI. 123) and in all the mythographical authorities I have been able to consult.

[3] Ovid, *Metam.*, VI. 117 and Hyginus, *Fab.*, clxxxviii.

[4] Hyginus, *Poet. astron.*, II. xviii. Spenser gives a necessary hint by referring to Arne as '*Aeolus* faire daughter.'

[5] Ovid, *Metam.*, VI. 116.

[6] Ibid., VI. 125 and X. 451. Christopher Middleton's *The historie of heaven* (London, 1596) is evidence of the interest in stellification myths in the sixteenth century.

[7] Hyginus, *Fab.*, cxxxviii.

[8] Lucian, *Somn. s. gall.*, iii.

[9] Taking the character-total range as 40, and the number of significant Ptolemaic totals as 4, the probability of chance occurrence of such an agreement is 1 : 16,000. Even if the count of metamorphoses is disallowed, the probability is still 1 : 400.

is challenged, the concurrence of the other two patterns still renders the possibility of coincidence inconceivably remote. Of course, it may be argued that the chances against any particular conformation occurring can be made to seem very great, if enough of its details are taken into consideration. The probability against chance occurrence can be made to increase indefinitely, simply by an arbitrary decision to regard more and more features of the passage as belonging to the numerological pattern. This argument fails, however, for several reasons. First, we are not concerned with an isolated conformation, but with a whole set of analogous conformations, occurring throughout the poem in similar positions (the descriptive cantos). Secondly, in this case the scheme is certainly duplicated, and perhaps triplicated. Finally, the features comprising the arrangement are not arbitrarily selected. Every feature considered can be assigned a definite significance in accordance with the system of Ptolemaic Catalogue numbers. This is even true of the partition of 33 into the sub-groups 1, 12, 1, 6, and 13. For we find that in Ptolemy's *Almagest* the 33 stars of Taurus are divided into sub-groups, according to their brightness. There are: 1 of the first magnitude; 6 of the third; 12 of the fourth; 13 of the fifth; and 1 of the sixth. In other words, the stars of Taurus are arranged in the same sub-groups 1, 6, 12, 13, 1.[1]

The interpretation of the tapestries thus amply corroborates that of the masque. There cannot be the slightest doubt that each is a numerological representation of Taurus. Nevertheless, the presence of Britomart in the earlier canto, as a spectator of the tapestries, again converts the thirty-three of Taurus into the thirty-four of Pisces. And to underline this Pisces total, we have four additional characters who participate in the action of the earlier part of the canto, but who do

---

[1] The probability against this particular arrangement of 33 characters occurring by chance can be arrived at by determining the total number of possible partitionings of 33. Now a positive integer r can be written as the sum of n positive integers in $\frac{(r-1)!}{(n-1)!\,(r-n)!}$ different ways (see W. Feller, *An Introduction to Probability Theory and its Applications*, Vol. I (New York, 1957), p. 37). Hence the number of ways in which 33 can be partitioned into five sub-groups is $\frac{(33-1)!}{(5-1)!\,(33-5)!} = \frac{32!}{4!\,28!} = \frac{32.\,31.\,30.\,29}{4.\,3.\,2} = 35,960$. Thus, even if we consider only partitions into five sub-groups, the probability against the particular arrangement in question occurring by chance is 35,960 : 1. If, however, we are reasonable enough to allow that partition into other numbers of sub-groups might have occurred, then of course the probability against chance occurrence becomes immensely greater.

153

not enter the house of Busyrane.[1] These correspond to the four *stellæ informatæ* of Pisces; they bring the larger total for the canto to thirty-eight, the inclusive figure for that constellation in the Ptolemaic catalogue.

While the repetition of the effect of Britomart's presence puts the numerological analysis on a strong footing, the significance of such a Taurus–Pisces conversion is still obscure. We may suspect, however, that the clue lies in the lines describing Cupid's usurpation of sovereignty in the tapestries:

> Whiles thus on earth great *Jove* these pageaunts playd,
> The winged boy did thrust into his throne,
> And scoffing, thus unto his mother sayd,
> Lo now the heavens obey to me alone,
> And take me for their *Jove*, whiles *Jove* to earth is gone.
>
> (III. xi. 35)

Both in the tapestries and the masque the importance of the central position of sovereignty is given repeated formal emphasis. In the masque, as we have seen, it is Cupid himself who occupies this position. In the tapestries the exactly central metamorphosis—coming seventeenth out of thirty-three—is that of Phaeton, whose crime it was to aspire wilfully to Phœbus' seat of power. Moreover, the gods whose amours are most elaborately treated, Jupiter, Phœbus, and Neptune, all had legitimate claims to cosmic power. This is a point crucial to any interpretation of the mythology of the episode. Spenser represents the cause of tragedy and of suffering in love as a displacement of Jupiter, the constitutional sovereign of the universe, by an evil Cupid—a Cupid wilful, tyrannical, desirous of mastery. I would, therefore, suggest that conversion of Taurus to Pisces by Britomart may be intended to symbolize a restoration of sovereignty to Jupiter. For Pisces is not only the Exaltation of Venus but also *the principal House of Jupiter*. Britomart's purpose is not to annihilate love, but only to end its destructive tyranny. In her, Venus finds her Exaltation, yet at the same time becomes part of an ordered universe acknowledging divine rule.

If, on the other hand, Britomart–Isis had failed—if she had succumbed to Taurus—she would have suffered her own metamorphosis. For the constellation Taurus was sometimes identified with the heifer

[1] I.e., Satyrane, young man, and Ollyphant (III. xi. 3–6); Scudamour (III. xi. 7–27).

into which Io–Isis, beloved of Jupiter, was changed. In the allegorization of that myth the imposition of the Taurus-form was interpreted as man's lapse into bestial vice; the recovery of human form (eventually the divine form of Isis), as man's moral reformation.[1]

[1] See, e.g., Sandys's commentary on *Metam.*, I: '*Jupiter*, the mind of man falling from Heaven, and joyning with *Io*, the body in a clowd is turned into a beast: as forgetfull of his owne originall; and captivated by his vices.' Later, when Io is retransformed, man 'is restored to his former beauty, and becomes like the Gods through his sanctity and integrity' (*Ovid's Metamorphosis* (London, 1632), p. 37).

155

XI

The Book of Mercury and Venus

i

Iₙ spite of critical opinion to the contrary, the fourth is in many
ways the most unified of all the books of the *Faerie Queene*. No doubt
this is in part the result of Spenser's deliberate effort to accord his
harmonious subject an appropriately harmonious treatment. But the
unity seems also to have been made possible by the conveniently
close, direct, and complete identity between the available myths, and
the philosophical and moral ideas Spenser wished to deal with.
Morally, the book is a 'Legend . . . of friendship'; in a wider sense,
its theme is concord—whether the concord of personal and political
relations, or of the world-order at large. Now, the guardian deity of
the fourth book is Mercury, the fourth god in the planetary week
(the guardian of Wednesday, or *dies Mercurii*); and Mercury is,
above all, the god of concord, and of that reason by which the world
is ordered.[1] Apparently because he was the fourth god of the week,
all the meaning with which the tetrad was endowed—such as its
doctrine of the true proportion of the double mean—accrued to
Mercury himself. Four was his number, and so he became known as
the *quadratus deus* and the god of true proportion.[2] In all the episodes

---

[1] See Tervarent, s.v. 'Mercure,' iii: 'La raison'; col. 269.

[2] This seems the most likely explanation; since the assignation of Mercury to
the fourth day of the week was the result of a purely mechanical permutation.
Nevertheless, Mercury was associated with the proportionate tetrad by quite
early Pythagorean authorities, and the association was never admitted to be a
post-factum rationalization. So Martianus Capella, *De nuptiis*, ed. Dick, sect. 734,
p. 369: 'hic numerus quadratus ipsi Cyllenio [i.e., Mercury] deputatur, quod
quadratus deus solus habeatur.' Cf. ibid., sects. 106–107, p. 44; Plutarch,

of the book, therefore, in which we have discerned an allegory of the tetrad of concord, Mercury must be thought of as exercising his office to produce a truly proportioned mixture. And, as we have seen, this tetradic pattern is sustained throughout the narrative episodes with great consistency. It is possible to go further, and to say that the whole movement of Book IV is from initial private contention and from the discord of societies reduced by Ate to travesties of tetradic order; through various reconciliations and achievements of concord in particular spheres of life; to a celebration of the 'blessed *Peace* and *Friendship* trew' of the universal Concord, in the Temple of Venus and in the spousal of Thames and Medway.[1] Venus joins Mercury in presiding over Book IV, because her influence and his are in Neo-platonic mythology very closely associated: 'Venus is the author of conciliation and friendship, Mercury of proportion and mingling.'[2]

The primary attribute of Mercury, symbolizing his character as a god of concord, is the caduceus. It is appropriate, therefore, that the caduceus should be introduced prominently and early into the action of Book IV. This is done in the most dramatic way possible when Cambina makes her sudden entry at the lists, in a chariot drawn by lions, to intervene between Cambell and Triamond. She carries, we are told, a caduceus like that of '*Maias* sonne' (Mercury):

> In her right hand a rod of peace shee bore,
> About the which two Serpents weren wound,
> Entrayled mutually in lovely lore,

---

[1] H. C. Notcutt ('*The Faerie Queene* and its critics,' *E & S*, XII (1926), 62–86) first drew attention to the book's movement from discord to concord. But his account of the symmetry with which episodes and images in its two halves match each other is forced, and he ignores the philosophical basis of the structure.

[2] Ficino, *In Timæum*, Ch. xix, 'Distinctio temporis, Planetarum motus': 'Venus enim conciliationis, et amicitiæ. Mercurius quoque proportionis, et commixtionis est author' (p. 1468); cf. Ch. xx, 'Planetarum dispositio, annus magnus': 'Per Mercurium mox præfectum Veneri tanquam proportionis commixtionisque fabrum formas mutuo formis, resque rebus rite commiscet' (ibid.). Ficino refers this close connection between the offices of the planets Mercury and Venus to the proximity and similar eccentricity of their orbits. On this point, see also Wind, *Pagan Mysteries*, p. 111 and n. 3. Mercury and Minerva were also often paired, or even united: see ibid., p. 166 f., and cf. Pl. 14a.

Sympos., IX. iii; and Macrobius, *Sat.*, I. xix. 15. In the Renaissance we find Giraldi still gathering reasons why Mercury should be the *quadratus deus* (*De diis*, 416A). A few authors also connect the number five with Mercury: see the *Commentariorum lib. sec.* appended to Valeriano's *Hieroglyphica*, Ch. xvii: 'Quinarius numerus, et quaternarius. Mercurius, et artium inventores' (p. 753C–D).

And by the tailes together firmely bound,
And both were with one olive garland crownd,
Like to the rod which *Maias* sonne doth wield,
Wherewith the hellish fiends he doth confound.
(IV. iii. 42)

The caduceus was a symbol dear to the mythologists and mystagogues of the Renaissance. Simple yet profound, it was ideally suited to iconographical speculation; so that a great many interpretations came to be attached to its several parts. To some extent Spenser indicates which of these symbolic traits of the caduceus emblem are relevant, by the emphasis that he lays, in his description, upon particular details. Cambina's caduceus (1) is a 'rod of peace'; (2) has serpents 'entrayled mutually in lovely lore' and (3) 'firmely bound' by the tails; and (4) is crowned with a single olive garland. In addition, we are shown something of the power of the caduceus in actual operation. When Cambell and Triamond are struck with it their swords fall from their hands, they stand astonished, and their 'mighty spirites' become 'bound with mightier band' (IV. iii. 48).

According to one interpretation, the caduceus was a rod of peace because of an incident that occurred when Mercury was visiting Arcadia:

Seeing two serpents with their bodies locked together, fighting one with another, he placed his staff [given him by Apollo, in exchange for the lyre] between them both, so that they were separated. Having done this, he said that the rod had been established for the sake of peace. And still, when some represent the caduceus, they make two serpents entwined with a rod, because the origin of peace was from Mercury.[1]

So Giraldi; while the more curious Valeriano, in a chapter authoritative enough to be quoted at length by Liceti, adds that the caduceus

has been applied as a symbol of peace and concord, because the image of a serpent is customarily used for war, hatred, and all other destructive injuries. That their kiss is a sign of peace and concord, none will deny. . . . The rod sometimes indicates discipline, sometimes the power of eloquence. If, then, any grave and pious person, endowed with eloquence, approaches combatants, teaches them that there is no safety in war . . . and shows

[1] Giraldi, *De diis*, p. 414B, citing Hyginus, *Poeticon astronomicon*, vii, 'Lyra'; cf. Alciati, *Emblemata*, p. 427, and our Pl. 14b, from Cartari. For other meanings of the caduceus, and for the classical authorities, see Tervarent, s.v. 'Caducée,' cols. 57–58, and 'Deux serpents,' col. 350. Particularly relevant, perhaps, in view of Spenser's connection with Van der Noodt, is the latter's use of the emblem to signify Amity (see 'Deux serpents,' i).

them that all wars are destructive and pernicious . . . he will courteously draw their discordant souls into concord, and will bind the two serpents— that is, their mutual hatred—into one, by the rod of his teaching.[1]

The olive wreath was also an emblem of peace; and olive appears with the caduceus on a Vespasian coin, described by Valeriano, that has the inscription 'PAX AUGUSTI.'[2]

These and similar interpretations of the caduceus do something to make the magical conclusion of Triamond's and Cambell's wrath more intelligible. It would appear that the iconography of Cambina's caduceus is intended as a silent comment upon her actions, explaining how her magical impact is in reality prepared for by her earlier eloquence. This eloquence itself displays the mercurial quality of *mixture*:

> Amongst her teares immixing prayers meeke,
> And with her prayers reasons to restraine.
>
> (IV. iii. 47)

The symbolism of the caduceus also underlies the statement that the mighty spirits of the pacified combatants are 'bound' with a yet mightier band. As for the description of the caduceus itself, its individual details assume a far more vital force when they are considered iconographically. Thus, at the moral level, 'lovely *lore*' recalls Valeriano's interpretation of the caduceus as a *doctrinæ virga*.

What is perhaps less obvious is that the mythography of the caduceus is also worked into the symbolism of the episode as a whole; and that it may lead to a solution of the important structural problems presented by this digressive yet titular section of Book IV. In his discussion of the caduceus serpents, Valeriano refers us to Philostratus 'who writes that the ring of Gyges had a stone of a sort that comes from the heads of certain crested serpents in the mountain

---

[1] *Hieroglyphica*, XV. xlv, 'Concordia' (p. 188); quoted in Liceti, *Hieroglyphica*, pp. 235–236. On the caduceus as an emblem of dialectic, see Alciati, loc. cit., and Giraldi, *De diis*, p. 414B, quoting Iamblichus: 'Revera . . . deus quispiam fuit, qui hominibus dialecticam ostendit, et e cœlo demisit: vel ut quidam dicunt, eloquens Mercurius, qui in manibus dialecticæ symbolum gestat, serpentes scilicet se invicem inspicientes.'

[2] *Hieroglyphica*, XV. xlvi, 'Pax': 'numismata tot caduceis insignita, pacis inscriptionem præferunt, ut in numo Caes. Vesp. August . . . sigillum est cum caduceo et ramo olivæ, inscriptione adiecta, PAX AUGUSTI.' Sawtelle (*Var. Sp.*, IV, 186) notes that olive was sometimes regarded as the gift, not of Minerva, but of Mercury. On the olive wreath as an attribute of Concordia in medieval iconography, see Mâle, p. 125, citing Prudentius, Alanus, etc.

parts of India.'[1] There is thus a connection between the caduceus and the ring found by Gyges in the brazen horse: the ring that plays so large a part in Chaucer's *Squire's Tale*, and that Spenser has taken over from there as his own ring of Canacee. Perhaps we should take more seriously than we previously have done Spenser's address to Chaucer, where he acknowledges this theft in a curiously elaborate way, and concludes with a statement of intention:

> I follow here the footing of thy feete,
> That with thy meaning so I may the rather meete,
> (IV. ii. 34)

Is it not possible that Spenser believed that he was taking more than just the names of characters, and a few narrative motifs, from the Squire's Tale? Certainly his complaint against the ravages wrought upon Chaucer's works by time has the effect of directing our attention to the point where the tale is broken off. And we find that the very last lines—the fragmentary 'pars tercia'—are these:

> Appollo whirleth up his chaar so hye,
> Til that the god Mercurius hous, the slye—[2]

More tangibly, the symbolism of the caduceus provides an explanation (indeed, the only available explanation) of the relevance of Agape's consultation of the Fates. The inclusion of a fairly elaborate treatment of the Fates in a Legend of Friendship is not readily seen to be appropriate. In consequence, the critic is tempted to regard this flash-back within a flash-back as a particularly culpable instance of narrative garrulity. Nevertheless, the positioning of the Fates has its structural significance; though a reader's understanding of this is made to depend, as so often with Spenser, on his initiation into a philosophic mystery. We recall that the serpents of Cambina's caduceus were 'by the tailes together firmely bound.' Now in addition to its moral meaning, as Valeriano notes, this knot binding the tails of the serpents has a philosophical significance:

For the caduceus signifies the power of Fate, or of a certain *afflatus* called divine, by which not only our minds, but also all created things, are moved and governed. And so it means the bond by which we are con-

---

[1] *Hieroglyphica*, XV. xliv, 'Concordia'; the reference is to Philostratus, *Life of Apollonius*, III. viii. The myth of Gyges' ring was, of course, a very familiar one, from Plato's use of it in *Republic*, Bk. II.

[2] The fragmentary conclusion was accessible to Spenser in Caxton's print.

nected with God, and the necessity of Fate itself, binding all things together.[1]

Thus, in addition to its purely narrative relevance, Agape's appeal to the Fates has a relevance to the symbolic centre of the whole episode —the caduceus. The positioning of the Fates in Book IV is in accordance with a definite scheme of thought, in terms of which the decorum governing the sequence of events becomes more rational and more satisfying.

The authority for the idea that the knot of the caduceus symbolizes Fate was *Saturnalia*, I. xix. Macrobius may be our sibyl, therefore, as we descend farther in our recovery of its 'lovely lore.' After describing the conformation of the caduceus, and emphasizing the different sex of its serpents, Macrobius tells us that it was anciently analysed into four principal elements:

The Egyptians also extend the symbolism of the caduceus to human generation, that is, to *genesis*; saying that four guardian deities are present to man as he is born: *Daimon*, *Tyche* [Fortune], *Eros*, and *Anangke* [Necessity]. And they think that the two first are to be understood as Sol and Luna. For Sol is the progenitor, the spirit of warmth and light, the begetter and guardian of human life; so that he is believed to be the *Daimon* of him who is born, that is, his god; while Luna is *Tyche*, because she presides over bodies, which are driven about by the vicissitudes of Fortune. Love is signified by the kiss of the serpents; Necessity by their knot.[2]

This passage suggests a further and much wider perspective of Spenser's poem. We may readily see that Macrobius' tetrad of powers governing human genesis corresponds to a distribution of themes among the first four books of the *Faerie Queene*. Thus, Books I and II, as has already been shown, are the books of Sol and Luna respectively; Book III is concerned with love; while Necessity appears in Book IV—and only in Book IV—unfolded in the triad of the Fates. At the same time, however, the fourth book seems to subsume all the books that precede it. Like the caduceus itself, it binds together in concord all four powers of genesis. For, first, it continues the narratives of several amours begun in the previous book; in two

[1] *Commentariorum lib. prior* (appended to the *Hieroglyphica*), Ch. xxvi, 'Potestas et vis fati' (p. 737).

[2] *Saturnalia*, I. xix. 16–17; ed. Eyssenhardt, p. 113. Spenser's 'mutually' (IV. iii. 42) perhaps renders Macrobius' *invicem*: 'hi dracones parte media voluminis sui invicem nodo quem vocant Herculis obligantur.' The whole passage is paraphrased by Valeriano as *Hieroglyphica*, XV. xlii, 'Genesis.'

instances carrying them to a peaceful resolution (the stories of Marinell and Florimell, and of Britomart and Arthegall). Indeed, the continuity between Books III and IV in this respect is so striking that critics have sometimes attempted to treat them 'as a single book on the subject of love.'[1] Secondly, the reconciliation between Britomart and Arthegall in IV. vi—which, as Professor Nottcutt observes, occupies a prominent position at the structural centre of the book— is an exact equivalent to the meeting of solar and lunar principles in the caduceus. This mythological identification, at least, need not rest on oblique suggestions and iconographical inferences: in the explanation of Britomart's dream at Isis Church we are directly informed that Arthegall is imaged by Osyris who 'signifies the Sunne,' and that Britomart has the rôle of Isis who 'doth the Moone portend' (V. vii. 4 and 22).

The union of male and female principles is further explored in one of the two core cantos of the book: the episode of the Temple of Venus. 'Right in the midst' of that Temple (and at the numerical centre of the stanzas devoted to the island) is placed the image that dominates the canto: an idol of *Venus Hermaphroditos*:

> But it in shape and beautie did excell
> All other Idoles, which the heathen adore,
> Farre passing that, which by surpassing skill
> *Phidias* did make in *Paphos* Isle of yore,
> With which that wretched Greeke, that life forlore,
> Did fall in love: yet this much fairer shined,
> But covered with a slender veile afore;
> And both her feete and legs together twyned
> Were with a snake, whose head and tail were fast combyned.

> The cause why she was covered with a vele,
> Was hard to know, for that her Priests the same
> From peoples knowledge labour'd to concele.
> But sooth it was not sure for womanish shame,
> Nor any blemish, which the worke mote blame;
> But for, they say, she hath both kinds in one,
> Both male and female, both under one name:
> She syre and mother is her selfe alone,
> Begets and eke conceives, ne needeth other none.
>
> (IV. x. 40–41)

[1] Lewis, *The Allegory of Love*, p. 338; cf. Kathleen Williams, 'Venus and Diana,' pp. 105–106.

Since the time of Upton, the connections between this Venus and the
Isis of Book V have been emphasized. These connections (through
Venus' 'slender veile' and her priestesses' linen: both attributes of
Isis) certainly exist, and indicate themes common to the two episodes,
such as the mystery of generation and of the female creative principle.
But this should not distract us from the more obvious features of
Spenser's description of Venus, nor from its more direct relation
to the themes we have been tracing. What is most strongly emphasized by Spenser himself is that this Venus unites in herself 'both
kinds in one,/Both male and female, both under one name.' As Upton noted, 'Venus in this double capacity, as male and female,
was named 'Ερμαφρόδιτος 'Ανδρόγυνος.[1] This double god, the *Venus
biformis*, was a mystery which Renaissance mythologists were so fond
of expounding that it might well provide matter for a separate enquiry.[2] For the present purpose, it will be enough to notice the
simple fact that the Venus of IV. x is not the Acidalian Venus of VI.
x, nor any of the ninety or so other Venuses distinguished by the
mythographers; but specifically the Paphian or Cyprian double-
sexed Venus.[3] She has male and female 'under one name' because she is *Venus Hermaphroditos*—a surname combining two
divine components of different sex, Mercury (*Hermes*) and Venus
(*Aphrodite*).

Notice that male and female principles are here united in a single
being; whereas earlier in the book they were represented by separate
characters, who experienced first opposition, then reconciliation and
concord. This more complete and perfect accord, realized in the
union between the persons of Venus Hermaphroditos, also finds

[1] *Var. Sp.*, IV, 231.

[2] The enquiry has already been opened by Wind: see his *Pagan Mysteries*,
pp. 112, 164, and 172 ff.

[3] Giraldi, who distinguishes the various Venuses at considerable length in his
De diis (*Syntagma* xiii; pp. 531–557), gathers the ancient authorities for the *Venus
biformis* or *androgynos* at pp. 542–543: cf. p. 533 on *Venus Hermaphroditos*. The
androgyne image was, of course, customarily interpreted as a symbol of sexual
henosis. Goulart, for example, commenting on Du Bartas' Sixth Day of the
First Week, defines the word *androgyne* as follows: 'This Greeke word, composed
of two divers names, signifieth a *Man–Woman*. . . . Man and woman lawfully
joyned in marriage, are two in one flesh: and an amorous, amiable, and venerable
Androgine, that is to say, a subject composed of Man and Wife, who are but one
body, one flesh, and one bloud, God having made of *Adam* onely, two bodies:
that is to say, *Adam* and *Eve*: and of these two bodies, one onely body, in tying
them together by the knot of holy marriage.'

reflection in the serpent twined round the legs of the idol. For the male and female serpents of the caduceus have now not only been 'bound into one,' but have actually become a single serpent, forming the figure of completion, the circle. In this serpent, 'whose head and tail were fast combyned,' there may, it is true, be intended an allusion to the eternal character of generation.[1] Moreover, in view of the mention of Janus at IV. x. 12, there seems to be a specific allusion to an image of Janus as the cosmic cycle of generation, described by Macrobius: 'the Phoenicians fashion a serpent brought together into a circle, devouring its own tail; so as to show that the world sustains itself out of its own self, and returns upon itself again.'[2] Nevertheless, within the context of the imagery of this particular book, clearly Venus' serpent must also be related to the serpents of the caduceus. That the latter might combine into one, and that this single androgynous serpent might symbolize the one flesh of sexual union, was, indeed, a possibility that had already been considered by the mythographers in the course of their prolonged erotic meditations upon the caduceus.[3]

The idea that *Venus Hermaphroditos* symbolizes an ideal union or henosis, achieved through concord, is given more direct expression in the account of Scudamour's approach to her Temple. In particular, the necessity that he should first pass through the porch where Dame Concord reconciles Love and Hate, before entering the 'inmost Temple,' conveys in the most forcible way possible the dependence of love's union upon an emotional accord. It appears that this part of the episode is especially original. The rest of the island may have its

---

[1] See Tervarent, s.v. 'Serpent en forme de cercle,' i, 'Éternité ou éternel.'

[2] *Saturnalia*, I. ix. 12–13; cf. Tervarent, s.v. 'Serpent en forme de cercle,' iii, 'L'univers.'

[3] See the citations in the *Collectanea* added to Valeriano's *Hieroglyphica*, p. 225. In Macrobius' description of the caduceus serpents these form a circle; and Valeriano relates this motif to sexual generation with the help of Pliny's account of the actual sexual habits of the serpent (*Hieroglyphica*, p. 188). The concealment of the extremities of the serpent twined round the lower part of Spenser's idol also points to a fundamental physiological symbolism—underlying all sexual interpretations of the caduceus—whereby the serpents represent the genital organs. They are 'entrayled' because they are entrails: 'Occultam sane rerum originem per Serpentis effigiem Valentiniani commonstrabant, positionem intestinorum nostrorum, per quæ esca infertur, in exemplum adducentes, quæ serpentinæ spiræ instar in utero delitescens, occultatæ in nobis genitricis substantiæ specimen habeat' (*Hieroglyphica*, p. 187).

resemblances to other Gardens of Harmony or Gardens of Pleasure,[1] just as the idol itself has a densely populated background of ancient and Renaissance mythology. But in his invention of the porch to the Temple, and in the whole radical allegory of Scudamour's difficult entry, to which this incident belongs, Spenser presents psychological insights in a highly original manner. Viewed as psychological allegory, the episode may be regarded as a more extended treatment of what, in the 1590 conclusion to Book III, is compressed into the three stanzas describing the union of Scudamour and Amoret into one 'faire *Hermaphrodite.*' The implication of the Temple of Venus allegory is that after successful passage through the gates of Doubt, Delay, and Daunger—traditional obstacles to the lover's enjoyment of his mistress's final *don de mercy*[2]—there is yet one more threshold to be passed before he attains the inmost temple of the one flesh. This further threshold, which has revealed itself only to a deeper psychological insight than that which discerned its predecessors, is occasioned by the ambivalence of sexual passion itself. We recall that it is with the utmost difficulty that the mature and amiable Dame Concord, whose appearance 'shewed great womanhood,' is able to achieve a reconciliation (hardly peace and friendship) between the brother impulses Love and Hate. The latter are portrayed as young men 'of contrarie natures,' strongly armed because mutually fearful. Love, who is the younger brother (presumably because in Scholastic analyses of the passions hatred and other feelings of repulsion were treated as modifications of more primary feelings of attraction; so that Hate had, as it were, a longer history than Love), is also stronger; if he were not, the lover would not now be approaching the Temple. Hate is strong enough, however, for Scudamour to be 'halfe dismayed' as he enters the gate open to receive him; so that Dame Concord has to entertain him 'in gentle wise,' allowing him to pass between her and Love, and making Hate refrain from his 'wicked

---

[1] In addition to the references given in *Var. Sp.*, IV, 222, see Wind's discussion of Gardens of Harmony and Gardens of Pleasure, in his *Bellini's Feast of the Gods*, p. 49. In such gardens Mercury not uncommonly presided.

[2] At least, Delay and Daunger were traditional (for their background in medieval love allegory, see *Var. Sp.*, IV, 220–221); Doubt, who is a more original figure, is discussed below. The nearest analogue to Spenser's porch of Concord is in Boccaccio's *La Teseide*, VII. 58 ff., imitated by Chaucer in *Parlement of Foules*, ll. 239–245 (see *Var. Sp.*, IV, 226); but there the figure in the porch is simply Peace, and no question arises of difficulty in passing the threshold.

will.' That is to say, it is only by the help of Concord, or, as we might put it, through the integration of aggressive and erotic impulses, that Scudamour can enter the Temple of *Venus Hermaphroditos*.

We may be at a loss to know how far Spenser's psychologizing is interiorized: to decide whether the aggression which causes 'perill' on the threshold of the open gate, and impedes Scudamour's penetration of the Temple, is his own; or whether it is that demonstrated by the woman he loves. But certainly we would be mistaken in merely referring the incident, as is sometimes done, to Empedocles' doctrine of Love and Hate as opposed metaphysical principles; or even (though this might have more plausibility) to 'the union of Discord and Concord . . . the Orphic-Neoplatonic "principle of generation." '[1] Everything points to a psychologizing mode, and to continuity between this gate and those on the bridge connecting the island with the mainland. And the bridge-gates undeniably represent psychological impediments. This is perhaps true even of Spenser's portrayal of Doubt with

> a double face,
> Th'one forward looking, th'other backeward bent,
> Therein resembling *Janus* auncient,
> Which hath in charge the ingate of the yeare:
> And evermore his eyes about him went,
> As if some proved perill he did feare,
> Or did misdoubt some ill, whose cause did not appeare.
>
> (IV. x. 12)

Janus, in his capacity as *Consivius a conserendo*, is in himself quite a proper guardian for a place of generation. But one wonders whether he is not also introduced, in this particular way, because the opening of his gate is associated with dire strife, and because the uncommitted fearfulness of Doubt inhibits the lover's entry upon a new generative cycle, a new year.[2]

ii

If the caduceus and its symbolic expansion provides Book IV with one centre of co-ordination, another is provided by Mercury's zodiacal house, Gemini (Pl. 15a). It is well known that the Heavenly Twins

---

[1] See Wind, *Pagan Mysteries*, p. 139, n. 3.

[2] The connection of Janus' open gate with war is too familiar to require documentation here. His bridge cult, which may be less so, has been studied by L. A. Holland in *Janus and the Bridge* (Rome, 1962).

were regarded in Neoplatonic mythology as implying the theme of Concord. Leda's four children, as Professor Wind has recently reminded us, were thought of as antithetical twins: Castor and Pollux represented *concordia*, Helen and Clytemnestra *discordia*.[1] Less familiar, perhaps, is the relation between Gemini and the hermaphrodite or androgyne. In medieval calendrical art Gemini was sometimes represented, not by two young men, but by linked male and female figures (Pl. 15b). It was this type which Du Bartas had in mind when, explaining the origin of each of the zodiacal signs in turn, he writes that 'In form . . . Of *Twins*' our elders put the third sign:

> because then, of two Sexes
> Kinde-cruell *Cupid* one whole body mixes:
> Then all things couple, then Fruits double growe.[2]

Signifying, as it does, both the theme of concord and that of generation, Gemini thus embraces the two main concerns of Book IV.

Throughout the action of the book, the motif of twinship and the related motif of physical likeness (apparent twinship) are prominent. So prominent, indeed, that one wonders how they can have passed without notice. Actual twins occur not only at the Temple of Venus, where Peace and Friendship are the twin daughters of Concord;[3] but also in the narrative allegory, much of which is devoted to the adventures of Amoret and Belphœbe. It was explained in the previous book that Amoret and Belphœbe are the twin daughters of

---

[1] See Wind, *Pagan Mysteries*, p. 139 and nn. The Twins were not always identified, however, as Castor and Pollux. Other possibilities are listed by the Jesuit astronomer Giovanni-Battista Riccioli (b. 1598, d. 1671) in his *Almagestum novum*, Vol. I (Bologna, 1651), p. 400; and the whole matter is dealt with at length in J. Rendel Harris' authoritative study, *The Cult of the Heavenly Twins* (Cambridge, 1906). Those who prefer their anthropology in fictional form will find a useful compendium of the lore of Gemini in John Barth's *The Sot-Weed Factor* (New York, 1960), Pt. III, Ch. ii: 'A Layman's Pandect of Geminology Compended by Henry Burlingame, Cosmophilist.'

[2] The origin of this type is obscure. We may either conjecture that it was based on a simple association of the month of May, and its sign, with love; or that (if it had any mythological basis) it was related to the Phœbus–Phœbe cult which, as Harris shows, displaced earlier Heavenly Twin cults such as that of Hilaeira and Phœbe. On medieval representations of Gemini, see Harry Bober, 'The zodiacal miniature of the *Très riches heures*.' Ruskin notes a representation of Gemini as bridegroom and bride in the north porch at Amiens (*The Bible of Amiens*, Ch. iv, sect. 147).

[3] IV. x. 34: '*Concord* she cleeped was in common reed, / Mother of blessed *Peace*, and *Friendship* trew; / They both her twins, both borne of heavenly seed.'

Chrysogone. Not until IV. vii, however, do the twins meet one another: a fact which makes their confrontation in that painful scene all the more dramatic.[1] The motif of perfect physical likeness is developed in the false Florimell's impersonation of the true, as well as in the story of Placidas and Amyas. The latter are such close doubles that Placidas is able to deceive even the infatuated Pœana (IV. viii. 56–59). These aspects of Book IV may be passed over briefly, since they have already received notice in our discussion of the tetrad. As we saw, Spenser modifies the Platonic tetrad of two means, by adding the feature of likeness between the centre terms. But now the reason for that modification emerges. It is really a synthesis of two different symbols of mercurian concord: the Twins and the tetrad.

When we pass beyond the fable of Book IV to its moral content we find again and again that the challenge Spenser is presenting resembles that presented by the myth of Castor and Pollux, the archetypal twins with whom the sign Gemini was usually identified. The geminologist Rendel Harris has remarked that the Greek mythologists added, to the fundamental myth of a mortal and an immortal twin,

a beautiful description of the discontent of the deified Polydeuces [Pollux] because his brother could not share his honours with him, and his determination not to enjoy Heaven alone, together with an account of the way in which Zeus rewarded the disinterested affection of Polydeuces and divided immortality for one between two, thus furnishing the Greek moralists with their classical instance of the higher forms of love in sacrifice.[2]

Spenser would never, of course, toy with the notion of human immortality. Yet there is an instance of the postponement of death by the sharing of *mortal* life, in his legend of Priamond, Diamond, and Triamond: a legend not, it is true, about twins, but about triplets 'borne at one burden' (IV. ii. 41). Moreover, it is self-sacrificing love that characterizes Book IV generally. This is what distinguishes it in emotional tone from Book III, where love is for the most part either

---

[1] Harris (*The Cult of the Heavenly Twins*, Ch. v) notes that female variants of the Heavenly Twins are common. His descriptions of the Hilaeira–Phœbe cult (mentioned by Pausanias) and the Apollo (Phœbus)–Artemis (Phœbe) cult are especially interesting in view of Belphœbe's characterization as an Artemisian figure.

[2] Ibid., p. 4.

unrequited, or selfish and predatory, or overmasteringly passionate. On the whole, there is more placidity about the loves of Book IV: more mutual generosity and altruism. When the wounded Triamond is unable to fight on the second day of Satyrane's tournament Cambell impersonates him and risks his life to 'purchase honour in his friends behalve'; only to be taken prisoner and rescued, in his turn, by Triamond:

> Then all with one consent did yeeld the prize
> To *Triamond* and *Cambell* as the best.
> But *Triamond* to *Cambell* it relest.
> And *Cambell* it to *Triamond* transferd;
> Each labouring t'advance the others gest,
> And make his praise before his owne preferd.
>
> (IV. iv. 36)

And it is in a similar spirit that Placidas allows himself to be taken for Amyas, and gives up his freedom for his friend. Such disinterested substitutions are so strongly reminiscent of Pollux's substitution for Castor that we can only conclude that the latter are omitted from the list of heroic friends at IV. x. 27, because to mention them there would have been supererogatory.

The fact that twins also occur as a subsidiary motif in Book III is not a serious difficulty.[1] While the procreation of Amoret and Belphœbe is recounted in flash-back at III. vi. 5–10, they are separated at birth, and their stories are never brought together until Book IV. Again, Argante and Ollyphant are twins (III. vii. 47), but twins of a perverse kind, bearing the same relation to those of Book IV as the evil Venus of the Bower bears to the good Venus of the Garden. These are instances of the overlapping of themes from book to book, which we meet at each stage of the poem. But an overlap is particularly natural between Books III and IV. These books are not only united by the close connection between their respective subjects, by narrative links, and by a shared guardian deity (Venus), but also by a bond of chronology. For, if the chronological structure of the poem were analysed it could be shown that, while the action of each of the other books occupies the space of a year, the actions of Books III and IV (delimited temporally as they are by the seven-month terms of

---

[1] *Pace* J. H. Walter, who assigns Bk. III to Gemini, ignoring the larger number of twins in Bk. IV ('*The Faerie Queene*: Alterations and Structure,' *MLR*, XXXVI (1941)).

Florimell's and Amoret's imprisonments) *together occupy only one year*.[1]

iii

The story of Marinell and Florimell, and the spousal of Thames and Medway, which have not yet been mentioned, in my view contain too much unrecognized political allusion to be susceptible to brief exposition. A few points with respect to their mythological and schematic content, however, may be ventured.

Marinell in his sickness is twice attended (at IV. xi. 6–7 and IV. xii. 23–24) by a leech called Tryphon. This marine surgeon was to some extent a mythological invention of Spenser's; Selden notices it as such in his illustrations to Drayton's *Poly-Olbion*.[2] But the point of the innovation has not been firmly grasped by modern commentators. The only note on Tryphon in the *Variorum Spenser* is Lotspeich's:

No god by this name appears in classical literature, nor, it would seem, anywhere before Spenser except in Boccaccio 7. 36, where the name occurs as a mis-reading for 'Trophonius' in Cicero, *Nat. Deor.* 3. 22. Boccaccio says: 'Cicero autem ubi de naturis (*sic*) deorum hunc Mercurium, qui Triphon appellatus est, filium dicit fuisse Valentis et Coronidis. Leontius autem addit, dicens eum fratrem fuisse Aesculapii medici. . . .' Spenser has built up his character from a mere name and from the remark that the one named was a brother of Aesculapius—hence probably a physician. The name itself, by its resemblance to Triton, is perhaps reason enough for giving it to a sea-god. (Vol. III, p. 243.)

That Spenser's allusion has far more point than this, soon appears. The family relationship between Æsculapius and Trophonius is not deployed merely to justify conferring upon the latter medical qualifications. It also, and far more significantly, draws our attention to the structural parallel between *Spenser's* Æsculapius and *Spenser's* Tryphon. Just as the wounded Sansjoy is taken to the underworld

---

[1] It will be gathered that I interpret the twelve days of Gloriana's feast (in the Letter to Raleigh) as twelve *annual* feast days: as a poetic rendering, in fact, of Elizabeth's Accession Day festival. Each day of the feast occasions an adventure, which occupies one year, and one book, of the poem—except that for Bks. III–IV there is only one adventure, Scudamour's. The 'naturalistic' chronology of the poem is really a separate subject; but I may mention here that the astronomical information given at II. ii. 44 and 46 is conformable with a mid-November date for Gloriana's feast. The date of Elizabeth's Accession Day anniversary festival was 17th November.

[2] See the note to *Poly-Olbion*, XI. 64: 'justifiable . . . as well as to make *Tryphon* their surgeon, which our excellent *Spenser* hath done.'

and entrusted to the care of Æsculapius (I. v. 36–44), so Marinell is attended by Tryphon. In each case the leechcraft is of a lower order when compared with the transcendent healing power of '*Apollo* King of Leaches' (IV. xii. 25); though even Apollo cannot cure the amorous wound of Marinell. Now, as we have seen, within the mythological pattern of Book I Æsculapius functions as a chthonic antitype to the book's Olympian guardian, Apollo. If our structural theory is correct, then, the parallel between the two episodes carries the implication that Tryphon similarly constitutes a chthonic antitype to Mercury. And this is precisely what we find Trophonius to be, when we look him up in Giraldi's *De diis gentium*. For Giraldi identifies Trophonius not only as an avatar of Mercury, but as '*Chthonius Hermes*, interpreted by many as an infernal Mercury, by others as an earthly or terrestrial Mercury.' This identification he bases on the same obscure Ciceronian passage that Boccaccio more perfunctorily adduced: 'One Mercury had Coelus for his father, and Dies for his mother; another, who is said to dwell in a cavern, and is the same as Trophonius, is the son of Valens and Phoronis.'[1]

The spousal of Thames and Medway has rightly been regarded as a celebration of the theme of concord. There has been little attempt, however, to attach any more precise meaning to the canto except at the purely descriptive and topographical level. Hardly anyone has asked the obvious question, why Spenser should make a comparatively small Kentish river such as Medway the 'proud Nymph' who for so long has rejected Thames's wooing. (Spousals of Thames and Medway had not been previously celebrated; though they were to be recelebrated in *Poly-Olbion*, XVIII.) Moreover, although much of the material of the canto is overtly political and historical, and although the English tradition of river epithalamia is also political and historical, only one scholar has put forward an overall interpretation of the wedding along these lines.[2] That interpretation is based

---

[1] *De diis*, *Syntagma* ix, pp. 420–421; cf. Cicero, *De nat. deor.*, III. xxii and Conti, *Mythologiæ*, V. v, p. 435. The spelling Triphonius can hardly have been peculiar to Boccaccio, as Lotspeich (*Var. Sp.*, III, 243) suggests; since Giraldi says that 'quidam Triphonium legant.' As usual, Spenser's mythology has not been understood because it has been read in the light of medieval and popular authorities, not Renaissance erudite authorities.

[2] A. M. Buchan, 'The political allegory of Book IV of *The Faerie Queene*,' *ELH*, XI (1944), 237–248; the following quotation is from p. 245. The background of river epithalamiums is discussed in this article, and in *Var. Sp.* (nn. to *F.Q.*, IV. xi; also *Minor Poems*, Appendix, '*Prothalamion*'). As Buchan points out (p.

on the assumption—first made by Upton—that the Medway is chosen because it flows past Penshurst, the seat of the Sidney family:

The Medway is Sidney and the policy he represented. It is married to the Thames, that is, it becomes the national policy of the country. To this marriage come, not only the rivers of England, but those of Ireland too. Spenser is saying that every section of England and Ireland must subscribe to this policy. But only harmony among the leaders, a renewal of friendship between Essex and Raleigh,—and this is the theme of Book IV,—will achieve the unity of purpose needed to guarantee success.

The arguments advanced in support of this thesis are interesting and ingenious—and very nearly plausible. They fail, however, to provide adequately for the damaging objections that Sidney was ten years dead when the second part of the *Faerie Queene* was published, and that the Medway had other and more obvious associations.

It is clear that, just as the Medway is representative of Kent, so the Thames is representative of England as a whole. The question we should ask, therefore, is, What spouse is most appropriate for England? If we follow the thought-forms of Spenser's time there is only one possible answer to this question: the English sovereign, Queen Elizabeth. Now, the poetic use of Kent as the home of Elizabeth (based on the fact that her royal palace at Greenwich was in that county) can be paralleled in *The Shepheardes Calender*. And in that poem, too, as Professor McLane has shown us,[1] the metonymy occurs in a political allegory about the English nation's wooing of its sovereign. The happier outcome of the lover's suit in *Faerie Queene*, IV, is no doubt due to the difference of genre, as well as to Elizabeth's adoption, in the intervening years, of a more militantly Protestant foreign policy.

At the same time, remembering that the spousal of Thames and Medway is closely related in kind to the 'Thamesis et Isis connubium' quoted in Camden's *Britannia*, which announces itself as a celebration of the union of 'Concord with Faith,'[2] we may reasonably take it that Spenser intended a moral or generalized meaning as well. It

[1] *Spenser's 'Shepheardes Calender,'* especially pp. 31–32, 37.

[2] '. . . tandem descenditur una / In thalamum, quo iuncta FIDE CONCORDIA sancta, / Splendida conceptis sancit connubia verbis': see Buchan, pp. 241–242.

242), there were traditional reasons for marrying Tama and Isis, none for marrying Thames and Medway. Note that Spenser has combined the convention of river marriage with the popular motif of the Feast of the Gods—on which, see Wind, *Bellini's Feast of the Gods*, and Henry Bardon, *Le festin des dieux* (Paris, 1960).

seems clear that this assumption is justified, when we find that
William Harrison explains the name Medway as descriptive of the
river's *mean position*: 'The Midwaie water is called in Latine Medevia
(as some write) bicause the course thereof is midwaie in a manner
between London and . . . Canturburie.'[1] Assuming, then, that Medway in some sense designates a mean, it seems natural to connect the
spousal of Thames and Medway with the philosophical subject of
Book IV: the double mean of stable concord. If we make this connection, and think of both Thames and Medway as means, the
former—who results himself from the confluence of many tributaries,
and who is accompanied by 'neighbour floods,' all of whom 'in
love agree' (xi. 40)—will correspond to the mean of Friendship;
while the latter will presumably correspond to the mean of Peace.
But is there any other reason why Medway should correspond to the
mean of Peace? Fortunately there is. Indeed, *only* if Medway represents Peace can we adequately account for the curious comparison by
which Thames, crowned with the towers of London, is likened to 'the
mother of the Gods . . . Old *Cybele*' (xi. 27–28). The Thames has to
be Cybele, that is, Ceres, because the Medway is Peace, and, as every
spectator at political festivals knew, *Pax Cereris amica.*[2] (Cartari, we
should note, discusses this motif under the heading 'Mercury.') After
the manner of the pageant composer, Spenser has worked together
several festival motifs, in themselves traditional, but original in their
fresh combination and their unusual river-god setting. In connection
with the idea that peace is the concomitant of (agricultural) prosperity,
it is perhaps relevant that Kent was regarded as the richest part of
England, 'Whose golden gardens seem th' *Hesperides* to mock.'[3]

[1] Cit. *Var. Sp.*, IV, 272.
[2] Cartari discusses this theme in the section headed 'Mercurius' (*Imagines
deorum* (Lyons, 1581), p. 212); cf. Pl. 14b. Though the iconography of Medua is
too complex to explore here, it may be noted that her 'vesture of unknowen
geare . . . seem'd like silver . . . wav'd upon, like water Chamelot.' It is this
argentum liquidum, or mercury, that manifests the divinity of the clothing 'to let
men plainely wot, / It was no mortall worke.'
[3] *Poly-Olbion*, XVIII. 671; cf. 659 ff.: 'O famous *Kent*, . . . / What country hath
this Isle that can compare with thee, / Which hast within thyself as much as thou
canst wish? / Thy conies, ven'son, fruit; thy sorts of fowl and fish: / As what with
strength comports, thy hay, thy corn, thy wood: / Nor anything doth want, that
anywhere is good.' The Flora-like appearance of Medua ('with flowres be-
scattered, / The which ambrosiall odours forth did throw / To all about, and all
her shoulders spred / As a new spring') points to a similar symbolism in the
Spenserian passage.

These significances may seem less disparate if we try to imagine the kind of peace Spenser is likely to have been celebrating, not long after 1588. Speaking in terms of caduceus symbolism, we might call it an armed or threatful peace—the caduceus as 'minæ et pax.'[1] And is it not in terms of precisely this ideal of armed peacefulness that Spenser portrays the Queen, under the image of Britomart? Supporting this hypothesis is the significance of the historical Medway. For its association with Penshurst and the Sidneys was merely in the nature of a happy accident for Spenser. It was far better known, in the 1590s, as the principal centre of naval and overseas military operations. By that time the Crown's naval activity had shifted from the Channel to the Thames estuary, and a new naval base had been established at Chatham on the Medway. (This position, facing the Spanish threat from the Netherlands, was more in accord with the altered European situation.[2]) Certainly the river had this significance for Drayton, who followed Spenser closely enough in his *Poly-Olbion* to include a wedding of Thames and Medway. Drayton's Medway is the river

> Whose bosom doth so please her Sovereign (with her pride)
> Whereas the Royal Fleet continually doth ride. . . .
>
> (*Poly-Olbion*, XVIII. 93)

> This *Medway* still had nurs'd those Navies in her road,
> Our Armies that had oft to conquest borne abroad;
> And not a man of ours, for arms hath famous been,
> Whom she not going out, or coming in hath seen:
> Or by some passing ship, hath news to her been brought,
> What brave exploits they did; as where, and how, they fought.
>
> (Ibid., XVIII. 109)

Accordingly, the bride is assigned a 535-line song recounting 'what to the *English* Name immortal praise should bring': in other words, a catalogue of the military heroes who have 'illustrated this *Isle*.'

Some such approach offers the best chance of accommodating Spenser's spousal of Thames and Medway within the schematic structure of Book IV as a whole. The canto, I would suggest, is far from being merely descriptive. It is a festival piece, celebrating a

[1] See Valeriano, *Hieroglyphica*, XV. xliii.
[2] On the naval importance of the Medway, see J. A. Williamson, *The English Channel* (London, 1959), pp. 180 f. Cf. Camden, *Annales*, s.v. 1576, where Medway is described as 'the road where the fleet usually anchors.'

visionary England—and Ireland—united in friendly alliance, and married to a sovereign whose policy promises a strong and prosperous peace.

iv

Throughout the narrative cantos of Book IV, as an earlier chapter has shown, the dominating number symbol is simply the concordant tetrad with two mean terms. However, in the three most elaborate episodes of the book—those of the tournament of Florimell's cestus, of the Temple of Venus, and of the spousal of Thames and Medway— the numerological patterns are by contrast somewhat complex. The last-named episode, indeed, is perhaps the most ambitious essay in this mode that Spenser ever attempted. Many subsidiary ideas naturally receive expression in the numerical composition of these 'set pieces.' Nevertheless, a common theme linking all three can be discerned: namely, the astrological influence of Mercury as a force reconciling and holding opposites in concord. In each case the astronomical number that conveys this idea is the Ptolemaic total for Gemini, the house of Mercury—the same sign that figures in the mythic structure of the book. This number is eighteen. As it happens, we have an independent instance of the use of this number, with a similar symbolic purpose, in *Prothalamion*. Much of that poem depends on an analogy between the two bridegrooms and 'the twins of Jove . . . Which decke the Bauldricke of the Heavens bright.'[1] As is well known, Spenser invented for *Prothalamion*, and for *Prothalamion* alone, a quite novel form of stanza. A stanza of how many lines? Why, as many as there are stars in the Heavenly Twins: eighteen.

The canto recounting the tournament, IV. iv, is divided into four almost equal parts, severally devoted to the approach to the tournament, and to the action of its first, second, and third days. The beginning of the following canto tells briefly how the tournament was adjudicated; then a longer account follows, of how the ladies in turn competed for the cestus or girdle of Venus—a competition in the sphere, not of courage and military prowess, but of chastity and

---

[1] Leda in Stanza 3 is related to the Twins theme, in that she is the mother of Castor and Pollux. Daniel H. Woodward ('Some themes in Spenser's "Prothalamion," ' *ELH*, XXIX (1962), 34–47) appears to have seen this, since he speaks of the bridegrooms as sons of the swan; but he fails to grasp the significance of the Twins as a symbol of concord, and their relevance in a bethrothal poem.

beauty. The complementary character of these two spheres of rivalry is made clear in the opening stanza of Canto v:

> It hath bene through all ages ever seene,
> That with the praise of armes and chevalrie,
> The prize of beautie still hath joyned beene;
> And that for reasons speciall privitie:
> For either doth on other much relie.
>
> (IV. v. 1)

That the two spheres are the domains of Mars and Venus, Spenser takes care to remind us: not only by introducing the periphrasis whereby the judges descend 'into the Martian field' (IV. v. 6) but also by recalling the love borne by the original owner of the cestus, Venus, for her 'beloved Paramoure, / The God of warre' (IV. v. 5). The complementary relationship between the martian and venerean fields of rivalry, we find, receives numerological expression in the numbers of male and female characters participating. Most obviously, perhaps, the unparticularized 'hundred knights' of IV. iv. 31 match the unparticularized 'hundred Ladies' of IV. v. 11. But it is more interesting to notice that, of the named characters, eight are female: Cambina, Canacee, Duessa, Lucida, Amoret, Snowy-Florimell, Ate, and Britomart. And eight, as we know, is the Ptolemaic number of Libra, the house of Venus. Complementary to this total is that of the knights particularized as jousting in the tournament. As the accompanying table shows, there are twenty-one such knights: the Ptolemaic number of Mars' house, Scorpio. This total includes the seven unnamed knights of IV. iv. 41, who undoubtedly take part in the jousting. A more dubious case, however, could also be made for including two guards who hold Cambell prisoner at IV. iv. 34; as well as Britomart, who is only apparently a knight. These three characters of doubtful status correspond to the three *stellæ informatæ* of Scorpio, and bring the most inclusive count to twenty-four, the larger Ptolemaic total for the constellation. (It should be noted that the total number of formal courses run in the tournament is also twenty-one.) Further, of the 17 challengers who defend the cestus of Venus, 8 are named and 9 unnamed—another allusion to the 8 + 9 stars of Libra, Venus' House. The 7 unnamed knights defeated by Arthegall on the last day clearly have little significance in terms of the fable: their function is as numerological makeweights.

Between the complementary values of Mars and Venus, it is the office of Mercury to strike a harmonious balance: to educe that Harmony who is mythologically the offspring of their union.[1] As we have already seen, the influence of Mercury at the tournament is expressed numerically in the tetradic grouping whereby 'the knights in couples marcht, with ladies linckt attone.'[2] But it is also expressed

THE TOURNAMENT OF THE CESTUS

	Location	Challenger		Opponent	Number of course
DAY I	Stanza 17	1. Satyrane	*v.*	2. Bruncheval	i
	Stanza 19	3. Ferramont	*v.*	4. Blandamour	ii
	Stanza 19	Ferramont	*v.*	5. Paridell	iii
	Stanza 20	(Ferramont	*v.*	6. Braggadocchio	not run)
	Stanza 20	Ferramont	*v.*	7. Triamond	iv
	Stanza 21	8. Devon	*v.*	Triamond	v
	Stanza 21	9. Douglas	*v.*	Triamond	vi
	Stanza 21	10. Paliumord	*v.*	Triamond	vii
	Stanza 24	Satyrane	*v.*	Triamond	viii
DAY II	Stanzas 26–36	Satyrane	*v.*	11. Cambell	
		(Two guards	*v.*	Cambell and Triamond)	
DAY III	Stanza 37	Satyrane			
	Stanza 40	12. Sanglier	*v.*	13. Arthegall	ix
	Stanza 40	14. Brianor	*v.*	Arthegall	x
	Stanza 41	15–21. Seven unnamed knights	*v.*	Arthegall	xi–xvii
	Stanza 44	Britomart	*v.*	Arthegall	xviii
	Stanza 44	Britomart	*v.*	Cambell	xix
	Stanza 45	Britomart	*v.*	Triamond	xx
	Stanza 45	Britomart	*v.*	Blandamour	xxi

through patterns based on eighteen, the Ptolemaic setting of Gemini. This total is reached by several independent counts. Most obviously, the total number of knights named as present at any time during the

[1] On Harmony as the daughter of Mars and Venus, see Wind, *Pagan Mysteries*, pp. 81 ff.; and Panofsky, *Studies in Iconology*, p. 163.

[2] IV. iv. 14. The table reveals similar conformations in the running of the tournament courses. Notice, e.g., the series of four challengers defeated by Triamond, which balances the series of four opponents defeated by Britomart: Arthegall, Cambell, Triamond, and Blandamour. The latter four form a tetrad whose mean terms are the friends Cambell and Triamond, and whose extreme terms are the erotic Blandamour and the (at this stage) anti-erotic Arthegall. (Cf. the similar tetrad at IV. ix. 20, discussed in Ch. iv above.) Also, on the middle day of the tournament Cambell is in a middle position between two guards, but is helpless to overcome them until he is joined by a second mean—again Triamond.

whole course of the episode, either at the tournament or the cestus contest, is eighteen.[1] Secondly, taking the cestus contest alone, the number of knights *and ladies* named is again eighteen. These are arranged, moreover, in such a way as to suggest a regular pattern: first come six couples (Cambell and Cambina; Triamond and Canacee; Paridell and Duessa; Ferramont and Lucida; Britomart and Amoret; Blandamour and Snowy-Florimell); then the Squire of Dames (13); Arthegall (14); Satyrane (15); Ate (16); Braggadocchio (17); and Erivan (18). Finally, taking the tournament by itself, it is probable (though not certain) that the eighteen of concord here makes yet another appearance. We note that the jousting of the first and third days is sharply distinguished from that of the second. The second day's fighting—no doubt in accordance with the nature of the dyad—is a disorderly mêlée. Spenser records only one distinct encounter on that day. On the uneven days, by contrast, separate courses, recounted in considerable detail, are run in an orderly manner by a limited number of knights. If, then, we consider the total numbers of male knights running courses on each individual day, we find that on the first day there are ten named knights, on the second day two, and on the last day six. In other words, a grand total of eighteen. The seven unnamed knights jousting on the last day correspond to the seven *stellæ informatæ* of the constellation Gemini.

The orderly ceremoniousness of the jousting and the cestus competition symbolizes the concord that should reconcile conflicting interests in a society. As the event proves, however, the forces of discord are in this instance too strong. In spite of the friendship and co-operative spirit with which Cambell and Triamond mutually assist and yield to one another, Ate's influence prevails, and the gathering breaks up in discord. Significantly, the last knight to be mentioned is Erivan, or Vain Strife. As a logical sequel, there follows the episode of Care's smithy. The jealousy of Vulcan, which must be excluded if Mars and Venus are to be brought into harmony, has returned, and threatens to rive even the 'rocke of Diamond' of the lover's faith.[2]

[1] 1. Satyrane, 2. Ferramont, 3. Devon, 4. Douglas, 5. Paliumord, 6. Bruncheval, 7. Blandamour, 8. Paridell, 9. Braggadocchio, 10. Triamond, 11. Cambell, 12. Sanglier, 13. Brianor, 14. Britomart, 15. Arthegall, 16. Scudamour, 17. Squire of Dames, and 18. Erivan.

[2] IV. v. 37: see Tervarent, s.v. 'Diamant,' ii: 'La bonne foi'; cf. Camden, *Remaines* (London, 1870), p. 356. On Vulcan's threat to the harmony of Mars

This breaking of concord is rendered numerologically in a most ingenious way. For the Gemini total, the eighteen of concord, is repeatedly impaired by significant departures from the pattern. In the count of knights running courses on the three separate days of the tournament Braggadocchio was included. He is unlike the other knights counted, however, in that when his turn comes he refuses to run his course (IV. iv. 20). Thus, the same knight whose claim to the snowy Florimell later occasions the disruption of the company, by his cowardice prevents the sum of the totals of male knights *actually completing their courses* from reaching eighteen. The number of concord is at once indicated and withheld. Similarly, the count of named knights present either at the tournament or the cestus contest also included the 'mock-knight' Braggadocchio. Finally, in the fifth canto Arthegall is present at Stanza 9, but when snowy Florimell is awarded to him at Stanza 21 he fails to come forward to take his prize, since he has already left, piqued by the result of the tournament adjudication. His failure to occupy the place of honour (which is usurped by Braggadocchio, just as at the later tournament in V. iii) prevents the number of characters named and present during the latter part of the adjudication from reaching the eighteen of concord.[1] In other words, the society portrayed lacks the justice and sovereignty, represented by Arthegall, that are necessary to concord. The fifth book, which sees the unmasking of Braggadocchio and the investiture of Arthegall with authority (V. iii. 36 and V. vii. 43), will supply this defect of justice.

Although several features of the tournament episode remain obscure, we can at least be sure that it is not intended merely as a portrayal of physical conflict. (If it were so, we might be excused for finding it boring.) It is meant rather as a poetic imitation of a *balletic* tournament, of a kind which actually took place in the sixteenth

---

[1] It is true that if we count Glauce, who may be *presumed* present during the cestus contest, the 18 of concord can be preserved. But she is not named until IV. v. 31, when the gathering has already broken up. In each of the cases considered the number *actually* produced by the default is 17: an '*infaustus*' number in Pythagorean lore, because it 'comes between' 16 and 18 (which form the tonic ratio 8 : 9) and disrupts their harmony; see Bongo, Pt. II, p. 41. It will be noted that Erivan ('Vain Strife') is the 17th *male* named in the episode.

---

and Venus, see Wind's discussion of Mantegna's *Parnassus*, in *Bellini's Feast of the Gods*, pp. 9–20.

century. Miss Frances Yates' recent account of tournaments at the Valois court has indicated some of the ways in which ideals of political and cosmic order were set forth by means of symbolic arrangements.[1] The symbolism of place and number in Spenser's tournament is in a similar mode.

V

The scheme of characters in the Temple of Venus episode is simpler, and should be intelligible almost as soon as it is set out in tabular form:

Locality	Division	Character	Number of characters	Sign	Planet
IV. x. 4–10	MAINLAND	Scudamour and twenty Knights	21	SCORPIO	MARS
IV. x. 11–20	Bridge	Doubt, Delay, and Daunger	3		
IV. x. 27	ISLAND	Scudamour	1	GEMINI	MERCURY
		Virtuous lovers: Hercules to Pythias	12		
IV. x. 31–36		Concord, Love and Hate	3		
IV. x. 39–42		Venus	1		
IV. x. 43		Worshipper	1		
IV. x. 49–52		Bevy of damsels: Womanhood, Shamefastnesse, Cherefulnesse, Modestie, Curtesie, Silence, Obedience, and Amoret	8	LIBRA	VENUS

The preliminary section (stanzas 1–20) is concerned with Scudamour's defeat of the twenty knights who guard the castle of Venus, and with his negotiation of the gates on the bridge leading to the 'island strong.' This first phase of the episode, marked by struggle and difficulty, is separated from those that follow by the passage across the river. Once across, Scudamour finds harmony and concord: 'having past all perill,' he is within the compass of an island that seems 'the onely pleasant and delightfull place . . . ever troden,' a 'second paradise,'

[1] Frances A. Yates, *The Valois Tapestries* (London, 1959).

a 'joyous place.' The character-totals are in keeping with the contrast in emotional tone between the milieux on either side of this main geographical division. For the mainland characters number twenty-one, the Ptolemaic total for Scorpio, the House of Mars.[1] (Since it is uncertain whether Doubt, Delay, and Daunger on the bridge should be included in the mainland count, these characters correspond to the three *stellæ informatæ* that bring Scorpio's more inclusive total to twenty-four.) Offsetting this Martian sign is a sign of Venus, Libra, represented at the other end of the canto by the bevy of eight damsels 'at the Idoles feet apart.' The damsels, it should be noticed, are described in four stanzas (49–52) that correspond to the four devoted to the knights (7–10).[2] Spenser's use here of the Ptolemaic total for Libra helps to relate the Temple to the other places of Venus in earlier books—especially the Bower of Bliss and the Garden of Adonis—with which he means it to be contrasted and compared.[3]

Between these groups symbolic of Mars and Venus sits Dame Concord, reconciling aggressive and erotic extremes. But the goddess worshipped on the island, as we have seen, is a hermaphroditic Venus, uniting the qualities of *Mercury* and Venus. This, too, is given numerological expression. For, if we confine our count to the characters on the island alone—to the sphere of harmony—we find that in addition to the eight damsels there are just eighteen others: that is, the Ptolemaic total for Gemini, Mercury's House. The

[1] The number may also conceivably contain a topical allusion: a Sir James Scudamore was one of twenty knights in the tournament described in Peele's *Anglorum Feriæ*. See *The Life and Minor Works*, ed. D. H. Horne (New Haven, 1952), pp. 270–274; and cf. the tournament list itself, in College of Arms MS. M.4, printed in S. Anglo, 'Archives of the English Tournament: Score Cheques and Lists,' *Journ. Soc. Archivists*, II (1961).

[2] A. C. Hamilton (*The Structure of Allegory*, p. 165) says that: 'The curious reader will find that this inward motion is carefully patterned in groups of four stanzas: 4–7, introduction; 8–11, the plain before the bridge; 12–15, Doubt and Delay at the first gate; 16–19, Danger at the second gate; 21–24, the description of the island; 25–28, the lovers; 32–35, the allegory of Love and Hate; 39–43, the Idol of Venus; 44–47, the address to Venus; 49–52, the bevy of maidens; 55–58, the actual rape of Amoret.' While this is something of an exaggeration—the allegory of Love and Hate, e.g., occupies Stanzas 32–36, or even 31–36, not 32–35—it is true that a four-stanza modulus of composition is common in Bk. IV generally.

[3] On the connections between the various places of Venus, see T. M. Gang, *'The Faerie Queene'*: *a Demonstration of its Unity* (Bodl. MS B.Litt. d. 604), Ch. ii.

character-total, like the goddess herself, combines Mercury and Venus.[1]

vi

The last of the core cantos of Book IV, that recounting the procession to the spousal of Thames and Medway, is a *tour de force* of numerical composition. Complicated numerology is so little to the modern taste, however, that it would be doing Spenser a disservice to indicate here more than the principal features of the symbolism. The latter is expressed through patterns of at least three different varieties: patterns of character-grouping, patterns of ordinal stanza numbers, and patterns of cardinal stanza numbers. I shall deal with the last variety first.

Since the first seven stanzas of the canto consist of narrative preliminaries not directly concerned with the wedding, the cardinal-number stanza pattern is principally confined to forty-six stanzas. Spenser draws attention to the limitations imposed by his numerical scheme of stanzas in the author-comment at IV. xi. 17:

> But what doe I their names seeke to reherse,
> Which all the world have with their issue fild?
> How can they all in this so narrow verse
> Contayned be, and in small compasse hild?

It is precisely because of the demands of numerical composition that the poet is unable to make his verse wider or his compass larger. As the accompanying table shows, this same stanza not only draws attention to the significance of stanza numbers but also itself marks the largest division in the canto. Up to and including the author-comment stanza, we have an account of 'some part of that great equipage, / Which from great *Neptune* do derive their parentage' (Stanza 17); after it we have those of 'Oceans seede.' The two large divisions thus formed occupy respectively ten and thirty-six stanzas; or, in Pythagorean terms, the decad and the great quaternion—both sacred numbers formed from the *tetractys*.[2] The last stanza of the canto, however, is also, as we shall see, an author-comment on its

---

[1] A further subtlety emerges if the bridge characters are counted with the island characters. Then we have, not $18 + 8$ (Mercury and Venus), but $21 + 8$ (Mars and Venus).

[2] See Plutarch, *De Iside*, 381A; also Adam's commentary on Plato's nuptial number. 36 is the sum of the first four even and the first four odd numbers $(1 + 2 + 3 + 4 + 5 + 6 + 7 + 8 = 36)$.

number symbolism. Thus, the thirty-five-stanza passage IV. xi. 18–52, describing both the groom's and bride's parties and the guests of Ocean's seed, and framed by two stanzas *in persona auctoris*, may be regarded as having a certain independent status. Now thirty-five was the Pythagorean number of harmony and resolution, and was known as the 'marriage age' number. It is with a similar symbolism that the same number is used again as the stanza-total of the suc-ceeding canto, which sees the resolution of the story of Florimell and Marinell, as a result of their presence at Proteus' house, where the spousal of Thames and Medway is celebrated. Thirty-five had this harmonious and generative significance for a particular reason: namely that it represents the sum of twenty-seven and eight, the final terms of the two 'lambda series' in the *Timæus* (1:3:9:27 and 1:2:4:8). As Macrobius puts it,

the first two cubes of all numbers are eight (even) and twenty-seven (odd), the odd being masculine and the even feminine. . . . Let the male and female numbers be joined together, meaning eight and twenty-seven. They make thirty-five. . . .[1]

If our interpretation is sound, then, we ought to find a division of the thirty-five-stanza passage into two sections, of twenty-seven and of eight stanzas; and we ought also to find that the contents of these sections have a masculine–feminine polarity. Both these require-ments are amply satisfied, for the passage devoted to Ocean's seed divides sharply after Stanza 44. The guests before this point belong to the bridegroom's party; those after it, to the bride's:

44

All which that day in order seemly good
Did on the Thamis attend, and waited well
To doe their duefull service, as to them befell.

45

Then came the Bride. . . .

[1] *In Somn. Scip.*, I. vi. 15–16; cf. Adam's Appendix on *Republic*, VIII. See also Plutarch, *The Morals*, tr. Holland (London, 1603), p. 1036, where additional reasons for the harmoniousness of 35 are given. The Pythagoreans term it 'a harmony' not only because it is composed of the first cubic numbers but also because it is the sum of $6 + 8 + 9 + 12$. These four numbers form an especially harmonious tetrad, whose middle terms are the arithmetic and harmonic means between the extreme terms, and in which all four terms bear proportionate relationships ($6:9::8:12$; also $6:8::9:12$, etc.). On the fertility of 35, see also Bongo, Pt. II, p. 87.

THE WEDDING OF THAMES AND MEDWAY

Locality	Section	Stanza total		Sub-section	Name	Character total	
Stanzas 8–10	NEPTUNE'S SEED	10		Introduction and invocation	Proteus	1	
Stanza 11					Neptune and Amphitrite	2	
Stanza 12				Sea-gods	Triton	1 } 18	30
Stanzas 13–14					Phorcys to Asopus	17 }	
Stanzas 15–16				Founders of nations	Ogyges to Albion	9	
Stanza 17				Author-comment	—	—	
Stanza 18	OCEAN'S SEED: rivers	36	27		Ocean and Tethys	2	
Stanzas 18–19					Nereus	1	
Stanzas 20–21				Famous rivers	Nile to Amazon	18	
Stanza 22				Author-comment	—	—	
Stanza 23					Arion	1	40+
Stanzas 24–26				Bridegroom's party	Isis, Churne and Charwell, Thame	4	40+
Stanzas 27–28				BRIDEGROOM	THAMES	1	10
Stanza 29				Pages	Kenet to Darent	6	
Stanzas 30–39				Neighbour floods	Severn to Lindus	34	
Stanzas 40–44				Irish rivers	Liffy to Oure	18	
Stanzas 45–46			8	BRIDE	MEDWAY	1	
Stanza 47				Bride's party	Theise to Frith	4	
Stanzas 48–52	OCEAN'S SEED: nymphs			Nereids	Proto to Nemertea	50	50
Stanza 53		1		Author-comment	—	—	

Moreover, the section before the division—a section that we may legitimately consider as masculine—consists of twenty-seven stanzas, that is, the cube of the first male number; while the feminine (bride's) section consists of eight, the female cube.

Next we observe a subsidiary division after Stanza 23. Ocean, Tethys, and their attendant 'famous rivers' of the world clearly belong to a different sub-class from the bridegroom's party of English rivers. This division is emphasized by the interpolation of another authorial stanza, Stanza 22, which introduces the theme of masculine and feminine qualities, and their mixture:

> Joy on those warlike women, which so long
> Can from all men so rich a kingdome hold;
> And shame on you, O men, which boast your strong
> And valiant hearts, in thoughts lesse hard and bold. . . .

The stanza immediately following brings the 'celestiall sound' of Arion's harmony—the same Arion who once 'drew / The eares and hearts of all that goodly crew,' calmed the seas, and caused the dolphin to stand still 'astonisht at his lore.' It seems reasonable to sup-

184

pose that this music 'which did next ensew / Before the spouse' symbolizes the harmonious union of male and female about to be celebrated; and that the 'lore' of Arion is thus akin to the 'lovely lore' of the harmonious caduceus. If this is so, then it is significant that the two sections that immediately follow the Arion stanza—that devoted to the groom and his party of English and Irish rivers, and that devoted to the bride and the nymphs—consist of twenty-one and of eight stanzas respectively. For these are the Ptolemaic totals of Scorpio and Libra, the same numbers that were used in the previous canto (though there in the pattern of character-grouping) to sym-bolize the harmony of Mars and Venus.[1] This overlapping of sec-tions, not to speak of the use of two quite different meanings for the number eight, may seem to us to confuse the numerology and throw all in doubt. Very probably, however, it was just this economy and involution that commended Spenser's numerology to his more in-genious contemporaries.

So far we have considered only cardinal stanza-numbers. If now we think in terms of *ordinal* numbers and stanza places it turns out that one of the patterns already distinguished makes a further appearance. Thus, although the bridegroom Thames figures in the flash-back stanza IV. xi. 8, he is only fully present in a single stanza: the twenty-seventh. This stanza receives very considerable numero-logical emphasis from the fact that it occupies the central position in the canto, the position of sovereignty. (It is therefore in the twenty-seventh place, counting from either end of the canto.) Nor does this exhaust the occurrences of the number. Spenser has yet further associated Thames with the male cube—if we may anticipate a little—by making him the twenty-seventh of Ocean's seed to walk in the procession. Finally, the comparison of Thames to 'old Cybele' main-tains the same symbolism. For cubic numbers were sacred to that goddess; as indeed her name was supposed to indicate.[2] Medway, on

[1] It is of interest that Ficino describes the resolution and union of Mars and Venus as a *concordia discors*, in the context of a discussion of the marriage age number, 35: see his *Expositio circa numerum nuptialem*, Ch. xvi: 'De habitu corporis, ætate, tempore ad generandum accommodatis' (p. 1424). It will not seem strange that Medway-Pax is assigned the number appropriate to Venus, if we recall that Cartari is at pains to show how closely Pax is associated with Venus.

[2] The source of this idea is Martianus Capella's discussion of the first cube, 8, in the *De nuptiis*: 'cybus autem omnis etiam matri deum tribuetur; nam ideo Cybebe nominatur' (ed. Dick, sect. 740, p. 374). In addition to the etymological argument, the association no doubt also drew strength from the identification of

the other hand, who is also mentioned in the eighth stanza from the beginning of the canto, appears in the eighth from the end.

The greater importance here assigned to the uneven cube calls for some explanation. Cubic numbers had several meanings which gave them symbolic relevance at this point in the poem. Most obviously, they occur in Book IV because four—as Du Bartas (p. 361) notes—was known as the 'cube's base.' Again, Plato had written that 'what brings solids into unison is never one middle term alone but always two'[1]—that is, continuous proportion of cubic numbers demands double mean terms (mean proportionals):

$$8 \; 12 \; 18 \; 27 \; 36 \; 48 \; 64 \text{ etc.}$$

All cubic numbers, then, are closely relevant to the philosophical preoccupation of Book IV with the double mean. Moreover, the first two cubes, the cubes of the *lambda* series, had also a generative significance. But between twenty-seven and eight, the numbers which generate life, there could be no parity of esteem. After all, the root of the male cube is three, which contains both monad and dyad, even and uneven, one and two (the root of the female cube).[2] Twenty-seven therefore came to be thought the more comprehensive and fundamental of the generative cubes; as such, it is given far more attention than eight in commentaries on the *Timæus*. Thus, the sovereign position Spenser gives to Thames, and the unequal matching of Thames with Medway (all England with a part of England) has a mathematical fitness.

Lastly, there is the numerology of the guests themselves, 'in order as they came' (IV. xi. 9). Spenser repeatedly draws attention to the numbers of guests in the different parts of the procession; and sometimes he even performs for us the chore of addition, as with the

---

[1] *Timaeus*, 32B (ed. Bury, pp. 58–59).

[2] I follow the argument of Ficino, p. 1419. Plutarch (*The Morals*, tr. Holland, p. 1037) points out also that in the *lambda* series, 27 is equal to the sum of all the preceding terms: $1 + 2 + 4 + 8 + 3 + 9 = 27$.

---

the geometric cube as earth, in *Timæus*, 55B. The cube 27 is discussed in relation to the generative cycle by Ficino, in his *Expositio circa numerum nuptialem* (see especially pp. 1422, 1424). Note that the goddess has made an earlier appearance in *F.Q.*, IV, in the person of Cambina. Cambina's chariot drawn by two lions was a distinctive attribute of Cybele or Earth: see, e.g., Valeriano, *Hieroglyphica*, I. xxxi, p. 16; and the engraving in Cartari (1556), p. 207 (our Pl. 16a: note also the cube prominently displayed in the foreground).

Nereids 'all which fifty are.' Moreover, he twice reminds us to look for a scheme based on constellation totals: first, in his concluding comment on the numerousness of the guests:

> The which, more eath it were for mortall wight,
> To tell the sands, or count the starres on hye,
> Or ought more hard, then thinke to reckon right,[1]

and then again in the opening stanzas of the following canto:

> O what an endlesse worke have I in hand,
> To count the seas abundant progeny,
> Whose fruitfull seede farre passeth those in land,
> And also those which wonne in th'azure sky?
> For much more eath to tell the starres on hy,
> Albe they endlesse seeme in estimation,
> Then to recount the Seas posterity:
> So fertile be the flouds in generation,
> So huge their numbers, and so numberlesse their nation.
>
> Therefore the antique wisards well invented,
> That *Venus* of the fomy sea was bred;
> For that the seas by her are most augmented.
> Witnesse th'exceeding fry, which there are fed,
> And wondrous sholes, which may of none be red.
> Then blame me not, if I have err'd in count
> Of Gods, of Nymphs, of rivers yet unred:
> For though their numbers do much more surmount,
> Yet all those same were there, which erst I did recount.
>
> (IV. xii. 1–2)

These comments may have been felt necessary because number symbolism by character-grouping was much less common than numerical composition by stanzas or lines. Simultaneously, however, they accomplish several other purposes; for they express the modesty of the poet with respect to his most ambitious numerological effort; provide a lyric recapitulation of the theme of oceanic fertility; and delimit the content of the number symbolism, by likening the count of guests to computation of the numbers of generation.

[1] The source of this simile seems to be Du Bartas, The Fourth Day of the First Week, ll. 201–204: a passage that leads straight into a catalogue of the zodiacal signs: 'Hee that to number all the Stars would seek, / Had need invent some new Arithmetick; / And who, to cast that Reck'ning takes in hand, / Had need for Counters take the Ocean's sand: / Yet have our wise and learned Elders found / *Foure-dozen Figures* in the Heav'nly Round. . . .' Goulart (p. 252) attributes the simile to Archimedes; but I think Spenser means us to have in mind Du Bartas' enumeration of the Ptolemaic constellations.

We notice that Spenser also describes the catalogue of guests as a 'count / Of Gods, of Nymphs, or rivers.' This triple division has already been encountered in the stanza pattern. Neptune and his progeny, the 'sea-gods' and 'founders . . . Of puissant Nations' (Stanzas 11–16) form the first class, 'gods'; the floods of Ocean's seed the second, 'rivers'; and the Nereids of Stanzas 48–51 the third, 'nymphs.' The authorial Stanza 17 separates the first two groups, while the substantive and formal break between the bridegroom's party and the bride's separates the last two after Stanza 44. (Except that the bride, her pages, and her handmaids are rivers, not nymphs: a point that I shall return to.) The symmetry of the arrangement receives further formal emphasis from the character-numbers. For in the middle section of the three, the 'rivers' section, the first and last sub-groups—the 'famous rivers' (Stanzas 20–21) and the 'Irishe Rivers' (Stanzas 40–44)—are of exactly equal number. What is more, the number of rivers in each of these flanking groups is eighteen: the Ptolemaic total for Gemini.[1] The same number appears as the total of the sea-god sons of Neptune. (Actually seventeen sea-gods follow Neptune and Tethys in the procession; but another son, Triton, who precedes his parents, is mentioned after them, so that in the count he falls together with his brothers.)

Next, we may take up the point that Medway and her attendants are rivers, while the rest of the guests named in this section (Stanzas 45–52) are 'Sea Nymphs.' This would seem to invite us to treat Medway's immediate party, five rivers in all, as a separate numerological unit. When we so treat it we find that this bride's party is matched by the bridegroom's immediate party, also of five rivers. The description of these two parties shows that each is arranged in the form of a quincunx:

	Thame		Doune		Frith
Churne	Isis	Charwell		Medua	
	Thamis		Theise		Crane

The meaning of these arrangements is not far to seek. Both bride and groom are accompanied by a quaternion of rivers; and the union of

[1] Since 18 is also one of the means between 8 and 27, we again have a double significance. By a happy coincidence, 18 could symbolize both the loving Twins, and the harmonious double mean. The latter allusion gains point in this particular context from the fact that, when the tetrad 8 : 12 : 18 : 27 was related to the four elements in a detailed way by schematizers such as Bongo (Pt. I, p. 140), 8 was assigned to Fire, 12 to Air, and 27 to Earth; while 18 was the term invariably assigned to Water.

the two parties forms the complete decad, the summation of the quarternion or *tetractys*. In Pythagorean symbolism the *tetractys* was called the 'fountain of nature' because it contains within itself, and generates, all other numbers.[1]

A similar intention partly accounts for the number of the tribute-paying (tributary) pages of Thames, who are named after, but attend 'round about him.' Six in number, they complete, together with the four who precede the bridegroom, another decad.[2] The six pages have, however, a further significance. Taken together with the thirty-four 'neighbour flouds' who next follow—as indeed they must be, since both pages and neighbours are attendant on Thames—they belong to a group of forty English rivers. This forty presents the *tetractys* in yet another form, well known from Plutarch's account of it in his commentary on the *Timæus*. For it is the sum of the terms produced by multiplying each of the digits of the tetractys by the last, by the tetrad itself:

$$40 = 1 \times 4 + 2 \times 4 + 3 \times 4 + 4 \times 4.$$

As Plutarch explains, these four terms of which forty is the sum (4, 8, 12, and 16) combine to produce all the principal harmonic proportions. Moreover, forty is the sum of the first two quadrates and the first two cubes $(1 + 4 + 8 + 27 = 40)$; and it is also the sum of the uneven *lambda* series $(1 + 3 + 9 + 27 = 40)$. In short, it is a number of great generative and harmonic properties, and is therefore appropriate to the middle section of the procession, which unfolds Arion's lore.[3]

Isolation of this forty gives the clue to a curious proportion that exists between the three main parts of the procession, the gods, the rivers, and the nymphs. Excluding the immediate parties of bride and

[1] See Appendix i, on the *tetractys* as the 'base' of the Castle of Alma, and the fountain of virtue in Bk. II. A subsidiary point about the numerology of Thames' party is the placing of Isis at the centre of a quincunx. This points forward to Bk. V, where Isis figures as a guardian deity, and where 5 is the nuptial number, her hieroglyph.

[2] They also complete a decad with Medway's attendants; with Thames himself they form the conformation of sovereignty $(1 + 6)$ which we have already encountered in the retinues of Lucifera and Busyrane.

[3] *De animæ procreat.*, xii–xiii (*The Morals*, p. 1037). Plutarch further explains that the sum of the uneven *lambda* series, 40, is composed of its last term, 27, and 13; these two numbers being the diesis and tonos by which mathematicians measure intervals of music. See also Hopper, *Medieval Number Symbolism*, p. 45.

groom as forming in themselves a complete unity, we arrive at a system of round-number groups:[1]

> 30 sea-gods
> 40 English rivers
> 40 others of Ocean's seed
> 50 nymphs

This is a tetradic system with double mean terms, such as I have shown in an earlier chapter to be a persistent philosophical theme of Book IV. Not only do the symbolic properties of forty make it a conventionally appropriate number to represent the harmoniously concordant double mean, but it is also *in fact* the arithmetic mean between thirty and fifty. (Hence the middle part of the procession equals the sum of the extreme parts: $40 + 40 = 30 + 50$.) Moreover, the numbers forming the tetrad are in the same proportion as the sides of the Pythagorean 3, 4, 5 right-angled triangle—the zoogonic triangle. Finally, as we know, the same 30, 40, 40, 50 tetradic system occurs again among the stanza-totals of Book V. [2]

Analysis of the numerical symmetries and symbolisms in the procession could be taken further still. One might explore, for instance, the subtleties that result from the counterpointing of two distinct sequences of guests: their order as enumerated (Medway before Doune and Frith, etc.), and their order as imaged (Doune and Frith before Medway). In the order of guests as imaged, there is a pattern of temporal numbers, the most obvious element of which may be schematized as follows:

> Neptune and Amphitrite
> 52 sea-gods and rivers
>
> Thames and pages
> 52 rivers
>
> Medway and pages
> 52 rivers and nymphs.

(A detailed temporal interpretation was often placed upon the generative numbers of the *Timæus*, on the strength of Plato's own dis-

---

[1] Proteus, mentioned at IV. xi. 9, is a son of Neptune, and must therefore be included in the first group, Neptune's seed.

[2] As the totals of Cantos i, iii, vi, and ix. See Ch. v, above, where it is noted that the positions of these cantos are designated by numbers in the *lambda* series.

cussion of them in relation to God's 'generation of Time' by the planets, which 'came into existence for the determining and preserving of the numbers of Time.'[1]) Or, again, one might pursue subsidiary patterns of astronomical numbers, such as that formed by the English and Irish rivers attendant on the bridegroom. Just as the Irish rivers represent Gemini (Mercury's House), so the English 'neighbour flouds' have significance of a similar category. They number thirty-four, the Ptolemaic total for Pisces: a sign particularly appropriate in this context, not merely because of its maritime associations but also more specifically because it is the Exaltation of Venus who 'of the fomy sea was bred' (IV. xii. 2). Thus, the two contiguous groups of rivers together allude numerically to the hermaphroditic Venus, by representing the signs of Hermes and Venus Aphrodite.

But it is not my purpose to push this line of enquiry to the limit. It will have been enough if I have given some idea of how Spenser used an overlapping proliferation of numerical patterns to imitate the fertile multiplication of Nature herself. Once even a part of the foregoing analysis is accepted, critical inferences of a far-reaching kind must follow. We can no longer speak of Spenser's formal construction as loose. If anywhere, we should expect to find looseness in a catalogue of rivers. But what we actually find in the wedding of Thames and Medway canto is a high degree of formal organization— 'narrow verse,' in which there would literally be no room for a single additional stanza or an extra river.

---

[1] *Timæus*, 38C–D (ed. Bury, pp. 78–79); and Ficino, pp. 1422 and 1414–16.

XII

The Book of Jupiter

i

Sᴘᴇɴsᴇʀ's astronomical content becomes unusually overt in the proem to Book V. These stanzas are concerned with the analogy between the moral or political disorder of human society and the progressive deterioration of cosmic order. In its political and macrocosmic aspects alike 'the world is runne quite out of square' and 'growes daily wourse and wourse' (Proem 1). Man's fall, by which he has degenerated from the justice and simple truth of the Golden Age, and become hardest stone in an age of stone, seems at first not surprising, since the heavens too are mutable:

> Right now is wrong, and wrong that was is right,
> As all things else in time are chaunged quight.
> Ne wonder; for the heavens revolution
> Is wandred farre from where it first was pight,
> And so doe make contrarie constitution
> Of all this lower world, toward his dissolution.
>
> (Proem 4)

Ostensibly as an illustration of the macrocosm's departure from original justice, Spenser next gives an account of the wandering of the zodiacal constellations 'from the point, where they first tooke/ Their setting forth' (Proem 5). The constellations have displaced one another in turn; so that the Ram (Aries) 'hath now forgot, where he was plast of yore,' and has shouldered the Bull (Taurus); the Bull has butted the Twins and made them crush the Crab (Cancer); and the Crab has been carried into the proper place of Leo. The phenomenon here described is, of course, the precession of

192

the equinoxes. In the time of Hipparchus (second century B.C.) the vernal equinoctial point had coincided with the first star in Aries; but since then it had regressed, until by Spenser's time it no longer coincided with Aries at all, but with a point about 5° from the beginning of the constellation Pisces. The zodiacal *signs* or houses, however, continued to be reckoned from the equinoctial point; hence the constellations could be regarded as roving 'out of their proper places farre away' (Proem 6).[1]

This passage is at the same time more than a mere illustration of cosmic disorder. Though the precession of the equinoxes appeared to alter the heavens irreversibly, it was known to be in reality a cyclical phenomenon with a very long period. Spenser therefore implies that behind the seeming mutability of the cosmos there is an underlying order. A fixed term is set to the process of deterioration. This precessional period, variously estimated at from 23,760 to 49,000 years,[2] was the longest cycle then known to science: as such, it attached the human imagination, and excited metaphysical speculations. It had early been identified with the Platonic Great Year, and with the cycles of *Politicus*; and so also with that succession of ages—golden to stony—which Spenser refers to in Proem 2. In consequence, it was often used as an apocalyptic symbol, holding promise (or threat) of a divine restoration of justice in a new cycle. So it is in the first stanza of Greville's *Caelica*, LXIX:

> When all this *All* doth passe from age to age,
> And revolution in a circle turne,
> Then heavenly Justice doth appeare like rage,
> The Caves doe roare, the very Seas doe burne,
> Glory growes darke, the Sunne becomes a night,
> And makes this great world feele a greater might.

[1] See Johnson, *Astronomical Thought in Renaissance England*, p. 23 n., the source of much of my information on this point. The conventional division of the heavens into twelve fixed zodiacal houses was established in the time of Hipparchus; but Spenser's statement that the spheres have wandered 'from the point, where they first tooke / Their setting forth, in these few thousand yeares' (Proem 5) makes it clear that he is looking back beyond that time, to the moment of creation itself. The aberration he refers to is an aberration from the *thema mundi*, or state of the heavens at the point of creation (cf. 'the world is runne quite out of square, / From the first point of his appointed sourse': Proem 1). On the *thema mundi*, see Robert Eisler, *The Royal Art of Astrology* (London, 1946), especially pp. 192 and 200.

[2] The estimates of various ancient, medieval, and Renaissance authorities are gathered by Riccioli in his *Almagestum novum*, Vol. I, p. 168.

Spenser's choice of illustration is thus well considered. The phenomenon of precession has relevance not only to the generative World Year that continues throughout the poem but also to the apocalyptic presentation of contemporary history that occupies Book V in particular. Moreover, the illustration directs our attention to the equinoctial points themselves, since it is solely with reference to these that the constellations can be said to have 'wandered.' And the equinoxes, as we shall see, have an important function in the astronomical symbolism of Book V.

Spenser's other, briefer, examples of cosmic disorder are: the alteration in the maximum declination of the sun during the fourteen centuries since Ptolemy's first measurement of it, the four legendary aberrations in the sun's rising and setting, and the eccentricity in the orbits of the maleficent planets Mars and Saturn. These illustrations are also thematic; for the shifts in the sun's rising and setting were sometimes regarded as effects of a transition from one Platonic cycle to another; while the change in solar declination had recently been adduced in contemporary complaints about the apocalyptic decline of the world.[1]

The mention, in the last illustration, of the planet Saturn 'that

---

[1] See J. L. Lievesay, 'An immediate source for *The Faerie Queene*, Book V, Proem,' *MLN*, LIX (1944). Hillard (*Var. Sp.*, V, 158) argues that Spenser's opinion that the sun 'is declyned from that marke of theirs, / Nigh thirtie minutes to the Southerne lake' (Proem 7) is erroneous; though he is courteous enough to suggest that for 'thirtie' we perhaps ought to read 'thirteen.' Gough (ibid.) explains that 'The obliquity of the ecliptic given by Ptolemy after Eratosthenes was 23° 51′ 20″, and in 1592 it was 23° 29′ 56″, the difference being nearly 21½ minutes. The sun had really declined less than eleven minutes since Ptolemy's time (A.D. 130), his estimate being 10′ 30″ too great.' We have also to take into account, however, errors in the *sixteenth-century* figures for maximum declination. Regiomontanus, for example, estimated 23° 28′ (giving a difference since Ptolemy of nearly 23½ minutes); and no doubt even lower readings were current. (See Riccioli, I, 160, where widely different estimates are quoted even from seventeenth-century authorities.) Spenser may not have been so expert in the use of ephemeral tables as Harvey would have liked; but his mastery of the elements of Renaissance astronomy was certainly so superior to that of his modern critics that it is stupid to try to fault him on such points of fact. A similar instance is his statement in *Amoretti*, LX, that Mars 'in three score yeares doth run his spheare.' The *Variorum* note treats this as an error for 'four score yeares,' thus displaying its author's ignorance of the fact that Mars had several different 'yeares.' As late as 1819, James Wilson (*A Complete Dictionary of Astrology*, p. 317) could write of Mars that 'his least year is 15, his mean 40, his great year 66, and greatest 214.' Riccioli (*Novum Almagestum*, I, 671) lists Great Years of 15, 17, 32, 47, and 79 natural years for Mars.

was wont be best' allows a transition to the mythological deity, Saturn, whose just rule (the *Saturnia regna*) constituted the Golden Age before the present Cycle of Deterioration. This in turn leads on to the myth of Astræa in Canto i; since it was just after Saturn's 'ancient raigne,' when 'sinne gan to abound' that she abandoned Earth. Before her departure Astræa instructed and armed Arthegall, and gave him the executive sanction of Talus. Thus, Arthegall's magisterial virtues represent a kind of remnant or memorial of Golden Age justice. The political corruption of Spenser's own age so oppressed him that in this book he felt an especial need to form the image of virtue according to 'the antique use' (Proem 3): the Republic must be ideal, for there can be no real justice without an apocalyptic change and the establishment of a new order. Nevertheless, justice has not left the cosmic order altogether; for Astræa

> hath now an everlasting place,
> Mongst those twelve signes, which nightly we doe see
> The heavens bright-shining baudricke to enchace;
> And is the *Virgin*, sixt in her degree,
> And next her selfe her righteous ballance hanging bee.
>
> (V. i. 11)

Now we can see why the five constellations Aries, Taurus, Gemini, Cancer, and Leo were used to illustrate equinoctial precession. The very next constellation in the zodiacal series is Virgo or Astræa, the righteous Virgin, who comes 'sixt in her degree' reckoning from Aries. And the next again is Libra, the constellation that in ancient times coincided with the autumnal equinoctial point, as indeed its visual representation signifies:

> After the *Maiden*, shines the *Balance* bright,
> Equall divider of the Day and Night.[1]

In Spenser's time, however, the equinoctial point had regressed into Virgo. Thus, the connection of Virgo with Libra, coming immediately after the account of precession in Proem 5–6, strongly reinforces that earlier allusion to the just apportioning of day and night at the equinoxes. Together with this specifically astronomical meaning,

---

[1] Du Bartas, The Fourth Day of the First Week, ll. 251–252 (p. 98). Eisler (p. 100) explains that the sign was invented at a time when the constellation rose heliacally at the autumnal equinox; at which season the water dropping from a waterclock into one scale of a balance during the day weighs as much as that dropping into the other scale at night.

there is a broader moral symbolism whereby the function of Libra is 'to weigh both right and wrong/In equall ballance with due recompence' (V. i. 7). Virgo-Astræa was often portrayed holding a balance: in fact, it was probably because of her contiguity with Libra that she got her name *Dike*, or Justice. We have a full analysis of this symbolism in Frances Yates' illuminating account of Astræa as a cult image of Queen Elizabeth.[1] In view of the popularity which Miss Yates shows the Astræa cult to have enjoyed, it is natural to expect an allusion to the Virgin Queen in *Faerie Queene*, V. i. 5–11; and surprising to find none. This is not, however, the only appearance of Astræa and her Balance in Book V.

The Balance, indeed, makes a further appearance almost immediately. It is a focal image in the episode of the extremist Giant in Canto ii. There the demonstration 'how badly all things present bee' (V. ii. 37) is closely related to the complaint in the proem, of whose surface meaning it offers a crude travesty. And the presumptuous attempt to reduce the world to order, without knowing 'the causes, nor their courses dew' (V. ii. 42)—that is, the great movements of history—is symbolized by the Giant's simplistic use of a balance. Arthegall's more complex counter-arguments, about the mysteriousness of cosmic order and its concealed compensations and imponderables, are interrupted when his revolutionary opponent is morally discredited. Talus discovers that the Giant is not really interested in justice, but is moved only by dislike of the Mean. Accordingly, 'he shouldered him from off the higher ground,' together with his balance: a fate that recalls the precessional displacement described in the proem. Just as Aries 'shouldered hath the Bull,' so Talus (Virgo's groom) shoulders the Giant and his balance (Libra). Spenser seems to imply that the term of the World Year (as we should say, the course of history) is not to be altered by crude or desperate measures. This rejection of opportunist political extremism may not appeal to every modern reader; but neither does it manifest (as is sometimes said) a specially reactionary attitude.[2]

Astræa also makes a further appearance in Book V; for, as Miss Yates has noticed,[3] she is reincarnated in Mercilla. The reader is

---

[1] Frances Yates, 'Queen Elizabeth as Astræa,' *JWI*, X (1947), 27–82.

[2] Other aspects of this episode are discussed by D. C. Allen in 'Spenser's Horology,' *MLN*, LXI (1946), 555 f.

[3] 'Queen Elizabeth as Astræa,' p. 67.

prepared for this by the last of the proem stanzas, in which Spenser addresses his patron as a goddess of justice:

> Dread Soverayne Goddesse, that doest highest sit
> In seate of judgement, in th'Almighties stead,
> And with magnificke might and wondrous wit
> Doest to thy people righteous doome aread,
> That furthest Nations filles with awfull dread,
> Pardon the boldnesse of thy basest thrall,
> That dare discourse of so divine a read,
> As thy great justice praysed over all:
> The instrument whereof loe here thy *Artegall.*

In retrospect, this stanza is seen to refer both to the Isis Church episode and to that of Mercilla's Court. Mercilla, who is clearly an image of the Queen, resembles Astræa in that she is a just virgin delivering righteous judgements. Her reign brings the return of a political Golden Age: kings and *cæsars* prostrate themselves before her (V. ix. 29) because she, more than Augustus, fulfils Virgil's prophecy: 'iam redit et Virgo, redeunt Saturnia regna.'[1] Moreover, her possession of the imperial virtues of *Iustitia* and *Clementia* is manifested by the several embodiment of these qualities in Arthegall and in Arthur respectively. When Mercilla ascends her throne and places the two knights 'th'one on th'one,/The other on the other side' (V. ix. 37) she is in effect *balancing* their virtues. She has assumed the posture of Virgo, and the scales of justice are in her hand.'[2]

A similar symbolism is expressed numerologically. The canto is divided into two exactly equal halves by the screen in Mercilla's palace: in the first half the knights are not yet in the Queen's court of justice; only in the second, after they have 'entred at the Scriene' are they 'guyded by degree/Unto the presence' (V. ix. 27). But the pattern of character-grouping is even more striking. In the first half of the canto eight characters participate—the Ptolemaic total for

---

[1] *Ecl.*, IV. 6. The imperial implications of Astræa as a political symbol are extensively treated by Frances Yates in 'Queen Elizabeth as Astræa,' p. 31 *et passim.*

[2] Spenser may possibly have received the suggestion for this emphasis on the physical disposition of Mercilla and her visitors from accounts of the trial of Mary Queen of Scots (see, e.g., Camden's *Annales* (1688 edn.), p. 353, and cf. *N & Q*, CCII (1957), 512, for the Cambridge Marginalian's note on the passage). On *Iustitia* and *Clementia* as imperial virtues, see Frances Yates, 'Queen Elizabeth as Astræa,' p. 67.

Libra;[1] while in the second half, that is, in the Queen's presence, there are twenty-six characters.[2] Within these twenty-six, moreover, an inner group may be distinguished, in immediate attendance on the throne: five *Litæ* and Virtues sit before Mercilla's feet, Arthegall and Arthur sit on either side, 'and neare them none' (V. ix. 37). The inner group thus consists of eight characters, balancing the total in the first half of the canto, and making yet another allusion to Libra. Finally, the positioning of Mercilla seems intended as a specific compliment to Elizabeth. She is mentioned at V. ix. 27, first of all the characters in the presence chamber; so that she comes between the main Libra group (V. ix. 1–26) and the Virgo group (V. ix. 27–52). There can be little doubt that we are meant to see in this placing a fulfilment of Virgil's prophecy of the stellification of Augustus:

between the Virgin and the grasping Claws, a space is opening (lo! for thee even now the blazing Scorpion draws in his arms, and has left more than a due share of the heaven!). (*Georgics*, I. 33–35.)

(The Claws of the Scorpion was an alternative name for Libra.) Thus, the mere physical array of the characters asserts Mercilla's imperial claim, and compares her with Augustus—a remarkably complex notion to be conveyed by such economical means.

We may digress here, to note that the number symbolism of the Mercilla episode can be paralleled in other Elizabethan authors. Symbolic application of the number twenty-six seems, indeed, to have been a persistent feature of the cult of Astræa. (Miss Yates, the

---

[1] 1. Arthur; 2. Arthegall; 3. damsel; 4. Malengin; 5. Talus; 6. Awe; 7. Order; and 8. Malfont. Both in the tournament for Marinell's spousal and in the subsequent adjudication ceremony (V. iii) the characters likewise form the total for Libra. In the tournament the seven challengers (Marinell and 'sixe knights more') are hard pressed until Arthegall joins them to complete the scales of justice. The characters participating in the adjudication are (in order named): 1. Florimell; 2. Braggadocchio; 3. Snowy Florimell; 4. Trompart; 5. Marinell; 6. Arthegall; 7. Guyon; and 8. Talus.

[2] 1. Mercilla; 2–6. *Litæ* and virtues; 7–8. Arthegall and Arthur; 9. Duessa; 10. Zele; 11. Kingdomes care; 12. Authority; 13. law of Nations; 14. Religion; 15. Justice; 16. Pittie; 17. Regard of womanhead; 18. Daunger; 19. Nobilitie; 20. Griefe; 21. Ate; 22. Murder; 23. Sedition; 24. Incontinence; 25. Adulterie; and 26. Impietie. 'The Peoples cry and Commons sute' (V. ix. 44) are not included in the count: they are not individually personified abstractions, and in none of the early editions were they accorded the italics that normally signalized proper names. Note that the six characters in the first half of the canto, who remain outside the screen, may be regarded as the six *stellæ informatæ* of Virgo.

historian of the cult, can only have missed noticing this through the accident of following Hyginus' rather than Ptolemy's description of the constellation Virgo.[1]) For example, Sir John Davies' *Hymnes to Astraea*, which is probably the most familiar and the most complete expression of Astraea-worship, consists of twenty-six poems, each of them an acrostic upon ELISABETHA REGINA.[2] As Miss Yates suggests, Elizabeth's Astraea rôle was a leading theme in the Accession Day tilts.[3] That the theme was sometimes presented at this festival in terms of number symbolism is perhaps to be concluded from George Peele's *Polyhymnia*, which celebrates the 1590 tilt, and which is arranged in sections corresponding to the courses run by 'six and twentie gallant Gentlemen.'[4] Moreover, astrological devices were common at the tilts. Several involving Astraea are described by Camden;[5] though we have no means of knowing whether any of these were numerical in character. It seems probable that some were, however, in view of the undoubtedly numerical portrayal of Virgo in the 1633 pageant staged for King Charles' entry into Edinburgh. This belated piece of Astraea pagentry is described for us by William Drummond of Hawthornden, who wrote the verses spoken on the occasion. At a narrow place in the 'great street' of the city, an arch was set up whose face

---

[1] 'Queen Elizabeth as Astraea,' p. 28. In Hyginus' setting, Virgo has only eighteen stars (*Poet. astron.*, III. xxiv; and see our Pl. 16b).

[2] The themes of the *Hymnes* are discussed by Frances Yates, ibid., pp. 63–65, 70, and 80.

[3] Ibid., p. 59, n. 4; cf. Roy C. Strong, 'The Accession Day of Queen Elizabeth I,' pp. 95–97.

[4] *The Life and Minor Works of George Peele*, ed. Horne, pp. 231–243. We know from Sir William Segar's account of the 1590 celebrations (reprinted in Horne's Introduction, pp. 167–169) that several of the themes of the Astraea cult found expression in the pageantry arranged for this particularly splendid occasion. Twenty-six knights actually ran in the 1590 tilt (as also in 1584): see Anglo, 'Archives of the English Tournament.' A much commoner number, however, was 20—the number tilting in 1585, 1586, 1587, 1598, and 1600, as well as in the important 1595 tilt described in Peele's *Anglorum Feriæ* (ed. Horne, pp. 265–275; cf. his Introduction, p. 97). Significantly, Peele ignores the inconvenient 1595 statistic, and ostentatiously enumerates 13 separate *encounters*, so as to get a total of $13 \times 2 = 26$ knight-courses. (Peele's mention of 20 knights is, of course, historically accurate; Horne (p. 282) queries this figure only because he mistakenly follows the H.M.C. *Report on Various Collections*, instead of the proper authority, Coll. of Arms MS. M.4.)

[5] See the *Remaines*, pp. 377, 378, and 381; discussed in Frances Yates, 'Queen Elizabeth as Astraea,' pp. 57 and 59.

represented a heaven, into the which appeared his Majesty's ascendant *Virgo*. She was beautified with six-and-twenty stars, after that order that they are in their constellation, one of them being of the first magnitude, the rest of third and fourth. By her was written,

HABET QUANTUM ÆTHER HABEBAT.[1]

ii

The *Litæ* who sit at Mercilla's feet are 'all lovely daughters of high *Jove*,'

> by him begot in loves delight,
> Upon the righteous *Themis*: those they say
> Upon *Joves* judgement seat wayt day and night,
> And when in wrath he threats the worlds decay,
> They doe his anger calme, and cruell vengeance stay.
>
> (V. ix. 31)

For several reasons we should expect Jupiter to preside over Book V, the Legend of Justice. Not only is he the fifth deity of the planetary week, but it was his reign that succeeded the *Saturnia regna*. The proem to Book V, which deplores the passing of 'Saturnes ancient raigne,' would thus seem a fit introduction to a book concerned with the reign of his son. And in fact Jupiter does turn out to be the book's guardian. His rule is discreetly administered, however, and is never allowed to become aggressively explicit. In consequence, it has seldom been enquired how far Jupiter's astrological influence determines the selection of material; nor to what an extent he constitutes the mythological focus for its imagery.

To begin with, it is from among the attributes of Jupiter that the book's principal emblematic objects are drawn. The first of these is the sword Chrysaor, which Astræa gave to Arthegall 'to make him dreaded more' (V. i. 9). It is true that the sword, like the balance, was an attribute of the righteous Virgin (as well as of the paler personification *Iustitia*): Mercilla's sword 'whose long rest rusted the bright steely brand' reminds us of this. But, after all, according to Hesiod's commonly accepted genealogy, Astræa was the daughter of Jupiter; and in any case the sword she gave to Arthegall is explicitly said to have come from '*Joves* eternall house.' It was

---

[1] *The Entertainment of the High and Mighty Monarch. Prince Charles, King of Great Britain, France, and Ireland, into his Ancient and Royal City of Edinburgh, the 15th of June, MDCXXXIII*, in *The Poems of William Drummond of Hawthornden*, ed. W. C. Ward, Vol. II (London, 1894), p. 86. The pageant is said to have been prepared by the Scottish painter Jamesone.

> gotten by her slight
> And earnest search, where it was kept in store
> In *Joves* eternall house, unwist of wight,
> Since he himselfe it us'd in that great fight
> Against the *Titans*, that whylome rebelled
> Gainst highest heaven; *Chrysaor* it was hight;
> *Chrysaor* that all other swords excelled,
> Well prov'd in that same day, when *Jove* those Gyants quelled.
>
> (V. i. 9)

The sword of justice is taken by sleight, because mortals—even mortals such as Astræa and Arthegall—can have no title to virtue. It remains as much Jupiter's by right as the cestus worn by Florimell remains Venus'. Even the sword's name speaks its true ownership; *Chrysaoreus* being a surname of Jupiter himself.[1] Since *Chrysos aor* also means 'golden sword,' Spenser is making an etymological pun when he writes that the sword was 'garnisht all with gold . . . whereof it tooke his name' (V. i. 10): the antecedent of *his* may be either 'steely brand' or 'Jove.'

The case is similar with Talus' iron flail. The flail can be given various topical interpretations;[2] or it can be regarded as appropriate to Astræa, on the ground that it is used for threshing ('With which he thresht out falshood'), the seasonal task in August, Virgo's month.[3] But above all the flail or whip is an attribute of Jupiter. The most familiar ancient *locus* for this iconographical feature is *Saturnalia*, I. xxiii, where Macrobius describes an image of Jupiter having the right hand raised with a whip (*dextera elevata cum flagro*). Later, the type became well established in astrological illustrations.[4] We begin to see that Spenser is using Astræa and her emblematic legacies to

---

[1] Strabo notices this surname of the Carian Zeus in his *Geography*, XIV. ii. 25 (tr. Jones, Vol. VI (1929), p. 297). Upton's association of *Chrysaor* with the Homeric epithet of Apollo is not, as we shall see, entirely irrelevant. The only other possibility is to connect the sword with the Chrysaor who fathered Geryon—Chrysaor the son of Neptune and Medusa. But no hint of this connection is given in Spenser's account of the sword's origin; besides, he is not likely to have believed, nor, even if he believed it, to have dared to imply, that the strict execution of justice begets rebellion and tyranny.

[2] See, e.g., *Var. Sp.*, V, 167; also Fr. J. P. Daly, in *N & Q*, CCV (1960), 49.

[3] See Tervarent, s.v. 'Fléau,' i: 'Le mois d'Août,' col. 185.

[4] See Seznec, p. 253, and his Figs. 98 (from Cartari) and 46 (from a bas-relief in the church of San Francesco of Rimini, whose iconography is also discussed in Charles Mitchell, 'The Imagery of the *Tempio Malatestiano*,' *Studi romagnoli*, II (1952), 77–90). Also Tervarent, s.v. 'Fouet,' i: 'Attribut de Jupiter,' col. 195.

unfold individual aspects of the sovereign deity. Jupiter himself, however, is left mysteriously implicit in the representatives and objects which are his divided images.

The principal attribute of Jupiter, the levin or thunderbolt, is reserved for Arthur, who uses it at a critical moment in his fight against the Soldan. The effect on the enemy's horses is devastating:

> Like lightening flash, that hath the gazer burned,
> So did the sight thereof their sense dismay.
>
> (V. viii. 38)

(The Soldan's chariot is also an attribute of Jupiter, in his solar *persona*;[1] it is appropriate here because, as the simile at V. viii. 40 explains,[2] the Soldan's rôle is that of a presumptuous Phaeton.) In the ancient myth of the Giant wars Jupiter's thunderbolt was borrowed, we recall, by Minerva. This detail, too, has been accommodated by Spenser; for, in another elaborate epic simile, he likens the power with which Britomart–Minerva charges against the sons of Dolon, to that of 'the flashing Levin . . . Uppon two stubborne oakes' (V. vi. 40). We could follow up other minor allusions to Jupiter's attributes—such as the description of Iris as 'the daughter of *Thaumantes* faire.'[3] But it seems more profitable to turn now to the broader themes of the book.

First and most obviously, Jupiter is the planetary deity whose function is to order and govern. In Ficino's account of the World Year of creation the contribution of Jupiter's planetary sphere is that it 'justly orders, divides, and distributes.'[4] It is hardly necessary to explain how the celestial law-giver and god of destiny came to be conceived of as presiding over human justice, giving it its moral authority and fostering it with his astrological influence. For

[1] See Macrobius, *Sat*. I. xxiii.

[2] 'As when the firie-mouthed steeds, which drew / The Sunnes bright wayne to *Phaetons* decay, / Soone as they did the monstrous Scorpion vew, / With ugly craples crawling in their way, / The dreadfull sight did them so sore affray, / That their well knowen courses they forwent . . . Such was the furie of these headstrong steeds, / Soone as the infants sunlike shield they saw.' As usual, the simile has a double aptness. The 'ugly craples' of the scorpion denote the constellation *chelæ scorpionis*, or Libra; so that in a sense the Soldan's horses are terrified by a vision of judgement.

[3] V. iii. 25, a periphrasis noted as unusually esoteric by S. K. Heninger (*A Handbook of Renaissance Meteorology* (Durham, N.C., 1960), p. 160).

[4] *In Timæum*, xx: 'Planetarum dispositio, annus magnus' (p. 1468).

Goulart, at least, it was enough to say that Jupiter is the star of justice because he is sovereign. Always an element in the meaning of Jupiter, this specifically legal function became more prominent when he was confused, in Arabic astrology, with the Babylonian god Marduk.[1] In medieval astrological texts Jupiter was even represented as a jurist: a conception that was not unacceptable to Renaissance scholars. Thus Ficino, writing to a jurisconsult, begins his letter with the premise that 'astronomers attribute the legal faculty to Jupiter'; though elsewhere he prefers to say, more abstractly, that 'Jupiter signifies law.'[2] Spenser's magistrate Arthegall, who is mythologically a foster-child of Jupiter's daughter, is therefore also a 'child of Jupiter' in the astrological sense.

More particularly, Jupiter was associated with the physical laws of nature, in that as governor of the universe he embodied the *necessitas naturæ*.[3] Astrologically, moreover, he fostered a propensity for natural philosophy.[4] It is fitting, then, that in Jupiter's book the mysterious laws of compensation operating in the physical universe should be invoked; as we find them to be, not only in Arthegall's arbitration between the sons of Milesio (V. iv) but also in his controversy with the Giant with the scales:

> What though the sea with waves continuall
> Doe eate the earth, it is no more at all. . . .[5]

More ironic is the decorum by which a complaint against cosmic disorder is made proem to the Book of Jupiter, the governing planet. The planetary ruler himself is apparently omitted from this survey of the heavens' anarchy; while three other planets—hasty Mars, tardy Saturn, and the declining sun—find notice in it. But appearances are deceptive. In actual fact Jupiter is covertly introduced at every stage of the enumeration of the wandering constellations, so

[1] See Seznec, pp. 156 and 158–159.

[2] *Epist.*, I (*Opera omnia*, p. 654): 'Legum facultatem Astronomi Iovi Solique attribuunt, quibus nihil in cœlis est pulchrius. Quid igitur in terris pulchrius est æquo æquitatis legumque interprete?' Cf. *Epist.*, V (p. 805): 'Intueatur quoque Iovem, hoc est, divinas humanasque leges, quas nunquam transgrediatur.'

[3] Ἀνάγκη φύσεως: see Conti, *Mythologiæ*, II. i (pp. 102–103), who cites Euripides' *Troades*.

[4] See, e.g., Ficino, *De vita*, III. xxiv (p. 568): 'Qui ad leges, vel naturalem communemque philosophiam est propensior, non ignoret Iovem se habere patronum.'

[5] V. ii. 39. The horological theory here combated is discussed in D. C. Allen's 'Spenser's Horology.'

that his very ubiquity conveys the notion of an ineluctable order; just as, in the *Cantos of mutabilitie*, the calendrical procession is itself the best refutation of the Titaness. This is most elegantly managed by a series of oblique allusions. Aries is described as 'that same golden fleecy Ram, which bore / *Phrixus* and *Helle* from their step-dames feares,' because Phrixus was often identified with Jupiter.[1] Similarly, Taurus is 'the Bull, which fayre Europa bore,' because that particular bull was Jupiter in amorous disguise. More explicitly, Gemini is referred to as 'those two twinnes of *Jove*'—out of many periphrases that might have been chosen.[2]

As I have mentioned, the conception of Jupiter as Law depended upon his sovereignty over the other gods. It is Jupiter 'who doth true justice deale / To his inferiour Gods' (V. vii. i). This sovereignty of Jupiter was a dominant theme of the various myths of warfare between the Olympians and the Giants—as these myths were understood, at least, in the Renaissance. Now the myths of the Giant war, together with those of the related Titan war, provided motifs, and even an overall frame of reference, throughout the *Faerie Queene*. Many of the poem's types of evil are Giants or Titans: Orgoglio, Disdayne, Argante, Ollyphant, and Mutabilitie. But it is noticeable that Book V has more than its share of Giants, and that Giant war motifs here dominate the action to an unusual degree. We have not only the Giant with the scales (V. ii) but also Geryoneo 'borne and bred / Of Gyants race, the sonne of *Geryon*' (V. x. 9) and Grantorto 'like to a Giant for his monstrous hight' (V. xii. 15). The Giants of mythology were evil precisely because they rejected the legal sovereignty of Jupiter. It should not be assumed, however, that Spenser's Giants always represent the evil of political rebellion. They may symbolize any threat to the just order of the commonwealth: if the

---

[1] See Conti, *Mythologiæ*, VI. ix (p. 593): 'Phrixus incolumis in Colchidem pervenit, ibique Iovi Phyxio cognomine, sive fugæ faventi immolavit. . . . Alii dicunt Dipsacum Phyllidis fluvii et nymphæ cuiusdam indigenæ filium Phrixum in hospitium accessisse, atque Phrixum ibi arietem Iovi cognomento Laphystio immolasse.' A different description of the constellation might have directed attention to Jupiter Ammon, who (according to an alternative theory) was stellified as Aries. But Spenser has chosen the less direct allusion to the god.

[2] The descriptions of the remaining constellations allude to Jupiter only indirectly, through his son Hercules. Thus Leo is 'the great *Nemæan* lion'; while the Crab is not merely displaced but 'crusht'—a reference to the slaying of its mythological forerunner by Hercules. The relevance of these Hercules allusions will appear shortly.

Giant with the scales is revolutionary, Geryoneo, and to some extent also Grantorto, are tyrannical. From Spenser's point of view, of course, the tyrant is in a sense rebellious, in that he overthrows the constitutional rule of law and rejects the authority of divine justice.

In the war against the Giants Jupiter's principal allies were Minerva and Dionysus.[1] And so it is in Book V, where, as we have seen, the rôle of Minerva is taken by Britomart. She has already pursued a Giant in III. xi (Ollyphant); now, her charge against the sons of Dolon borrows the power of Jupiter's levin. As for the dionysiac rôle of Arthegall, it is announced in the opening stanzas of the first canto, which recall the heroic originators of the imperial line of sovereignty:

> Such first was *Bacchus*, that with furious might
> All th'East before untam'd did overronne. . . .

> There Justice first her princely rule begonne.
> Next *Hercules* his like ensample shewed,
> Who all the West with equall conquest wonne,
> And monstrous tyrants with his club subdewed;
> The clube of Justice dread, with kingly powre endewed.

> And such was he . . .
> The Champion of true Justice Artegall.
>
> (V. i. 2–3)

Like Dionysus, Arthegall fights on behalf of justice against Jupiter's mythic opponents, the Giants. Hercules belongs in the same category, because he, too, is a son of Jupiter, and because it was through him alone that the Giants—or, as they are called here, 'monstrous Tyrants'—were defeated. As in earlier books, the rôle of Hercules in Book V is taken by Arthur. This is indicated, for example, by the way in which Geryoneo's ancestry is presented. We are told that the father's genocidal herdsman had a dog, Orthrus, begotten by the monster Echidna and 'great *Typhaon*'—the latter a particularly dangerous enemy of Jupiter until '*Hercules* them all did overcome in fight' (V. x. 10). When it is said that Geryoneo

> after that his monstrous father fell
> Under *Alcides* club, streight tooke his flight
> From that sad land, where he his syre did quell,
> And came to this, where *Belge* then did dwell,
>
> (V. x. 11)

[1] '. . . Gigantes Diis adversarios, quos Iupiter adiuvantibus Pallade et Dionyso una cum Diis aliis deballavit' (Conti, *Mythologiæ*, IV. v (p. 305)).

the inference is that, just as Geryon fell to Alcides (Hercules), so now Geryoneo will, to Arthur. More obviously, Arthegall's submission to Radigund is conceived as an analogue to Hercules' submission to Omphale.[1] Finally, we may note yet another allusion to the Giant war in the account of Isis Church. The priests there drink no wine,

> for wine they say is blood,
> Even the bloud of Gyants, which were slaine,
> By thundring *Jove* in the Phlegrean plaine.
> (V. vii. 10)

Earth, angry with the Olympians, brought forth from the blood the vine, whose liquor still stirs in men 'old rebellious thought,/ To make new warre against the Gods againe.'[2]

As an earlier chapter has shown, the theme of sovereignty receives expression in the number symbolism of Book V; its modulus is throughout pental, from the five constellations of the proem to the five *Litæ* and groups of five witnesses at Mercilla's Court. We can now appreciate the mythological aspect of this symbolism; which depends on the fact that Jupiter, the sovereign god, is fifth among the deities of the planetary week. In accordance with this position he performs the offices of the Pythagorean pentad, including its equal division of the nine digits. As Ficino puts it, 'through Jupiter, [the Sun] justly orders, divides, and distributes.[3] Now, the distribution of the material substance of the earth is a well-developed theme of Book V. It is particularly prominent in Arthegall's controversy with the extremist Giant, and in the dispute between the sons of Milesio. In the latter episode topical legal issues are no doubt

---

[1] An analogy that is made explicit at V. v. 24. For the conflation of Iole and Omphale, see *Var. Sp.*, V, 203–204.

[2] An idea borrowed from Plutarch's account of the Egyptian priests of Isis (see *Var. Sp.*, V, 219). Much more might be said about the Giant war as a mythological frame of reference in Bk. V, and about the political symbolism of Giants in sixteenth-century literature. But I am unwilling to encroach on a field covered by two unpublished theses: T. M. Gang's '*The Faerie Queene*': *a Demonstration of its Unity* and Roger O. Iredale's *Book Five of Spenser's 'Faerie Queene'* (Univ. of Reading M.A. Thesis (1959)).

[3] *In Timæum*, xx ('Planetarum dispositio, annus magnus'): 'Per Iovem motus insuper vitales adhibens, quæcunque moventur, iuste dirigit, atque distribuit' (p. 1468). Throughout this chapter, Ficino considers the actions of the planets as various modes of operation of the sun, who is the *præcipuus temporum declarator*.

touched on;[1] but there is also an argument of wider import, which is closely related to the earlier debate. Arthegall's statement to the Giant, that 'whatsoever from one place doth fall, / Is with the tide unto an other brought' (V. ii. 39), is taken up and developed in his arbitration between Bracidas and Amidas. Their dispute, too, concerns the diminishing of the land by 'the devouring sea'; and, as before, Arthegall's verdict takes the form of a vindication of the strange compensatory justice of Providence. What is really in question in both cases is the effects of Jupiter's *distribution*. The god himself may be mysteriously concealed; yet he is recognizably Jupiter the divider, Jupiter *providentia dei*, Jupiter *Fortuna maiora*.[2] The last-mentioned epithet is hinted at by Bracidas when he says:

> what so good or ill
> Or God or Fortune unto me did throw,
> Not wronging any other by my will,
> I hold mine owne, and so will hold it still.
> (V. iv. 14)

But the force of this beautifully enigmatic allegory is completely missed, unless a much more direct participation of Jupiter in it is noticed. The father who 'did equally bequeath his lands in fee' to Bracidas and Amidas was none other than Jupiter himself; for the name *Milesio* is simply one of the god's many surnames.[3] In short, the disputed possessions are not possessions at all, but divine gifts.

In certain other episodes the influence of Jupiter is felt astrologically. So it is when Sir Burbon abandons his shield of faith in order to obtain Fleurdelis' love. This is usually, and probably correctly, interpreted as a topical allusion to Henry IV's attempted pacification of France by abandoning the Protestant faith and hypocritically accepting that of Rome. Sir Burbon errs from justice, and therefore needs Arthegall's help, because he places the values of politic sovereignty before his duty as a godly prince: he is ready to compromise his religious principles to get peace. In this he manifests one of the effects of the planet Jupiter in an unfortunate

[1] For the legal background of the incident, see H. B. Nelson, 'Amidas v. Bracidas,' *MLQ*, I (1940).
[2] On Jupiter as Providence, see Conti, I. viii (p. 20); also II. i (p. 104): 'Iovem datorem omnium bonorum . . . vocarunt antiqui, et patrem omnium, quia viros bonos multis beneficiis prosequeretur; at temerarios et scelestos per calamitates et bonorum iacturam . . . revocaret.'
[3] See ibid., II. i (p. 98).

position: religious hypocrisy.[1] The belief that Jupiter had this effect is possibly to be traced to Ptolemy's *Tetrabiblos*. There we learn that Jupiter in a dishonourable position endows the soul 'instead of reverence for the gods, with superstition'; while subjects of Jupiter allied with Mars in a dishonourable position are 'quickly changeable, light, readily changing their minds.'[2]

iii

In view of Jupiter's covert omnipresence in Book V, we naturally expect a fuller manifestation of the god in the overtly mythological canto recounting Britomart's visit to Isis Church. The canto begins promisingly enough with the reflection that justice is a sacred virtue because it is especially related to Jupiter's office of cosmic regulation:

> Nought is on earth more sacred or divine,
> That Gods and men doe equally adore,
> Then this same vertue, that doth right define:
> For th'hevens themselves, whence mortal men implore
> Right in their wrongs, are rul'd by righteous lore
> Of highest Jove, who doth true justice deale
> To his inferiour Gods, and evermore
> Therewith containes his heavenly Commonweale:
> The skill whereof to Princes hearts he doth reveale.
>
> (V. vii. 1)

What follows, however, turns out to be a description of the cult of Isis and Osiris, and a strange dream-allegory in which Britomart and Arthegall become identified with these two Egyptian deities. Moreover, although planetary gods are involved in the episode, these do not seem to include Jupiter. Instead we are given the not obviously relevant information that Isis has a lunar, Osiris a solar, rôle. The priests of Isis

> wore rich Mitres shaped like the Moone,
> To shew that *Isis* doth the Moone portend;
> Like as *Osyris* signifies the Sunne.
>
> (V. vii. 4)

Thus, while the moral allegory about justice and clemency is fairly clear, from a mythological point of view the canto presents difficulty. The solution to the problem lies in a series of identifications,

---

[1] See W. Lilly, *An Introduction to Astrology*, ed. Zadkiel (London, 1933), p. 38.
[2] *Tetrabiblos*, III. xiii (ed. Robbins, pp. 347 and 349).

or equations, of one god with another. These equations were originally made in late antiquity, in an attempt to find an underlying order in the confusion of polytheistic myths. The result was a remarkable coalescence of the Olympian with the exotic deities: even, sometimes, of the Olympian deities with each other. The tendency was to reduce the myths to their common denominator; which often meant, their cosmological or seasonal element. Spenser may have learned about this syncretism either from such familiar ancient sources as Macrobius' *Saturnalia* and the studies of Egyptian religion in Plutarch's *Moralia* (especially the *De Iside*); or from Renaissance mythologists such as Conti, Cartari, Giraldi, and Valeriano.

The identification most necessary to an understanding of the mythology of Isis Church is that of Jupiter with Sol. This identification was commonplace among the syncretistic mythologists. To Macrobius it appears evident 'by clear indications';[1] and Conti, discussing *Phaedrus* 246E, expects only one answer to the rhetorical question: 'What is that great ruler Jupiter, unless what we call the sun?'[2] The Renaissance writer fashionably cites an Orphic hymn; but his main authority is the Platonic passage, where Jupiter's ordering of the gods (stars) in twelve bands is described[3]—a clear reference, he thinks, to the sun's course through the twelve parts of the zodiac. By the same authors, Osiris, too, is equated with the sun, just as he is by Spenser. Plutarch's treatment of the cult of Osiris, in the *De Iside*, is based throughout upon this interpretation.[4] Macrobius, more recklessly syncretistic, finds resemblances also between the cults of Osiris and Adonis: both are sun gods, whose myths of successive sorrow and joy represent the alternating winter and

[1] *Sat.* I. xxiii. 1 (ed. Eyssenhardt, p. 124): the 'clear indications' include an esoteric interpretation of Homer, *Il.*, I. 423.

[2] *Mytholog.*, II. i (p. 102).

[3] 'Zeus, the mighty lord, holding the reins of a winged chariot, leads the way in heaven, ordering all and taking care of all; and there follows him the array of gods and demi-gods, marshalled in eleven bands; Hestia alone abides at home in the house of heaven; of the rest they who are reckoned among the princely twelve march in their appointed order' (tr. Jowett). Macrobius, in his discussion of the equation, cites the same passage.

[4] See especially 372A and 372C–E, the direct source of *F.Q.*, V. vii. 4. Much of Spenser's Egyptian mythology seems to be derived from the *De Iside*. For example, the Pythagorean explanation why the priests of Isis drink no wine is to be found there, at 353B–C; and the wind swallowed by Osiris–Arthegall in Britomart's dream (V. vii. 14–15) seems to reflect Plutarch's statement that 'the power assigned to the wind some call Osiris' (375F; ed. Babbitt, p. 145).

summer seasons.[1] Finally, to complete the circle of equations, Osiris was commonly taken to be the Egyptian name of Jupiter. According to Diodorus, for example, Osiris is Jupiter the righteous, the father, ruler, and counsellor of all men.[2] And sometimes all three equations are combined; as when Macrobius explains that Osiris' emblem is an eye, because he is the eye of Jupiter, the sun.[3]

We can now see that when Spenser, in the introduction to the Isis Church episode, begins with Jupiter's divine justice, then continues:

> Well therefore did the antique world invent,
> That Justice was a God of soveraine grace . . .

> Calling him great *Osyris*, of the race
> Of th'old Ægyptian Kings, that whylome were;
> With fayned colours shading a true case:
> For that *Osyris*, whilest he lived here,
> The justest man alive, and truest did appeare,
>   (V. vii. 2)

he intends us to see a close link between the two reflections. Osiris is not just any god of justice, but a 'fayned' version of Jupiter himself, under a mortal's name. An anthropological foundation, as it were, is being laid for Arthegall's assumpion of a divine rôle in the generative dream of Britomart. Dionysus and Hercules, with whom Arthegall was earlier compared (V. i. 2–3), were likewise semi-divine avatars of Jupiter; and, as solar demi-gods, were also identified with Osiris and with the planet Sol himself.[4] All these identifications are involved in the mythic rôle of Arthegall. As one might expect in a hero of Book V and a patron of justice, his rôle is primarily Jovian. Like Jupiter, he fights Giants, delivers judgements, and apportions the goods of the earth. Clarinda, sent to woo him, must use charms which can 'even Jove himself to love entise' (V. v. 34). At the same time his identification with the sun is also close: at the spousal tournament, for example, his device is 'the Sunne brode blazed in a golden field'

[1] *Sat.*, I. xxi. 11–12 (ed. Eyssenhardt, p. 119).

[2] Cit. Valeriano, *Hieroglyphica*, XXII. xxiii (p. 268). See also Valeriano's Index, under the heading 'Osiris.'

[3] *Sat.*, I. xxi. 12 (p. 119).

[4] E.g., Plutarch (*De Iside*, 364E) equates Osiris and Dionysus; while Macrobius (*Sat.*, I. xx. 10–11 (pp. 115–116) and I. xviii. 7–9 (p. 105)) interprets Hercules as the power of Sol, and Dionysus as Sol in the lower or nocturnal hemisphere.

(V. iii. 14). The comparison of Arthegall to Osiris (V. vii. 22) unites both these components; for Osiris—who 'signifies the Sunne' (V. vii. 4)—is at once a mythological Jupiter and a planetary Sol.[1] The same comparison also has the effect of setting up a mythological complex of a type that was usually given seasonal or temporal interpretations: a point to which I shall shortly return.

Britomart's mythic rôles present less difficulty, because it has already been fully established, in our discussion of Books III and IV, that she represents a synthesis of Diana and Minerva (Athena). Moreover, we know that Minerva sprang from the head of Jupiter and signifies the wisdom or experienced counsel of that deity.[2] The remaining equations are again derived from such well-known authorities as Plutarch's *De Iside*; where we learn that the Egyptians 'oftentimes call Isis by the name of Athena.'[3] For the notion that Isis is the Moon, as well as for the 'Moone-like Mitre' worn by the priests and by Britomart in her dream, Spenser seems to have drawn on another Plutarchan passage, already cited:

There are some who without reservation assert that Osiris is the Sun . . . and there are those who declare that Isis is none other than the Moon; for this reason it is said that the statues of Isis that bear horns are imitations of the crescent Moon, and in her dark garments are shown the concealments and the obscurations in which she in her yearning pursues the Sun.[4]

The mythological rôles assumed by Britomart and Arthegall thus form a set of equated or associated pairs, that may be tabulated as follows:

Britomart : Isis   : Luna : wisdom of Jupiter : Athena ⎤ allies of Jupi-
Arthegall : Osiris : Sol   : Jupiter   : Dionysus ⎬ ter against
                                        Hercules ⎦ the Giants

The syncretistic character of the mythology of Book V invites comment. In no previous book has there been a comparable fusion

[1] For Osiris as an opponent of Giants, see Valeriano, *Hieroglyphica*, XXXII. xxxix (p. 387).

[2] Minerva sprang from the head, because that is the seat of intellect, the supreme work of nature. Alternatively, the birth of Minerva may signify that wisdom and experience are born out of the conduct of affairs and government: activities symbolized by Jupiter. See Conti, IV. v (p. 304).

[3] 376A; cf. Plato, *Timæus*, 21E (ed. Bury, pp. 30–31).

[4] *De Iside*, 372D–E (ed. Babbitt, pp. 128–129). According to other theories, Isis was interpreted as the Earth; as Proserpine; as Venus (cf. the iconographical links between Isis Church and the Temple of Venus); as Bellona; etc.

of the guardian deity with a cluster of other gods, demi-gods, and heroes. This change, which is signalized by the modulation into Egyptian mythology, is in itself thematic. For Isis and Osiris were identified with so many other gods, precisely because together they comprehended the totality of nature, the sum of individual deities. It is highly appropriate that the Book of Jupiter—ruler of all the gods, and himself an all-embracing god of nature or *mundus*— should include a synthesized pantheon of this kind. Now that the sphere of Jupiter has been reached, a more comprehensive and generalized view of the cosmos becomes possible.

We are still left with the problem why Spenser should choose to 'unfold' his Jupiter into a pair of deities. True, the idea that Jupiter contained both sexes was by no means unheard of. Conti, for instance, quotes an Orphic hymn: 'Jupiter is both male and female, unacquainted with death.' What is this Being, at once male and immortally female, asks Conti, unless the *anima mundi*, which has within itself the power to generate all things?[1] Nevertheless, Spenser's development of a relatively obscure idea constitutes an artistic choice, and one which is only partially explicable in the terms of my previous paragraph. Among other discernible motives is the need in Book V for another member in the series of female divinities who are to celebrate and inspire the poet's patron. Cœlia (I), Medina and Alma (II), Venus Architis (III), and Venus Hermaphroditos (IV): all the poem's images of perfected virtue have been feminine. This no doubt helps to account for the relative predominance of Isis in V. vii. If a female lawgiver was required Isis was a natural choice; for she not only presided over the law of nature but also under the guise of Ceres the 'inventress of laws' dispensed justice to men.[2] (The lawgiving of Ceres–Isis was always connected with her establishment of the peaceful arts of agriculture: a notion that finds reflection in Book V's many images of sowing and threshing.[3]) An added harmony, which should not be missed, is the schematic relation between the guardian goddess and Virgo-Astræa. For, in the Manilian system, the guardian deity of Virgo's month was none other

---

[1] *Mytholog.*, II. i (p. 104).

[2] See Valeriano, *Hieroglyphica*, XXXVIII. ii: 'Institutio' (p. 469): 'They commemorate Isis, or rather Ceres, as the inventress of laws (*legum inventricem*)'; and cf. ibid., I. xxvii (p. 15) and III. xvi (p. 35) on *Ceres Legifera*.

[3] V. vi. 29, e.g.: Talus 'in his hand his thresher ready keight.'

than Ceres. And Astræa herself, who was usually portrayed bearing an ear of corn, had a close affiliation with Ceres and Isis.[1]

But one senses a far deeper reason than these for the substitution of Isis and Osiris for Jupiter. One of the most remarkable features of the *Faerie Queene* is the strain of cosmogonic myth running through the poem. Whatever the aspect of man or of nature being represented, Spenser's conception of it is marked by the introduction of a metaphysic of love. In his vision—which is informed with Orphic as well as with traditional Christian ideas, yet remains highly individual—a polarity of male and female principles characterizes all natural processes and patterns of life. It is not only that love, in various forms, produces and constitutes and transforms the cosmic order; but also that that love is sexually differentiated. From this point of view, the unfolding of Jupiter into male and female aspects can be regarded as a simple statement of a theme communicated elsewhere in the *Faerie Queene* more cryptically: in the Garden of Adonis, for example; in the caduceus; in the Hermaphroditic Venus; and in the Dame Nature of the *Cantos of mutabilitie*, whose veil hid 'whether she man or woman inly were' (VII. vii. 5). These mythological constructions display more than a mere predilection for certain bisexual images. It is not too much to say that the best parts of the poem express a sexual mysticism: a mysticism which perceives, in the most exalted forms of nature, even in nature's Creator, a generative play of male and female.

This vision receives its expression mythically, in the loves of solar and lunar gods. It is the pattern of cosmic amour, indeed, which constitutes one of the most characteristic features of Spenser's fairyland. Now in this respect Book V has an especial function, in that for the first time it sets forth the pattern directly. Its use of Egyptian deities, in whom so many of the mythological rôles developed in preceding books are assimilated, implicitly co-ordinates what has gone before. At the same time the unifying myth is now 'explained.' Whereas in earlier books the planetary rôles were conveyed obliquely through imagery or tropic language, now we are told directly: '*Isis* doth the Moone portend; / Like as *Osyris* signifies the Sunne' (V. vii. 4). This has the effect of retrospective illumination; so that

---

[1] See Riccioli, I, 400; also Frances Yates, 'Queen Elizabeth as Astræa,' pp. 28 and 30, where, however, the connection between Astræa and Ceres in the Manilian system is not noticed.

earlier separate fictions are seen as parts of a single fiction. Una worshipped by the Satyrs is recognized as Isis veiled, the Isis of the *asinus portans mysteria* emblem.[1] The Red Cross Knight's fight with Orgoglio becomes a cosmic conflict between Osiris and Typhon.[2] And if we have not yet accredited Hamilton's suggestion that the dionysiac Verdant is a winter sun god whose release 'gives spring,' then the solar rôle assigned to the dionysiac Arthegall in Britomart's dream gives reason why we should.[3] Similarly, it could be shown that all the generative couples of Books III–IV—Venus and Adonis, Florimell and Marinell, Amphitrite and Neptune, Tethys and Oceanus, Thame and Isis, and the rest—find a common relation in the primary conjugates Isis and Osiris.[4] Even types of evil are brought within the ambit of the cosmogonic myth. They are seen to have been presented either as analogues of the Giant or monstrous adversaries of Isis and Osiris (forces of chaos, darkness, or winter); or else as antitypes to the beneficent divinities. Sometimes the two possibilities coincide: Argante and Ollyphant, the twin children of Typhœus (Typhon), 'ere they into the lightsome world were brought,/ In fleshly lust were mingled' (III. vii. 48), thus repeating an act which was anciently attributed to Isis and Osiris themselves, but which Spenser was understandably anxious to transfer to other agents.[5] Finally, the linking narrative of Arthur and Gloriana is almost certainly intended to display a similar solar–lunar pattern; though no doubt at a more fundamental level than that of Arthegall and Britomart. Certainly Arthur has the rôle of a sun-god hero; as is shown by particular incidents such as his battle with Orgoglio–Typhon, by the frequent analogies drawn between his achievements and the archetypal labours of Hercules (the Sun's annual twelve-part

---

[1] I. vi. 16–19. J. M. Steadman has studied the significance of the satyrs' worship of Una's beast from this point of view in 'Una and the Clergy: the Ass Symbol in *The Faerie Queene*,' *JWI*, XXI (1958), 134–137.

[2] Indications of the analogue implicit in the incident itself are discussed by S. K. Heninger ('The Orgoglio Episode in *The Faerie Queene*,' *ELH*, XXVI (1959), 171–187).

[3] For a discussion of Verdant as *ver dant*, see Hamilton, *The Structure of Allegory*, p. 137. Arthegall is compared to Bacchus (Dionysus) at *F.Q.*, V. i. 3.

[4] The amours of some of the couples mentioned are shown by Hamilton to carry a seasonal symbolism. It would be tedious to list ancient authorities for their several identifications with Isis and Osiris.

[5] See Plutarch, *De Iside*, 356A; and cf. Harrison, 'Divinity in Spenser's Garden of Adonis,' p. 50 and n., where the same two Giants are treated as antitypes of Adonis.

task), and by such iconographical details as his 'sunshiny shield' (I. viii. 20) or the dawn-tree emblem of his aspiration.[1] From what we know of the poem's other main *personæ* of the Queen—Belphœbe and Britomart—we may suppose that Gloriana, too, would in the continuation have assumed the rôle of a Lunar goddess. We already have an indication of this in Arthur's dream of her nocturnal visitation (I. ix. 13–15), which re-enacts the amour of Endymion with Diana. Who is the Faery Queen, after all, but the Queen of Night?

iv

But I am reluctant to pursue these analogies farther than is necessary to my argument. Nothing is more boring than demonstrations that all the myths in a poem are variations of a single myth; and I fully sympathize with the view that the interest of the *Faerie Queene* lies in its variety, not its uniformity. Moreover, it is proper to ask whether it makes any difference to our literary response, to know that Arthegall is 'like to' a god who 'signifies the Sunne.' When Spenser indicates that Arthegall's rôle is a solar one is this anything more than a vague cosmic gesture? Whatever planetary rôles may be adumbrated, clearly these are of interest only for their effects on the action, the imagery, or the other elements of the imitation; only in so far, that is, as they contribute to a realized poetic vision. Now such effects exist in the case of the *Faerie Queene*, and can be variously demonstrated. Unfortunately, it is beyond the scope of the present work to explore the poem's realization of cosmic rôles in terms of seasonal myth. Such developments, which have been provocatively described by Hamilton, do not seem, on the whole, to issue in numerological expression; except in such immediately intelligible substantive numbers as the seven-month terms of

---

[1] For the common interpretation of the labours of Hercules as a symbol of the sun's zodiacal course, see, e.g., Conti, VII. i (p. 704). (The same author interprets a shield closely similar to Arthur's as 'the power of the sun' (ibid., IV. v; p. 308); though I am aware that the latter shield has also a theological meaning.) Note that a poplar branch is carried by Prays-desire, who is shown to be the fountain of Arthur's moral action at *F.Q.*, II. ix. 37–39. Valeriano (*Hieroglyphica*, LII. xix: 'De populo: Tempus') associates the poplar with Hercules, and regards it as a symbol of time: 'Per eam tempus etiam indicabant; propterea quod arbor ea bicoloribus sit foliis prædita, ex quo præcipuas ipsius temporis partes, quippe diem ac noctem referre videatur. Ideoque Probus Herculi dicatam ait, quod Physici tempus per Herculem interpretantur. . . .'

215

Amoret's and Florimell's imprisonments.[1] In Book V, however, the solar–lunar symbolism is worked out structurally in a different way that concerns us directly.

No one can read in Book V for long without being struck by the prominence given to temporal images and to the reckoning of time. The *Litæ* or Hours at Mercilla's Court remind us that it is time which interposes between Jupiter's anger and 'the worlds decay,' and which, by cooling the wrath of mortal princes, is a means of grace to the offender (V. ix. 31–32). The union of Arthegall–Osiris and Britomart–Isis has as its progeny the Lion of Horus—signifying not only the political generation of an 'hour' or era of justice through the mingling of righteousness and peace, justice and equity; but also, more largely, the creation of time by the interaction of sun and moon.[2] And, in the narrative allegory, much importance attaches to the expiry of the term within which Grantorto's challenge must be answered by Arthegall.

But perhaps the most striking instance of the concern with time is the expression of Britomart's anxiety when the agreed three-month period of Arthegall's absence elapses without his return:

> her griefe with errour to beguyle,
> She fayn'd to count the time againe anew,
> As if before she had not counted trew.
> For houres but dayes; for weekes, that passed were,
> She told but moneths, to make them seeme more few:
> Yet when she reckned them, still drawing neare,
> Each hour did seeme a moneth, and every moneth a yeare.
>
> (V. vi. 5)

There may well be an allusion here to the term of the Platonic Great Year. Britomart's confusion of shorter and longer temporal periods recalls the fact that one year of the *annus magnus* cycle corresponded to a day in the individual human life.[3] In the fable she is waiting for

---

[1] Cf. Macrobius, *In somn. Scip.*, I. vi. 57 (p. 111): 'The sun, too, upon which everything depends for life, varies its course in the seventh sign: it reaches the summer solstice in the seventh sign after leaving the winter solstice and reaches the autumn equinox in the seventh sign after leaving the spring equinox.'

[2] On the connection between Horus and the Horæ, see Valeriano, *Hieroglyphica*, XXXIII. xlix (405); on the generation of Time, Plato, *Timæus*, 38C and 39C.

[3] See Adam, *The Republic*, II, 301. The ideal duration of human life was reckoned by Plato as 100 years; each year consisting of 360 days. Thus a human life is 36,000 days, the *annus magnus* 36,000 years.

the return of Astræa's foster-child; in the allegory, for something akin to the return of justice with the inception of a new Great Year period and a new Golden Age.

On the other hand, the temporal periods actually mentioned in the stanza may also be relevant. One is reminded that in his account of the making of time in *Timæus* 39B–D Plato relates the 'complete Year [the *annus magnus*] when all the eight circuits, with their relative speeds, finish together and come to a head' very closely with the shorter cycles of night and day, the month, and the natural year, all of which are determined by the two principal luminaries. These cycles, too, imitate the eternal nature of the 'intelligible living Creature': night and day, for example, are 'the revolution of the one and most intelligent circuit.'[1] Plato's further statement that a month is accomplished 'every time that the Moon having completed her own orbit overtakes the Sun' is clarified by Macrobius' account of the disparity between the moon's synodic and sidereal periods.[2] During the moon's sidereal circuit, he explains, the sun has moved on through one part of the zodiac; thus the moon 'pursues' the Sun during the last two days of her synodic period, when she is catching up with him for a new conjunction. Precisely similar ideas are invoked in Spenser's mention of the 'Moon-like Mitre' worn by the priests of Isis, and by Britomart in her dream:

> They wore rich Mitres shaped like the Moone,
> To shew that *Isis* doth the Moone portend;
> Like as *Osyris* signifies the Sunne.
> For that they both like race in equall justice runne.
> (V. vii. 4)

As we have seen, these lines allude to Plutarch's identification of Isis with the moon, in a passage which not only introduces the crescent emblem but also interprets the dark garments of Isis as

[1] 39C; cf. 47A–B.

[2] 'The sun . . . passes through one sign of the zodiac in a month's time. Let us suppose that the sun is in the first part of Aries when the moon leaves its conjunction with it or, as we say, "is born." After twenty-seven days and nearly eight hours the moon returns to the first part of Aries but does not find the sun there, for it, meanwhile, has gone on, according to its own fixed course. Consequently we do not think of the moon as having yet returned to its starting point because our eyes saw it at that time not starting out from the first part of Aries, but leaving the sun. For two days, more or less, it pursues the sun, catches up with it, and then proceeds from it again, a new moon' (*In somn. Scip.*, I. vi. 50; p. 110).

'the concealments and the obscurations in which the Moon in her yearning pursues the Sun.'[1] Spenser's Isis, like Plutarch's, is the *crescent* moon: the moon *in conjunction with the sun*. The conjunction itself, out of which the new mensal cycle is perpetually born, is symbolized in the generative dream of Britomart. But, equally, the time before conjunction has its correlative in the narrative allegory. For Britomart's anxiety about Arthegall's delay prompts her to look for him, and thus to re-enact the yearning search of Isis for Osiris.

This does not exhaust the book's astronomical symbolism, however. Arthegall's absence, after all, is measured in months as well as days and hours; so that his period of inactivity, which seems related to the winter captivity and idleness of Dionysus, suggests an annual, as much as a monthly or daily, phenomenon. Again, Spenser's startling substitution of long-haired priests of Isis for the traditional shaven priests is another allusion to the annual cycle; since the cutting of hair anciently signified the withdrawal of the sun in winter.[2] These features fall into place, if full weight is given to Spenser's statement that Isis–Luna and Osiris–Sol 'like race in equall justice runne.' In the context of the proem's repeated emphasis on the equinox, the statement has a very precise astronomical meaning. The 'races' of moon and sun are alike at the equinox, in

---

[1] *De Iside*, 372D–E. That Britomart looks towards her lover through a window 'that opened West' (V. vi. 7) and is led by Dolon to his house 'but little wide by West' (V. vi. 22) are details to be explained not only in terms of the political allegory but also by reference to the spatial relations of sun and moon as conjunction is approached; cf. Du Bartas' address to the moon: 'When the Imperiall Star / Beholds thee just in one Diameter, / Then by degrees thy *Full* face falls away, / And (by degrees) Westward thy Horns display: / Till fall'n again betwixt thy Lovers arms / Thou wink'st again, vanquisht with pleasures charms' (The Fourth Day of the First Week; pp. 110–111). It is just possible that Spenser intends a specific numerical allusion to the moon's sidereal and synodic periods in the lines 'Yet when she reckned them, still drawing neare, / Each hour did seeme a moneth, and every moneth a yeare.' For the difference between the 27-day 8-hour and the 29-day 12-hour periods, that is, the time during which the moon 'expects' conjunction, is 52 hours—a year, as it were, of hours.

[2] See Goulart, *A Learned Summary*, pp. 165–166. Cf., however, Macrobius, *Sat.*, III. viii. 3, where the worship of Attis by men in women's clothes and women in men's clothes is said to signify that the moon goddess contains within herself both sexes. In Arthegall's womanish phase, which corresponds to the sun's loss of virility at night and in winter, Spenser explores another aspect of the transvestist image. It should be noted that Radigund, who dominates Arthegall, bears a shield 'with stones, that shined wide, / As the faire Moone in her most full aspect, / That to the Moone it mote be like in each respect' (V. v. 3; cf. V. v. 12, but also V. v. 11. 8).

the sense that then night and day are equal. The cult celebrated at Isis Church is thus in some sense a cult of the equinox.[1]

It is clear that this symbolism of the equinox draws together many of the themes of the book. In the first place, the equinox is a supreme cosmic example of Equity. The 'like race' of the luminaries is run, we are told, in *equal* justice. The natural laws of compensation invoked by Arthegall find here their grandest manifestation, in the balancing of night and day, winter and summer. For the hours of daylight exceed the hours of darkness in the six-month period before the autumnal equinox by exactly the same amount as they are exceeded in the six-month period after it; a just proportion is maintained. Secondly, from a schematic point of view, the equinox expresses the nature of the zodiacal signs allotted to Book V, Virgo and Libra. Virgo is the constellation in which the autumnal equinoctial point actually lay in Spenser's time; while the sign Libra, more directly, is the 'equall divider of the Day and Night.'[2] Thirdly, the symbolism comprehends Britomart's Minervan rôle: as guardian of Aries, Minerva was known as the 'ruler of the equinoctial circle.'[3] Finally, since the precessional period and the *annus magnus* are one and the same, the equinox is an earnest of the eventual return of the Golden Age of justice. Britomart's commitment to equity and justice at Isis Church, which gives rise to the dream of a new political era, rebuts the superficial meaning of the proem, but confirms its deeper implication.

The foregoing interpretation places a good deal of weight, it is

---

[1] Plutarch testifies to the importance of the equinox in the historical cult of Isis and Osiris: 'on the thirtieth of the month Epiphi they celebrate the birthday of the Eyes of Horus, at the time when the Moon and the Sun are in a perfectly straight line, since they regard not only the Moon but also the Sun as the eye and light of Horus. On the 8th of the waning of the month Phaophi they conduct the birthday of the Staff of the Sun following upon the autumnal equinox, and by this they declare, as it were, that he is in need of support and strength, since he becomes lacking in warmth and light, and undergoes decline, and is carried away from us to one side' (*De Iside,* 372B; ed. Babbitt, p. 127). Britomart's reckoning of the time of Arthegall's absence (V. vi. 5) may contain another allusion to the equinox, besides that already noted. The variation in the apparent length of the hour ('each hour did seeme a moneth') may perhaps be intended to suggest the seasonal variation of the 'unequal' or 'temporal' hour—that is, the hour arrived at by dividing the period of day (or of night) by twelve. Only at the equinoxes is a temporal diurnal or nocturnal hour equal to a natural hour.

[2] Du Bartas, The Fourth Day of the First Week, l. 252 (p. 98).

[3] See Ficino, *Opera omnia*, p. 1439.

true, on a single stanza. But this is not done without formal warrant from Spenser. For the importance of the astronomical stanza is emphasized numerologically in the strongest possible way. It is placed at the exact centre of the book; being the 294th out of 588 stanzas.[1] The parallel with a numerical pattern already analysed is most striking. Just as Books I and II together are divided equally at the meeting of the Red Cross Knight and Guyon, to symbolize the 'like race' of sun and moon, so the single Book of Jupiter (who embraces both sun and moon) is divided in equity at the equinoctial stanza. In each case the point of division is indicated verbally, by a cryptic allusion to the planets' equal courses (II. i. 32 and V. vii. 4).

Once the temporal significance of the Isis Church episode is grasped, it becomes natural to see it as a terminus for numerological measurements. And calculation soon reveals that several solar and lunar periods arrive at their complete term in this canto. For example, at III. ii. 45 Glauce tells Britomart that the body of her lover 'wheresoever that it light, / May learned be by cyphers.' A reader alert to the possibility of number symbolism will immediately catch the hint that the principal appearances of Arthegall in relation to Britomart have been placed numerologically. Arthegall's first appearance is in Britomart's magic glass (III. ii. 24–25), from which his face looks out 'as *Phœbus* face out of the east.' But, in spite of the legend ciphered upon his armour in this vision, Britomart learns the full identity of her destined lover only by consulting Merlin, who 'could call out of the sky / Both Sunne and Moone, and make them him obay' (III. iii. 12). Merlin names Arthegall, and describes his origins, at III. iii. 26). Before doing so, however, he affirms the historical destiny that determines the match (while not removing the need for moral action):

> Indeed the fates are firme,
> And may not shrinck, though all the world do shake:
> Yet ought mens good endevours them confirme,
> And guide the heavenly causes to their constant terme.
> (III. iii. 25)

This is an even broader numerological challenge, encouraging us to reckon the 'term' or period of the relationship from this point. Now clearly the destined union comes to a fulfilment (albeit a wish-fulfil-

---

[1] Counting both proem and argument stanzas.

ment) at V. vii. 16, where Britomart–Isis dreams that she is impregnated by Arthegall–Osiris. The 'constant terme' fixed by the fates is there accomplished, in the visionary conception and birth of 'a Lion of great might.' If, then, we regard the stanzas from III. iii. 25 to V. vii. 16 as constituting the 'term,' their total ought to represent some period of generation or some political cycle. The total[1] is found, in fact, to be 1460: a number which would be immediately recognizable to an educated Elizabethan as one of the principal values assigned to the Great Year by Firmicus, Censorinus, and other authorities. For the benefit of the modern reader, it should be explained that the arbitrary or standard Egyptian year of 365 days lost one day in every four of the canicular or sothic years.[2] In the 'canicular period' of 1460 years, consequently, the Egyptian new year's day travelled completely round the canicular year. Hence both the quadrennial period (1460 days) and the canicular period (1460 years) were identified as Great Years or generative cycles.[3] What is even more significant, these periods were associated especially with Isis. Valeriano tells us that her image 'among other things signifies the Egyptian year itself, which lasts for four solar years.'[4]

There are other instances of the convergence of planetary terms upon the Isis Church canto; but they are either less striking or less certain than the one just described. For example, the first meeting of Britomart with Arthegall in Book V comes after exactly 328 stanzas, the number of days in the sidereal lunar year. But it is perhaps less important now to follow out all the individual harmonies of this order than to recognize in general their existence. The excitement is in first becoming aware that the poem's adventures not only enact planetary courses symbolically but also mime them numerologically by observing appropriate temporal limits. A fresh aspect of Spenser's formal structure reveals itself: a new species, even, of poetic form.

---

[1] Counting both proem and argument stanzas.

[2] Reckoned from the annual heliacal rising of Sirius (also known as Sothis or Canicula), the canicular year was close to the Julian year of $365\frac{1}{4}$ days.

[3] See Censorinus, *De die natali*, xviii–xix (ed. Otto Jahn (Berlin, 1845), pp. 51–52, 54–55, 56, and 58); Riccioli, I, 130 with references; and Giraldi, *Opera omnia* (Basel, 1580), II, 549.

[4] *Hieroglyphica*, XXXIX. ii: 'De Iside: Quadrennium' (p. 484A–B).

XIII

The Book of Venus

Recent criticism of the sixth book of the *Faerie Queene* has represented it as modulating to a fictive method different from that of its predecessors. Hamilton describes this new mode as romantic and literal; Berger, as aesthetic, casual, and introspective.[1] From our own point of view, perhaps the most striking departure is the seeming absence of any complexities of number symbolism. While the distribution of themes according to the Pythagorean series of symbolic numbers continues in Book VI, the patterns of character-grouping do not; nor can one find any significance in its stanza-totals. Instead of the numerological virtuosities of Book IV, and the careful balance of Book V, we have here an informality of arrangement.[2] In consequence, I shall have less to say of this book than of any other.

From a schematic stand-point, Book VI belongs to Venus, the sixth deity of the planetary week. In accordance with this guardianship, the core canto portrays the Graces dancing in the pleasance of the Acidalian Venus:

> the Graces, daughters of delight,
> Handmaides of *Venus*, which are wont to haunt
> Uppon this hill, and daunce there day and night:
> Those three to men all gifts of grace do graunt,
> And all, that *Venus* in her selfe doth vaunt,
> Is borrowed of them.
>
> (VI. x. 15)

[1] Hamilton, *The Structure of Allegory*, p. 204; Harry Berger, 'A Secret Discipline: *The Faerie Queene*, Book VI,' in *Form and Convention in the Poetry of Edmund Spenser*, ed. Nelson, p. 38.

[2] Though it is always unsafe to make such a statement about *F.Q.* If we had the seventh book in its entirety, the adventures of Bk. VI might well present different structural aspects.

The Graces grant, most obviously, the gift of beauty: physical beauty (gracefulness) and beauty of manners (graciousness). The book's preoccupation with this particular gift is displayed in the stories—and even in the names—of Calidore, Calepine, and Mirabella. Gifts of other kinds, however, are also the province of Venus. Just as the guardian of the preceding book was Jupiter the *Fortuna maiora*, so the guardian of this is Venus the *Fortuna minora*. And fortune, we find, is one of the most persistent themes of Book VI. It appears, for example, in the various treatments of heredity. Thus, the child presented by 'good fortune' to Matilda raises the question how much in the achievement of civility and honour is due to 'linage' and how much to nurture (VI. iv. 35–36)—the question, that is, how far what is given by fortune can be altered by 'what ever formes ye list thereto apply.' Offsetting this instance are the stories of Tristram, Pastorella, and the Salvage Man: all of them courteous, and all foundlings (fortune's children), whose humble circumstances fail to obscure their inheritance of nobility. These stories are often taken as demonstrations of the ineffaceable gentility that distinguishes those of 'heroicke sead.' But in fact they far more positively exemplify a stoic triumph over adverse *external* fortune in the outward circumstances of life. Certainly fortune in this sense of outward circumstances is the theme of Meliboe's story. In the focal canto VI. ix, a discourse by Meliboe himself explicitly treats the power of mind to conquer unfortunate circumstances: 'in vaine,' he says,

> doe men
> The heavens of their fortunes fault accuse,
> Sith they know best, what is the best for them:
> For they to each such fortune doe diffuse,
> As they doe know each can most aptly use.
> For not that, which men covet most, is best,
> Nor that thing worst, which men do most refuse;
> But fittest is, that all contented rest
> With that they hold: each hath his fortune in his brest.
>
> It is the mynd, that maketh good or ill,
> That maketh wretch or happie, rich or poore . . .
>
> For wisedome is most riches; fooles therefore
> They are, which fortunes doe by vowes devize,
> Sith each unto himselfe his life may fortunize.
> (VI. ix. 29–30)

223

Seen rightly, man's fortune is a gift of grace: an inner reality, 'in his brest,' independent of the conventional external criteria of what makes 'good' and 'bad' fortune. (Unaccountably, Berger despises Meliboe as a failed gardener, and his philosophy as sour grapes.[1] Boethian stoicism was not Spenser's whole creed; but neither is there any reason to doubt that he meant Meliboe's 'sensefull words' (VI. ix. 26) as the expression of one facet of an acceptable attitude.) Finally, fortune also has a bearing on the book's subsidiary topic, reputation. This topic appears in several of the narratives, but especially in the stories of Priscilla and Calepine (VI. iii) and of Serena and Timias (VI. v–vi). The honour of these characters is put in jeopardy in such a way as to demonstrate the dependence of reputation upon the contingencies of fortune. Thus Priscilla reflects 'how great a hazard she at earst had made / Of her good fame.'[2]

The guardianship of Venus is more clearly manifested in the romantic character of the book: almost every one of its stories has an erotic element. It is not surprising, therefore, to find that the most direct and the most fully elaborated appearance in the whole poem of Cupid 'the sonne of Venus' is in Book VI. Elsewhere, even where we might expect to find him, the god is either specifically said to be absent (e.g., IV. x. 42); or is only briefly mentioned (e.g., II. ix. 34); or is present in a perverse form (e.g., III. xii). Only in the incident of Mirabella's sentence (VI. vii. 28–32) does he enter the poem directly and beneficently. That the goddess of love herself makes no personal appearance seems to be in keeping with the book's preference for philosophical consideration of the origins of love. Instead of portraying amorous passion in the manner of Book III, Spenser here treats desire in a generalized manner, as response to beauty. More broadly still, civilization—indeed, every form of culture, savage and pastoral as well as courtly—is presented as an effect of *eros*. In this connection, Berger's comment on Serena and the cannibals can hardly be bettered:

The savages have nothing but a woman on which to project their primitive *eros*, and the Petrarchan catalogue describing Serena suggests that their *eros* demands new objects, different modes of expression, more

[1] 'A Secret Discipline,' p. 61 and n. 25.
[2] Incidental references to Fortune are far more frequent in this than in any other book: see, e.g., VI. i. 6, 39, and 41; ii. 33; iii. 5, 12, and 21; iv. 21 and 25–26; vii. 50; viii. 10; and xi. 1 and 29.

refined forms. However obscure, the primitive *eros* is the response to God which the Neoplatonists call love, 'the desire of beauty.' It is a desire which involves not only passive pleasure, not only the urge for generation in nature, but also the urge to create, in Diotima's words, 'that which is proper for the soul to conceive or contain,' *i.e.*, wisdom and virtue. . . . The soul is driven by its very confusion before the poverty of the actual— the mere gifts of nature—to create the symbolic forms which embody its desire and shadow its goal; objectifying these forms into an environment it may better understand its own energy by gazing at its diverse cultural images. Therefore, *eros* produces a cultural dialectic between the soul and its environment: each soul is born into a world of institutions, traditions, and conventions which are external to it and impersonal, yet which are the work of previous souls; they supply the vocabulary through which the soul defines its desire, the forms through which it articulates its experience. The soul internalizes these forms, makes them personal, makes them new.[1]

As Berger points out, the art of Colin Clout is also a function of *eros*. But the poet's own persona is not introduced merely to allow consideration of poetry as one of the forms of courtesy. It is also an introspective return to the origin, the 'nursery' of the *Faerie Queene* itself.[2] As he approaches the halfway stage of his epic, Spenser pauses to contemplate its course, as he does also in *Amoretti*, LXXX:

> After so long a race as I have run
> Through Faery land, which those six books compile,
> give leave to rest me being halfe fordonne,
> and gather to my selfe new breath awhile.

Significantly, the images serving as the focus of this contemplative act of Colin's are the Graces, and the starry crown of Ariadne to which these are compared. The Graces, because they constitute the supreme and most universal image of the triple returning rhythm of *emanatio*, *conversio*, and *remeatio*, the rhythm that activates the whole poem.[3] The crown of Ariadne, because it embodies the perfection of cosmic order, which the *Faerie Queene* celebrates. The constellation Corona is assigned by Ptolemy to Venus;[4] so that Spenser locates love at the centre of the cosmos when he exclaims:

[1] 'A Secret Discipline,' pp. 58–59.
[2] On the book's concern with origins, which is announced in the proem ('Revele to me the sacred noursery / Of vertue'), see Berger, ibid., pp. 69–75.
[3] Wind discusses the Graces as a fundamental cosmic triad in *Pagan Mysteries*, Ch. iii.
[4] *Tetrabiblos*, I. ix; ed. Robbins, p. 55.

225

Looke how the Crowne . . .

Being now placed in the firmament,
Through the bright heaven doth her beams display,
And is unto the starres an ornament,
Which round about her move in order excellent.

Such was the beauty of this goodly band,
Whose sundry parts were here too long to tell.

(VI. x. 13–14)

Berger is perhaps nearer the mark than he realizes, when he comments: 'The comparison unites the heavenly and imaginary dances, the physical and mental orders, the actual zodiac and the zodiac of the poet's wit. . . . The pastoral dance . . . resonates with the full amplitude of the cosmic harmony.'[1] He believes that 'the subject of the simile is the imaginary rather than the actual cosmos, the dance rather than the constellation.' But we are in a position to understand that the crown of Ariadne is indeed a hieroglyph of the whole starry firmament and of the planets in their circular courses. Colin's pipe evokes the music of the spheres as directly as poetry well can. For his art is one of astronomical symbolism, miming the courses and dispositions of the stars in all their 'order excellent.'[2]

[1] 'A Secret Discipline,' p. 67. Both Berger and Hieatt rightly connect the crown, and the dance of the Graces, with other circular conformations in Bk. VI, such as the 'girland . . . Of lovely lasses' around Pastorella (VI. ix. 8).

[2] Cf. Hieatt, 'The Daughters of Horus,' pp. 119–121: 'garlands, rings, ring-dances, and the revolution of heavenly bodies about a common center become for him the image of his great creative gesture—the image of the sun tracing his circles around the earth and imposing in the day, the seasons, and the year that eternity in mutability upon which all created life depends, and which is, as well an abstract of human life, particularly at the high point of marriage.'

XIV

The Book of Saturn

A NUMEROLOGICAL foundation has already been laid for the view that the *Cantos of mutabilitie* form part of an unfinished seventh book. We may expect this book, therefore, to belong to the seventh guardian deity of the planetary week. And it accords well with the substance of the *Cantos*, we find, and with the announced subject of the book, that they should be presided over by Saturn, the god of time. For most of the seventh canto is occupied with Dame Mutabilitie's evidence, which takes the form of a procession of the 'times and seasons of the yeare that fall' (VII. vii. 27): namely, the four Seasons, the twelve Months, Day and Night, and the twenty-four Hours. The Titaness herself is actually an embodiment of time; though time regarded in a special way, as alteration or inconstant change. Thus she believes that her case is proved by a demonstration that '*Time* on all doth pray,' while Jupiter, in his speech for the defence, tells her that the planetary deities rule the times and seasons 'and in them also thee' (VII. vii. 47–48). Indeed, both of Spenser's immediate sources for Mutabilitie's claim to ultimacy—Petrarch's *Trionfi* and Hawes' *Pastime of Pleasure*[1]—make Time himself the claimant. As for the titular subject of the book, Constancy, it was a virtue that Saturn was often thought to personify. In Ficino's account of the Great Year of creation, for instance, this is the very property assigned to the planet:

---

[1] Cf. especially the 'Trionfo del tempo' and the 'Trionfo dell' eternità'; and *The Passetyme of Pleasure*, ll. 5684–90: 'Do not I tyme cause nature to augment / Do not I tyme cause nature to decay / Do not I tyme cause man to be present / Do not I tyme take his lyfe away / Do not I tyme cause dethe take his say / Do not I tyme passe his youth and age / Do not I tyme every thynge aswage' (ed. W. E. Mead, E.E.T.S. (London, 1928), p. 218).

Through Saturn, he [that is, Sol] maintains perseverance in motions and constancy in changes, and brings to completion all his other planetary offices throughout the firmament.[1]

This same passage helps us to understand why the seventh book of the *Faerie Queene* brings together for the first time all the planetary deities. It is in keeping with a philosophical conception of Saturn such as Ficino's, that Spenser should make the book he devotes to this outermost planetary deity have the most comprehensive reference. With the completion of the planetary week the whole cosmic order is now unfolded, and can be reviewed in its entirety.

It may be objected, however, that in the extant fragment of the seventh book Saturn is a far less prominent deity than Jupiter. It is Jupiter, as king of the gods, who receives the complaint of the aspiring Mutabilitie in the first of the *Cantos* (VII. vi. 24–35), and who attempts to answer it at Arlo Hill in the second (VII. vii. 48). The complaint itself is not, in the main, against Saturn, but against 'this same *Jove*,' the alleged usurper of the principality of the gods. Besides, we cannot help noticing that several of those who march in the procession of times and seasons are pointedly related to Jupiter. The Hours, for example, 'faire daughters of high *Jove*,' were by him made porters of heaven's gate; and Leo, the sign of July, is the same beast slain by Hercules 'th'Amphitryonide'—that is, by the son of Jupiter, who, under the guise of Amphitryon, begot him upon Alcmena (VII. vii. 36 and 45).

It is true that Mutabilitie's case is principally against Jupiter; and in this very feature lies the point that I wish to make about the *Cantos*. As ruler of the planetary deities and representative of cosmic order, as *Mundus* and Destiny,[2] Jupiter is certainly the power whom Dame Mutabilitie must seek to depose. Indeed, she might almost have appeared as an evil character in Book V, the Book of Jupiter. But we feel that, if she had appeared there, her rebellion would have been put down more summarily: Jupiter or his representative would have briskly countered her arguments, and turned her over to Talus. In the poem as we have it—in the *Cantos of mutabilitie*—things turn

---

[1] *In Timæum*, xx (p. 1468): 'Per Saturnum et motibus perseverantiam, et motis firmitatem præstat, per firmamentum hæc omnia complet.' As previously explained, Ficino imagines Sol as acting through each of the planets in turn.

[2] The relevance to the *Cantos* of Jupiter's role as Destiny is well brought out by Sherman Hawkins ('Mutabilitie and the Cycle of the Months,' in *Form and Convention in the Poetry of Edmund Spenser*, ed. Nelson, especially pp. 80–82).

out differently. Admittedly, Jupiter is 'confirm'd in his imperiall see' by the judgement of the great goddess, Dame Nature; but he cannot be said to make a very impressive showing at the trial. More strangely still, Nature's verdict is mysteriously ambivalent. At first she even seems to find for the plaintiff: 'all things stedfastness doe hate / And changed be' comes very near to a decision that Mutabilitie has made her case. Moreover, though Jupiter's power is confirmed, yet it is revealed to be only a temporary and partial jurisdiction, within a larger scheme of things. By one of those fine mythological *peripeteias* which are Spenser's greatest contribution to our literature, the judgement of Nature discloses that Jupiter's authority, in spite of its supremacy in all that has gone before, is nevertheless neither ulti-mate nor unqualified. If Mutabilitie is 'put downe,' this is not be-cause the universe is judged to have a static and unchangeable order; but because all things 'by their change their being doe dilate; / And . . . worke their owne perfection,' and because a 'time shall come that all shall changed bee.' All nature is indeed subject to continual change; though this change is not a haphazard flux, as Dame Muta-bilitie asserts. Instead, it is the constant process of development that brings creation to its fulfilment; and so to the *eschata*, and the even more radical change from corruptible to incorruptible. Mutabilitie's unsuccessful suit has thus led to a new understanding of the world-order, as dependent upon temporal and historical processes—which are themselves dependent, in turn, upon the larger events of the redemptive history. A new aspect of nature, not directly considered before in the poem, has emerged: namely, its temporal extension.

All this is eminently compatible with the view that the guardian of Book VII is Saturn, the god of time. It befits his guardianship, too, that time (in Nature's, not Mutabilitie's, sense) should here be presented in a favourable light. Whereas in the Garden of Adonis it was 'wicked *Time*' 'great enimy' to the 'faire flowre of beautie'—a mere personification of the law of decay to which 'all that lives, is subject' (III. vi. 38–40)—in the *Cantos of mutabilitie* time is far from being simply destructive. Even the personification is rehabilitated: Father Time reappears as 'an hory / Old aged Sire' at Cynthia's silver gates (VII. vi. 8). Nevertheless, although Saturn's guardian-ship provides the readiest explanation of all these features, a subtler possibility should also be kept in mind. It is possible that, just as Venus *Fortuna minora* partially displaced the maleficent Mars from his proper guardianship of Book III, so Jupiter *Fortuna maiora* may have been meant to displace Saturn (the other astrologically maleficent planetary deity) in Book VII. Some support for this speculation is perhaps to be found in the twice-stated kinship of Mutabilitie to Bellona her sister (VII. vi. 3 and 32). But our knowledge of the seventh book is probably too incomplete for us to decide between these alternatives.

Instead, let us trace in greater detail Saturn's implication in the *Cantos*. From a mythological standpoint, one of the first noticeable features is that Spenser calls Dame Mutabilitie a Titaness. While in the fifth book, as we have seen, Jupiter's adversaries were monsters or Giants, Mutabilitie is

> a daughter by descent
> Of those old *Titans*, that did whylome strive
> With *Saturnes* sonne for heavens regiment.
>
> (VII. vi. 2)

Titans and Giants should by no means be confused. The latter fought against Jupiter; the former, in a different though related war, rebelled in the first instance against Saturn, Jupiter being involved only secondarily in defence of his father's authority. And in the *Cantos*, both Jupiter and Dame Mutabilitie herself trace their dispute back to the archetypal conflict of the *Titan* War.[1] The mythological justification of Mutabilitie's plaint is that

> *Titan* (as ye all acknowledge must)
> Was *Saturnes* elder brother by birth-right;
> Both, sonnes of *Uranus*: but by unjust
> And guilefull meanes, through *Corybantes* slight,
> The younger thrust the elder from his right:
> Since which, thou *Jove*, injuriously hast held
> The heavens rule from *Titans* sonnes by might;
> And then to hellish dungeons downe hast feld:
> Witnesse ye Heavens the truth of all that I have teld.
>
> (VII. vi. 27)

In the same connection it is significant that Jupiter is twice referred to by the periphrasis 'Saturnes son.'[2]

---

[1] See *F.Q.*, VII. vi. 27–30 and 33.

[2] VII. vi. 2: '*Titans*, that did whylome strive / With *Saturnes* sonne'; VII. vi. 34: 'Ceasse *Saturnes* sonne . . . t'allure mee to thy side.' Cf. VII. vii. 29, where Mutabilitie emphasizes that Jupiter was begotten in the world; though the point here is that, if he was begotten, he cannot be eternal, unchangeable, or ultimate.

More remarkable still are certain ingenious formal transpositions of Jupiter and Saturn, which imply a close yet concealed interdependence between the two deities. In Mutabilitie's demonstration of the changeableness of the planetary deities the order of attack is as follows:

LUNA   MERCURIUS   VENUS   SOL   MARS   SATURNUS   IUPPITER

That the order is not a random one is shown by Mutabilitie's beginning: 'And first, concerning her that is the first' (VII. vii. 50). In fact, the planets are arranged according to a quite conventional order. It is the order of proximity to Earth in the Ptolemaic system—except for one peculiarity. *The postons of Jupiter and Saturn have been interchanged.* The familiar Ptolemaic order of proximity is:

LUNA   MERCURIUS   VENUS   SOL   MARS   IUPPITER   SATURNUS

It might, of course, be argued that Mutabilitie's single departure from this sequence is made merely in the interest of rhetorical emphasis. No doubt she wishes to lead into her *peroratio* (VII. vii. 54–56) from a *climax*, and therefore leaves her chief opponent, Jove, to be dealt with last. This approach must seem inadequate, however, as soon as we notice similar transpositions of the same two planets, in the procession of times and seasons—a procession marshalled, be it noted, by '*Natures* Seargeant (that is *Order*).' November's mount, we are told,

> not easie was to deeme;
> For it a dreadfull *Centaure* was in sight,
> The seed of *Saturne*, and faire *Nais*, *Chiron* hight;
> (VII. vii. 40)

while December rides 'upon a shaggy-bearded Goat':

> The same wherewith *Dan Jove* in tender yeares,
> They say, was nourish by th'*Idæan* mayd.
> (VII. vii. 41)

Now the zodiacal sign entered by the sun in November is Sagittarius, which was customarily represented by a centaur. But, whereas Sagittarius is the House of *Jupiter*, Spenser here relates it mythologically to *Saturn*. This he does by imagining that the centaur is Chiron.[1]

---

[1] There was a convenient tradition to this effect, transmitted, e.g., by Natale Conti (*Mythologiæ*, IV. xii: 'Conversus est igitur Chiron in signum illud cœleste, quod nunc etiam a sagitta illa nomen retinet, atque ita formatur ut videatur

There were two traditions, here conflated, with respect to Chiron's parentage: according to one, he was the son of Saturn and Philyra; according to the other, of Magnes and Nais. Well may Spenser warn us that the description needs special attention, that the mount is 'not easie . . . to deeme'. Conversely, December's Goat, Capricorn, is the House of Saturn; yet it is here mythologically related to Jupiter.[1] There could be no way more elegantly oblique of conveying the mysterious interrelation, in the fabric of nature, of Jupiter and Saturn, permanence and change, order and mutability.

The procession of times and seasons, which the Titaness expects to provide evidence of universal flux, ironically has an opposite effect. In spite of its ostensible purpose, the method of narration is such that it persuades both the court and the reader of the measured governance and direction of time's course. This point has been so well dealt with by Sherman Hawkins[2] that it need not detain us here. What does deserve attention is that the passage presents, in the form of direct personifications, entities whose mythological and numerological representations we have been tracing in previous books. For example, the figures of Day and Night and Life and Death convey the same idea of an alternation of opposed cosmic principles that is expressed throughout the poem in its temporal and cosmological myths. More particularly, the portrayal of Day and Night as 'riding together both with equall pase'[1] and followed by the Hours alludes briefly to the seasonal balancing of diurnal and nocturnal hours about the equinoxes: a phenomenon developed symbolically, as we have seen, in the numerology of Books I, II, and V.

---

[1] This transposition is particularly pointed, in view of the fact that Saturn's guardianship of the *Cantos* has already been alluded to by a representation of Capricorn. Faunus, whose story is related in VII. vi, was commonly identified with that constellation. His only other appearance in *F.Q.*, we note, was at II. ii, where also he symbolizes the influence of Saturn.

[2] See his 'Mutabilitie and the Cycle of the Months,' pp. 87–99.

[3] VII. vii. 44; cf. Du Bartas' account of the equinoctial circle: 'while Apollo drives his Load of Light / Under this *Line*, the Day and dusky Night / Tread equall steps' ('The Columnes,' p. 366).

---

sagittam e vulnere extractam ostendare.' His stellification shows that God does not neglect the pious: that the man of virtue and integrity will be elevated, after his earthly afflictions are over, to a perpetual blessedness and glory). According to the more familiar view (based on Hyginus, *Poet. astron.*, II. xxvii and xxxviii), Chiron was translated to the heavens not as Sagittarius but as Centaurus; and the former constellation was identified instead with Crotus.

Indeed, all the temporal measures that are mimed in the formal structure of the poem are personified here; with one significant exception. Order marshals the four seasons, the twelve months of the year, day and night, and the hours; but the week is conspicuously absent. It is with rich import, therefore, that Jupiter asks, at the conclusion of the procession:

> But, who is it (to me tell)
> That *Time* himselfe doth move and still compell
> To keepe his course? Is not that namely wee
> Which poure that vertue from our heavenly cell,
> That moves them all, and makes them changed be?
> So them we gods doe rule, and in them also thee.
>
> (VII. vii. 48)

More directly, the effect of Dame Mutabilitie's immediately subsequent review of the seven planets is to recall the omitted measure of time, the planetary week. And it is the consideration of this temporal measure—the most fundamental of the structural series of the poem, but one only now, with Saturn's day, completed—that is Mutabilitie's undoing. For contemplation of the great week of creation leads inevitably to Nature's verdict about time's eternal conclusion. We are thus inclined to attach a new and more exact value to the last lines of the imperfect eighth canto. Is Spenser's meaning not at once poetic and personal, at once present and ultimate, when he prays for vision of the world's eternal Sabbath?—

> thence-forth all shall rest eternally
> With Him that is the God of Sabbaoth hight:
> O that great Sabbaoth God, graunt me that Sabaoths sight.

PART THREE

XV

Numerological Criticism

i

O<small>NE</small> predictable attitude to the foregoing analyses of numerical patterns in *The Faerie Queene* will be that of comprehensive disbelief. There are those who hold that, while such an approach may be valuable in studying medieval literature, in the case of Renaissance poetry it can never be taken seriously, until the day when a contemporary notice of the practice of numerical composition is produced: preferably an explanation in plain prose of the compositional method of a particular poem. That day has now arrived; and, as luck will have it, the number symbolism involved is like Spenser's astronomical, and based on Ptolemy's star catalogue. It is true that the evidence concerns a work that is neither well known to us now nor possessed of any literary worth. But even a bad poem may serve the cause of science. 'Christianus Proteus,' a protean poem to the Virgin by the Flemish Jesuit Bernard Bauhuis,[1] is a piece of pious ingenuity, of a kind that was once more highly prized than it is now. It consists of a verse TOT TIBI SUNT DOTES, VIRGO, QUOT SIDERA CÆLO, whose words can be permuted, its author believed, in only 1022 ways accommodable in hexameter verse. The line-total thus arrived at happened also to be an accepted estimate of the total

[1] The full title or description of the poem, which first appeared in Bauhuis (Bauhusius') *Epigrammatum libri IX* (Antwerp, 1615), reads: 'Divæ, optimæ, maximæque matri-virgini Mariæ, admirabilem hunc, unius libri versum, unius versus librum, Christianum Proteum, tot ora scilicet, quot cælum sidera gerentem (verti enim potest, millies, bis et vicies, sensu salvo et Heroici carminis lege) nostri in cæli Reginam affectus monumentum hoc ponimus sempiternum' (1634 Antwerp edn., p. 39).

237

number of stars in the whole firmament—a harmony which is expounded at great length in *Pietatis thaumata*, an elaborate commentary on the poem, by Hendrik Van der Putte.[1] In the course of his essay in number mysticism, Van der Putte specifically connects the line-total with Ptolemy's enumeration of the stars. Chrysippus, he tells us, had earlier estimated 1058 stars: 'but Hipparchus and Ptolemæus reduced the number, reckoning that the court of heaven was sufficiently bright, starred with 1022 lights.'[2]

Evidence that numerical composition based on astronomical numbers was practised by at least one Renaissance poet can thus be produced: evidence that will satisfy the most stringent demands of the sceptic. It cannot be too strongly insisted, however, that such demands are altogether unreasonable. No comparable authorization is required for our custom of analysing, say, melopœia, or syntactical ambiguities; though notices of these poetic elements can hardly be said to lie thick on the ground of Renaissance or earlier literary criticism. We have to remember that descriptive criticism of any kind was rare, until the late seventeenth century. (Even so, two of the earliest pieces of Spenser criticism, Digby's and Austin's, discuss his substantive number symbolism.) Moreover, numerical composition was essentially an arcane practice in the Renaissance; so that the last thing we should expect to find is an unveiled authorial exposition.[3]

The more one studies the literature and ideas of the Renaissance,

---

[1] *Eryci Puteani pietatis thaumata in Bernardi Bauhusi e Societate Iesu Proteum parthenium, unius Libri Versum, unius Versus Librum, Stellarum numero, sive formis M.XXII. variatum* (Antwerp, 1617). Hendrik Van der Putte (otherwise Ericius Puteanus or Henri (or Éric) Dupuy), b. 1574, d. 1646, a Flemish philologian. In his edition, the variations of the 'Christianus Proteus' are printed in full, and numbered in the margin. His commentary (itself a numerical composition, being divided into chapters corresponding to the letters of the Greek alphabet) also discusses at great length the symbolism involved in the number of words in Bauhuis' verse. No doubt as a result of Van der Putte's exposition the 'Christianus Proteus' enjoyed some fame in the seventeenth century. It attracted several other commentaries, among them one by the celebrated astronomer Bernouilli—who demonstrated, however, that far more hexameter permutations than 1022 are in fact possible. See *Nouvelle Biographie Générale*, s.v. 'Bauhusius,' and Michaud's *Biographie Universelle*, s.v. 'Bauhuis.'

[2] *Pietatis thaumata*, p. 82.

[3] Medieval poets did not always regard their numerology as a Pythagorean mystery, and were consequently less reticent: Curtius is able to adduce many explicit references to formal numbers. But even in the Middle Ages it was usually the less serious poet who divulged the secrets of his creation.

the more probable it seems that our reluctance to admit the existence of numerical composition stems from an ignorance of the thought-forms of that period. Indeed, the burden of proof ought properly to rest on the sceptic. For, while literary numerical composition was an obscure practice, the widespread application of number symbolism in other spheres of life and art was either more openly acknowledged or has since been uncovered through the labours of scholarship. We know that the intelligent Elizabethan was accustomed to look for a meaning in all manner of formally applied numbers; even if it is difficult for us fully to imagine the state of his sensibility when he did so. His awareness of the symbolic value of number is demonstrated, for example, by the way in which festivals were presented and recorded. We have already joined Drummond in counting the stars 'beautifying' Astræa in the 1633 Edinburgh *Entertainment*; earlier, we find Spenser's contemporary Blenerhasset keeping a careful tally of the numbers of actors in each part of a procession—numbers that had, for him, a 'learned intent.'[1] A similar consciousness of number was displayed in architectural design. Several recent studies have drawn attention to the use made by Renaissance architects of mathematical theories of proportion, involving microcosmic symbolism as well as abstract numerical harmonies. Although the mode of symbolism had changed, the number mysticism embodied in the formal design of the sixteenth-century palace was no less intricate than that of the medieval cathedral.[2] In this field too we meet with astronomical numbers.

[1] Thomas Blenerhasset, *A revelation of the true Minerva*, ed. Josephine Waters Bennett, Scholars' Facs. and Repts. (New York, 1941), sig. E4r: 'First *Saturne* and vii. sages past before, / Then mightie *Mars* with him ix. worthies went, / *Neptune* he had three saylers and no more, / *Apollo* two for a learned intent [side-note: 'Castor and Pollux'] / *Silenus* v. all v. from heaven were sent [side-note: 'Preachers']. . . .' The close relation between Elizabethan festivals and Spenser's poetry is studied in Frances Yates, 'Queen Elizabeth as Astræa'; C. R. Baskervill, 'The Genesis of Spenser's Queen of Faerie,' *MP* XVIII (1920–21); and I. L. Schulze, 'Elizabethan Chivalry and the Faerie Queen's Annual Feast,' *MLN*, L (1935), 'Reflections of the Elizabethan Tournaments in *The Faerie Queene*,' *ELH*, V (1938), and 'Blenerhasset's *A revelation*, Spenser's *Shepheardes Calender*, and the Kenilworth Pageants,' *ELH*, XI (1944). These articles only scratch the surface of a large subject, however. For example, the whole question of the relation between the tournaments in Bks. IV and V and contemporary festivals (not to speak of contemporary political history) has still to be explored in detail.

[2] On number mysticism in medieval cathedral design, see Otto von Simson, *The Gothic Cathedral*, and George Lesser, *Gothic Cathedrals and Sacred*

At Knole House (1570), the home of the Sackvilles, there are said to have been 365 rooms corresponding to the days of the year, 52 staircases corresponding to the weeks of the year, and 7 courts corresponding to the days of the week.[1] In music, again, the practice of numerical composition was highly developed, and seems to have persisted longer than in other arts.[2] In particular, the existence of a well-established numerological tradition in vocal music may have been a decisive factor in the growth of literary numerology; though our knowledge of this influence is not yet full enough to permit detailed conclusions.

Elizabethan sermons,[3] works of popular devotion, and folk-songs[4] all reflect the habit of associating numbers and meanings; even sport had its number symbolism, if we can credit Sir Thomas Browne's remark about the game based on the sovereignty of the fifth place. Number symbolism was primarily, however, the domain of the serious scholar. Almost universally, it was accorded a philosophical and theological status that may now seem fantastic: expressions of scepticism comparable with John Selden's would not be at all easy to find.[5] In this connection, the mass of Renaissance literature devoted to number symbolism is a large fact that speaks for itself. Nearly every work with a universal scope, from Valeriano's

[1] V. Sackville-West, *Knole and the Sackvilles* (London, 1958), p. 19. This tradition seems quite plausible, considering the interest that ancient examples in a similar symbolic mode aroused in the Renaissance. See, e.g., the discussion by Valeriano (*Hieroglyphica*, XXXIX. xi; p. 486) of the sepulchre of Simandius, which had a circumference of 365 cubits. Astrological orientation of monuments, which Valeriano discusses in the same chapter, was a common practice: see F. Saxl, *La Fede astrologica di Agostino Chigi* (Rome, 1934), pp. 22–23.

[2] A good introduction to this aspect of numerology is Manfred Bukofzer's 'Allegory in Baroque Music,' *JWI*, III (1939–40), 1–21.

[3] J. E. Neale (*Queen Elizabeth* (London, 1938), p. 217) records an illuminating anecdote of a sermon on the climacteric numbers which annoyed the Queen.

[4] Lina Eckenstein, *Comparative Studies in Nursery Rhymes* (London, 1906), gathers many examples of folksongs based on number symbolism—including the still surviving 'Green Grow the Rushes, O.'

[5] Selden's *Table Talk*, in *Opera*, Vol. III (London, 1726), cols. 2048–49: 'All those mysterious things they observe in numbers, come to nothing . . . because number in it self is nothing, has not to do with nature, but is merely of human imposition, a meer sound.'

Geometry, 2 vols. (London, 1957); on Renaissance theories of symbolic proportion, Rudolf Wittkower, *Architectural Principles in the Age of Humanism* (London, 1949), and Milutin Borisavljević, *The Golden Number and the Scientific Aesthetics of Architecture* (London, 1958). Wittkower includes an extensive critical bibliography of recent studies.

Hieroglyphica to Cornelius Agrippa's *De occulta philosophia*, had its section setting out the meanings of the digits in the Pythagorean system, or explaining the traditional allegorizations of numbers in the Bible. Particularly influential, among poetical works of this kind, was a passage in 'The Columnes,' the Fourth Part of the Second Day of the second of Du Bartas' *Devine Weeks*; it is given close attention, we note, in the commentary by Goulart. There were also many more specialist works. The ancient, patristic, and medieval authorities on number symbolism—Plato (*Timæus*), Iamblichus (*Theologoumena arithmeticæ*), Philo, Macrobius (*In somnium Scipionis*, I. vi), Censorinus, Martianus Capella, Saint Augustine, and Raban Maur—not to speak of compilers such as Bersuire—were now joined by a host of Renaissance mystagetes, many of them Neoplatonists or Jesuits, who accorded their curious subject a more systematic treatment than it had yet received. In this category belong Nicholas of Cusa's *De docta ignorantia*, Pietro Bongo's *Mysticæ numerorum significationis liber*, Francesco Giorgio's *De harmonia mundi*, and Athanasius Kircher's *Musurgia universalis*. Certain Platonic commentaries of Ficino[1] and Barozzi,[2] and the *Conclusiones*[3] drawn by Pico from Iamblichus, Proclus, and Pythagoras, also deserve mention.

At a time when men were in general disposed to regard number as significant, it was natural that poetic 'numbers' in particular should be approached in this frame of mind. Thus, literary theorists commonly based their treatment of prosody on the notion that the numerical organization of poetry concealed wisdom akin to that of Pythagorean philosophy.[4] Poetic form, they argued, is just as much

[1] Especially his 'Expositio circa numerum nuptialem in octavo de Republica' (*Opera omnia*, pp. 1414–24).

[2] Francesco Barozzi (Franciscus Barocius), *Commentarium in locum Platonicum obscurissimum* (Bologna, 1566).

[3] *Opera omnia*, Vol. I (Basel, 1573), pp. 75–79; see also his *Apologia*, ibid., 172–174, Kircher's *Arithmologia* (Rome, 1665), Jodocus Clichtoveus' *De mystica numerorum significatione* (Paris, 1513), and Joannes Meursius' *Denarius Pythagoricus* (Leyden, 1631). Among modern introductions to the study of number symbolism, the most useful are Hopper, *Medieval Number Symbolism*; Wittkower, *Architectural Principles in the Age of Humanism*; E. Bindel, *Les éléments spirituels des nombres* (Paris, 1960); B. Pick, *The Cabala, its Influence on Judaism and Christianity* (London, 1913); and J. L. Blau, *The Christian Interpretation of the Cabala in the Renaissance* (New York, 1944).

[4] A characteristic statement will be found in Minturno, *De poeta*, ii ((Venice, 1559), pp. 89–91). Since poets constantly occupy themselves in counting words

governed by principles of mathematical harmony as the form of music is, or the cosmos at large. Accordingly, Puttenham considers metre and stanzaic forms under the heading 'Of proportion poetical'; while Kircher, nearly a century later, attempts a sophisticated (though already slightly eccentric) calculus of metrical patterns, in his enormous treatise on the mathematics and philosophy of music. Even at its most nebulous level of generality, this metaphysical conception of poetic numbers must have encouraged the cultivation of abstract harmonies and symmetries—possibly the more important, because the more universal in its applications, of the two varieties of numerology.

It is mainly, however, with the other variety, with symbolic numerology, that we are concerned. In symbolic numerology the formal dimensions of the literary work have connotative value, in accordance with some system of number symbolism. Nowadays such numerology is usually regarded (when its existence is admitted at all) as a trifling caprice of pious monks. This attitude has probably been confirmed quite unintentionally by the same two works of scholarship that have offered the most revealing glimpses of the extent to which literary form expressed theological symbolisms in the Middle Ages: Vincent Hopper's *Medieval Number Symbolism* and Ernst Curtius' XVth *Excursus* on 'Numerical Composition.'[1] Valuable as they are, these studies accidentally give the false impression that numerological composition was a specially medieval phenomenon.[2]

In actual fact, it seems to have been widespread in the literature of antiquity. The *locus classicus* for the theory of numerology signi-

---

[1] *European Literature and the Latin Middle Ages*, pp. 501–509.

[2] Though Curtius draws grudging attention to a few instances of round-number line-totals in late antiquity: 'Numerical composition occurs even in Roman poetry from the *Appendix Virgiliana* to Claudian and Ausonius.'

---

and measuring feet, they must be familiar with the great power that the sages of antiquity believed to reside in numbers: 'quia vero magnam in numeris vim sapientes illi veteres posuerunt, hanc perspectam esse poetis oportere. . . . Doctrina autem, ac sapientia illa, quæ a fonte Orpheo ad Pythagoram, ac deinceps ad Platonem permanavit, mundum musica ratione constituit. Atque cum omnis musica in vocibus, et corporis motione versetur . . . vocum autem ratio dividatur in numeros, et cantum; has omneis quidem parteis in poetica profecto reperies. Neque enim dubitandum est numeros quidem omnibus Poetis cum musicis semper fuisse communes.' In support of the poet's claim to numerical wisdom, Minturno also offers a demonstration of Virgil's substantive use of Pythagorean symbolic numbers, such as the monad and dyad.

ficantly comes in an architectural work influential in the Renaissance: Vitruvius' *De architectura*. Here we find mention of an established tradition of numerological composition that is said to have received its impetus from the Pythagorean philosophy of number. Discussing the formal design of his own work, Vitruvius invokes precedent:

> Pythagoras also, and those who followed his sect, decided to write their rules, cube fashion, in their volumes, and fixed upon a cube—216 lines—and they thought that not more than three cubes should be in one treatise. Now a cube is a body with all its sides squared and their surfaces equal. When a cube is thrown, on whatever part it rests, it retains its stability unmoved so long as it is untouched, like the dice which players throw in a tray. Now this analogy they seem to have taken from the fact that this number of verses, like a cube upon whatever sense it falls, makes the memory there stable and unmoved. Greek comic poets also, interposing the canticum sung by the chorus, divided the spaces of their plays. Thus making the parts cube fashion, they relieve by intervals the delivery of the author's words.[1]

Like the Renaissance commentators on Vitruvius, we are unable to say which Greek authors he refers to here. Recent scholarship has, however, disclosed extensive indications of numerical composition in the work of certain Latin poets. Virgil, for example, seems to have used line-count numerology in organizing the structural sections of his *Eclogues*. Professor Jacques Perret,[2] who has analysed Virgil's

---

[1] Bk. V, Pref., 3–4; ed. and tr. F. Granger, Vol. I (London and Cambridge, Mass., 1955), p. 253. Marino may have taken a hint from the specification of three cubes of six when he composed his *Epitalami* in 648 (= 3 × 216) lines. In this case, of course, there is also a symbolic correspondence with the content, in that 216 is the generative or psychogonic cube.

[2] *Virgile l'homme et l'œvre* (Paris, 1952), pp. 17–29; see also pp. 111–120, where the structure of the *Aeneid* is compared with that of the *Eclogues*, and C. G. Hardie's review in *JRS*, XLIII (1953), 221–223. Perret synthesizes the results of previous researches into this aspect of Virgil's architectonics, by P. Maury ('Le secret de Virgile et l'architecture des Bucoliques,' *Lettres d'Humanité*, III (1944), 71–147), L. Herrmann ('La double symétrie dans la Septième Bucolique de Virgile,' *Rev. belge de philol. et d'hist.*, V (1926), 944–949), and K. Witte ('Vergils Georgica,' in *Die Gesch. d. röm. Dichtung im Zeitalter des Augustus* (Erlangen, 1927), I, 2). See also G. E. Duckworth, 'Mathematical Symmetry in Vergil's *Aeneid*,' *TAPhA*, XCI (1960), 184–220. The same author's comprehensive book, *Structural Patterns and Proportions in Vergil's Aeneid: a Study in Mathematical Composition* (Ann Arbor, 1962), which analyses instances of numerical composition in several classical Latin authors, came to my notice too late to be used in the present study. If its findings are accepted they will certainly do nothing to weaken my argument that Renaissance numerical composition is often to be seen as a neoclassical phenomenon.

numerical patterns in an admirably critical manner, treats them as abstract symmetries. Nevertheless, their complexity, and the comparatively infrequent occurrence in them of round numbers, suggest that they may also contain symbolisms as yet obscure.

In the Middle Ages numerology based upon theological symbolism was admittedly dominant; and the finest example of a work composed in this mode is also the greatest poem of the period: Dante's *Divina Commedia*.[1] At the same time this should not be allowed to obscure the fact that abstract symmetrical numerology is also common in medieval vernacular literature. It has been observed not only in lyric poems (where it is most to be expected) but also in the French epic and the German *leich*.[2] What seems to me an even more important qualification, however, is that neither kind of numerology was primarily an indigenous form. Numerical composition was first of all Latin and learned; only subsequently did it appear in vernacular literature.

Once this is grasped, it becomes easier to appreciate the true significance of the efflorescence of complex numerology in the Renais-

---

[1] See Hopper, *Medieval Number Symbolism*, pp. 155, 164 f., 180, *et passim*; H. D. Austin, 'Number and Geometrical Design in the Divine Comedy,' *The Personalist*, XVI (1925), 310–330; Howard Candler, 'On the Symbolic Use of Number in the Divine Comedy and Elsewhere,' *Royal Soc. of Lit.*, ser. 2, XXX (1910), 1–29; Ferdinand Koenen, 'Dantes Zahlen-symbolik,' *Deutsche Dante-Gesellschaft*, VIII (1924), 26–46; Hermann Gmelin (ed.), *Dante: Die göttliche Komödie*, Vol. III (Stuttgart, 1957), index, s.v. 'Parallelismus' and 'Symmetrie'; P. Petrocchi, 'Del numero nel poema dantesco,' *Rivista d'Italia*, III (1901); and Rodolfo Benini, *Dante tra gli splendori de' suoi enigmi risolti* (Rome, 1952), especially pp. 25–44 and 177–202. Renaissance commentaries on Dante have a good deal to say about certain aspects of his symbolic numbers: e.g., the dimensions of the *bolge* in the *Inferno*.

[2] See C. O. Chapman, 'Numerical Symbolism in Dante and *The Pearl*,' *MLN*, LIV (1939); O. Greenwood's Introduction to *Sir Gawain* (London, 1956); C. A. Robson, 'The Technique of Symmetrical Composition in Medieval Narrative Poetry' in *Studies in Medieval French Presented to Alfred Ewert* (Oxford, 1961); and Denis Stevens, 'Ars Antiqua' in *Ancient Forms to Polyphony*, Vol. I of *The Pelican History of Music* (London, 1960), p. 256. We should also notice here the common medieval practice of composing in units of 30 lines (or multiples of 30). According to one theory, Mr. Robson's, this habit was chirographical in origin: it arose simply because 30 was a suitable round-number of lines for a manuscript page. The 30-line modulus was still followed by certain sixteenth-century poets, such as Raleigh (see *The Poems*, ed. Agnes Latham, The Muses' Library (London, 1951), Nos. IV, V, XIX, and XXX). This point may have a bearing on the textual criticism of 'The passionate mans Pilgrimage,' for the concluding couplet occurring in Raleigh's *Remains* and in MS. Add. 18044, which completes the poem's 60 lines, is generally thought spurious.

sance. It was really a result of the Humanist effort to recover what were believed to be the springs of strength in ancient poetry. Such, indeed, are the very terms in which Henry Reynolds summons his fellow poets to relearn the art of number:

> *Pythagoras* . . . was made the Master of Silence; And who, as all the doctrines hee delivered were (after the manner of the *Hebrewes*, *Ægyptians*, and most auncient Poets) layd downe in enigmaticall and figurative notions, so one among other of his is this: *Give not readily thy right hand to every one*, by which Precept (sayes the profound *Iamblicus*) that great Master advertiseth that wee ought not to communicate to unworthy mindes, and not the practized in the understanding of occulte doctrines, those misterious instructions that are only to bee opened (sayes he) and taught to sacred and sublime wits, and such as have beene a long time exercised and versed in them.

Now, from this meanes that the first auncients used of delivering their knowledges thus among themselves by word of mouth; and by successive reception from them downe to after ages, That Art of mysticall writing by Numbers, wherein they couched under a fabulous attire those their verball Instructions, was after called *Scientia Cabalæ*, or the Science of reception,— *Cabala* among the *Hebrewes* signifying no other than the Latine *receptio*: A learning by the auncients held in high estimation and reverence, and not without great reason; for if God (as the excellent *Io: Picus* rehearses) *nihil casu, sed omnia per suam sapientiam ut in pondere et mensura, ita in numero disposuit*, did nothing by chance, but through his wisdome disposed all things as in weight and measure, so likewise in number; and which taught the ingenious *Saluste* [side-note: '*Sig*ʳ *du Bertas* in his Columnes.' to say that—

> *Sacred harmony*
> *And law of Number did accompany*
> *Th' allmighty most, when first his ordinance*
> *Appointed Earth to rest and Heaven to daunce.*

Well might *Plato* consequently affirme that, *among all liberall Arts and contemplative Sciences, the chiefest and most divine was the Scientia numerandi*; and who likewise questioning why Man was the wisest of Animalls, answers himselfe againe, as *Aristotle* in his Problemes observes, *quia numerare novit*, because hee could number; no lesse than *Avenzoar* the *Babylonian*, whose frequent word by *Albumazars* report, as *Picus Mirandula* notes, was *eum omnia nosse qui noverat numerare*, that hee knowes all things that knowes numbers: But howsoever an Art thus highly cried up by the Auncients, Yet a Learning (I say) now more than halfe lost, or at least by such as possesse any limbe of it rather talked of than taught,—*Rabanus*, a great Doctor of the Christian Church, only excepted, who hath writ a particular booke *de Numerorum virtutibus*; by diverse others, as *Ambrose, Nazianzen, Origine, Augustine*, and many more (as the learned *Io*: *Picus* at large in his Apology showes), reverendly mentioned, but never published in their writings. And I am fully of opinion (which till I find reason to recant, I will not bee ashamed to owne) that the Ignorance of this Art, and the worlds mayme in the want or not understanding of it, is insinuated in the Poets generally-sung fable of *Orpheus*, whom they faigne to have recovered his *Euridice* from Hell with his Musick, that is, Truth and Equity from darkness of Barbarisme and Ignorance with his profound and excellent Doctrines; but, that in the thicke caliginous way to the upper-earth, she was lost againe, and remaines lost to us that read and understand him not, for want meerely of the knowledge of that Art of Numbers that should unlocke and explane his Mysticall meanings to us.[1]

I have quoted Reynolds at length because, although *Mythomystes* did not appear until 1633, it expresses with unusual fullness an attitude typical of sixteenth-century Humanism.[2] In particular, we should note the vital connection that is drawn between the Pythagorean mysteries and the practice of numerology. Van der Putte, similarly, calls Bauhuis an *alter Pythagoras*, and directly compares Pythagorean science with computistic poetry.[3]

It is now well known that the enthusiastic revival of Pythagoreanism played a considerable rôle in the development of Renaissance scientific thought. The Pythagorean conception of the universe in mathematical terms helped to open the way to a truer and more scientific description of nature than was possible within the concrete enclosure of Aristotelian thought.[4] It seems unreasonable to suppose, therefore, that the numerological Pythagorean element in Renaissance literature reflects an obscurantist cleaving to outmoded thought-forms. On the contrary, we should see it as the resultant of neo-realist impulses, and the expression of sensibilities in touch with the best thought of the age. In the belief that *omnia conveniunt numero*, poets were trying to accommodate the form of their works to the form of nature, as nature was then revealing herself. Numerology, in common with other expressions of Neo-Pythagorean en-

[1] *Mythomystes*, reptd. in *Critical Essays of the Seventeenth Century*, ed. J. E. Spingarn, Vol. I (Oxford, 1908), pp. 157–159.
[2] Although the emphasis on Cabbalism, or ciphered numerology, is perhaps more characteristic of the seventeenth century—in spite of the reference to Pico.
[3] *Pietatis thaumata*, p. 111: 'in cælo Pythagoras, in versu Bauhusius.'
[4] This point is fully developed in Prof. Giorgio de Santillana's brilliant essay 'Space, Time and Understanding,' *New World Writing*, XIII (1958), 294–302; see also Johnson, *Astronomical Thought in Renaissance England*, pp. 100–101, and Alexandre Koyré, *From the Closed World to the Infinite Universe* (Baltimore, 1957), *passim*.

thusiasm, might be the recourse of minds dissatisfied with the Aristotelian and medieval world-picture.

In the eighteenth century the practice of numerical composition seems to have been abandoned (though a late instance is possibly to be found in Collins' 'Ode to Evening'[1]); and when Hopkins, in the next, once more based his metrical patterns on Pythagorean symbolism, this could easily appear an eccentric whim. From Renaissance numerology, however, we get a different impression. The method was then normal and consonant with the right reason of the time.

ii

If we try to determine which Renaissance poems are numerologically designed it is admittedly far from easy to come to a firm conclusion. The better the poem, the more organic and subtle, and therefore also the less obvious, its numerology is likely to be. Nevertheless, the indication from current research is that the method of composition which Hieatt shows Spenser to have adopted in *Epithalamion*, and which the present study shows him to have adopted also in the *Faerie Queene*, was not an unusual one. Gunnar Qvarnström has reported an elaborate numerical arrangement of stanzas in Benlowes' *Theophila*, and an extensive line-count numerology in *Paradise Lost*;[2] while Maren-Sofie Röstvig has gathered many similar examples, especially in Milton's shorter poems and in Henry

---

[1] It has 52 lines, the number of weeks in the year. The purpose of this allusion, if indeed it is an intentional allusion, can be understood in the light of Merle E. Brown's explanation of the poem's seasonal structure ('On William Collins' "Ode to Evening," ' *EC*, XI (1961), 136–153).

[2] *Dikten och den nya vetenskapen. Det astronautiska motivet*. Acta Reg. Soc. Humaniorum Litterarum Lundensis, No. LX (Lund, 1961); reviewed by Maren-Sofie Röstvig in *Seventeenth-Century News*, XIX (1961). An English translation of the numerological sections of Qvarnström's book, under the title *The Enchanted Palace*, is soon to appear. Qvarnström demonstrates that *Paradise Lost* has a numerically symmetrical structure, its exact centre being Christ's ascent of his chariot during the war in heaven. (We may compare Spenser's similar focus on the sovereign midpoint, in the fifth book of *F.Q.*) Moreover, the line-count of speeches in *P.L.* is shown to be appropriate to their contents. E.g., of Christ's 12 speeches in the poem, 4, symmetrically disposed about the centre, are each of 23 lines; this is in accordance with a symbolism (based on the Vulgate version of Exod. xxxii. 28, and developed at length by Bongo), whereby 23 denotes vengeance upon sinners. Less-illustrious numerological poems discussed by Qvarnström include Chamberlaine's *Pharonnida* (1659), More's *Psychozoia* (1647), and Fane's *Otia sacra* (1648).

More's epics.[1] To these instances we must add all of Spenser's shorter poems, several of Chapman's, and at least one of Shakespeare's.[2] It seems safe to predict that before long it will turn out that most good poems of the period—certainly most poems that make any pretence to craft or learning—are numerologically organized. We are now at a threshold, I believe, and have the opportunity of crossing into a new phase of Renaissance literary scholarship.

This very hope makes it urgent that excessive claims for the numerological approach should be avoided. I have no wish to encourage illusory notions about its importance and critical status. Thus, we must allow that numerological analysis will seldom alter our evaluation of a poem; nor is it likely to overthrow our previous understanding of the meaning. Certainly the knowledge that a bad poem is composed numerically should not make us think it good. Usually, the perception of a numerical correspondence will at most add a little to our pleasure in reading; just as appreciation of an

[1] Maren-Sofie Röstvig, 'The Hidden Sense: Milton and the Neoplatonic Method of Numerical Composition,' in *The Hidden Sense and other Essays*, Norwegian Studies in English, No. 9 (1963), 1–112. Unfortunately Dr. Röstvig's paper did not appear in time for me to use it, or to give it the notice it deserves.

[2] The most elaborately structured of Spenser's shorter poems (other than *Epithalamion*) appears to be *Daphnaida*. Appropriately for an elegy, it uses 7, the number of mutability, as its modulus. Not only is a 7-line stanza employed, but the centre section consists of a complaint in 7 numbered strophes, each of 7 stanzas. The remainder of the poem is so arranged that 28 (i.e., 4 × 7) stanzas precede the complaint, and a coda of 4 stanzas or 28 (i.e., 4 × 7) lines follow it: an arrangement reminiscent of that adopted in Virgil's fourth Eclogue (3 : 7 : 7 : 28 : 7 : 7 : 4; see Perret, p. 25). Thus, the complaint section of the elegy, in 7 × 7 stanzas, is offset by the 9 × 9 stanza-count of the whole. A similarly elegiac scheme is used in *The Ruines of Time*, which consists of 686 (i.e., 7 × 7 × 7 × 2) lines, and contains two pageants, each of 6 plus 1 separately numbered stanzas. *Virgil's Gnat* has 700 lines, counting the introductory stanzas, but not the concluding epigraph. Without the introductory stanzas its line-total is 686: the same scheme as in *The Ruines of Time*. *Ruines of Rome*, on the other hand, has the 33-stanza scheme (based on a symbolic interpretation of the 33 years of Christ's life) that was made famous by Dante's use of it for the *Divina Commedia*. For a more elaborate account of the numerology of Spenser's shorter poems, see Röstvig, 'The Hidden Sense,' 82–92.

Vincent Hopper ('Spenser's "House of Temperance," ' p. 966 n.) analyses numerical patterns in Maurice Scève's *Délie*; and Miss Joan Grundy (*The Poems of Henry Constable* (Liverpool, 1960), pp. 220 f.) draws attention to Constable's explanation of the symbolic division of his sonnets into '3 parts, each parte contayning 3 severall arguments, and every argument 7 sonnets.' (Drayton, we may note, used the same scheme of 9 × 7 sonnets.) Donne has several numerological poems: the most obvious case, perhaps, is his XIIth Elegy, with its extended conceit of the year's passage; it consists of 52 couplets.

instance of melopœia will, or of a rhetorical figure. The numerology will merely belong to the routine operation of the decorum we are accustomed to expect in Elizabethan poetry. In a few of the better poems of the period, however, numerological structures have a more crucial significance. It is no exaggeration to say that one can hardly begin to appreciate the form of Shakespeare's *Venus and Adonis*, or to grasp its philosophical content, until one has read it numerologically.

In such cases, of course, the numerical structures are intricate, and would elude any brief demonstration here.[1] Only trivial instances are immediately obvious. Nevertheless, Chapman's 'The amorous zodiack' may be considered as belonging to an intermediate category.[2] Its numerology is easily grasped, yet it is not without some complications and subtleties. The poem consists of 180 lines, disposed as twenty-eight six-line stanzas, together with an *envoi* of two further stanzas. Rhetorically, the arrangement is a fairly simple one: each of the twelve zodiacal signs in turn is developed symbolically, or paired off with the physical excellencies of the beloved by means of an astrological melothesia. Now, it is not left entirely to the reader of this calendrical love-lyric to draw the conclusion that its stanza-totals, twenty-eight and thirty, correspond respectively to the number of days in the lunar month and to the average number of days spent by the sun in each sign, during its apparent twelve-month journey round the 360° of the ecliptic circle. For Chapman draws attention to the former correspondence by frequent mentions of the monthly term; as in the twenty-eighth stanza, the last stanza of the lunar month: 'Sliding on thy smooth thighs to thys months end.' The latter correspondence is also hinted at, in such lines as:

[1] A numerological analysis of *Venus and Adonis* is attempted by Mr. I. C. Butler and the present author in 'Time-Beguiling Sport,' forthcoming in the Brown University Shakespeare Memorial Volume.

[2] *The Poems of George Chapman*, ed. Phyllis B. Bartlett (New York and London, 1941), pp. 87–92, and 434; though Chapman's authorship of the poem is debated. What is certain is that whoever wrote it imitated, and in places directly translated, Gilles Durant's 'Le zodiac amoureux.' The latter first appeared in 1587 and 1588 anonymously; then in 1594 under Durant's own name in *Les œvres poétiques du Sieur de La Bergerie* [= Durant], *avec les imitations du latin de J. Bonnefons*; later also with Bonnefons', i.e., Joannes Bonefonius' *Basia* (Leyden, 1659). The English imitator selects the directly zodiacal part of Durant's longer poem, and endows it with many of the numerological features discussed below. The equal residence in the signs, however, and the idea of making appropriate departures from this modulus, is taken over from the original.

With thee Ile furnish both the yeare and Sky
(St. 4, 1. 1)
Keeping even way through every excellence,
Ile make in all, an equal residence
Of a newe Zodiack. . . .
(St. 5, ll. 5–6)

The promise to 'make in all [the signs], an equal residence' is adhered to formally; since as a rule the same number of stanzas, two, is allotted to each sign. (The last signs, Aquarius and Pisces, are given only one each; but this is immediately compensated for, in a way that recalls Spenser's *Epithalamion*, by the two *envoi* stanzas). Two striking departures from this arrangement, however, allow some display of numerological virtuosity. First, the poet-sun dwells on the sign Gemini for three stanzas instead of two; thus alluding to the fact that the astronomical sun does in reality remain in this sign longer than in any other. Here again the numerology is sign-posted: 'But nowe I feare . . . I should be mov'd to dwell there thirty days' (St. 12). Secondly, the sign visited in November is Corona, an extrazodiacal sign, instead of the expected Sagittarius—an aberration duly noticed in the phrase 'leaving a little my ecliptick lyne.' This, the poem's sole mention of the ecliptic, occurs in the twenty-third stanza. And, as we know, the ecliptic is inclined to the celestial equator at an angle of $23\frac{1}{2}°$.

iii

From a preliminary survey of Renaissance numerological literature, certain considerations of a general nature emerge.

A broad distinction may be made between formal numerology and substantive number symbolism. In the latter the numbers occur in the grammatically expressed meaning of the literary work. The 'mysterious number' five in Donne's 'The primrose,' and the dimensions of Rabelais' Abbey of Thelema,[1] are examples of substantive number symbolism. In formal numerology, on the other hand, significance attaches to the numerical patterns of non-grammatical elements. It would appear that the variety of possibilities within this kind is far wider than has been supposed. Not only may the cardinal numbers of lines, stanzas, and books be meaningful, as in earlier numerological poetry, but also the ordinal numbers, or positions, of

[1] Discussed in M. A. Screech, *The Rabelaisian Marriage* (London, 1958), pp. 29–34.

these units. Nor need the pattern be limited to external divisions; the line- or stanza-measure of any passage may be symbolically appropriate to its content. Further, any similar elements forming a distinct set—events, images, characters, even words—may be numerologically arranged. Thus, the characters participating in each descriptive canto in the *Faerie Queene* are meant to be counted, and so are the kisses in *Venus and Adonis,* and the days occupied by the action of *Paradise Lost.* These examples show that in practice the distinction between substantive and formal numerology is not always easy to maintain. Equally, however, formal numerology shades off at the opposite extreme into stanzaic organization. The construction of a sestina might be considered as a mathematical operation of some intricacy.

Leaving aside abstract symmetry, we find at least four principal modes of symbolism, in accordance with which the formal numbers of a literary work might be ordered. (1) Theological number symbolism, derived mainly from Biblical allegorizations: a characteristically medieval mode, which nevertheless survived vigorously in the Renaissance period. (2) The more philosophical and self-consistent symbolism of Pythagoreanism and Platonism. (In practice modes (1) and (2) were often combined; nor had they altogether distinct origins, since patristic exegesis of the Bible drew heavily on Platonic ideas.) (3) The temporal or astronomical mode, in which formal numbers alluded to the measurements of cosmic phenomena. This mode is perhaps the most interesting of all, in that it enabled the form of a poem to participate in the action dynamically. (4) The least interesting mode, round-number composition. It was generally otiose; though we should remember that some round numbers had significance in Pythagorean or in Biblical number synbolism. A striking feature of Renaissance numerology is the emergence, and eventual predominance, of modes (2) and (3).

In the conduct of numerological criticism the temptation to project illusory patterns is so seductive that a strict procedural method is indispensable. Speculative puerilities can sometimes be avoided by observing the following principles:

The critic should confine his attention to the external sections of the work, or to passages that are clearly defined by discontinuities or prominent features in their contents. The units counted should also be determinate. (The method of Whaler's numerological analysis of

251

Paradise Lost, for example, is faulty by this criterion; since it depends on computation of rhythmic units whose existence is open to debate.[1]) No licence should ever be allowed in setting the termini of the count.

'Type fallacies' are to be avoided. Thus, if the stanza-count of a passage is asserted to have an astronomical value the stanza-counts of complementary passages ought to have complementary astronomical values, not Pythagorean or Biblical ones.

No formal number should be broken down into component symbolic numbers (for example, by factorization) unless a precedent for the operation can be found in some probable source. We may feel it desirable to avoid such manipulation altogether; but unfortunately certain Renaissance authors, among them Milton, seem not to have shared this feeling.

The significance of formal numbers is properly in the nature of a correspondence. No numerological interpretation can carry conviction, therefore, unless the text supports it. There must be congruence between the meaning assigned to the formal number and the meaning of the passage it measures. Thus, there would be no point in seeing an allusion to the lunar year in the formal measure of Guyon's adventure, unless we had substantive reason to suppose his rôle lunar. Occasionally a Renaissance poet will hint at his numerological intention, in some cryptic utterance that can be interpreted as a direct rubric to the reader; as when Shakespeare makes Venus say 'There shall not be one minute in an hour / Wherein I will not kiss my sweet love's flower' or 'Ten kisses short as one, one long as twenty: / A summer's day will seem an hour but short'; or when Chapman announces the end of his twenty-eight-stanza month in the line 'Sliding on thy smooth thighs to thys months end.' Interpretation of such ambiguities is subject to the ordinary criteria of literary and scholarly analysis.

[1] James Whaler, *Counterpoint and Symbol, an Inquiry into the Rhythm of Milton's Epic Style, Anglistica*, VI (Copenhagen, 1956). This is not to say that Whaler's interpretation is not a brilliant construction. No doubt many of his findings with respect to Milton's rhythm will eventually be accepted: already we may allow him to have established, e.g., that the grouping of books in the first edition of *P.L.* (I, II, III, and IV; V, VI, and VII; VIII and IX; X) follows the reversed, destructive form of the Pythagorean *tetractys* 4 : 3 : 2 : 1. But most of his hypotheses await rigorous demonstration; not only as regards the prosodic analyses presupposed but also the symbolic values attached to numbers without contemporary authority. What seems to be called for is a revision of Whaler's work in the light of seventeenth-century musical and arithmological theory.

Finally, every numerical pattern deemed intentional must be examined statistically, to determine the probability of its occurrence by mere chance. Patterns discussed in the present work have been so examined; and in certain cases we have been able to arrive at definite estimates of the maximum probabilities of chance occurrence. Invariably these probabilities are exceedingly slight. On any reasonable view, patterns with less than 5% probability of chance occurrence are worth considering; but the patterns we have been discussing range in probability from one in several hundreds to one in many thousands.[1] These are chances that some opposed to numerological criticism may be prepared to take; for my part, I should not like to be so foolhardy. At the same time, while a routine caution about probabilities should certainly be observed, we should also remember that, unless it is observed in moderation, many intentional patterns will be neglected. For a Renaissance poet was not in any way obliged to construct statistically improbable configurations. The pattern he intended might well be one that had a good chance of occurring at random. For example, the probability against 'The amorous zodiack' having the same number of stanzas as there are days in the lunar month—a correspondence we know to be intended—is not very great. In other words, there can be no question of the numerological critic submitting his findings unreservedly to the judgement of the statistician. The latter is incompetent to measure the degree of congruence between form and content, or to assess the structural prominence of features defining a pattern. Judgements about numerology are ultimately the responsibility of the literary critic *per se*. Nor, when a critic makes such judgements, is he engaging in any special activity divorced from the rest of critical discourse. Instead, he is simply recovering the context of the literary event in one more direction, the direction of mathematics and number symbolism. After all, numerological criticism is not much more dependent on statistical probability than, for example, prosody is. We are accustomed to say with assurance that 'Western wind, when will thou blow' rhymes ABCB; but this statement is only justified because of the probability that the phonetic resemblance between 'rain' and 'again' did not occur fortuitously. On reflecting how many simple words there were that rhymed with 'rain,' and how restricted was the diction of the

[1] E.g., see above, p. 144, n. 1, p. 152, n. 9, and p. 153, n. 1.

sixteenth-century popular lyric, we might well conclude that the probability of the assertion was less than we had assumed. Judging, that is, by purely statistical criteria. Of course we never think of so judging. We always take into account the historical—though statistically imponderable—fact that rhyming was common practice during the period to which the poem belongs; and this fact decides us. But similar imponderables ought similarly to influence our statements about numerological patterns. Not only do we know that numerical composition was once commonly practised; but we have also to attach due weight to congruences between form and content.

If the above principles are adhered to it seems to me that numerological criticism has a valuable and necessary contribution to make. Necessary, because it treats an element in poetry intermediate between the metrical and the syntactical; so that it throws a unique light on the relation between form and substance. Moreover, it can sometimes assist interpretation of a difficult poem. *The Faerie Queene* is a notable instance: in the fourth book in particular, as we have seen, numerology provides an essential key to the philosophical content. Finally, where numerical patterns are highly developed the results of analysing them must affect any final critical evaluation; a finely structured poem may seem loose, so long as we fail to grasp the principles of its form.

One of the most interesting features of the rediscovery of numerology is that it raises fresh problems in critical theory. For example, it has a bearing on the intentionalist controversy. For we can sometimes speak with propriety of numerological patterns as intended by the author, and see in them independent yet poetically realized statements of his overall meaning. Just as our first communication with an intelligent species on an alien planet would be through number (that most permanent and universal mode of intellection), so the formal numbers of a poem communicate the poet's creative purpose across the gulf of time. As Spenser believed, numerical construction can make a poem an 'endless monument.'

iv

If our interpretation of the number symbolism of the *Faerie Queene* is correct—if even a part of it is correct—then the common conception of the poem will have to be drastically revised. It will no longer be possible to think of it as lacking in structural organization.

Indeed, Spenser may almost be judged to have erred in the opposite direction, and to have produced an overwrought and excessively patterned work. Moreover, any theory about the poem's development that posits casual or widespread revisions at a late stage of composition has a new obstacle to overcome: the necessity that the revisions must have been such as to satisfy the demands of a comprehensive numerical scheme. I do not imply that the scheme was devised first and then implemented (though this is by no means inconceivable); but at least there can be no question of complex numerology being hastily added at the last moment. Another consequence of our findings is that the temporal and seasonal element of the poem's content will now have to be considered as occupying a more central place than it has occupied in the view of any previous critic except Hamilton.

Aesthetically, Spenser's numerology seems to me far superior to that of other English poets, with the exception of Shakespeare, and possibly of Milton. For one thing, it is unusually organic, and constitutes an essential element in the unity of his work. It is internally functional, not externally decorative. By this criterion Jonson, with his fondness for composition in round numbers or in the traditional computistic number twenty-two, must be judged Spenser's inferior. Again, the numerology of the *Faerie Queene* is unusual in being continuous and dense, to such an extent that it seems a texture rather than a superimposed surface pattern. Constantly presenting the resistance of its exigencies to the flow of language and narrative, it produces a massive effect of deliberation and of intelligent fitness, until one might almost say the poem's body thinks. There is something impressive, too, about a poet with the virtuosity to fulfil the requirements of so many different schemes, while maintaining the appearance of *sprezzatura*, of ease and casual mastery. (On the other hand, Spenser's numerology may positively have assisted his sureness of touch: it may help to explain the impression he gives of always knowing precisely what ought to come next.)

The success of Spenser's numerology depends heavily on his choice of astronomical numbers. This is not only because such a mode is more susceptible to numerological subtlety, and because its symbolism is less arbitrary. More striking is the cumulative impression we get that the poem's world is extended in time; that it accomplishes, with deliberate speed, a miniature imitation of cosmic periodicities.

The numbers Spenser deploys in scintillating variety—the numbers of the planetary week, of the solar and lunar years, of the zodiacal constellations—all combine to adumbrate an essentially temporal and dynamic world. By comparison, Dante's seems static and hieratic.

It is natural for us to imagine that such an extensive use of astronomical numerology was new in Spenser's time, even that it was his invention. Possibly, of course, only our ignorance makes us think so. The poem that Chapman translated as 'The amorous zodiack'— Gilles Durant's 'Le zodiac amoureux'—first appeared in 1587; and there were no doubt others like it earlier. Valeriano mentions a belief going back to Aristotle, that the circularity of certain stanza forms was originally intended as an image of the year's recurrence.[1] And the whole tradition of hexaemeral poetry, which received a powerful new impulse in the sixteenth century from Du Bartas' *Sepmaines*, depended on the use of a temporal schema. Nevertheless, it is unlikely that any Renaissance or earlier poet will be found to have used astronomical numerology with a subtlety equal to Spenser's, or to have carried it to comparable heights of artistry. We can be almost certain that the influence of the *Faerie Queene* and of *Epithalamion*, together with that of *Venus and Adonis*, determined the subsequent fashion of writing in this form. It is probably right, too, to think of the form as a correlate of the preoccupation with time and mutability which characterizes Elizabethan thought.

Experimental and tentative though our approach has been, it may have succeeded in reopening a large area of meaning in the *Faerie Queene*, further exploration of which will improve our understanding of the poem. Already it appears to be a work more continuously philosophical than has been thought. Its temporal and seasonal mythology, as well as its numerical philosophy, ought now to receive more critical attention; though this need not mean neglect of the moral and historical allegory. As a good Pythagorean and Platonist, 'thoroughly versed in the mathematical sciences,'[2] Spenser knew that number contained all aspects of reality, the moral and spiritual as well as the physical and abstract. Moreover, his imitation of cosmic order was not without political implications: it owed much to a tradition of Tudor pageantry, in which astronomical symbolism was used

---

[1] *Hieroglyphica*, XXXIX. xii; p. 487.
[2] As Sir Kenelm Digby thought him to be: see Digby's *Observations*, reptd. *Var. Sp.*, II, 472.

to develop the notion of cosmic kingship.[1] Primarily, however, the world-order of the *Faerie Queene* is the outcome of a personal vision and aspiration above the flux of mutability. To fashion a noble person or a nobler self, Spenser had to fashion a true microcosm; and to do that he had to imitate in his poem, *in parvo*, the whole macrocosm, with each sphere that forms the emerging soul. How could this be done, without numbers? Was not all creation effected *ut in pondere et mensura, ita in numero*? The numbers of astronomy were uniquely suited to convey Spenser's vision of a nature constantly renewed and eternized in the cyclic repetitions that bring it ever nearer to the fulfilment of the great week of creation.

[1] We shall understand this connection better when Dr. Sydney Anglo's analysis of the 1501 pageants is published. Certain of these pageants develop a symbolic correspondence between Arthur and Arcturus, and introduce substantive number symbolism based on the enumeration of the constellation *Ursa maior*.

A LIST OF STUDIES WHOLLY OR PARTLY DEVOTED TO NUMERICAL CRITICISM

AUSTIN, H. D. 'Number and Geometrical Design in the Divine Comedy.' *The Personalist*, Vol. XVI, 1925.

BENINI, RODOLFO. *Dante tra gli splendori de' suoi enigmi risolti, ed altri saggi.* Rome, 1952.

BUKOFZER, MANFRED. 'Allegory in Baroque Music.' *Journal of the Warburg Institute*, Vol. III, 1939.

BULATKIN, E. W. 'The Arithmetical Structure of the O.F. *Vie de Saint Alexis*,' *PMLA*, Vol. LXXIV, 1959.

CANDLER, HOWARD. 'On the Symbolic Use of Number in the Divine Comedy and Elsewhere,' *Transactions of the Royal Society of Literature*, Ser. 2, Vol. XXX, 1910.

CHAPMAN, COOLIDGE OTIS. 'Numerical Symbolism in Dante and *The Pearl*.' *Modern Language Notes*, Vol. LIV, 1939.

CURTIUS, ERNST ROBERT. *European Literature and the Latin Middle Ages.* Tr. Willard R. Trask. London, 1953.

DUCKWORTH, GEORGE E. 'Mathematical Symmetry in Vergil's *Aeneid*.' *Transactions of the American Philological Association*, Vol. XCI, 1960.

——. *Structural Patterns and Proportions in Vergil's Aeneid: a Study in Mathematical Composition.* Ann Arbor, 1962.

GMELIN, HERMANN (ed.). *Dante: Die göttliche Komödie.* 3 vols. Stuttgart, 1954–57.

GREENWOOD, O. (ed.). *Sir Gawain and the Green Knight.* London, 1956.

HARDIE, COLIN G. Rev. of Perret (q.v. below). *The Journal of Roman Studies*, Vol. XLIII, 1953.

HATTO, A. T. 'On Beauty of Numbers in Wolfram's Dawn Songs.' *Modern Language Review*, Vol. XLV, 1950.

HERRMANN, L. 'La double symétrie dans la Septième Bucolique de Virgile.' *Revue belge de philologie et d'histoire*, Vol. V, 1926.

HIEATT, A. KENT. *Short Time's Endless Monument.* New York, 1960.

——. 'The Daughters of Horus: Order in the Stanzas of *Epithalamion*.' *Form and Convention in the Poetry of Edmund Spenser.* Ed. William Nelson. Selected Papers from the English Institute. New York and London, 1961.

HOPPER, VINCENT FOSTER. *Medieval Number Symbolism.* New York, 1938.

——. 'Spenser's "House of Temperance." ' *PMLA*, Vol. LV, 1940.

HUISMAN, J. A. *Neue Wege zur dichterischen und musikalischen Technik Walthers von der Vogelweide, mit einem Exkurs über die symmetrische Zahlenkomposition im Mittelalter.* Utrecht, 1950.

STUDIES DEVOTED TO NUMERICAL CRITICISM

KOENEN, FERDINAND. 'Dantes Zahlensymbolik.' *Deutsche Dante-Gesellschaft*, Vol. VIII, 1924.

MAURY, P. 'Le secret de Virgile et l'architecture des Bucoliques.' *Lettres d'Humanité*, Vol. III, 1944.

PETROCCHI, P. 'Del numero nel poema dantesco.' *Rivista d'Italia*, Vol. III, 1901.

PERRET, JACQUES. *Virgile l'homme et l'œvre*. Paris, 1952.

QVARNSTRÖM, GUNNAR. *Dikten och den nya vetenskapen. Det astronautiska motivet.* Acta Reg. Soc. Humaniorum Litterarum Lundensis, LX. Lund, 1961.

ROBSON, C. A. 'The Technique of Symmetrical Composition in Medieval Narrative Poetry.' *Studies in Medieval French Presented to Alfred Ewert.* Oxford, 1961.

RÖSTVIG, MAREN-SOFIE. 'The Hidden Sense: Milton and the Neoplatonic Method of Numerical Composition.' *The Hidden Sense and Other Essays.* Norwegian Studies in English, No. 9. Oslo and London, 1963.

WALKER, J. D. 'The Architectonics of George Herbert's "The Temple." ' *ELH*, Vol. XXIX, 1962.

WHALER, JAMES. *Counterpoint and Symbol, an Inquiry into the Rhythm of Milton's Epic Style. Anglistica*, Vol. VI. Copenhagen, 1956.

WITTE, K. 'Vergils Georgica.' *Die Geschicht des römisch Dichtung im Zeitalter des Augustus.* Erlangen, 1927.

Appendix I

The Arithmological Stanza,
The Faerie Queene, II. ix. 22

Since the early seventeenth century this stanza has attracted more commentary than any other in the poem;[1] and because of its relevance to our present theme it claims yet further attention now.

> The frame thereof seemd partly circulare,
> And part triangulare, O worke divine;
> Those two the first and last proportions are,
> The one imperfect, mortall, fœminine;
> Th'other immortall, perfect, masculine,
> And twixt them both a quadrate was the base
> Proportioned equally by seven and nine;
> Nine was the circle set in heavens place,
> All which compacted made a goodly diapase.

The first thing to notice about these lines is the remarkable polyvalency of their meaning. While not among Spenser's greatest, they nevertheless represent a *tour de force* of ambiguity, for they can simultaneously be approached either as an architectural description of Alma's Castle or as a geometrical description of the human body, or as generally allusive arithmology, or as step-by-step instructions for a specific geometrical construction or arithmetical operation.

[1] Sir Kenelm Digby, *Observations on the 22. Stanza in the 9th Canto of the 2d. Book of Spencers Faery Queen* (London, 1644); William Austin, *Hæc Homo wherein the Excellency of the Creation of woman is described by way of an Essaie* (London, 1637) ('discovered' by Carroll Camden: see 'The Architecture of Spenser's "House of Alma," ' *MLN*, LVIII (1943), 262–265); commentaries by Upton, Dowden, Morley, Kitchin, Robin, and Naylor, reptd. (as are Digby's *Observations*) or paraphrased in *Var. Sp.* II, Appendix xi, 'The twenty-second stanza of canto 9'; and Vincent Foster Hopper, 'Spenser's "House of Temperance," ' *PMLA*, LV (1940), 958–967.

Thus, a seventeenth-century commentator William Austin, to whom attention has been redirected by Carroll Camden,[1] could see the stanza simply as an account of the physical proportions of the human body. The structure of man's nature, says Austin, was made after God's image: 'but, whether this *building* (for the *Form*) were *square*; like a castle, or *cornerd* like a *triangle*: or *round*; like a

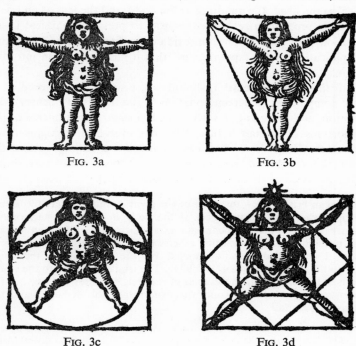

FIG. 3a   FIG. 3b

FIG. 3c   FIG. 3d

tower: or, like a *Roman* H. according to *most* of our *modern ædifices*, is partly questionable.'[2] The crude diagrams that he offers, to show how the body's dimensions bear the proportions either of the mystic square, the mystic triangle, the mystic circle, or the astrological horoscope diagram of the zodiacal houses, will explain his drift (for drift it is) sufficiently clearly.[3] Austin was something of an ass, and

[1] For reference, see previous n.

[2] *Hæc Homo*, p. 75.

[3] Reproduced in our Figs. 3a–3d. The diagrams are briefly defined in *Hæc Homo*, pp. 75–79. The significance of the '*Roman* H' as a corporeal symbol can perhaps be referred to a passage in Macrobius (*In somn. Scip.*, I. vi. 45), where it

although he asserts that all his *discourse* concerning the severall proportions of the body, are [*sic*] very elegantly and briefly contracted, by the late dead Spencer' in the stanza under discussion, it is impossible to take his remarks very seriously as literary criticism. Nevertheless, they illustrate one level of contemporary interpretation. Two centuries later Henry Morley—who saw the 'circle set in heavens place' as the head, the quadrate as the body, and the legs as an open, and therefore 'imperfect' triangle—was to press the physical interpretation with such fanciful and ridiculous literalism, and so naïve an application of the tape-measure, that it has since fallen into disrepute.

This line of interpretation should not, however, be ignored. It is more complete in its accommodation of the details of Spenser's description, and more in line with other Renaissance treatments of the proportions of human nature, than has ever been recognized. In Francesco Giorgio's *De harmonia mundi*, for example, we find the notion that man's body is so designed that its proportions correspond to the intervals of the musical scale, including the diapason:

Let us scan briefly a few instances of the great Architect's care to dispose the proportions of the members of the body in the most harmonious manner; in which every concord and every harmony will be seen to have been brought together—omitting others, where the intermediate intervals are, as it were, filled in and completed. For the proportion of the whole body to the trunk is sesquioctave [9 : 8]. The trunk or thorax to the whole length of the legs, as far as the soles of the feet, is as four to three . . . the proportions in which the tone, the diatessaron, the diapente, and the diapason resound.[1]

[1] *De harmonia mundi totius cantica tria* (Paris, 1545), fol. 101^r; cf. also fols. 335^v–336^r. The Jesuit Athanasius Kircher has a similar but more fully tabulated passage showing that all the musical proportions of perfect consonance can be

is observed that the number 7 'is now called [*h*]*eptas*, the first letter no longer being in use; but the ancients used to call it *septas*, the Greek word testifying to the veneration owing to the number' (ed. Stahl, pp. 108–109; see further Stahl's note on Pythagorean discussions of the form of the word). Probably the most interesting of Austin's diagrams is the last, which he directs us to construct as follows: 'elevate the *hands* againe, so that the *feet* '(stradling) may imitate a *Saint Andrews Crosse*, and you may draw this figure or true form of the *twelve houses* of the *seven Planets* in Heaven; All which *discourse* concerning the severall proportions of the body, are very elegantly and briefly contracted, by the late dead Spencer [in *F.Q.*, II. ix. 22, which is quoted].' Austin seems to regard the geometrical figures of Spenser's stanza as *alternative* constructions drawn from the whole human body, rather than as representations of its parts.

The same author compares the human head with the geometrical figure of the circle. Not having seen a head himself (or perhaps foreseeing the objections of those more instructed in theology than in craniometry), he feels that this comparison needs the authority of Lactantius:

Since therefore God is an intelligible sphere, and this whole world offers itself to our attention in a spherical form, man also, who holds the mean place between God and this world, must necessarily terminate in the same figure; and must imitate the intellectual sphere in his soul, the sensible in his body.[1] [Here follows a traditional diagram—similar to that used by

FIG. 4

Austin—which shows that the circumference of the circle with man's navel 'or, more accurately, his pubis' as centre passes through the extremities of his outstretched limbs. See our Fig. 4.] It will be seen that the whole modulus of the body proceeds from and tends towards rotundity. For Lactantius says that the head is round like a sphere or a circle; and the body too is rounded, with extremely well-proportioned dimensions.[2]

[1] This notion of a double circularity—both mental and physical—seems to provide a satisfactory basis for reconciling the views of two commentators on Spenser's stanza. Robin (who takes Spenser's circle as man's head: cf. Giorgio's Lactantius citation immediately below) and Hopper (who follows the more traditional identification of the circle as the soul) may well both be right.

[2] *De harmonia mundi*, fol. 100ᵛ. The reference in the last sentence is presumably to Lactantius' *De opificio dei, vel formatione hominis* (Patrolog. Lat., VII, 34): 'Eius prope divina mens, quia non tantum animantium, quæ sunt in terra, sed etiam sui corporis est sortita dominatum, in summo capite collocata, tanquam in arce sublimis speculatur omnia, et contuetur. Hanc eius aulam, non obductam

derived from the numbers denoting the magnitudes of the various parts of the body (*Musurgia universalis sive ars magna consoni et dissoni* (Rome, 1650), X. i: tom. II, p. 405). On Francesco Giorgio, see Wind, *Pagan Mysteries*, p. 182 n., and Wittkower, p. 102 n., where references to recent discussions of his architectural theory and philosophical connections are gathered.

APPENDIX I

The strand of architectural meaning is also more complete than it seems at first. Not only were the words *frame, quadrate, base*, and *compacted* architectural terms; but also, less obviously, the numbers 7 and 9 had similar associations. Vitruvius mentions them, in juxtaposition, as the modules of columns of the Doric and Ionic orders respectively.[1] Moreover, these modules, which determined the

[1] *De architectura*, IV. i. 8 (ed. Granger, I, 206–207). The Doric column is seven measures of the diameter in height, the Ionic nine: one is 'manlike in appearance, bare, unadorned; the other feminine' (IV. i. 7). The probability that Spenser intended a secondary reference to these pillar proportions is somewhat strengthened by the fact that earlier in Bk. II he described Belphœbe's legs as 'faire marble pillours . . . Which doe the temple of the Gods support' (II. iii. 28), thereby disposing the reader to catch later allusions to what was a *topos* of very wide distribution in the Renaissance—the image of the human body as a temple standing upon pillar-legs. These pillars were, of course, associated with the twin pillars emblem of virtue: cf. Giles Fletcher, *Christs victorie*, II, St. 13, where Christ's legs are 'as two white marble pillars that uphold / Gods holy place'; Chapman, 'The amorous zodiack,' St. 27, where thighs are pillars upholding '*Venus* Phane'; and the same author's *Hymnus in Cynthiam*, ll. 188 ff., where the pillars lead on to a geometrical description of the body: 'Forme then, twixt two superior pillers framd / This tender building, Pax Imperii nam'd, / Which cast a shadow, like a Pyramis / Whose basis, in the plaine or back part is'; also R. H. Perkinson's discussion of these passages, in 'The body as a triangular structure in Spenser and Chapman,' *MLN*, LXIV (1949). One of Spenser's principal sources throughout Bk. II, Giangiorgio Trissino's *La Italia liberata da Gotthi* (Rome, 1547), contains a description of a Palace of Areta (Virtue) that in some ways resembles the House of Alma (the Palace is built, e.g., 'd'una materia eterna, / Che vincea di belleza ogni altro marmo' (fol. 93): compare and contrast *F.Q.*, II. ix. 21). In this description great emphasis is laid on the Vitruvian proportions governing the number and arrangement of pillars. Of the four *logge* surrounding the *cortile* within the Palace, 'le piu lunghe fur distinte / In trentadui pilastri, e trentun vano, / Si come l'altre, che chiudeano i capi, / Ogniuna in ventun foro era divisa / . . . quel palazo tutto era composto / Con gran giudizio in dorica misura.' Trissino no doubt chooses the Doric style because of its masculinity, and because of the notorious difficulty involved in working out its proportions (on this point,

porrectamque formavit, ut in mutis animalibus, sed orbi et globo similem; quod omnis rotunditas perfectæ rationis est, ac figuræ': a passage which brings together several of the images developed in Spenser's allegory of the Castle of Alma. But the lofty citadel idea was taken by Lactantius from Cicero's *Tusculan Disputations* (I. x), a text that I believe to be one of Spenser's main sources for *F.Q.*, II; while, as Robin percipiently observes (*Var. Sp.*, II, 482), the conception of the head as imaging a divine sphericality goes back directly to Plato's *Timæus*. What we should note in Giorgio, however (and here the appeal to patristic authority is significant), is the Christian modulation of Pythagorean and Platonic notions, which is very characteristic of his period. The context of the passage is a prolonged discussion of the microcosmic nature of man, and of his endowment with the distinctive stylistic qualities of the divine architect in whose image he is made.

264

dimensions of every element of a building in either style, were supposed to have been derived from the proportions of the female (Artemisian) and male (Apolline) statures.[1] As we know, Renaissance architectural theory frequently linked the modules of building construction with the dimensions of the human body, and with the intervals of the musical scale. The element common to all (and connecting also the various semantic strands in Spenser's stanza) was, of course, proportion, mystically understood.[2]

The more convincing commentators upon Spenser's stanza always recognized that it does not merely present a physical description; but that it is also meaningful in terms of Pythagorean and Platonic arithmology—a context to which lines 4–5, in particular, seem to allude. In this context circle and triangle have a definite symbolic meaning, which the architectural and anatomical interpretations of the stanza fail to embrace. As Vincent Hopper puts it:

> Morley's measurements . . . miss entirely the philosophical concept of man as a mean between corruptible and incorruptible which is certainly implied. On the other hand, by accepting the philosophical implication at its face value, we can construct an exact reproduction of Spenser's body-castle on purely mathematical lines.

> At the outset, it is agreed that the circle and the triangle which compose the castle must be considered as first principles. This is sound Aristotelian mathematics:

> > Every plane figure must be either rectilinear or curvilinear. Now the rectilinear is bounded by more than one line, the curvilinear by one only. But since in any kind the one is naturally prior to the many and the simple to the complex, the circle will be the first of plane figures. Again, if by complete, as previously defined, we mean a thing outside of which no part of itself can be found, and if addition is always possible to the straight line but never to the circular, clearly the line which embraces the circle is complete. If then the complete is prior to the incomplete, it follows on this ground also that the circle is primary among figures. . . .

[1] *De architectura*, IV. i. 6–7.

[2] On the various applications of Renaissance theories of proportion see Wittkower, *Architectural Principles in the Age of Humanism*.

---

see Vitruvius, *De architectura*, IV. iii. 1–3). In an earlier passage, describing the palace of Acratia (Concupiscence), he deals directly with the proportion of the individual pillar (ratio of height to diameter); see Rudolf Wittkower, 'Principles of Palladio's Architecture,' *JWI*, VII (1944), 102 (where, however, 'sono grosse anchora / L'ottava parte, *e piu*, di quella alteza' (my itals.) is translated 'their thickness is their height by eight divided'; so that the moral point of the passage—the pillars' disproportionate excessiveness—is lost).

If, again, one orders figures according to their numbers, it is most natural to arrange them in this way. The circle corresponds to the number one, the triangle, being the sum of two right angles, to the number two.[1]

Here are 'the first and last proportions,' the *One* and the *Many*, *Una* and *Duessa*, *Unity* and *Diversity*. The circle is 1, 'immortall, perfect, masculine.' The triangle, by its likeness to 2, is 'imperfect, mortall, fœminine.' In all Pythagoreanism the distinction was made between these two principles, and by them the relative perfection or imperfection of numbers and figures was determined. Immortality, perfection, and masculinity were considered the fundamental attributes of unity. Diversity, represented in the decad by the number 2, was stigmatized by the opposite characteristics. The conjunction of circle and triangle would therefore suggest to the Pythagorean the universal equipoise maintained by the eternal opposition of spiritual perfection and material imperfection.[2]

Here Hopper is in effect following the argument of one of Spenser's earliest and best expositors, Sir Kenelm Digby. In Digby's commentary, however, Aristotelian and Pythagorean mathematics are sometimes fused with a sort of anagogical geometry after the manner of Cusanus:

By these Figures [the circle and triangle], I conceive that [Spenser] means the mind and body of Man; the first being by him compared to a Circle, and the latter to a Triangle. For as a Circle of all Figures is the most perfect, and includeth the greatest space, and is every way full and without Angles, made by the continuance of one onely line: so mans soul is the noblest and most beautifull Creature, that God hath created, and by it we are capable of the greatest gifts that God can bestow, which are Grace, Glory, and Hypostaticall Union of the Humane nature to the Divine, and she enjoyeth perfect freedome and libertie in all her Actions, and is made without composition, which no Figures are that have Angles (for they are caus'd by the coincidence of severall lines) but of one pure substance which was by God breath'd into a Body made of such compounded earth as in the preceding *Stanza* the Author describes. And this is the exact Image of him that breathed it, representing him as fully as tis possible for any creature which is infinitely distant from a Creator. For, as God hath neither beginning nor ending: so, neither of these can be found in a Circle, although that being made of the successive motion of a line, it must be supposed to have a beginning some where, but his circum-

[1] Aristotle, *De cælo*, II. iv, tr. J. L. Stocks, in *Works*, ed. W. D. Ross (Oxford, 1922), II, 286b–287a.

[2] Hopper, pp. 961–962. As our quotations from Giorgio have shown, however, the meanings of the triangle and the circle were not so invariable as Hopper suggests. It is all the more necessary, therefore, to examine closely the significance of 7 and 9.

ference no where: But mans soul is a Circle, whose circumference is limited by the true center of it, which is onely God. . . . By the Triangular Figure he very aptly designes the body: for as the Circle is of all other Figures the most perfect and most capacious: so the Triangle is most imperfect, and includes least space.[1]

It is already apparent that the arithmological stanza presents in brief compass the same Pythagorean ideas that we have found to govern much of the formal disposition of the first two books of the poem. We still miss the specific moral point, however, if we regard the geometrical images merely as illustrating the metaphysical divisions into which human nature falls. As Digby recognizes very clearly, the marvel implicit in the Castle's architectural design consists in the 'joyning together' of completely disparate components:

Certainly of all Gods works, the noblest and perfectest is Man, and for whom indeed all others were done. For, if we consider his *soul*, it is the very Image of God. If his *bodie*, it is adornd with the greatest beautie and most excellent symmetry of parts, of any created thing. . . . But in all this, me thinks, the admirablest work is the joyning together of the two *different* and indeed *opposite* substances in Man, to make one perfect compound; the *Soul* and the *Body*, which are of so contrary a nature, that their *uniting* seems to be a Miracle. For how can the one inform and work in the other, since there's no mean of operation (that we know of) between a spirituall substance and a corporeall? yet we see that it doth: as hard it is to find the true proportion between a Circle and a Triangle; yet, that there is a just proportion, and that they may be equall, *Archimedes* hath left us an ingenious demonstration; but in reducing it to a Probleme, it fails in this, that because the proportion between a crooked line and a straight one, is not known, one must make use of a Mechanick way of measuring the *peripherie* of the one, to convert it to the side of the other.[2]

One of the intentions of Spenser's stanza, in fact, is to draw attention to the *incommensurateness* of mind (circle) and body (triangle), and the difficulty of establishing proportion between them: a fact with painfully real psychological and moral consequence. This use of a geometrical image to illustrate the mysterious indeterminateness of man's nature can be paralleled in Giorgio's *De harmonia mundi*. In his discussion of the correspondence between the four elements and the quaternion in its square form Giorgio observes that we can never make the square commensurate with the circle:

Neither is any coequal with the circle of divine essence known to us . . . nor will its diameter (which unless I err is man) be found commensurate

[1] *Observations*, reptd. in *Var. Sp.*, II, 473.　　　　　[2] Ibid., 474.

with any side [of the square]. For man, like a diameter placed in the middle of the universe, does not harmonise with any determinate creature; an animal of changeable and dissolute nature, he passes freely into any form.[1]

In Digby's account of the circular part of the frame occurs the most interesting passage in his commentary, and the most obscure:

mans soul is a Circle, whose circumference is limited by the true center of it, which is onely God. For as a circumference doth in all parts alike respect that indivisible Point, and as all lines drawn from the inner side of it, do make right Angles within it, when they meet therein: so all the interiour actions of mans soul ought to have no other respective Point to direct themselves unto, but God; and as long as they make right Angles, which is, that they keep the exact middle of virtue, and decline not to either of the sides where the contrary vices dwell, they cannot fail, but meet in their Center.[2]

This appears to mean that all radii of a circle are at right angles with one another, which is nonsense. A little reflection, however, will show that Digby refers to that property of a circle by which a tangent will form a right angle with the radius drawn through its point of contact with the circumference: in other words, 'all lines drawn from the inner side of it [of the circumference], do make right Angles within it [right angles with the tangents touching the circumference at the points from which the first lines were drawn; or, what is the same thing, with the circumference itself at those points], when they meet therein [that is, when and only when the lines meet in the centre of the circle; in other words, on condition that they are radii].' The metaphor receives further development in Digby's comment on the concluding line of Spenser's stanza:

when a mans Actions are regular, and directed towards God, they become like the lines of a Circle, which all meet in the Center, then his musick is most excellent and compleat, and all together are the Authors of that blessed harmony which maketh him happie in the glorious vision of Gods perfections, wherein the minde is filled with high knowledges and most pleasing contemplations; and the senses, as it were, drowned in eternall delight; and nothing can interrupt this Joy, this Happinesse, which is an everlasting Diapase.[3]

[1] *De harmonia mundi*, fol. 51ʳ. A not dissimilar symbolism of elemental square and virtuous, incorporeal circle underlies the architectural passage in Marvell's 'Upon Appleton House, to my Lord Fairfax,' Sts. 6–7: 'Let others vainly strive t'immure / The *Circle* in the *Quadrature*! / These *holy Mathematicks* can / In ev'ry Figure equal Man. / . . . where he comes the swelling Hall / Stirs, and the *Square* grows *Spherical*.'

[2] *Observations*, in *Var. Sp.*, II, 473.   [3] Ibid., 477.

The harmony of the well-tempered nature depends, once again, on the virtuously 'regular' and radial orientation of its moral action.

As Digby himself modestly explains, his treatise was hastily put together; so that it contains many notions incompletely or obscurely expressed. Perhaps we can reconstruct his meaning, however, and understand his emphasis on the symbolic angle between radius and tangent, if we give full force to his allusion (already quoted above) to a demonstration of Archimedes', by which the circle and the triangle can be brought to proportion and equality. Digby must mean the First Proposition of Archimedes' *Measurement of the Circle*, which states that—

a triangle rectangle, of whose two sides (contayning the right angle) one is equal to the semidiameter of the circle, and the other to the circumference of the same, is equall to the Area of that circle.[1]

This demonstration, we notice, once more involves the right angle between radius and circumference; though the latter has now assumed a rectilinear form. Thus, in Digby's view, the difficult and mysterious integration of the incommensurate mind and body of man—the discovery of a 'just proportion' between them—depends throughout on the maintenance of the right angle that symbolizes mean virtue and the orientation of the soul.

'And twixt them both a quadrate was the base, / Proportioned equally by seven and nine.' As Hopper, following Robin, rightly observes, 'the juxtaposition of these two numbers is immediately reminiscent of the astrological theory of the "grades" of human life': a theory whose medieval *locus classicus* is Censorinus' *De die natali* (xiv), and which was widely known, from this and other sources, in the Renaissance.[2] According to the theory, 7, the number of the body, and 9, the number of the mind, have power to determine certain critical stages in human life. The first and last of these climacterics are 49 and 81, because of the special power of square numbers. The most critical, however, is the median climateric, 63 (that is, 7×9); since it pertains to both parts of human nature (*quod et ad corpus et ad animum pertineat*). Hopper continues:

[1] I give the enunciation as it is stated in the 1570 English Euclid (tr. Billingsley), fol. 357.

[2] Hopper (962) cites Campanella, William Harrison, Bodin, and Sir Thomas Browne; one could add almost all arithmological works from the fifth-century Macrobius' *In Somn. Scip.* to the seventeenth-century Kircher's *Musurgia*, as well as a host of commentaries on Plato, encyclopædias, *summas*, and the like.

Even apart from this widespread recognition of the combination of the two numbers together with their implications, 9 is readily identified as the angelic number, and 7 as the number of man (ruled by 7 planets, living through 7 days and 7 ages). In short, the two numbers appear to express the same duality as the two figures: 7 as the number of the body and mortality, 9 as the immutable number of spiritual perfection. By the phrase, 'set in heaven's place,' may be meant either a reference to the 9 circling heavens or the usage of 9 as symbolic of heavenly things. The Pythagoreans originally held that all numbers above 10 were merely reflections of the basic decad, produced by multiplication or addition; but with the introduction of arabic numerals 9 was considered by some to be the 'boundary' of number (since in 10 the monad is repeated) and so might be represented by a circle. Simultaneously, the number 9 took on the spiritual attributes of circularity and incorruptibility because, however often multiplied, it always returns to, or reproduces, itself [in every multiple of 9, the sum of the digits is also 9]. In any case 'this sacred number nyne' and the circle both clearly represent the spirit or heaven: 'Nine *was* the circle.'

While we may readily accept the general drift of these elucidations, they may be thought a little vague, perhaps even remote from Spenser's particular intention. His concern here, after all, is not with the stages of life, but with the parts of man. What we need are illustrations that will give specific content to the general associations of the digits 7 and 9 with body and mind respectively.

This is what Digby is attempting to supply when he connects the two numbers with the operations of the planets and the intelligences in forming man's nature. Spenser, he says,

meanes the influences of the superior substances (which governe the inferiour) into the two differing parts of Man; to wit, of the *Starres* (the most powerfull of which, are the seven Planets, into his body: and of the Angels divided into nine Hierarchies or Orders) into his soul: which in his *Astrophel*, he saith is

By soveraigne choice from th'heavenly Quires select,
And lineally deriv'd from Angels race.

And as much as the one governe the Body, so much the other do the Minde. Wherein is to be considered, that some are of opinion, how at the instant of a childs conception, or rather more effectually at the instant of his Birth, the conceived sperme or tender Body doth receive such influence of the Heavens as then raigne over that place, where the conception or birth is made: And all the Starres or virtuall places of the celestiall Orbes participating the qualities of the seven Planets (according to which they are distributed into so many Classes, or the compounds of them) it comes to passe, that according to the varitie of the severall Aspects of the one and of the other, there are various inclinations and qualities in mens bodies, but all reduced to seven generall heads and the compounds of them, which being to be varied innumerable wayes, cause as many different effects, yet the influence of some one Planet continually predominating. But when the matter in a womans wombe is capable of a soul to inform it, then God sendeth one from Heaven into it. . . . Which whether it have been created ever since the beginning of the world, and reserv'd in some fit place till due time, or be created on emergent occasion; no man can tell: but certain it is, that it is immortall, according to what I said before, when I spake of the Circle which hath no ending, and an uncertain beginning. The messengers to conveigh which soul into the bodie, are the Intelligences which move the Orbes of Heaven, who according to their severall natures communicate to it severall proprieties: and they most, who are Governours of those Starres at that instant, who have the superioritie in the planetary aspects. Whereby it comes to passe, that in all inclinations there's much affinitie betweene the Soul and the Body, being that the like is betweene the Intelligences and the Starres, both which communicate their vertues to each of them. And these Angels, being, as I said before, of nine severall Hierarchies, there are so many principle differences in humane souls, which participate most of their proprieties, with whom in their descent they made the longest stay, and that had most active power to work on them, and accompanied them with a peculiar *Genius* (which is according to their severall Governments) like the same kind of water that running through various conduits wherein severall aromatike and odoriferous things are laid, do acquire severall kinds of tastes and smels. For it is supposed, that in their first Creation, all Souls are alike, and that their differing proprieties arive to them afterwards when they passe through the spheres of the governing Intelligences. So that by such their influence, it may truly be said, that 'Nine was the Circle set in Heavens place.'[1]

From his following references to passages in the Garden of Adonis canto (especially III. vi. 2 and 32), it appears that Digby thinks of the arithmological stanza in relation to the continuing concern of the *Faerie Queene* with actual *fashioning* of 'a gentleman or noble person' —with the inner processes, that is, by which the mind is implanted, formed with particular virtues, and brought to perfection.

But Digby's *Discourse* was made without the aid of books, 'the first halfe quarter of an houre' after he saw the stanza: it is natural to expect fuller illumination from the more considered writings of the various medieval and Renaissance arithmological authors. From them, we learn that the heptad and the ennead, while interpreted

[1] *Observations*, in *Var. Sp.*, II, 476–477.

along the general lines indicated by Digby, were frequently given more specific applications.

For the corporeality of the heptad we have an obvious and fully adequate authority in Macrobius' *Commentary on the Dream of Scipio*. After a passage concerned with the appearance of 7 in the phases of development of the human embryo and in the hebdomads of the ages of man,[1] Macrobius tells us how 'the number 7 also marks the members of the body.' There are 7 inner or 'dark' members (tongue, heart, lungs, liver, spleen, and two kidneys); 7 other members which receive and expel food and air (pharynx, œsophagus, stomach, bladder, and three principal intestines); 7 tissues of the body (marrow, bone, sinew, vein, artery, flesh, and skin); 7 visible parts of the body (head, trunk, two arms, two legs, and the generative organ); 7 divisions in each jointed member; 7 openings in the citadel of the body (mouth, two eyes, two nostrils, two ears); and, finally, 7 motions of the body (forward, backward, left, right, up, down, and rotatory). As Stahl (p. 108 n.) remarks, the significance assigned to the heptad by Macrobius and other writers in the same tradition was probably derived from the fact that this number marks the lunar quarters.[2]

The human significance of the ennead is a little more elusive. Fortunately, however, Giorgio devotes a whole chapter to this very topic.[3] His ultimate purpose is to find psychological and theological equivalents for the number 27, the last of the seven numbers of the *Timæus* series, from whose mixture the Word-Soul was generated. To this end he distinguishes three separate novenaries in man. The first (which is of interest in view of Spenser's concern, in The Legend of Temperance, with the mortification of the flesh and the edification of a new nature) results, we are told, from the replacement of man's

---

[1] I. vi. 62–75. See Stahl's note (p. 115) on the difference between Macrobius' scheme of 10 hebdomads and the scheme implied in, e.g., Jaques' speech on the 7 ages of man in *As You Like It*, II. vii; also Ptolemy, *Tetrabiblos*, IV. x, with Robbins' nn., pp. 61 and 440.

[2] *In somn. Scip.*, I. vi. 77–82, with Stahl's notes, which list many parallels in other antique and patristic arithmologies. The division of the body into 7 was also connected with the development of physiological theories based on a planetary melothesia (that is, assignment of the governance of various parts of the body to one or another of the 7 planets). The passage from Digby's *Observations* quoted above contains an allusion to such theories.

[3] *Cant. prim.*, *ton. quint.*, Ch. x: 'Quomodo tres illi novenarii reperiantur in homine.'

272

mortal, corruptible body by a spiritual, incorruptible one. The two-fold mortal body (*bifarius corpus*) consists of two quaternions, since each of its moieties is composed of four elements: an 8 therefore, 'to which is added a certain unified life; so that the body may be integrated, and may live';[1] that is, $9 = 2 \times 4 + 1$:

> But the second novenary is in the soul; composed of the five exterior senses, and the four interior senses—that is, the imaginative, cogitative, phantastic, and common senses [or faculties]; and it terminates at the intellect, as at the decad. Within the latter (the intellect), there is another, purer nine, in simple numbers, with which the nine orders of angels is in accord. This novenary terminates at that [other] decad which is the supreme fount and parent of all.[2]

In the remainder of the chapter Giorgio attempts to find, in a dichotomy between the active and passive parts of the human soul, a parallel with the odd and even divisions of the *Timæus* double series of the World-Soul.[3]

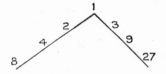

Giorgio's third novenary, that of the intellect, is turned to good account, as we have seen, by Digby. His second novenary, that of the exterior and interior 'senses,' was if anything the commoner scheme among the arithmologists,[4] and seems very relevant to the allegory of the Castle of Alma—which, we recall, includes an elaborate treatment of the interior senses, as well as a representation of the exterior senses in the 'five great Bulwarkes' assailed by Maleger's troops. Giorgio's first novenary is apparently peculiar to himself, and can be

---

[1] 'Quibus (ut compaginatum sit corpus, et vivat) inest vita quædam unica' (*De harmonia mundi*, fol. 91ʳ).

[2] 'In anima vero est secundus novenarius collectus ex quinque sensibus exterioribus, et quatuor interioribus, videlicet imaginativa, cogitativa, phantasia, et sensu communi: terminaturque ad intellectum, tanquam ad decimum' (ibid.). It should be remembered that in all arithmologies of this tradition the decad and the monad could be interchanged at will.

[3] Known to the Renaissance in the form of the *lambda* diagram; though as Stahl (p. 109, n. 48) points out, this diagram was probably not used by Plato himself.

[4] Cf., e.g., Kircher, *Musurgia*, II, 459. A different scheme again occurs in Bongo (I, 241), who lists nine *complexions* derived from four humours.

left out of consideration. The other two novenaries, however, correspond to the two sides of an ambiguity in Spenser's stanza. Does nine there designate the intellect (*mens*), in harmony with the angelic orders; or the soul (*anima*), with its nine senses? This question must be deferred for the present, though we may note here that Spenser mentions the number 9 twice. 'Nine was the circle' must refer to the ninth or celestial sphere, above the errant seven and the starry eighth, from which bodiless spirits began their descents—as Digby, following Macrobius, explains.[1] It follows that this 9 also refers to the angelic, incorporeal part of man: the intellect. It is not yet certain, however, that the 9 by which the quadrate is proportioned carries exactly the same meaning.

It is thus possible to substantiate the broad lines, at least, of Hopper's identification of 7 as the number of the body and 9 as the number of the mind. And for his view that 'the two numbers appear to express the same duality as the two figures'—the duality, that is, between the first and last proportions—support can also be found. A connection is indeed intended between 7 and 9, on the one hand, and the two fundamental series, of the odd and even numbers, on the other. For, as Giorgio observes, the heptad is formed out of $1 + 2 + 4$, the first three terms in the series of even numbers (the monad, as usual, counting as both even and odd).[2] And in the same way 9 is formed from $1 + 3 + 5$, the first three odd numbers. Thus, on the basis of purely mathematical symbolism, Spenser's two numbers correspond to the opposed principles of odd and even, masculine and feminine, limited and unlimited.

It is the identification of Spenser's 'quadrate' that has given rise to most controversy; which is not surprising, since even in this context it stands out as a word that is especially ambiguous and laden with associations. Digby is at first sight disappointingly unhelpful here. He says only that Spenser means—

the foure principall humors in mans Bodie, viz. *Choler*, *Blood*, *Phleme*, and *Melancholy*: which if they be distempered and unfitly mingled, dissolution of the whole doth immediately ensue: like to a building which falls to ruine, if the foundation and Base of it be unsound or disordered. And in some of these, the vitall spirits are contained and preserved, which the other keep in convenient temper; and as long as they do so, the soul

---

[1] For Macrobius' account of the descent see *In somn. Scip.*, I. ix and xii.
[2] *De harmonia mundi*, fol. 90^v.

and bodie dwell together like good friends: so that these foure are the Base of the conjunction of the other two.[1]

Upton, like Digby, takes the quadrate as a tetrad,[2] but gives it a much wider interpretation:

the sacred ΤΕΤΡΑΚΤΥΣ, the fountain of perpetual nature, (as called in the Pythagorean verses) the mysterious quadrate, was the base. This quadrate or sacred quaternion, comprehended all number, all the elements, all the powers, energies, and virtues in man: Νοῦς, Ἐπιστήμη, Δόξα, Αἴσθησις; Temperance, justice, fortitude, prudence. Hope, fear, joy, grief. Cold, hot, moist, dry. Fire, air, earth, water. . . .[3]

Though tantalizing in its brevity, this interpretation is more plausible, particularly in its mention of the 'powers, energies, and virtues in man.' For the whole point and formal relevance of the stanza must lie in the moral power of the quadrate: its power to integrate the diverse frame of man.

This was well understood by Francis Webb, whose 'Letter from the author . . . to a friend. On the 22nd Stanza of the 9th canto of the 2nd book of Spenser's Faerie Queen' is one of the few considerable pieces of Spenser commentary to have eluded the *Variorum* editors' drag-net.[4] Webb develops at some length—though without documentation from authors accessible to Spenser—the notion that the quadrate's function is a unifying one. The quadrate is applied, he says, like the '*tertiam animam* by which matter and soul are united.' Like Upton, he identifies the quadrate as the Pythagorean quaternion or *tetractys*:

This philosophy considered the Quadrat as a principle of union between numbers and proportions; and therefore may well be considered in the present instance to be so meant respecting the quadrat being placed, as a mean, or connecting principle, between the circle and triangle; and therefore may properly be considered and treated of in the same manner as the Platonists did the *tertiam quandam naturam*, which partaking of the quality of body and mind, was the bond by which these were united.[5]

This seemingly arbitrary endowment of the *tetractys* with just the moral qualities needed to explain Spenser's quadrate at first arouses

[1] *Observations*, in *Var. Sp.*, II, 475–476.
[2] *OED*, s.v. 'quadrate,' sb. 1. c: 'a group of four things = QUATERNION, 1,' with an instance from Saltonstall (1637): 'By the number of twice two, hee invented the quadrate of the foure Elements.'
[3] Reptd. in *Var. Sp.*, II, 479.
[4] Printed together with the same author's *Panharmonicon* (London, 1815?).
[5] 'A Letter,' p. 39. The whole passage (pp. 39–41) is relevant.

methodological suspicion. When we consult the Renaissance authorities, however, we find that the virtuous power of the *tetractys*, and its mediating and co-ordinating functions, were indeed common topics. Moreover, these interpretations were based on definite arithmological arguments. We may draw our illustrations from Giorgio and Bongo; since the pedantically full explanations of the latter conveniently offset the allusive style of the former.[1]

If we would learn about the Pythagoreans, writes Giorgio, and the precepts of the esoteric theologians, we must begin with the quaternion, 'the root and beginning of all numbers' (*omnium numerorum radix et exordium*). This title has its justification in the quaternion's special properties. Nothing goes beyond it, he explains, since it embraces all numbers, provided that the base of numeration is 10, the sum of its separate digits. It contains every kind of number: 'par et impar, quadratum, quadrantalem, longum, planum, cubalem, pyramidalem, primum et compositum.'[2] Moreover, it yields four cubic numbers that bear a relation to, or have the proportions of, the decad. With the help of Bongo,[3] we can make out what is meant here, namely that

$$1 + 2 + 3 + 4 = 10$$
$$10 + 20 + 30 + 40 = 100$$
$$1^3 + 2^3 + 3^3 + 4^3 = 100$$

Finally, the *tetractys* contains every proportion and every musical consonance; since between its several members there may be 'proportio dupla, tripla, quadrupla, sesquialtera, sesquitertia.'[4] Taking the last and first digits of the *tetractys*, for example, we get the ratio

---

[1] I purposely use Renaissance, rather than ancient, authorities; though, of course, much of their material was derived from such sources as Hierocles' commentary on Pythagoras' *Carmina aurea*.

[2] *De harmonia mundi*, fol. 50ᵛ. Bongo writes to similar effect, but follows Macrobius in emphasizing the quaternion's inclusion of the first odd and first even numbers, and the fact that the digits contained in it sum to ten, the fount of number $(1 + 2 + 3 + 4 = 10)$.

[3] Pt. I, p. 136. Kircher bases an elaborate world-scheme on the same formulæ. In his scheme (which in its essentials goes back to Renaissance Neoplatonism) the monad or unity signifies God, the denary Intelligence, the centenary Soul, and the millenary Body (*Musurgia*, II, 451). This is of some relevance here, in view of the obscure passage in Digby's *Observations* concerning denaries and centenaries (*Var. Sp.*, II, 475). Perhaps, after all, Digby did associate Spenser's quadrate with the quaternion.

[4] *De harmonia mundi*, fol. 50ᵛ; cf. ibid., fols. 423ʳ⁻ᵛ, and Bongo, I, 156—where, of course, each of the ratios is painstakingly worked out.

4:1, or *quadrupla*, which yields the musical interval *bisdiapason*. All these unique properties are summed up in the *symbolum* of Hierocles: 'nothing can be said or done, unless it proceeds from the four-fold number, as from the root and foundation of all' (*nihil dici aut fieri potest, nisi a quaternario numero tanquam a radice et fundamento omnium proveniat*).[1] Or, as Bongo puts it, 'from the quaternion arise the roots of the whole world' (*A quaternario quippe manarunt totius mundi radices*).[2]

Throughout his chapter on the quaternion, Giorgio strains to discover correspondences with the four elements. Now this is a line of thought that can illuminate Digby's odd connection of Spenser's quadrate with the four humours; for the Franciscan writer uses *element* in the most expansive possible sense, tracing a pattern of four-fold 'elements' through every level of the cosmos. He mentions the four metaphysical elements (*essentia, esse, virtus, actio*); the four *seminaria naturæ* (*virtus, pullulatio naturalis, adulta forma, et compositum*); the four mathematical elements (point, line, plane, solid); the four *seminaria virtutum* (justice, temperance, fortitude, prudence); and the four powers of judgement, according to Hierocles (*intellectus, disciplina, opinio, sensus*).[3] Just as architects, imitating nature, arrange their buildings with four corners, in order that the structure will be firm, so 'the Creator rightly lays a four-fold foundation for every mundane fabric.' Underlying Giorgio's whole chapter—and underlying also, I believe, Spenser's stanza—is this notion that the quaternion is the foundation ('base') of all being, because it is a principle of order common to different levels of existence.

In Bongo's chapter on the quaternion we find that it is assigned a similar co-ordinative function; but for the reason that it symbolizes soul. Having cited Plato's view that the soul is a harmonic number composed from the *tetractys*, Bongo surveys several theories of the four-fold nature of the soul; such as the theory that there are four souls *veluti fundamenta*: namely *mens, scientia, opinio,* and *sensus*.[4] The Pythagoreans, he notes, postulate a different correspondence between the soul and the quaternion; for they say that the soul is composed of four spiritual elements, and that it exerts a four-fold spiritual force: concupiscible, irascible, rational, and voluntary (*liberumque,*

---

[1] *De harmonia mundi*, fol. 51^r.   [2] *Numerorum significationis*, I, 137.
[3] *De harmonia mundi*, fol. 51^r.   [4] Cf. Plato, *Republic*, VI, 511.

sive voluntarium). Next he returns to Plato's *Republic*, and to the idea of four virtues controlling the four powers of the soul.[1]

Bongo's identification of the quaternion with virtue is worked out in even greater detail. He justifies this very ancient association by adducing the special virtue of square numbers; among which 4 is pre-eminent, in that it is equal to the sum of its factors ($4 = 2 \times 2 = 2 + 2$): 'pulcherrimam quandam præseferens consonantiæ speciem.' All the angles of a square are right angles which 'signify "right" reason; and right reason is the perennial font of virtue.'

Nevertheless, while 4 is a symbol of virtue, and thus incorporeal, it is also at the same time a corporeal number. This double nature of the quaternion (a feature to which Bongo devotes much intricate arithmological pseudo-reasoning) explains its special fitness to symbolize the co-ordinative function of the virtuous *anima* that mediates between *mens* and *corpus*. The most important of the arguments supporting the double characterization of the quaternion depends upon a contrast between two geometrical representations of the number in Pythagorean mathematics. It could be expressed either as four dots placed at the corners of a square or as three dots at the apices of a triangle, with a fourth dot placed above them, so as to form a tetrahedron. In the latter case, by comparison with its triangle base, the tetrahedral or pyramidal quaternion is solid and corporeal.[2] In the former case, however, 'when the same number as a square is compared with the cube 8, then the quaternion is incorporeal, and simply a surface (base) of 8: a quadrate, raising no solid mass.' Thus the quaternion—

[1] *Numerorum significationis*, I, 168 f. Another approach to the same conclusion, in an earlier passage (I, 141), should be noticed. There Bongo cites the view of Philolaus and Pythagoras, that the soul consists in a harmony and temperature of complexions and qualities, whose dissolution leads to the separation of the body from the soul, and to death. Moreover, the life of the soul depends on 'geometrical proportion' (*cuius vita omnis alioqui nonnisi per istam temperaturam, et proportionem geometricam*). These matters are probably discussed in connection with the *tetractys* because it contains the geometrical series 1 : 2 : 4, as well as all the ratios of perfect musical consonance.

[2] Ibid., p. 135. The close relevance to Spenser's stanza of this notion of the pyramidal quaternion is best understood by comparison with Chapman's Geometrical Man: 'This tender building, Pax Imperii nam'd, / Which cast a shadow, like a Pyramis / Whose basis, in the plaine or back part is / Of that queint worke: the top so high extended, / That it the region of the Moone transcended' (*Hymnus in Cynthiam*, ll. 189–193; cited, but not explained, by Perkinson). The comparison suggests that Spenser's triangular figure ought perhaps to be regarded as one of the plane faces of a pyramid.

comprehends both kinds of nature, namely, the corporeal, and that which is free from body: the incorporeal, in the plane surface that fills the square; but the corporeal, in the other dimension that cubes complete. . . .[1]

In Renaissance arithmology, then, the quadrate (quaternion: *tetractys*) was regarded: (1) as a base (base of numeration, fundamental principle, root or foundation of all existence); (2) more particularly, as a mean quantity (often the soul, *anima*), partaking of both corporeal and incorporeal natures, and therefore able to unify mind and body; (3) as a principle of harmony in nature (to 'quadrate' meant to harmonize[2]); and (4) as the fountain of all virtue. Once this context of Spenser's stanza is known, the identity of his quadrate is established beyond any reasonable doubt. For it, too, is said to be the 'base' or foundation of the human frame. Secondly, it is 'twixt' (that is, in an intermediate position between, or else, shared in common by) the opposed parts of man's nature—mortal and immortal, corporeal and incorporeal. And finally, when all the parts of the frame are 'compacted' the result (thanks to the operation of the quadrate) is the harmony of 'a goodly diapase.'

It will be noticed that in Spenser's stanza the word *twixt* has two possible meanings. According to the first of these, the quadrate is in a mean position *between* the other two parts; just as the square comes above the triangle but below the circle, in degree of capaciousness, and therefore of perfection. But according to the second meaning, the foundation is *twixt* the other parts in the sense that it is 'shared between' them. These meanings correspond to two complementary ways of regarding the *anima*. Either we can think of it as a mean between the mortal *corpus* and the angelic *mens*; or we can think of it as sharing in both natures—as part corporeal, part incorporeal. Following the latter approach, we can discern a level of significance at which the numbers 7 and 9 participate mathematically as well as symbolically. For, if the quaternion be represented in linear form, as a straight line 4 units long, then the square described with this line as base will have an area that exactly contains two other areas, denoted by the

---

[1] *Numerorum significationis*, I, 135. Another of Bongo's arguments for the double nature of the quaternion is based on that property of a geometrical progression by which every third term (counting inclusively) is a square number—and therefore virtuous and incorporeal—while every fourth term is a cubic number, at which 'we fall towards corporeal nature.'

[2] *OED*, s.v. 'quadrate,' vb. 3. b.

numbers 7 and 9. That is, $4^2 = 16 = 7 + 9$. As Hopper explains,[1] this was—

the usual demonstration for the formation of square or quadrate numbers which, by definition, are generated by the successive addition of the sequence of odd numbers to the sequence of quadrates so produced: 1 (considered a quadrate) + 3 (first odd number) = 4; 4 (quadrate) + 5 (second odd number) = 9; 9 (quadrate) + 7 (third odd number) = 16.

The square on the quaternion (denoting the soul) is thus composed of two numbers which, as we have seen, symbolize its corporeal and incorporeal aspects. 7 and 9 may also, however, contain specific allusions to the different numerical divisions of the *anima*. If so, then Spenser's stanza is in line with a passage in the *De harmonia mundi*, where Giorgio, discussing the double nature of the *anima*, shows that it can be considered as characterized either by the 9 senses mentioned above or by 7 spheres corresponding to the influences of the 7 planets.[2]

As it happens, the relation of 16 to 9 (and of 9 to 4) is directly treated by Giorgio in another passage, as an illustration of the incommensurateness of the circle and the quaternion in its square form. Although no direct proportion can be found between them, he says,

Nevertheless a proportion is mediated by raising the lower square of the elements into a better square [*Est tamen proportio mediata reducendo elementorum quadraturam infimam in quadratum meliorem*]. . . . And so by a marvellous proportion these four-fold elements harmonise; like square numbers, that are rounded off with the proper number, and harmonised by a mean proportional to both. For example, 4 and 9 are square numbers, and the mean between them is 6. 6 : 4 is *proportio sesquialtera*, and so is 9 : 6. In the same way, 9 and 16 harmonise, and so it is with the whole series of square numbers.[3]

In each case the proportion (and therefore the musical interval) between the larger quadrate and the mean is the same as that between the mean and the smaller quadrate; thus giving rise to a unison (often loosely called *diapason*) of intervals. Spenser's 'goodly diapase' may also allude to the relation of the quaternion with 7, a number which was frequently given a musical application. Thus, Giorgio, as we have

---

[1] P. 963; he notes that the two squares of 9 and 16 units 'are the traditional figures employed for illustration of the use of the *gnomon* (the L-shaped section) in the formation of squares. [Cites Allman, and Nicomachus.] The first English Euclid (London, 1570) uses these two squares as illustrations throughout the definitions of Book X (fols. 228–232).'

[2] Fol. 90ʳ.   [3] *De harmonia mundi*, fol. 51.ʳ

seen, observes that the sum of the series of even numbers, up to and including the term 4 (that is, $1 + 2 + 4$), is 7; and in the same passage follows Macrobius in the view that the 7 spheres form a heptachord, with a total interval of a diapason.[1] While these associations explain the stanza's final line satisfactorily enough, its precise phrasing ('All which compacted') suggests that there may be yet another, neater solution, depending upon the *compacting* (that is, 'composition') of proportions or intervals.[2]

Perhaps the foregoing covers all that we can be sure the numerological stanza is intended to mean. We must not, however, omit Vincent Hopper's interesting suggestion that it additionally contains detailed instructions for the mathematical demonstration of the mean proportional; in keeping with 'Spenser's own definition of the castle as a "House of Temperance" together with his earlier references [at II. i. 58 and II. ii. 2] to the golden mean as the measure of temperance.'[3] This familiar demonstration called for—

a right triangle inscribed in a circle whose diameter is the hypotenuse of the triangle. The figure, 'partly circulare' and 'part triangulare,' thus necessitates one quantity, the hypotenuse-diameter, 'twixt them both' and, since the lower part of the circle is omitted in the actual demonstration, this quantity gives the appearance of a base on which both circle and triangle rest. Spenser has given precisely the necessary data for such a construction:

[1] *De harmonia mundi*, fol. 90^v, after Macrobius *In somn. Scip.*, II. i–iv (on a Ciceronian passage, cit. at II. i. 3, that itself states the same notion). Cf. also Upton, in *Var. Sp.*, II, 480, who cites Pliny to similar effect.

[2] This was a familiar operation in musical theory; the stock example being the composition of the fifth (3 : 2) and the fourth (4 : 3) to form the diapason (6 : 3 or 2 : 1). In his discussion of the numbers adding to 7, Macrobius (*In somn. Scip.*, I. vi. 43) remarks that 'all wise men admit that the soul was also derived from musical concords. Among these an important one is the diapason, which consists of two others, the fourth and the fifth.' In one of these ratios, he points out, 'the first term is three, and in the other, four.' A specific moral application of this composition of intervals is noted among Pico della Mirandola's *Conclusiones secundum mathematicam Pythagoræ*, Nos. 8–10. The fifth or *diapente* is there identified as the proportion between the irascible and the concupiscible faculties; while the proportion between the reasonable soul (*ratio*) and the irascible faculty is *diatessaron*, that is, a fourth. Added together, these intervals yield the *diapason* —the proportion between the rational soul and the concupiscible faculty (*Opera omnia* (Basel, 1573), I, 79). Hopper (p. 965) isolates, and consequently misapplies, the last of these correspondences only. If the Pythagorean notion is in fact relevant Spenser's meaning may be that in its corporeal (heptadic) aspect the soul (*ratio*) yields a diapason by preserving the right proportions with the irascible and concupiscible faculties: a meaning which would be quite in accord with the overall allegory of Bk. II.   [3] Hopper, p. 964.

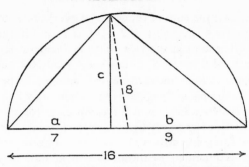

Diagram showing Hopper's reconstruction of the Castle
of Alma.

If this construction is checked with the stanza it will be agreed that the
'frame' seems 'partly circulare' (*N.B.* not a circle) and 'part triangulare.'
'Twixt them both' the quadrate 16 is the base 'proportioned equally by
seven and nine.' Line c is the mean between 7 and 9, joining the two numbers at one end and the two figures at the other. The radius of the circle is
8, which is the octave or, precisely, the 'goodly diapase' of Spenser's
concluding line, and a perfect measure for the circle of the universe, 'the
harmony of the spheres.' For 8 is the number of harmony, it is the number
of emanations in Spenser's *Hymne of Heavenly Beauty*, it is Henry More's
'steddy Cube, all propping Adonai,' it is the proportion between reason
and concupiscence according to Pico della Mirandola.[1]

This interpretation, while it incorporates many valuable ideas,
presents also several difficulties.[2] For example, although Hopper
earlier went to some trouble (rightly, as I have shown) to connect the
number 7 with the triangular part of the frame, and 9 with the circular
part, he has now abandoned these connections. The triangular and
circular (or semicircular) areas in his diagram do not bear any recognizable proportion to each other, or to any third quantity.[3] More-

[1] Hopper, pp. 964–965.

[2] Among the latter I do not, however, include the obscurity of the symbolism
of the number 16, which puzzles Hopper (p. 966, n. 28). Apart from its use by
Giorgio mentioned above, we may cite Vitruvius' characterization of it as a
doubly perfect number, on the grounds that it is composed of the decad plus the
perfect 6 (*De architectura*, III. i. 8; in a passage debating whether 6 or 10 is the
more perfect number); or Bongo's *Numerorum significationis*, II, 38–40, where
Vitruvius' argument is repeated, and supported by the further reflection that 16
is virtuous because it is the square of the virtuous 4.

[3] The ratio between the triangular and semicircular areas is in fact $21\sqrt{7} : 88$.
In these formulations of the difficulties of Hopper's theory—and, indeed,
throughout this Appendix—I owe much to the assistance of Dr. D. P. Walker.

over, Hopper's demonstration actually introduces a different con-nection between numbers and figures, quite unsupported by arithmo-logical authority. Whereas Spenser says 'nine was the circle,' Hop-per's circle has a radius of 8 units, and an area of about 201½ units. 8 may be (though it has not been shown to be) 'a perfect measure for the circle of the universe'; but it is not the measure of Spenser's circle. Finally, the geometric mean between 7 and 9 (c in Hopper's diagram) is $\sqrt{63}$, an irrational number which as far as I can tell was accorded no special symbolic significance in the Renaissance. This seems a serious difficulty; though of course it could be argued that the point of the stanza lies in the irrationality of the elusive mean and the in-commensurateness of the circle and the triangle. All this is not to deny that the stanza contains directions for a specific geometrical construction. It may very well be found to do so. But, if it is, the con-struction will not be identical with Hopper's; and one suspects that it may be a good deal more complex.[1]

Nevertheless, Hopper is right in his general contention that the stanza expresses the capacity of man (especially, we may add, man's soul) to act as 'the Neo-Platonic *copula mundi*, joining heaven and earth, circle and triangle, 9 and 7, spirit and body'; and that this unique function depends on the fact that the 'operation of this ethical golden mean is found only in man, who, in his ideal state, is a mean between excess and defect, between reason and concupiscence, be-tween heaven and earth.'[2] The human *anima* could only act as the *vinculum*, it was believed, if it was itself in harmony.[3]

And we can go further with Hopper, agreeing that, within the stanza's terms of reference, *some* geometrical demonstration of the mean is positively called for. The assumption that Spenser intended the *geometric* mean, moreover, is a natural one; for this mean was especially richly endowed with symbolic meanings in Renaissance cosmology. It had a prominent place both in the theory of musical

---

[1] A geometrical demonstration relating the triangle, quadrate, and circle *as proportional areas* might be found, for example; perhaps, even, one that includes the construction of a mean proportional. In this connection it is worth noting that Hopper's diagram was used in the construction of a square equal in area to a triangle (Euclid, II. xiv).

[2] Hopper, p. 966.

[3] Cf., e.g., Kircher, *Musurgia*, I, 534: 'ut anima vinculum mentis et corporis esset in sua essentia, nil nisi harmonia exque harmoniis composita.' This passage follows a discussion of the *lambda* series, and precedes one on the *tetractys*.

proportion and in arithmological accounts of the formation of the soul from the geometric series of the *Timæus*. We ought not to assume too readily, however, that this is the only variety of mean alluded to in Spenser's stanza. The other means had also symbolic values. Giorgio, indeed, devotes a long discussion to the moral significance of each in turn: geometric, arithmetic, and harmonic.[1] In support of his solution, Hopper cites a passage in Dee's Preface to the 1570 English Euclid, which touches on the application of numerical proportion to moral philosophy:

> Aristotle in his *Ethikes* (to fatch the sede of Justice, and light of direction, to use and execute the same) was fayne to fly to the perfection, and power of numbers: for proportions arithmeticall and Geometricall.[2]

Turning to Aristotle himself, however, we find that the arithmetic mean plays a more prominent part in the *Ethics* than the geometric. True, the geometric mean is used as an illustration of distributive justice. But rectificatory justice is illustrated by the arithmetic mean; and—what is far more relevant to our present purpose—*the mean of temperance is compared to an arithmetic mean*.[3] Moreover, returning to Dee, we notice his discussion of the medical theory that the temperate state is represented by the mean between the qualities Hot, Cold, Moist, and Dry. As he explains at some length, the reading of a particular mixture of humours is arrived at by calculating the arithmetic means between the observed degrees of the various qualities, as these are represented in the separate humours concerned.[4]

I am thus encouraged to propose a simple (though admittedly incomplete) numerical solution of the latter part of Spenser's stanza, based on the assumption that it alludes to the *arithmetic* mean. As we have seen, the quaternion was regarded as having a dual nature,

---

[1] *De harmonia mundi*, fols. 91^v–92^r; the property of the arithmetic mean, we are told, is that it 'leads to peace.' This notion stems from a Pythagorean tradition, transmitted also by Pico, in which the three means were identified with the three daughters of Themis: 'Triplex proportio, Arithmetica, Geometrica et Harmonica, tres nobis Themidos filias indicat, iudicii, iustitiæ, pacisque existentes symbola' (Pico della Mirandola, *Conclusiones sec. math. Pythag.*, No. 6; in *Opera omnia*, I, 79). All the means were also given elaborate politico-philosophical applications in Renaissance arithmology—a line of thought that survived as late as Kircher (*Musurgia, lib.* X, *Registrum* vii, 'Symphonismus Mundi politici sive de Musica politica'; II, 432–440).

[2] Hopper, p. 967, quoting Dee's Pref., sig. a. ii.

[3] See *Nicomachean Ethics*, 1106^{a-b} and 1131^b–32^a.

[4] Dee, Pref., sig.$_*$ iii^v.

corporeal and incorporeal, in that it could be represented geometric-
ally either as a pyramid or as a square (quadrate). In the former case
it was three-dimensional, and therefore corporeal by comparison
with the plane triangle forming the base of its pyramid; while in the
latter case it was incorporeal, by comparison with a cubic number
(8) which had the quaternion (in its virtuous, square, plane, two-unit-
sided form) as its base. My proposed solution, stated mathematically,
is that *8 is the arithmetic mean between 7 and 9*. That is to say, the
corporeal substance that has the virtuous quaternion as its foundation
—that is based on virtue—maintains a temperate state by occupying
a mean position between the mortal mutable 7 and the wholly
spiritual 9. As is appropriate where the virtue of temperance, or
where the temperature of bodies, is concerned, the mean is an arithmetic one. While this solution does not accommodate the triangular
and circular areas of the first part of the stanza, it should be noted that
the geometrical demonstration of the arithmetic mean (here the
bisection of a line $7 + 9 = 16$ units long) would depend on the use of
the all-important right angle, symbolic of virtue.[1]

Although this disquisition on a single stanza has been disproportionately long, I hope it will have served to show, beyond any reasonable doubt, not only that Spenser was conversant with Platonic and
Pythagorean mathematics but also that he stood in close relation to
the Renaissance tradition of moralized arithmology. It may have
shown, too, that some even of Spenser's less impressive lines can
stand up to detailed analysis and continue to reveal, underneath an
apparently simple explicitness, layer after layer of densely textured
allusion and association. I am not thinking here merely of the stanza's
microcosmic reflection of the poem's continuing concern with 'soul-
making'—with the processes by which the virtuous *anima* achieves its
emergence.[2] Rather do I have in mind the many specific connections

[1] Moreover, the numbers 7 and 9, as well as their arithmetic mean 8, can be
arrived at by adding the sides of the Pythagorean right-angled triangle (the
'zoogonic' 3, 4, 5 triangle) in pairs, taken in order. I.e., $3 + 4 = 7$; $4 + 5 = 9$;
and $5 + 3 = 8$. The area of the same triangle is 6 units: the geometric mean
between the lower quadrate 4 and the 'better square' 9. I mention this as a
promising line of inquiry that might lead a deeper searcher to a solution embracing both geometric and arithmetic means.
[2] Even the numerical placing of the stanza (i.e., II. ix. *22*) is in keeping with
this theme. For 22 is the number of terms in the *Timæus* 'double interval' series,
that is, the series $1 : 2 : 4 : 8$ expanded by the interpolation of harmonic and
arithmetic means, and by the further interpolation of $9 : 8$ intervals (see *Timæus*,

that relate the stanza (once its number symbolism is understood) to the symbolic structure of Book II, and that serve to illuminate the meaning of widely separated images. These connections operate both in a forward direction: so that we recall the virtuous quaternion-base of Alma's castle in our reading of the lines that open the twelfth canto:

> Now gins this goodly frame of Temperance
> Fairely to rise . . .
> Formerly grounded, and fast setteled
> On firme foundation of true bountihed;

and in a backward direction: enabling us to identify the 'golden squire,' with which Guyon hoped to 'measure out a meane' between the extremes of passion,[1] as the Pythagorean *gnomon* used to raise a lower square to a higher.[2] The pleasurable discovery of such wholly

---

[1] *F.Q.*, II. i. 58. Cf. II. ii. Arg.: 'the face of golden Meane.' Since E. Buyssens has shown that *face* here means 'a curtain wall between bastions,' and that the arrangement of Medina's castle is therefore linear or triangular ('Aristotelianism and Anti-Puritanism in Spenser's Allegory of the Three Sisters,' *Eng. Studies*, XVIII (1936), p. 69), we may regard this episode too as belonging to the structure of mathematical symbolism.

[2] In geometry the *gnomon* is the figure which, when it is added to any figure, preserves that figure's original form. The term was specially applied, however, to the case of the square—hence the Pythagorean 'gnomonic numbers,' that is, the

---

tr. Bury, pp. 66–70). According to Plato's mathematical myth, this series is one of the two constituent elements in the formation of the Soul. Consequently, the number 22 came to be associated with the Soul, and with the principle of order informing the cosmos. It was sometimes on account of this association, rather than merely because there were 22 letters in the Hebrew alphabet (Curtius' explanation), that the number figured so prominently in numerical composition. (On the medieval use of the number, in which the Biblical association was usually the operative one, see Curtius, *European Literature and the Latin Middle Ages*, pp. 505–506.) The same *Timæus* series is also alluded to, though in a different manner, in Spenser's model for the House of Alma, Trissino's Castle of Areta. It will be remembered that the shorter sides of its *cortile* were divided into 21 intervals by 22 pillars. Trissino's emphasis on *intervals*, which play so important a part in Plato's description of the series, puts the allusion beyond doubt. It is almost equally certain that the arcades of 32 pillars forming the longer sides of Areta's *cortile* are meant to correspond to the terms of the enlarged 'triple interval' series in the *Timæus*, that is, the second constituent in the formation of the World-Soul (the series from 1 to 27: see Bury's edn., p. 70). That series, however, contains 34, not 32, terms. If, as seems probable, we are meant to imagine the outer pillars on the short sides of the *cortile* as situated at the corners and included in both counts, then we may conclude that Trissino based his symbolism on a misreading of a later section of the *Timæus* (36B–C), describing the joining together of the two bands into which the Soul-series is split.

implicit connections gives a strong impression of the organic consistency of Spenser's symbolism. So it is when we perceive that the foundation of the castle of Alma—the quaternion, or *fons virtutis*—is none other than the virtuous fountain of the book's opening episode; and, conversely, that the 'sacred vow' made by Guyon beside that fountain (II. i. 60–61) echoes the ancient oath of the Pythagoreans, which they were said to have taken on the *tetractys*.[1]

The quadrate 16, symbolic of virtue,[2] and in particular of virtue's integration of the contrary natures represented by the numbers 7 and 9, is further applied in the arrangement of the Alma episode by stanzas:

Location	Subject	Number of stanzas
II. ix. 1–16	The castle approached	16 16
17–20	Alma: the rational soul	4⎫
21–32	A tour of the castle: the vegetable soul	12 ⎬28
33–44	The parlour: the sensitive soul	12⎭
45–48	A tour of the turret	4⎫16
49–60	The three counsellors: the rational soul unfolded	12⎭

It will be seen that the modulus of the stanza-arrangement is 16: a total which not only appears in the 'approach' section (II. ix. 1–16) and in the clearly demarcated section devoted to the head or turret (II. ix. 45–60); but also—more significantly—when the Alma section (II. ix. 17–20) is combined with either of those devoted to the two inferior souls. If we remember that Alma is the rational soul (or, as Digby has it, the Reason) we can see why her stanzas, together with those of each other part of the soul, should compose the quadrate of just order, the square of the number of concord, 16. Further, we notice that each of the souls, in its extended description (like Medina and her sisters, whose 'equal shares' (II. ii. 13. 4) have a similar symbolism), is allotted the same space, namely 12 stanzas—making

[1] Most of the arithmological authorities repeat the information that the Pythagoreans swore by the *tetractys*; Macrobius' mention of the tradition (*In somn. Scip.*, I. vi. 41; ed. Stahl, p. 107) ensured its wide dissemination.
[2] See p. 282 n. 2 above.

odd numbers, which, added to squares, generate the series of square numbers. Originally, *gnomon* had the concrete meaning of a carpenter's square (*norma*); and the latter in consequence came to be an emblem of virtue, and in particular of temperance (see my 'Emblems of Temperance,' p. 143).

36 in all, a number associated in Pythagorean thought with the development of the soul in the embryo.[1] Again, the section devoted to the body with which these souls is compounded occupies 28 stanzas; and 28:36::7:9. The same proportions also obtain between the ordinal numbers of two stanzas in which Alma's authority is specifically acknowledged: II. ix. 28, where Appetite and Diet 'attone / Did dewty to their Lady,' and II. ix. 36, where the emotions of the Parlour 'all attonce out of their seates arose, / And to her homage made.'

[1] See Adam, *The Republic of Plato*, II, 293 f.

Appendix II

The Horoscope of Phantastes

> Emongst them all sate he, which wonned there,
> That hight *Phantastes* by his nature trew;
> A man of yeares yet fresh, as mote appere,
> Of swarth complexion, and of crabbed hew,
> That him full of melancholy did shew;
> Bent hollow beetle browes, sharpe staring eyes,
> That mad or foolish seemd: one by his vew
> Mote deeme him borne with ill disposed skyes,
> When oblique *Saturne* sate in the house of agonyes.
>
> (II. ix. 52)

Upton cites in explanation the fine passage in Chaucer's *Knight's Tale* (I (A) 2450–69) where Saturn describes the dire effects of which he is capable, especially 'whil [he] dwelle[s] in the signe of the leoun.' Kitchin gives the same reference, adding that ' "Agonyes" refers to the belief . . . that under Saturn strife and contention (ἀγῶνες) largely prevail'—a belief which he illustrates from the *Compost of Ptolemæus*: 'the children of the sayd Saturne shall be great jangleres and chyders . . . When he doth reygne, there is moche debate' (*Var. Sp.*, II, 300). The astrology of the Chaucerian passage has since been discussed by Curry (*Chaucer and the Medieval Sciences*, pp. 128–130), who directs us to Guido Bonatus: 'If Saturn be in the fixed signs, he is powerful in producing destitution and death for those born upon the earth. But in Leo he is stronger, hardier, and more persistent than in the other signs.' Neither Upton, Kitchin, nor Curry explains that Saturn is particularly unfortunate in Leo because there the planet is in its Detriment—i.e., the sign opposite its House Aquarius (on the meaning of Detriment, see Wilson, *A Complete*

289

Dictionary of Astrology, p. 26). As we have already seen, this dia-metric relationship of the signs Leo and Aquarius is of thematic importance in Spenser's poem.

While the horoscope of Phantastes is perhaps sufficiently glossed by the Chaucerian passage, we should mention the possibility that it may contain additional details of a technical order. Spenser's choice of the term 'oblique' seems too careful for the passage to be merely equivalent to, say, Digby's 'Saturn looked askance [i.e., "unfavourably"] in the geniture' (*Observations* on Browne's *Religio medici*). Certainly the phrase 'oblique *Saturne*' alludes to the notorious indirectness of the god's action (Calepinus, *Dictionarium*, s.v. *obliquus*: 'indirectus'), as well as to his froward or perverse nature (Cooper, *Thesaurus*, s.v. *obliquus*: 'crooked, awrie'; *OED*, s.v. *oblique*, adj. 4: 'deviating from right conduct or thought; morally or mentally one-sided or perverse'); while Calepinus' further equivalent for *oblique*, 'non rectus,' suggests a secondary allusion to the ubiquitous Pythagorean metaphor of the morally right angle. We cannot help asking, however, whether *oblique* may not also be intended in a more technical astronomical sense (*OED*, s.v. *oblique*, adj. 1: 'having a slanting or sloping direction or position: declining . . . from the horizontal'). If it is so intended, we may be able to reconstruct Phantastes' horoscope in more detail. For 'oblique *Saturne*' will then mean 'Saturn declining below the western horizon': that is, Saturn in the seventh House of the horoscope, the Occident, the House diametrically opposite to the Ascendant. (For an account of the fixed Houses of the horoscope, see Eisler, *The Royal Art of Astrology*, p. 39; and Ptolemy, *Tetrabiblos*, ed. Robbins, pp. 272–273.) Assuming that Saturn is in the sign Leo, then Leo will be in the Occident; so that the sign in the Ascendant will be Aquarius, the dominating sign in Spenser's Bk. II.

In the foregoing we have accepted Kitchin's interpretation of the phrase 'house of agonyes,' which will stand, so long as we add the (perhaps more primary) derivation from ἀγωνία, = 'fear,' 'perturbation,' 'suffering'; and also 'sterility,' 'impotence' (see Calepinus, s.v. *agonia*)—all meanings that aptly describe Saturn's influence as it is portrayed by Spenser. We have also taken for granted the relevance of the Chaucerian passage, and hence the identification of the 'house of agonyes' as the sign Leo. But a caveat must now be entered. Dr. C. H. Josten warns me that the phrase may not refer to a zodiacal House at all, but to a House of the horoscope. The twelfth House of the horoscope—named in Greek 'Evil Daemon.' in Latin *Carcer*—was associated with adversity, disease, enmity, illnesses, and suffering of all kinds. Moreover, since it was situated low on the eastern horizon, Saturn in this twelfth House might well be described as oblique, in the sense that he was not in the right-angle position which made his influence tolerable, but was 'disjunct' (see *Tetrabiblos*, III. xiii; pp. 339–341). There has thus remained enough uncertainty about the details of the horoscope to prevent their inclusion in my main argument.

BIBLIOGRAPHY OF REFERENCES CITED

The following is not a full bibliography, but is designed merely to clarify the brief foot-note references. Only works cited on at least two separate occasions are listed.

ABARBANEL, GIUDA. See under EBREO.

ADAM, JAMES. See under PLATO.

AGRIPPA, H. C. *De occulta philosophia libri tres*. Antwerp and Paris, 1531.

ALCIATI, A. *Emblemata . . . cum C. Minois . . . commentariis et notis posterioribus*. Lyons, 1600.

ALLEN, DON CAMERON. 'Spenser's Horology.' *Modern Language Notes*, Vol. LXI, 1946.

ANGLO, SYDNEY. 'Archives of the English Tournament: Score Cheques and Lists.' *Journal of the Society of Archivists*, Vol. II, 1961.

ANON. 'MS Notes to Spenser's *Faerie Queene*.' *Notes and Queries*, Vol. CCII, 1957.

AUSTIN, WILLIAM. *Hæc Homo wherein the Excellency of the Creation of woman is described by way of an Essaie*. London, 1637.

BARTAS, DU. See under DU BARTAS.

BENNETT, JOSEPHINE WATERS. *The Evolution of 'The Faerie Queene*.' Chicago, 1942.

BERCHORIUS, PETRUS. See under BERSUIRE.

BERGER, HARRY. *The Allegorical Temper: Vision and Reality in Book II of Spenser's 'Faerie Queene*.' Yale Studies in English, CXXXVII. New Haven, 1957.

————, 'A Secret Discipline: *The Faerie Queene*, Book VI.' *Form and Convention in the Poetry of Edmund Spenser*. Ed. William Nelson. Selected Papers from the English Institute. New York and London, 1961.

BERSUIRE, PIERRE (PETRUS BERCHORIUS). *Dictionarium seu repertorium morale*. Nuremberg, 1489.

BOBER, HARRY. 'The Zodiacal Miniature of the *Très Riches Heures* of the Duke of Berry—its Sources and Meaning.' *Journal of the Warburg Institute*, Vol. XI, 1948.

BONGO, PIETRO. *Mysticæ numerorum significationis liber*. Bergamo, 1585.

BUCHAN, A. M. 'The Political Allegory of Book IV of *The Faerie Queene*.' *ELH*, Vol. XI, 1944.

CAMBRIDGE MARGINALIAN. See under ANON.

CAMDEN, CARROLL. 'The Architecture of Spenser's 'House of Alma.' *Modern Language Notes*, Vol. LVIII. 1943.

CAMDEN, WILLIAM. *Britannia sive florentissimorum regnorum, Angliæ, Scotiæ Hiberniæ, et Insularum adiacentium ex intima antiquitate Chorographica descriptio. . . . Nunc postremo recognita, et . . . adaucta.* London, 1600.

——. *Remaines of a greater worke concerning Britaine.* Library of Old Authors. London, 1870.

CENSORINUS. *De die natali liber.* Ed. Otto Jahn. Berlin, 1845.

CONTI, NATALE (NATALIS COMES). *Mythologiæ, sive explicationis fabularum, Libri decem.* Lyons, 1653.

CORNFORD, F. M. 'Mysticism and Science in the Pythagorean Tradition.' *Classical Quarterly,* Vol. XVII, 1923.

CURRY, WALTER CLYDE. *Chaucer and the Medieval Sciences.* London, 1960.

CURTIUS, ERNST ROBERT. *European Literature and the Latin Middle Ages.* Tr. Willard R. Trask. London, 1953.

DIGBY, SIR KENELM. *Observations on the 22. Stanza in the 9th Canto of the 2d. Book of Spencers Faery Queen.* London, 1643 or 1644. Reptd. in *Variorum Spenser* (see below).

DRAPER, J. W. 'Classical Coinage in the *Faerie Queene.*' *PMLA,* Vol. XLVII, 1932.

DREYER, J. L. E. *A History of Astronomy from Thales to Kepler.* Formerly titled *History of the Planetary Systems from Thales to Kepler.* Revised by W. H. Stahl. London, 1953.

DU BARTAS. *Devine Weekes and Workes.* Tr. Joshua Sylvester. London, 1613.

——. See also under GOULART.

EBREO, LEONE (GIUDA ABARBANEL). *Dialoghi d'amore.* Ed. S. Caramella. Bari, 1929.

EISLER, R. *The Royal Art of Astrology.* London, 1946.

ELLRODT, ROBERT. *Neoplatonism in the Poetry of Spenser.* Travaux d'Humanisme et Renaissance, XXXV. Geneva, 1960.

FICINO, MARSILIO. *Opera omnia.* Facs. rept. of 1576 Basel edn. Ed. Mario Sancipriano and Paul Oskar Kristeller. Turin, 1959.

FOWLER, ALASTAIR D. S. 'Six Knights at Castle Joyous.' *Studies in Philology,* Vol. LVI, 1959.

——. 'Emblems of Temperance in *The Faerie Queene,* Book II.' *Review of English Studies,* N.S., Vol. XI, 1960.

——. 'The River Guyon.' *Modern Language Notes,* Vol. LXXV, 1960.

——. 'The Image of Mortality: *The Faerie Queene,* II. i–ii.' *The Huntington Library Quarterly,* Vol. XXIV, 1961.

GANG, T. M. *The Faerie Queene: a Demonstration of its Unity.* Bodleian MS. B.Litt. d. 604.

GIORGIO, FRANCESCO. *De harmonia mundi totius cantica tria.* Paris, 1545.

GIRALDI, L. G. *De diis gentium varia et multiplex historia.* Basel, 1548.

GOMBRICH, E. H. 'Botticelli's Mythologies: a Study in the Neoplatonic Symbolism of his Circle.' *Journal of the Warburg Institute,* Vol. VIII, 1945.

[GOULART, SIMON.] *A Learned Summary Upon the famous Poeme of William of Saluste Lord of Bartas.* Tr. T[homas]. L[odge]. London, 1621.

GYRALDUS. See under GIRALDI.

HAMILTON, A. C. *The Structure of Allegory in 'The Faerie Queene.'* Oxford, 1961.

HANKINS, JOHN E. 'Spenser and the Revelation of St. John.' *PMLA*, Vol. LX, 1945.

HARRIS, J. RENDEL. *The Cult of the Heavenly Twins.* Cambridge, 1906.

HAWKINS, SHERMAN. 'Mutabilitie and the Cycle of the Months.' *Form and Convention in the Poetry of Edmund Spenser.* Ed. William Nelson. Selected Papers from the English Institute. New York and London, 1961.

HIEATT, A. KENT. *Short Time's Endless Monument: the Symbolism of the Numbers in Edmund Spenser's 'Epithalamion.'* New York, 1960.

——. 'The Daughters of Horus: Order in the Stanzas of *Epithalamion.*' *Form and Convention in the Poetry of Edmund Spenser.* Ed. William Nelson. Selected Papers from the English Institute. New York and London, 1961.

HOPPER, VINCENT FOSTER. *Medieval Number Symbolism.* New York, 1938.

——. 'Spenser's "House of Temperance." ' *PMLA*, Vol. LV, 1940.

HORNE, DAVID H. (Ed.). *The Life and Minor Works of George Peele.* New Haven, 1952.

IAMBLICHUS (i.e., PSEUDO-IAMBLICHUS). *Theologoumena arithmeticæ.* Ed. V. de Falco. Leipzig, 1922.

JOHNSON, F. R. *Astronomical Thought in Renaissance England.* Baltimore, 1937.

KIRCHER, ATHANASIUS. *Musurgia universalis sive ars magna consoni et dissoni in x. libros digesta.* Rome, 1650.

LEWIS, C. S. *The Allegory of Love.* Oxford, 1938.

——. Rev. of Ellrodt (q.v. above). *Études Anglaises*, Vol. XIV, 1961.

LICETI, FORTUNIO. *Hieroglyphica, sive antiqua schemata gemmarum anularium quæsita Moralia, Politica, Historica, Medica, Philosophica, et Sublimiora.* Padua, 1653.

LODGE, THOMAS. See under GOULART.

LORD, GEORGE DE F. *Homeric Renaissance: the Odyssey of George Chapman.* London, 1956.

MCLANE, PAUL E. *Spenser's 'Shepheardes Calender.'* Notre Dame, Ind., 1961.

MACROBIUS. *Commentary on the Dream of Scipio.* Tr. and ed. William Harris Stahl. Records of Civilization, Sources and Studies, XLVIII. New York, 1952.

——. *Saturnalia,* Ed. F. Eyssenhardt. Leipzig, 1893.

MÂLE, ÉMILE. *The Gothic Image: Religious Art in France of the Thirteenth Century.* Tr. Dora Nussey. London, 1961.

MANILIUS. *M. Manilii Astronomicon.* Ed. A. E. Housman. 5 vols. Cambridge, 1937.

MARTIANUS CAPELLA. *De nuptiis Philologiæ et Mercurii.* Ed. A. Dick. Leipzig, 1925.

PALINGENIUS, MARCELLUS (P. A. MANZOLLI). *The Zodiake of Life.* Tr. Barnabe Googe. Ed. Rosemond Tuve. Scholars' Facsimiles and Reprints. New York, 1947.

PANOFSKY, ERWIN. *Meaning in the Visual Arts.* New York, 1955.

——. *Studies in Iconology.* New York and Evanston, 1962.

PERRET, JACQUES. *Virgile: l'homme et l'œvre.* Paris, 1952.

PEELE, GEORGE. See under HORNE.

PLATO. *Plato VII: Timæus, Critias, Clitopho, Menexenus, Epistulæ.* Tr. R. G. Bury. Loeb Classical Library. London, 1952.

——. *The Republic of Plato.* Ed. James Adam. 2 vols. Cambridge, 1929.

——. *The Republic of Plato.* Tr. B. Jowett. Oxford, 1881.

PLUTARCH. *Moralia.* Tr. and ed. Frank Cole Babbit and Harold North Fowler. Loeb Classical Library. 15 vols. London, 1927–.

——. *The Morals.* Tr. Philemon Holland. London, 1603.

PTOLEMY, CLAUDIUS (PTOLEMÆUS). *Omnia quæ extant opera, præter Geographiam . . . summa cura et diligentia castigata ab Erasmo Osualdo Schrekhenfuchsio, et ab eodem Isagoica in Almagestum præfatione.* Basel, 1566.

——. Μαθηματική σύνταξις: *Composition Mathématique.* Tr. and ed. M. Halma. 2 vols. Paris, 1816.

——. *Tetrabiblos.* Tr. and ed. F. E. Robbins. Loeb Classical Library. London, 1940.

PUTTE, VAN DER. See under VAN DER PUTTE.

RATHBORNE, ISABEL E. 'The Political Allegory of the Florimell–Marinell Story.' *ELH*, Vol. XII, 1945.

RICCIOLI, GIOVANNI-BATTISTA. *Almagesti novi tomus primus.* 2 pts. Bologna, 1651.

ROBBINS, F. E. 'The Tradition of Greek Arithmology.' *Classical Philology,* Vol. XVI, 1921.

SALUSTE DU BARTAS. See under DU BARTAS.

SEZNEC, JEAN. *The Survival of the Pagan Gods.* Tr. Barbara F. Sessions. Bollingen Series, XXXVIII. New York, 1953.

SIMSON, VON, OTTO. *The Gothic Cathedral.* Bollingen Series, XLVIII. New York, 1956.

TERVARENT, DE, GUY. *Attributs et symboles dans l'art profane 1450–1600.* Travaux d'Humanisme et Renaissance, XXIX. Geneva, 1958.

TRISSINO, G. G. *La Italia liberata da Gotthi.* Rome, 1547.

THORNDIKE, LYNN. *A History of Magic and Experimental Science.* 6 vols. New York, 1923–41.

VALERIANO, PIERIO. *Hieroglyphica, sive de sacris Ægyptiorum aliarumque gentium literis, Commentariorum Libri LVIII. cum duobus aliis ab eruditissimo viro annexis. Accesserunt loco auctarii, Hieroglyphicorum Collectanea, ex veteribus et recentioribus auctoribus descripta, et in sex libros digesta.* Frankfort, 1613.

VAN DER PUTTE. *Pietatis thaumata in Bernardi Bauhusi e Societate Iesu Proteum parthenium, unius Libri Versum, unius Versus Librum, Stellarum numero, sive formis M.XXII. variatum.* Antwerp, 1617.

[VARIORUM SPENSER.] *The Works of Edmund Spenser: a Variorum Edition.* Ed. Edwin Greenlaw *et alii.* 10 vols. Baltimore, 1932–57.

VITRUVIUS. *On Architecture.* Tr. and ed. Frank Granger. Loeb Classical Library. 2 vols. London, 1931.

WILLIAMS, KATHLEEN. 'Venus and Diana: Some Uses of Myth in *The Faerie Queene*.' *ELH,* Vol. XXVIII, 1961.

WILSON, E. C. *England's Eliza.* Cambridge, Mass., 1939.

WILSON, JAMES. *A Complete Dictionary of Astrology.* London, 1819.

WIND, EDGAR. *Bellini's Feast of the Gods.* Cambridge, Mass., 1948.

——. *Pagan Mysteries in the Renaissance.* London, 1958.

WITTKOWER, RUDOLF. *Architectural Principles in the Age of Humanism.* London, 1949.

YATES, FRANCES A. 'Queen Elizabeth as Astræa.' *Journal of the Warburg Institute,* Vol. X, 1947.

Index

297

Date Due

NO 18 '67			
NO 26 '73			
DE 10 '73			
DE 10 '73			
OCT 27 '77			

Demco 293-5